LATIN Made Simple

The Made Simple series has been created primarily for self-education but can equally well be used as an aid to group study. However complex the subject, the reader is taken step by step, clearly and methodically through the course. Each volume has been prepared by experts, using throughout the Made Simple technique of teaching. Consequently the gaining of knowledge now becomes an experience to be enjoyed.

In the same series

Accounting
Acting and Stagecraft
Additional Mathematics
Advertising
Anthropology
Applied Economics
Applied Mathematics
Applied Mechanics
Art Appreciation
Art of Speaking
Art of Writing
Biology
Book-keeping
British Constitution
Business and Administrative Organisation
Calculus
Chemistry
Childcare
Commerce
Commercial Law
Company Administration
Company Law
Computer Programming
Cookery
Cost and Management Accounting
Data Processing
Dressmaking
Economic History
Economic and Social Geography
Economics
Electricity
Electronic Computers
Electronics
English
English Literature
Export
Financial Management
French
Geology
German
Human Anatomy
Italian
Journalism
Latin
Law
Management
Marketing
Mathematics
Modern Electronics
Modern European History
New Mathematics
Office Practice
Organic Chemistry
Philosophy
Photography
Physical Geography
Physics
Pottery
Psychology
Rapid Reading
Retailing
Russian
Salesmanship
Secretarial Practice
Social Services
Soft Furnishing
Spanish
Statistics
Transport and Distribution
Typing
Woodwork

LATIN Made Simple

Rhoda A. Hendricks, M.A.

Advisory editor
A. V. Kelly, M.A.(Oxon)

Made Simple Books
W. H. ALLEN London
A Howard & Wyndham Company

Made and printed in Great Britain
by Butler & Tanner Ltd, Frome and London,
for the publishers W. H. Allen & Company Ltd,
44 Hill Street, London W1X 8LB

First edition, October 1969
Reprinted, April 1975
Reprinted, September 1978

ISBN 0 491 00333 1 Paperbound

Foreword

To study Latin is to study one of the most important influences on English language and literature as well as the languages and literature of most Western European countries. Anyone who seeks to understand the origins of our own culture and civilization must turn to the language of the people whose ideas played such a major part in its development.

The influence of the Romans is still with us in our everyday lives—the inscriptions on the coins in our pockets, the motto of our school or regiment, the indecipherable writing on our doctor's prescription. It is also there in our system of law, our religion (which flourished and spread because of the ease of communication the Roman Empire provided), in the best of our literature, which owes so much to the great writers of Greece and Rome, and in our language.

In English education Latin has, since mediaeval times, been the foundation of all learning. In the eighteenth and nineteenth centuries a study of the Classics was considered essential to the education of any cultivated gentleman, and until very recently a competence in Latin or Ancient Greek was a *sine qua non* of entry to the Universities of Oxford and Cambridge. Now, as a result of vocational and technological pressures on the curriculum of schools and universities, Latin has come to play a less central role in education, although, since these pressures have also resulted in a wider extension of educational opportunity, there has been no reduction in the number of those who have the opportunity to learn it.

Today much re-thinking is taking place in Latin teaching. As a result of research like that of the Cambridge Schools Classics Project, people are beginning to realize that although there are undoubted advantages for the man who can master the art of Latin composition, much that is equally valuable can be gained by learning to read Latin texts. It is not necessary to become a Cicero in order to be able to read and appreciate the prose of Cicero. In the past many a student has been deterred from learning Latin by the idea of its being 'difficult'. This idea is justified only if the student wants to become proficient in Latin composition. *Reading* it is an entirely different matter.

Through concentrating on learning to read Latin, Latin can be 'made simple', and this, therefore, is the central feature of the book. It is designed for those, whether in school or no longer in school, who wish to read the works of the great Latin authors in the original and to discover all that is lost even in the most sensitive translations. Selected passages from the works of most of the greatest figures of Latin literature are given throughout the text. It may be beyond the competence of the student to understand fully many of the extracts at the point at which they occur. But we hope he will gain sufficient from them to have his appetite whetted to return to them again and again, understanding more at each reading.

The student who works through to the final chapters will find he is able to read extracts from the more straightforward Latin authors with some fluency, that he has mastered the major elements of Latin grammar and syntax in their less complex forms, and that he has, in fact, reached a standard equivalent to that of 'O' level G.C.E. If he wishes to submit his new-found skills to the test of a public examination, he will find he is well prepared for the examinations of those boards which are now concentrating on testing a candidate's ability to read and understand Latin literature, providing he prepares himself adequately in the set texts that the board requires.

A. V. KELLY

Contents

CHAPTER 1

INFLECTION

In English, the use of a word is generally indicated by its position in the sentence, without any change in spelling. Sometimes, however, a word changes its form or spelling to show a corresponding change in its grammatical use and meaning.

singular:	boy	subject:	I	present:	does
plural:	boys	object:	me	past:	did

This process is called *Inflection.* You will notice that the change can take place either at the ending of the word or within the word.

In Latin, *Nouns, Pronouns, Adjectives,* and *Verbs* are inflected and the inflection usually takes place at the end of the word. Because Latin is a highly inflected language, the ending of a Latin word is of primary importance and must be considered as carefully as the stem of the word, which shows only the basic vocabulary meaning. Inflection will be clearly explained throughout this book and ample practice will be given.

PRONUNCIATION

Pronunciation, of course, is not necessary in the reading of Latin, but it is helpful in the comparison of Latin words with those of English and other languages. The consonants are pronounced as in English, except:

c and **ch** are always like k, as in coop.
g is always hard, as in go.
i-consonant is like y, as in you.
s is always s, as in so, not like z.
t is always like t, as in tie, not like sh, as in fiction.
v is always like w, as in woman.
x is like x, as in example.
gu, qu are like gw, qw, as in queen.

The vowels are either long or short (e.g. 'a' is sometimes pronounced as in 'cat' and sometimes as in 'father'). There are no fixed rules for the length of vowels, and the proper pronunciation can be learned best by paying close attention to the phonetic pronunciation given in the practice below and by hearing someone pronounce Latin correctly. The diphthongs (two *vowels*, pronounced as one) are pronounced:

ae like ai, as in aisle.
au like ou, as in ouch.

ei like ei, as in eight.
oe like oi, as in soil.
ui like we.

Practise reading aloud, following the English sound guide, until you can read this passage clearly and without hesitation. Remember that every consonant and vowel is pronounced in Latin. Syllables in bold type should be stressed.

Pater noster qui es in **pah**-*tehr* **naws**-*tehr qwee ehs in*	Our father who art in
caelis, sanctificetur **kai**-*lees* **sahnk**-*tih-fih*-**kay**-*toor*	heaven, hallowed
nomen tuum. Adveniat **noh**-*mehn* **too**-*uhm. ad*-**weh**-*nee-at*	be thy name. Thy
regnum tuum. Fiat **reg**-*nuhm* **too**-*uhm.* **fee**-*at*	kingdom come. Thy will
voluntas tua sicut in *woh*-**luhn**-*tahs* **too**-*a* **seek**-*uht in*	be done on earth as it is
caelo et in terra. Panem **kai**-*loh eht in* **tehr**-*rah.* **pah**-*nehm*	in heaven. Give us this day
nostrum cotidianum da **nohs**-*truhm* **koh**-*tee-dee*-**ah**-*nuhm dah*	our daily bread.
nobis hodie. Et dimitte **noh**-*bees* **hoh**-*dee-ay. eht dee*-**miht**-*e*	And forgive us
nobis debita nostra sicut **noh**-*bees* **deh**-*biht-a* **naws**-*tra* **seek**-*uht*	our debts as
et nos dimittimus *eht nohs dee*-**miht**-*ti-muhs*	we forgive
debitoribus nostris. Et *deh-bih*-**taw**-*rih-buhs* **naws**-*trees. eht*	our debtors. And
ne nos inducas in tentationem *nay nohs in*-**doo**-*kahs in* **ten**-*tah-tee*-**oh**-*nehm*	lead us not into temptation
sed libera nos a malo. *sehd* **lee**-*beh-rah nohs ah* **mah**-*loh.*	but deliver us from evil.
Amen. **ah**-*mehn.*	Amen.

The Lord's Prayer. Matthew VI, 9–13

THE PARTS OF SPEECH

The parts of speech are the same in Latin and English, but Latin has no article (the, a, an). The article must, therefore, be supplied in English.

Noun—the name of a person, place, or thing, e.g., *Caesar*, *Rome*, *town*
Pronoun—a word used instead of a noun, e.g., *he*

Adjective—a word that describes a noun or pronoun, e.g., *good*
Verb—a word that shows action or state of being, e.g., *run, is*
Adverb—a word that modifies a verb, adjective, or adverb, e.g., *quickly, very*
Preposition—a word used in conjunction with a noun or pronoun to make an adverbial or adjectival phrase, e.g., *in, by, with*
Conjunction—a word that joins words, phrases, clauses, or sentences, e.g., *and*
Interjection—an exclamation showing emotion, e.g., *oh*

WORD DERIVATION

Many of our English words have been inherited directly from Latin, with little or no change in spelling.

animal	**labor**	**captivus**	**fortuna**	**multitudo**	**natio**
animal	labour	captive	fortune	multitude	nation

Other English words come from Latin in the form of Derivatives.

Latin	*English*	*English Derivative*
agricola	farmer	agriculture
stella	star	constellation
terra	earth	terrace
filia	daughter	filial

You will find that you are familiar with a large number of Latin words already. Watch for Latin words that have come directly or indirectly into English, for English Derivatives, and for Latin phrases and expressions in everyday use. These will be brought to your attention throughout the book.

SOME GIRLS' NAMES OF LATIN ORIGIN AND THEIR MEANINGS

Rosa, rose
Victoria, victory
Beatrice, making happiness
Barbara, foreign
Amabel, lovable
Amy, beloved
Amanda, worthy of love
Regina, queen
Gloria, glory
Celestine, heavenly
Viola, Violet, violet
Clara, bright
Laura, laurel
Stella, Estelle, star
Flora, flowers
Augusta, majestic
Letitia, happiness
Alma, beautiful
Miranda, worthy of admiration
Sylvia, of the forest
Gratia, Grace, grace, gratitude

CHAPTER 2

Vocabulary

amo, amare, like, love (amateur)
porto, portare, carry (portage, deportment)
laudo, laudare, praise (laudable)
laboro, laborare, work (laboratory)
voco, vocare, call (vocation, vocative)

The first form of each verb given here is the first person singular of the present tense. For example, **amo,** 'I like', I am liking', 'I do like'. The second form is the present infinitive. For example, **amare,** to like. The infinitive furnishes the stem on which the present tenses are formed. Stem: **ama-, porta-, lauda-, labora-, voca-.**

THE VERB: FIRST CONJUGATION

Inflection

1. The change in the ending of a verb to show tense (time), person (the subject of the verb) and number (singular or plural) is called **conjugation.**
2. Verbs that have **-a-** in the infinitive are **a-conjugation** or 1st conjugation.
3. **a-conjugation** Verbs have **-a-** in most of the forms.

Present Tense of **a-conjugation** verbs.

Singular

1st person	**amo**	I like; I am liking; I do like
2nd person	**amas**	you like; you are liking; you do like
3rd person	**amat**	he, she, it likes; he, she, it is liking; he, she, it does like

Plural

1st person	**amamus**	we like; we are liking; we do like
2nd person	**amatis**	you like; you are liking; you do like
3rd person	**amant**	they like; they are liking; they do like

Grammar Practice No. 1

Conjugate the Present Tense of **porto, laudo, laboro,** and **voco** in the same way, giving the Latin form and its English meaning, and then check your answers below. Do this until you can give all the forms easily and quickly. The ability to read Latin depends on the rapid recognition of the meanings of the endings and of the vocabulary and so it is essential that these should be mastered.

Example: **porto,** I carry, I do carry, I am carrying; **portas,** you carry, you do carry, you are carrying; **portat,** he, she, it carries, he, she, it does carry, he, she, it is carrying; etc.

Check on Grammar Practice No. 1

porto, I carry, do carry, am carrying
portas, you carry, do carry, are carrying
portat, he, she, it carries, does carry, is carrying
portamus, we carry, do carry, are carrying
portatis, you carry, do carry, are carrying
portant, they carry, do carry, are carrying

laboro, I work, do work, am working
laboras, you work, do work, are working
laborat, he, she, it works, does work, is working
laboramus, we work, do work, are working
laboratis, you work, do work, are working
laborant, they work, do work, are working

laudo, I praise, do praise, am praising
laudas, you praise, do praise, are praising
laudat, he, she, it praises, does praise, is praising
laudamus, we praise, do praise, are praising
laudatis, you praise, do praise, are praising
laudant, they praise, do praise, are praising

voco, I call, am calling, do call
vocas, you call, are calling, do call
vocat, he, she, it calls, is calling, does call
vocamus, we call, are calling, do call
vocatis, you call, are calling, do call
vocant, they call, are calling, do call

Vocabulary

stella, stellae, *f.*, star (stellar, constellation)
puella, puellae, *f.*, girl
casa, casae, *f.*, cottage, house
femina, feminae, *f.*, woman (feminine)
aqua, aquae, *f.*, water (aquarium)
terra, terrae, *f.*, land, earth (terrace, territory)
agricola, agricolae, *m.*, farmer (agriculture)

In giving the vocabulary, two forms of a noun are given, as above, as well as its gender. The first form is the case of the subject, the **Nominative** case. The second form is the case of possession, the **Genitive** case, and furnishes the stem to which the rest of the case endings are added. Stem: **stell-, puell-, cas-, femin-, aqu-, terr-, agricol-.**

THE NOUN: FIRST DECLENSION

Inflection

1. The change in the ending of a noun to show its use in the sentence is called **declension.** The different forms of the noun are called **cases.**
2. Nouns that have **-ae** as the ending of the Genitive form are **a-declension,** or **1st declension.**
3. **1st declension** nouns have **-a-** in most of the case endings.
4. **1st declension** nouns are all feminine, unless the word indicates a male.

	Singular		*Use*
Nominative	**stella**	the star	Subject
Vocative	**stella**	O star	Addressing
Accusative	**stellam**	the star	Direct Object
Genitive	**stellae**	of the star	Possession
Dative	**stellae**	to, for the star	Indirect Object
Ablative	**stella**	by, with, from, etc., the star	Prepositional Phrases

	Plural		*Use*
Nominative	**stellae**	the stars	Subject
Vocative	**stellae**	O stars	Addressing
Accusative	**stellas**	the stars	Direct Object
Genitive	**stellarum**	of the stars	Possession
Dative	**stellis**	to, for the stars	Indirect Object
Ablative	**stellis**	by, with, from, etc., the stars	Prepositional Phrases

Grammar Practice No. 2

Decline **puella, casa, femina, aqua, terra,** and **agricola** in the same way, giving the Latin form and its English meaning, and then check your answers below. Do this until you can give all the forms easily and quickly.

Example: puella, the girl; **puella,** O girl; **puellam,** the girl; **puellae,** of the girl; **puellae,** to, for the girl, etc.

Check on Grammar Practice No. 2

puella	the girl	**puellae**	the girls
puella	O girl	**puellae**	O girls
puellam	the girl	**puellas**	the girls
puellae	of the girl	**puellarum**	of the girls
puellae	to, for the girl	**puellis**	to, for the girls
puella	by, with, from, etc., the girl	**puellis**	by, with, from, etc., the girls
casa	the cottage	**casae**	the cottages
casa	O cottage	**casae**	O cottages
casam	the cottage	**casas**	the cottages
casae	of the cottage	**casarum**	of the cottages
casae	to, for the cottage	**casis**	to, for the cottages
casa	by, with, from, etc., the cottage	**casis**	by, with, from, etc., the cottages
femina	the woman	**feminae**	the women
femina	O woman	**feminae**	O women
feminam	the woman	**feminas**	the women
feminae	of the woman	**feminarum**	of the women
feminae	to, for the woman	**feminis**	to, for the women
femina	by, with, from, etc., the woman	**feminis**	by, with, from, etc., the women
aqua	the water	**aquae**	the waters
aqua	O water	**aquae**	O waters
aquam	the water	**aquas**	the waters
aquae	of the water	**aquarum**	of the waters
aquae	to, for the water	**aquis**	to, for the waters
aqua	by, with, from, etc., the water	**aquis**	by, with, from, etc., the waters
terra	the land	**terrae**	the lands
terra	O land	**terrae**	O lands
terram	the land	**terras**	the lands
terrae	of the land	**terrarum**	of the lands
terrae	to, for the land	**terris**	to, for the lands
terra	by, with, from, etc., the land	**terris**	by, with, from, etc., the lands
agricola	the farmer	**agricolae**	the farmers
agricola	O farmer	**agricolae**	O farmers
agricolam	the farmer	**agricolas**	the farmers

agricolae	of the farmer	**agricolarum**	of the farmers
agricolae	to, for the farmer	**agricolis**	to, for the farmers
agricola	by, with, from, etc., the farmer	**agricolis**	by, with, from, etc., the farmers

Practice Exercises

No. 1. For each of these singular forms give the corresponding plural.

Example: stellam, the star — **stellas,** the stars
vocas, you call — **vocatis,** you call

1. **aquam,** the water
2. **puellae,** of the girl
3. **terra,** the land
4. **agricolae,** for the farmer
5. **stella,** by the star
6. **vocat,** he calls
7. **laboras,** you work
8. **porto,** I carry
9. **laudo,** I praise
10. **amat,** he likes

No. 2. What is the English pronoun shown by each of the following?

1. **-mus** 2. **-t** 3. **-o** 4. **-tis** 5. **-nt** 6. **-s**

No. 3. What use in the sentence would each of these pairs of noun endings have?

1. **am, as** 2. **a, is** 3. **a, ae** 4. **ae, is** 5. **ae, arum**

No. 4. Change the following to the singular or plural.

Example: portat — portant

1. **porto**
2. **amant**
3. **portamus**
4. **laudo**
5. **vocat**
6. **laboras**
7. **portant**
8. **vocatis**
9. **amo**
10. **laudas**

CHAPTER 3

THE SIGNS OF THE ZODIAC

The Signs of the Zodiac are all Latin words and are easily remembered by associating their meanings with the way in which they are depicted.

Aries, the Ram	**Leo,** the Lion	**Sagittarius,** the Archer
Taurus, the Bull	**Virgo,** the Maiden	**Capricorn,** the Goat
Gemini, the Twins	**Libra,** the Scales	**Aquarius,** the Water Bearer
Cancer, the Crab	**Scorpio,** the Scorpion	**Pisces,** the Fishes

Many of the Planets are named after Roman deities, as:

Jupiter, King of the gods
Saturn, god of Sowing
Mercury, the Messenger god
Venus, goddess of Love
Mars, god of War
Neptune, god of the Sea
Pluto, god of the Lower World

Vocabulary

Nouns

insula, insulae, *f.*, island (insular, insulate)
patria, patriae, *f.*, native country (patriot)
paeninsula, paeninsulae, *f.*, peninsula
copia, copiae, *f.*, supply, abundance (copious, cornucopia). In the plural, **copiae** means forces, troops
filia, filiae, *f.*, daughter (filial)
silva, silvae, *f.*, forest, woods (sylvan)
Germania, Germaniae, *f.*, Germany
Britannia, Britanniae, *f.*, Britain
Italia, Italiae, *f.*, Italy
Iulia, Iuliae, *f.*, Julia
nauta, nautae, *m.*, sailor (nautical)

Verbs

pugno, pugnare, fight (pugnacious)
oppugno, oppugnare, attack
iuvo, iuvare, help, aid
do, dare, give (datum)

THE USE OF THE CASES

As indicated above, the changes in the ending of a noun show its use in the sentence.

The Nominative Case

The Nominative case indicates that the noun is the *subject* of the sentence.

puella laborat	*The girl* works
feminae vocant	*The women* call

puella is the subject of **laborat; feminae** is the subject of **vocant;** both are in the Nominative case.

Note that when a verb has a noun as subject, it must be put in the 3rd person—he, she, it or they.

The Vocative Case

The Vocative case is used when we are *calling to* or *addressing* someone.

laboro, agricola	I am working, *O farmer*
vocatis, feminae	You are calling, *O women*

The Accusative Case

The Accusative case indicates that the noun is the *direct object* of the sentence.

aquam amas	You like *water*
feminas laudamus	We praise *women*

aquam is the direct object of **amas; feminas** is the direct object of **laudamus;** both are in the Accusative case.

The Genitive Case

The Genitive case shows *possession* and is, therefore, to be translated by 'of', 'belonging to' or by 's or s'. It is usually related to the noun next to it.

terra agricolae	The land of the farmer—*the farmer's* land
terra agricolarum	The land of the farmers—*the farmers'* land

Practice Exercises

No. 5. Complete these sentences by adding the correct subject. Choose your answer from the words in brackets.

1. .... **laborant (Feminae, Feminas)**
2. .... **aquam portat (Puella, Puellam)**
3. .... **puellas amant (Agricolarum, Agricolae)**
4. .... **pugnant (Copiae, Copiis)**
5. .... **insulam oppugnat (Nauta, Nautae)**
6. .... **aquam amat (Agricolae, Agricola)**
7. .... **feminas laudant (Filiis, Filiae)**
8. .... **pugnant (Nautis, Nautae)**
9. .... **feminam iuvant (Puellae, Puellas)**
10. .... **laborat (Filiam, Filia)**

No. 6. Complete these sentences by adding the correct Direct object. Choose your answer from the words in brackets.

1. .... **laudo (Puellam, Puellae)**
2. .... **oppugnant (Insulas, Insula)**
3. .... **portas (Aquae, Aquam)**
4. .... **amamus (Britanniam, Britannia)**
5. .... **vocatis (Feminae, Feminas)**
6. .... **oppugnamus (Paeninsula, Paeninsulam)**
7. .... **laudat (Silvas, Silvae)**
8. .... **amas (Patriae, Patriam)**
9. .... **vocat (Agricolas, Agricolae)**
10. .... **oppugnatis (Copia, Copias)**

No. 7. Complete these sentences, choosing your answer from the words in brackets.

1. **Casam** .... **laudas (puellae, puellas)**
2. **Copiam** .... **portamus (aquae, aqua)**
3. **Terram** .... **oppugnant (agricolis, agricolarum)**
4. **Casas** .... **laudamus (feminarum, feminam)**
5. **Patriam** .... **amamus (nauta, nautae)**
6. **Insulam** .... **amo (nautam, nautae)**
7. **Filiam** .... **laudatis (agricola, agricolae)**
8. **Casam** .... **laudo (nautarum, nautis)**
9. **Copiam** .... **amatis (stellarum, stellis)**
10. **Patriam** .... **amas (feminam, feminae)**

THE DATIVE AND ABLATIVE CASE

The Dative Case

The Dative case shows the *Indirect Object* of the verb. The Indirect Object indicates **to whom** or **what** something is given, said, shown, etc.

puellae aquam do	I give water *to the girl*
agricolis terram damus	We give land *to the farmers*

Puellae (to the girl) and **agricolis** (to the farmers) are the indirect objects of **do** and **damus** respectively. Both are, therefore, in the Dative case.

Note that the word 'to' is sometimes omitted in English (e.g. 'I give the girl water').

The Ablative Case

The Ablative case has several uses. We will concern ourselves here only with its use in prepositional phrases. Certain prepositions in Latin must always be followed by the Ablative case.

cum puellis	*with the girls*
in aqua	*in the water*

Prepositional Phrases

Latin prepositions are followed by either the Accusative or the Ablative case. It is important to remember which case must be used with each preposition.

1. The Accusative case is used with these prepositions:

ad, to, towards	**Ad casam ambulo.**	I walk *towards the cottage.*
	Ad casas ambulo.	I walk *towards the cottages.*
in, into	**In casam ambulo.**	I walk *into the cottage.*
	In casas ambulo.	I walk *into the cottages.*

2. The Ablative case is used with these prepositions:

cum, with	**Cum puella ambulo.**	I walk *with the girl.*
	Cum puellis ambulo.	I walk *with the girls.*
in, in, on	**In casa sum.**	I am *in the cottage.*
	In casis sunt.	They are *in the cottages.*
	In terra sum.	I am *on land.*
	In viis sunt.	They are *on the streets.*
e or **ex,** from, out from	**ex via**	*out of the street*
	ex viis	*out of the streets*

a or **ab,** from, away from **a silva** *away from* the forest
a silvis *away from* the forests

a and **e** are not used before a vowel or h. **ex** and **ab** must be used.

Vocabulary

Nouns

fabula, fabulae, *f.*, story (fable, fabulous)
via, viae, *f.*, road, way, street (via, viaduct)
incola, incolae, *m.* or *f.*, inhabitant
fama, famae, *f.*, rumour, renown, report (fame)
Europa, Europae, *f.*, Europe

Verbs

ambulo, ambulare, walk (ambulance, perambulator)
narro, narrare, tell, relate (narrate)
monstro, monstrare, point out, show (demonstrate)
habito, habitare, dwell, live (habitation)
navigo, navigare, sail, cruise (navigate)

Prepositions

ad (with the Accusative case), to, towards (advance)
a or **ab** (with the Ablative case), from, away from (abdicate)
e or **ex** (with the Ablative case), from, out of (emit, expel)
cum (with the Ablative case), with
in (with the Accusative case), into, onto
in (with the Ablative case), in, on

Practice Exercises

No. 8. Give the English for the following:

Example: in vias, into the roads

1. **ad viam**	6. **ab terra**	11. **in silvas**	16. **ad insulam**
2. **in casa**	7. **a casis**	12. **cum puella**	17. **ex terra**
3. **cum femina**	8. **e silvis**	13. **in aqua**	18. **cum agricola**
4. **in silvam**	9. **in insulas**	14. **ad aquam**	19. **in patria**
5. **ex casis**	10. **ad vias**	15. **ab puellis**	20. **cum puellis**

No. 9. Complete these sentences by adding the correct Indirect Object. Choose your answer from the words in parentheses.

1. .... **silvas monstramus (Feminae, Feminam)**
2. .... **aquam dat (Nauta, Nautae)**
3. .... **fabulas narrant (Nautarum, Nautis)**
4. .... **viam monstrat (Puellam, Puellae)**
5. .... **fabulam narrat (Puellis, Puellas)**
6. .... **casas monstratis (Feminis, Feminarum)**
7. .... **terram dant (Agricolam, Agricolis)**
8. .... **casam das (Femina, Feminae)**
9. .... **silvas monstrat (Puella, Puellis)**
10. .... **fabulas narratis (Agricolae, Agricolas)**

CHAPTER 4

ROMAN NUMERALS

The basic Roman numerals, and the corresponding Arabic numerals, are:

I 1 **V** 5 **X** 10 **L** 50 **C** 100 **D** 500 **M** 1000

These Roman numerals are used in various combinations to form any desired numeral:

1. A smaller numeral placed in front subtracts from the larger. For example, **IV,** 4; **IX,** 9; **XC,** 90; **CM,** 900.
2. A smaller numeral placed after adds to the larger. For example, **VI,** 6; **XI,** 11; **CX,** 110; **MC,** 1100.
3. Repeated numerals double, triple, and so on. For example, **XX,** 20; **XXX,** 30; **CC,** 200; **CCC,** 300.
4. When a line is drawn over a numeral, it multiples that numeral by 1000. For example, $\overline{\mathbf{V}}$, 5000; $\overline{\mathbf{X}}$, 10,000; $\overline{\mathbf{C}}$, 100,000; $\overline{\mathbf{D}}$, 500,000.

A GUIDE TO ROMAN NUMERALS

I	1	**XX**	20	**CCI**	201
II	2	**XXI**	21	**CCC**	300
III	3	**XXX**	30	**CCCI**	301
IV or **IIII**	4	**XXXI**	31	**CD**	400
V	5	**XL** or **XXXX**	40	**CDI**	401
VI	6	**XLI**	41	**D**	500
VII	7	**L**	50	**DI**	501
VIII	8	**LI**	51	**DC**	600
IX or **VIIII**	9	**LX**	60	**DCI**	601
X	10	**LXI**	61	**DCC**	700
XI	11	**LXX**	70	**DCCI**	701
XII	12	**LXXI**	71	**DCCC** or **CCM**	800
XIII	13	**LXXX** or **XXC**	80	**DCCCI** or **CCMI**	801
XIV	14	**LXXXI** or **XXCI**	81	**CM**	900
XV	15	**XC**	90	**CMI**	901
XVI	16	**XCI**	91	**M**	1000
XVII	17	**C**	100	**MI**	1001
XVIII	18	**CI**	101	**MM**	2000
XIX	19	**CC**	200	**MMI**	2001

Roman Numeral Practice No. 1

Give the corresponding Arabic numerals for the following:

XIII	MC	XLIII	DII	CXX
CCC	XXV	DCX	CDXX	$\overline{\text{X}}$CCC
IX	CM	XXXVI	XCV	LXXIV

Check on Roman Numeral Practice No. 1

13	1100	43	502	120
300	25	610	420	10,300
9	900	36	95	74

Vocabulary

Verbs

nato, natare, swim

Adjectives

magna, large, great (magnify)
parva, small
bona, good (bonanza)
mala, bad, evil (malice)
mea, my, mine
tua, your, yours
Romana, Roman
pulchra, pretty, beautiful (pulchritude)
longa, long (longitude)
lata, wide (latitude)
multa, much. In the plural **multae** means many (multicoloured)
clara, clear, bright, famous (clarity)
antiqua, old, ancient (antique)

Adverbs

non, not (non-stop)
bene, well (benefactor)
male, badly (malformed)

ADJECTIVES

1. An adjective describes a noun.

filia	**filia pulchra**	**filia bona**
daughter	pretty daughter	good daughter

2. An adjective must be in the same *gender* (masculine, feminine, or neuter), *number* (singular or plural), and *case* as the noun it modifies.

	Singular		*Use*
Nom.	**casa magna**	large cottage	Subject
Voc.	**casa magna**	O large cottage	Addressing

Acc.	**casam magnam**	large cottage	Direct Object
Gen.	**casae magnae**	of the large cottage	Possession
Dat.	**casae magnae**	to, for the large cottage	Indirect, Object
Abl.	**casa magna**	by, with, from the large cottage	Prepositional Phrases

	Plural		*Use*
Nom.	**casae magnae**	large cottages	Subject
Voc.	**casae magnae**	O large cottages	Addressing
Acc.	**casas magnas**	large cottages	Direct Object
Gen.	**casarum magnarum**	of the large cottages	Possession
Dat.	**casis magnis**	to, for the large cottages	Indirect Object
Abl.	**casis magnis**	by, with, from the large cottages	Prepositional Phrases

ADVERBS

As the name suggests, an adverb usually adds something to the meaning of a verb, although adverbs are used to modify other words too.

Agricola non natat	The farmer does not swim
Puella bene natat	The girl swims well

Practice Exercise

No. 10. Supply the correct ending for each adjective.

Example: aquam mal............, bad water **aquam malam**

1. **casam parv**............, small cottage
2. **me**............**filiarum,** of my daughters
3. **pulchr**............**stellas,** pretty stars
4. **tu**............**terra,** your land
5. **filiae mal**............, to the bad girl
6. **casis Roman**............, for Roman cottages
7. **puellas parv**............, small girls
8. **aquam bon**............, good water
9. **feminae parv**............, to the small woman
10. **casarum pulchr**............, of pretty cottages

FAMILIAR PHRASES

Many Latin Phrases are in everyday use and can be recognized and used easily with a little practice.

1. **nota bene,** note well, is used in writing and speaking to draw attention to something that should be noticed especially. It is often abbreviated: **N.B.**
2. **bona fide,** with good faith or honesty. Example: It is a **bona fide** certificate. Thus, a genuine certificate. The opposite is **mala fide,** in bad faith.
3. **adsum,** I am present, is sometimes used in roll call answering.
4. **meum et tuum,** mine and thine, is sometimes used in place of the English phrase.
5. **terra firma,** firm land. Example: They were glad to step on **terra firma.**
6. **aqua** occurs frequently in English: **aqua pura,** pure water. **aqua vitae,** water of life, meaning brandy or alcohol. **aqua fortis**, literally strong water, is nitric acid.

CHAPTER 5

READING

Italia	Italy
1. **Italia est paeninsula in Europa.**	1. Italy is a peninsula in Europe.
2. **Paeninsula est longa et lata.**	2. The peninsula is long and wide.
3. **Incolae multae sunt agricolae et nautae.**	3. Many inhabitants are farmers and sailors.
4. **Italia est clara et antiqua.**	4. Italy is famous and old.
5. **Magna est fama Italiae.**	5. The fame of Italy is great.
6. **In Italia sunt viae multae et pulchrae et longae.**	6. In Italy there are many beautiful and long roads.
7. **Sicilia et Sardinia et Corsica sunt magnae et pulchrae insulae.**	7. Sicily and Sardinia and Corsica are large and pretty islands.
8. **Incolae patriam amant et bene laborant.**	8. The inhabitants love their country and work hard.

THE VERB 'TO BE'

Present tense of **sum, esse,** to be

	Singular		*Plural*	
1st person	**sum**	I am	**sumus**	we are
2nd person	**es**	you are	**estis**	you are
3rd person	**est**	he, she, it is; there is	**sunt**	they are; there are

The verb 'to be' does not have an object; it has a *complement.* The complement will normally be a noun or an adjective that describes or tells us something about the subject. It must, therefore, be put into the same case as the subject, i.e. normally the Nominative case.

Pulchra est	She is beautiful
Casae sunt magnae	The cottages are large

Practice Exercises

No. 11. What is the English for each of the following?

1. **estis** 2. **est** 3. **sunt** 4. **sum** 5. **es** 6. **sumus**

No. 12. Pick out and translate the complements.

Example: Insula est pulchra. pulchra, pretty

1. **Insula est magna.**
2. **Silvae sunt pulchrae.**
3. **Filiae sunt bonae.**
4. **Casa est mea.**
5. **Copiae sunt Romanae.**
6. **Terra est mala.**
7. **Paeninsula est tua.**
8. **Casae sunt parvae.**
9. **Silva est pulchra.**
10. **Femina est bona.**

No. 13. Pick out and translate the complements.

Example: Sunt agricolae. agricolae, farmers

1. **Est agricola.**
2. **Sunt nautae.**
3. **Germania est patria mea.**
4. **Sicilia est insula.**
5. **Sunt casae.**
6. **Sum nauta.**
7. **Estis feminae.**
8. **Es puella.**
9. **Sumus agricolae.**
10. **Non est silva.**

FAMILIAR QUOTATIONS

Many quotations from Latin authors are in use today, either in their Latin form or in translation. If you become so familiar with these quotations and their meanings that you know them by memory, you will have acquired some of the real flavour of the Latin language and thought.

Roma aeterna, Eternal Rome. *Tibullus*

Laborare est orare, To labour is to pray. *Motto of the Benedictine Monks*

Errare humanum est, To err is human. *Seneca*

Dira necessitas, Dire necessity. *Horace*

Aurea mediocritas, The golden mean. *Horace*

Rara avis. A rare bird. *Horace*

Ars longa, vita brevis, Art is long, life is short. *Seneca*

Fortuna caeca est, Fortune is blind. *Cicero*

FIRST REVISION (CHAPTERS 1–5)

VOCABULARY REVISION

Nouns

1. agricola
2. aqua
3. Britannia
4. casa
5. copia
6. copiae
7. Europa
8. fabula
9. fama
10. femina
11. filia
12. Germania
13. incola
14. insula
15. Italia
16. Iulia
17. nauta
18. paeninsula
19. patria
20. puella
21. silva
22. stella
23. terra
24. via

1. farmer
2. water
3. Britain
4. cottage
5. supply, abundance
6. troops
7. Europe
8. story
9. rumour, renown, report
10. woman
11. daughter
12. Germany
13. inhabitant
14. island
15. Italy
16. Julia
17. sailor
18. peninsula
19. native country
20. girl
21. forest, wood
22. star
23. land, earth
24. road, way, street

Adjectives

1. antiqua
2. bona
3. clara
4. lata
5. longa
6. magna
7. mala
8. mea
9. multa
10. multae
11. parva
12. pulchra
13. Romana
14. tua

1. ancient, old
2. good
3. clear, bright, famous
4. wide
5. long
6. large, great
7. bad, evil
8. my, mine
9. much
10. many
11. small
12. pretty, beautiful
13. Roman
14. your, yours

Verbs

1. ambulo
2. amo
3. do
4. habito
5. iuvo
6. laboro
7. laudo
8. monstro
9. narro
10. nato
11. navigo
12. oppugno
13. porto
14. pugno
15. sum
16. voco

1. I walk
2. I love, like
3. I give
4. I dwell, live
5. I help, aid
6. I work
7. I praise
8. I point out, show
9. I tell, relate
10. I swim
11. I sail, cruise
12. I attack
13. I carry
14. I fight
15. I am
16. I call

Adverbs

1. **bene**	2. **male**	3. **non**
1. well	2. badly	3. not

Prepositions

1. **a, ab** 2. **ad**	3. **cum** 4. **e, ex**	5. **in**
1. from, away from 2. to, towards	3. with 4. from, out from	5. in, on; into

Practice Exercises

No. 14. Complete the following sentences by adding the appropriate ending to the adjective.

1. **Europam antiqu............ laudamus.**
2. **Aquae pulchr............ et bonae sunt.**
3. **In silvis parv............ habitat.**
4. **Stellas clar............ amas.**
5. **Incolae insularum mult............ sumus.**
6. **Magna est terra Roman............**
7. **Feminae filias bon............ amant.**
8. **Fabulam mal............ narrat.**
9. **Pulchr............ sunt filiae feminarum.**
10. **Aquam incolis mult............ dat.**

No. 15. Give the Genitive Singular and Gender of these nouns.

Example: casa, casae, *f.*

1. **casa**	6. **insula**	11. **terra**	16. **patria**
2. **femina**	7. **puella**	12. **Britannia**	17. **incola**
3. **stella**	8. **copia**	13. **fama**	18. **Europa**
4. **aqua**	9. **filia**	14. **Italia**	19. **agricola**
5. **fabula**	10. **nauta**	15. **silva**	20. **via**

No. 16. Give the Infinitive for each of these verbs.

Example: amo, amare

1. **amo**	4. **sum**	7. **monstro**	10. **porto**	13. **nato**
2. **laudo**	5. **voco**	8. **do**	11. **narro**	14. **pugno**
3. **navigo**	6. **oppugno**	9. **habito**	12. **laboro**	15. **ambulo**

No. 17.

1. Make a list of the Latin cases and give the use of each.

2. Give the complete declension of these phrases, with the English meaning of each form.

   insula lata, the wide island **via longa,** long road

3. Give the complete Present Tense of these verbs, with the English meaning of each form.

   laboro, I work; I am working; I do work
   laudo, I praise; I am praising; I do praise
   sum, I am

ADESTE, FIDELES

The author of this hymn is unknown, but it was composed in the seventeenth century and translated by Frederick Oakley in the nineteenth century.

Adeste, Fideles

Adeste, fideles, laeti triumphantes,
Venite, venite in Bethlehem;
Natum videte regem Angelorum;
Venite adoremus Dominum.

Deum de Deo, Lumen de Lumine,
Gestant puellae viscera;
Deum verum, genitum non factum;
Venite adoremus Dominum.

Cantet nunc hymnos Chorus Angelorum;
Cantet nunc aula caelestium,
Gloria in excelsis Deo!
Venite adoremus Dominum.

Ergo Qui natus die hodierna,
Iesu, tibi sit gloria;
Patris aeterni verbum caro factum;
Venite adoremus Dominum.

Oh Come All Ye Faithful

Oh come, all ye faithful, joyful and triumphant,
Oh come ye, oh come ye to Bethlehem;
Come and behold him, born the King of Angels;
Oh come, let us adore him, Christ the Lord.

God of God, Light of Light,
Lo! he abhors not the Virgin's womb;
Very God, begotten, not created;
Oh come, let us adore him, Christ the Lord.

Sing, choirs of angels, sing in exultation,
Sing, all ye citizens of heaven above:
'Glory to God in the highest!'
Oh come, let us adore him, Christ the Lord.

Yea, Lord, we greet thee, born this happy morning,
Jesu, to thee be glory given,
Word of the Father, now in flesh appearing;
Oh come, let us adore him, Christ the Lord.

CHAPTER 6

READING

Proserpina	Proserpina
1. **Dea agricolarum est Ceres.**	1. The goddess of the farmers is Ceres.
2. **Filia est Proserpina. Ceres filiam pulchram amat.**	2. Her daughter is Proserpina. Ceres loves her beautiful daughter.
3. **Ceres et Proserpina terram et silvas amant et agricolas iuvant.**	3. Ceres and Proserpina love the land and woods and help the farmers.
4. **Proserpina est clara. Incolae terrarum multarum Proserpinam bene amant et laudant.**	4. Proserpina is famous. The inhabitants of many lands love Proserpina well and praise her.
5. **Pluto Proserpinam ad terram infernam[1] portat quod[2] puellam amat.**	5. Pluto carries Proserpina to the lower world because he loves the girl.
6. **Dea Ceres filiam vocat quod misera est. Agricolae non laborant et terra non bona est.**	6. The goddess, Ceres, calls her daughter because she is unhappy. The farmers do not work and the land is not good.
7. **Pluto agricolis Proserpinam dat et terra est pulchra et bona quod bene laborant.**	7. Pluto gives Proserpina to the farmers and the earth is pretty and good because they work hard.
8. **Aestate[3] Proserpina est cum agricolis et hieme[4] est in terra inferna.**	8. In summer Proserpina is with the farmers and in winter she is in the lower world.

NOTES: 1. **inferna,** lower. 2. **quod,** because. 3. **aestate,** in summer. 4. **hieme,** in winter.

Vocabulary

Nouns

provincia, provinciae, *f.*, province (provincial)
gloria, gloriae, *f.*, glory (glorious)
praeda, praedae, *f.*, booty, plunder (predatory)
victoria, victoriae, *f.*, victory (victorious)
Graecia, Graeciae, *f.*, Greece
Hispania, Hispaniae, *f.*, Spain
fossa, fossae, *f.*, ditch (foss)

Adjective

alta, high, deep (alto, altitude)

Verbs

supero, superare, surpass, overcome, conquer (insuperable)
aedifico, aedificare, build (edifice)
sto, stare, stand
exspecto, exspectare, to await, expect, wait for

Adverbs

saepe, often
ubi, where, when (ubiquitous)
ibi, there, in that place
hic, here, in this place
cur, why

Prepositions

ante (with the Accusative case) before, in front of (antedate, antecedent)
post, (with the Accusative case) behind (postdate, postpone)

ORDER OF WORDS

Because the meaning of an English sentence is shown by the position of the words, any change in the position of the words changes the meaning of the sentence. For example, 'the farmer calls the girl', or 'the girl calls the farmer'.

Since the inflection or form of the endings of Latin words shows their use in the sentence, a change in the position of the words in a Latin sentence does not change the actual meaning of the sentence.

Agricola puellam vocat
Agricola vocat puellam
Puellam agricola vocat
Puellam vocat agricola
Vocat agricola puellam
Vocat puellam agricola
} The farmer calls the girl

There is a normal order of words in a Latin sentence.

a. The Subject usually stands first.

Puella fabulas narrat.	The girl (subject) tells stories.
Femina silvas amat.	The woman loves the woods.

b. Adjectives and Genitives stand next to their nouns.

filia pulchra -or- **pulchra filia**	pretty daughter
filia agricolae -or- **agricolae filia**	the farmer's daughter

c. Adverbs precede the word they modify.

non narrat	she does not tell
non multae puellae	not many girls
non saepe	not often

d. An Indirect Object usually precedes the Direct Object.

Puella agricolae fabulas narrat.	The girl tells stories to the farmer.

e. Verbs stand at the end of their clauses. The verb 'to be', however, usually has the same position as in English.

Puella fabulas narrat.	The girl tells stories.
Puella est pulchra.	The girl is pretty.

Any change in the normal word order of a Latin sentence is usually for emphasis or a special effect.

Puellam femina amat.	It is the girl the woman loves.

Note. The word 'there'.

Be careful to distinguish between the two uses of the word 'there'.

1. With the third person of the verb 'to be', *there is* or *there are.*

Est femina in casa.	There is a woman in the cottage.
Sunt feminae in casa.	There are women in the cottage.

2. The adverb **ibi,** *there* or *in that place.*

Ibi pugnant.	They are fighting there.
Ibi stant feminae.	There stand the women.

FAMILIAR QUOTATIONS

Many of the words in these quotations belong to the **a-declension** or to the **a-conjugation.**

Sed non culpa mea est. But the blame is not mine. *Ovid*

Licentia poetica. Poetic licence. *Seneca*

Summa summarum. The total of totals. *Plautus*

Periculum in mora. Peril in delay. *Livy*

Si qua via est. If there is any way. *Virgil*

Tanta potentia formae est. So great is the power of beauty. *Ovid*

Sollicitae tu causa, pecunia, vitae. You, money, are the cause of an anxious life. *Propertius*

Practice Exercises

No. 18. Give the English meanings for these forms.

1. **sumus**
2. **superant**
3. **stat**
4. **est**
5. **exspectatis**
6. **aedificat**
7. **sunt**
8. **natamus**
9. **superat**
10. **navigant**
11. **datis**
12. **vocas**
13. **aedificamus**
14. **ambulant**
15. **statis**

No. 19. Translate these prepositional phrases.

1. **in Italia**
2. **ad Britanniam**
3. **cum feminis**
4. **ad Italiam**
5. **in provincia**
6. **cum copiis**
7. **in paeninsula**
8. **ante casas**
9. **post casas**
10. **cum puella**
11. **in silvis**
12. **ad viam**
13. **ad insulam**
14. **in casas**
15. **ante fossam**

No. 20. Give the English translations for the following.

1. **incolae**
2. **Cur laborant?**
3. **Patriam tuam iuvas.**
4. **Praedam portat.**
5. **Bene pugnat.**
6. **Sunt pulchrae.**
7. **victoria est magna.**
8. **patria clara**
9. **fabulam longam narrat.**
10. **ex casa**
11. **ab via**
12. **Ubi est?**
13. **ante insulam**
14. **post victoriam**
15. **cum copiis**
16. **ex provinciis**
17. **ad vias**
18. **Britannia est insula.**
19. **Sunt multae puellae.**
20. **Ubi sunt?**

CHAPTER 7

SOME BOYS' NAMES OF LATIN ORIGIN AND THEIR MEANINGS

Rex, king, ruler
Sylvester, of the woods
Victor, conqueror
Claude, lame
Augustus, majestic, august
Lucius, light
Constant, firm, true
Valentine, healthy, strong
Felix, happy, lucky
Patrick, patrician, noble
Dominic, of the Lord
Septimus, the seventh child
Octavius, the eighth child
Martin, of Mars
Aurelius, golden
Dexter, on the right, fortunate
Vincent, conquering
Benedict, blessed
Pius, devoted, faithful
Rufus, red
Clement, kind, mild
Leo, Leon, lion
Clarence, Clare, bright
Paul, small

Vocabulary

Nouns

amicus, amici, *m.*, friend (amicable)
inimicus, inimici, *m.*, (personal) enemy (inimical)
puer, pueri, *m.*, boy (puerile)
vir, viri, *m.*, man (virile)
ager, agri, *m.*, field (agriculture)
bellum, belli, *n.*, war (bellicose)
oppidum, oppidi, *n.*, town
arma, armorum, *n. pl.*, arms, weapons (armoury)
castra, castrorum, *n. pl.*, camp (castle)
periculum, periculi, *n.*, danger (peril)
socius, socii or **soci,** *m.*, ally, comrade (social)
gladius, gladii or **gladi,** *m.*, sword (gladiator)
nuntius, nuntii or **nunti,** *m.*, messenger, message (announce)
proelium, proelii or **proeli,** *n.*, battle
auxilium, auxilii or **auxili,** *n.*, help, aid (auxiliary)

Adjective

angusta, narrow (anguish)

Verbs

aro, arare, plough (arable)
occupo, occupare, seize, take possession of (occupy)
armo, armare, arm (army)
neco, necare, kill
nuntio, nuntiare, announce, report (pronounce)

Prepositions

per (with the Accusative case), through, across (persevere, permeate)

de (with the Ablative case), about, concerning, down from (descend)

Adverb

etiam, even, also

Conjunction

sed, but

THE NOUN: SECOND DECLENSION

1. Nouns that have **-i** as the ending of the Genitive form are **2nd declension.**
2. **2nd declension** nouns that end in **-us** or **-er** or **-ir** in the Nominative case are masculine.
3. **2nd declension** nouns that end in **-um** in the Nominative case are neuter.

2nd declension nouns fall into two main groups—the masculine and the neuter.

1. masculine **2nd declension** nouns.

	Singular		*Use*
Nominative	**amicus**	the friend	Subject
Vocative	**amice**	O friend	Addressing
Accusative	**amicum**	the friend	Direct Object
Genitive	**amici**	of the friend	Possession
Dative	**amico**	to, for the friend	Indirect Object
Ablative	**amico**	by, with, from, etc., the friend	Prepositional Phrases

	Plural		*Use*
Nominative	**amici**	the friends	Subject
Vocative	**amici**	O friends	Addressing
Accusative	**amicos**	the friends	Direct Object
Genitive	**amicorum**	of the friends	Possession
Dative	**amicis**	to, for the friends	Indirect Object
Ablative	**amicis**	by, with, from, etc., the friends	Prepositional Phrases

Other masculine **2nd declension** nouns are spelled with an **-i-** in the stem. Compare **socius** with **amicus:**

	Singular		*Plural*	
Nom.	**socius**	the ally	**socii**	the allies

Voc.	**soci**	O ally	**socii**	O allies
Acc.	**socium**	the ally	**socios**	the allies
Gen.	**socii** or **soci**	of the ally	**sociorum**	of the allies
Dat.	**socio**	to, for the ally	**sociis**	to, for the allies
Abl.	**socio**	by, with, from, etc., the ally	**sociis**	by, with, from, etc., the allies

Some masculine **2nd declension** nouns end in **-er.** Of these, some keep the **-e-** in all forms and others drop the **-e-** after the vocative singular. Notice these nouns and compare them with **amicus** and **socius** above:

	Singular		*Plural*	
Nom.	**puer**	the boy	**pueri**	the boys
Voc.	**puer**	O boy	**pueri**	O boys
Acc.	**puerum**	the boy	**pueros**	the boys
Gen.	**pueri**	of the boy	**puerorum**	of the boys
Dat.	**puero**	to, for the boy	**pueris**	to, for the boys
Abl.	**puero**	by, with, from, etc., the boy	**pueris**	by, with, from, etc., the boys

	Singular		*Plural*	
Nominative	**ager**	the field	**agri**	the fields
Vocative	**ager**	O field	**agri**	O fields
Accusative	**agrum**	the field	**agros**	the fields
Genitive	**agri**	of the field	**agrorum**	of the fields
Dative	**agro**	to, for the field	**agris**	to, for the fields
Ablative	**agro**	by, with, from, etc., the field	**agris**	by, with, from, etc., the fields

Notice that English derivatives often provide a clue as to whether particular nouns retain the **-e-** or lose it (e.g., puerile, agriculture).

2. Neuter **2nd declension** nouns.

	Singular		*Plural*	
Nom.	**bellum**	the war	**bella**	the wars
Voc.	**bellum**	O war	**bella**	O wars
Acc.	**bellum**	the war	**bella**	the wars
Gen.	**belli**	of the war	**bellorum**	of the wars
Dat.	**bello**	to, for the war	**bellis**	to, for the wars
Abl.	**bello**	by, with, from, etc., the war	**bellis**	by, with, from, etc., the wars

Some neuter **2nd declension** nouns are spelled with an **-i-** in the stem. Compare **proelium** with **bellum:**

	Singular		*Plural*	
Nom.	**proelium**	the battle	**proelia**	the battles
Voc.	**proelium**	O battle	**proelia**	O battles
Acc.	**proelium**	the battle	**proelia**	the battles
Gen.	**proelii** or **proeli**	of the battle	**proeliorum**	of the battles
Dat.	**proelio**	to, for the battle	**proeliis**	to, for the battles
Abl.	**proelio**	by, with, from, etc., the battle	**proeliis**	by, with, from, etc., the battles

PREFIXES

In both Latin and English, prefixes are used to modify the basic meaning of a word. These prefixes are usually Latin prepositions. An understanding of the meaning of the prefix makes the meaning of the Latin or English compound word clearer. Prefixes occur most frequently in verb forms. These are some of the most common Latin prepositions and their meanings as prefixes:

a, ab, abs, away	**absum,** be away, be absent
ad, to, towards	**advoco,** call to
ante, before, in front	**antecedo,** go before
post, after, behind	**postpono,** put after, put behind
de, down, from, away	**depono,** put down, put away

Practice Exercises

No. 21. Complete these sentences with the correct word, choosing your answer from the words in brackets.

1. **In** .... **agricolae laborant (agro, agrum)**
2. .... **feminae non amant (Bella, Belli)**
3. **Boni sunt filii** .... **(amicis, amicorum)**
4. .... **in aqua natant (Pueros, Pueri)**
5. .... **arma damus (Viro, Viri)**
6. .... **aramus (Agris, Agros)**
7. .... **auxilium dant (Sociis, Socios)**
8. **In** .... **casas aedificamus (oppidum, oppido)**
9. .... **magnum est (Pericula, Periculum)**
10. .... **filia pulchra est (Viro, Viri)**

No. 22. Change each of these forms to the plural, and give the English.

1. **amicus**
2. **pueri**
3. **agro**
4. **belli**
5. **oppidum**
6. **vir**
7. **periculum**
8. **gladi**
9. **nuntium**
10. **auxilio**
11. **nuntio**
12. **viro**
13. **periculo**
14. **ager**
15. **bellum**

No. 23. Fill in the blanks with the correct English.

1. **castrorum,** .... the camp
2. **socius,** .... ally
3. **gladium,** .... sword
4. **de bello,** .... the war
5. **per periculum,** .... the danger
6. **oppidi,** .... the town
7. **viri,** .... the man
8. **inimici,** .... enemies
9. **agros,** .... fields
10. **pueri,** .... the boy

No. 24. Give the English translation for the following.

1. **ex agro**
2. **armant**
3. **angusta via**
4. **amicos**
5. **cum puero**
6. **ibi arat.**
7. **post castra**
8. **amicorum**
9. **cum viro**
10. **gladiis pugnant.**
11. **oppida monstrant.**
12. **viro arma dant.**
13. **fabulas de bello narramus.**
14. **pericula amat.**
15. **castra sunt in agro.**
16. **per agros ambulatis.**
17. **sunt oppida.**
18. **auxilium das.**
19. **gladii necant.**
20. **in castris habitant.**

CHAPTER 8

READING

Servi	Slaves
1. **Romani servos multos in bello occupant.**	1. The Romans seize many slaves in war.
2. **Ex oppidis Graeciae ad Italiam servos portant.**	2. They carry the slaves to Italy from the towns of Greece.
3. **Servi sunt boni, sed in Italia saepe non sunt laeti.**	3. The slaves are good, but in Italy they are often not happy.
4. **Servi sunt praeda belli et multi**[1] **servos bene curant, sed multi servos male curant.**	4. Slaves are the booty of war and many people care for their slaves well, but many care for them badly.
5. **Servi in agris et in casis et in viis laborant.**	5. The slaves work in the fields and in the houses and on the roads.
6. **Saepe aegri sunt, sed multi**[1] **servos aegros bene curant.**	6. They are often sick, but many people take good care of the sick slaves.
7. **Romani servis multa**[1] **dant et curam bonam dant.**	7. The Romans give many things to the slaves and give them good care.
8. **Servi dominos bonos et dominas bonas amant.**	8. The slaves like good masters and good mistresses.
9. **Multi servi sunt clari et filios dominorum iuvant.**	9. Many slaves are famous and aid the sons of their masters.
10. **Multi domini servos liberant et multi servi liberi sunt viri clari.**	10. Many masters free their slaves and many free slaves are famous men.

[1] NOTE: **multi** (without a noun), 'many people'; **multa** (without a noun), 'many things'.

Vocabulary

Nouns

filius, filii or **fili,** *m.*, son (filial)
cura, curae, *f.*, care (curate)
equus, equi, *m.*, horse (equestrian)
frumentum, frumenti, *n.*, grain
servus, servi, *m.*, slave, servant (servitude)
dominus, domini, *m.*, master (dominate)
domina, dominae, *f.*, mistress

Adjectives

miser, misera, miserum, wretched, unhappy (miserable)
laetus, laeta, laetum, happy
liber, libera, liberum, free (liberal)
aeger, aegra, aegrum, sick, ill

Verbs

libero, liberare, free, set free (liberate)
curo, curare, care for, cure (curator)

Adverbs

hodie, today

ADJECTIVES

A. Inflection

You have already had **1st declension** adjectives. These adjectives also belong to the **2nd declension. 1st declension** and **2nd declension** adjectives have the same endings as the nouns of these declensions.

Singular

	Masculine	*Feminine*	*Neuter*
Nominative	**bonus**	**bona**	**bonum**
Vocative	**bone**	**bona**	**bonum**
Accusative	**bonum**	**bonam**	**bonum**
Genitive	**boni**	**bonae**	**boni**
Dative	**bono**	**bonae**	**bono**
Ablative	**bono**	**bona**	**bono**

Plural

Nominative	**boni**	**bonae**	**bona**
Vocative	**boni**	**bonae**	**bona**
Accusative	**bonos**	**bonas**	**bona**
Genitive	**bonorum**	**bonarum**	**bonorum**
Dative	**bonis**	**bonis**	**bonis**
Ablative	**bonis**	**bonis**	**bonis**

Singular			
Nominative	**miser**	**misera**	**miserum**
Vocative	**miser**	**misera**	**miserum**
Accusative	**miserum**	**miseram**	**miserum**
Genitive	**miseri**, etc.	**miserae**, etc.	**miseri**, etc.

Singular			
Nominative	**pulcher**	**pulchra**	**pulchrum**
Vocative	**pulcher**	**pulchra**	**pulchrum**
Accusative	**pulchrum**	**pulchram**	**pulchrum**
Genitive	**pulchri**, etc.	**pulchrae**, etc.	**pulchri**, etc.

B. Agreement of Adjectives.

Adjectives must agree with the nouns they modify in *Gender*, *Number*, and *Case*. Note that they do not necessarily agree in declension or spelling.

cura bona, good care (*fem.*)
nauta bonus, good sailor (*masc.*)
equus bonus, good horse (*masc.*)
puer bonus, good boy (*masc.*)
servus miser, wretched slave (*masc.*)
equus pulcher, pretty horse (*masc.*)
frumentum bonum, good grain (*neut.*)
bellum miserum, wretched war (*neut.*)
oppidum pulchrum, pretty town (*neut.*)

C. Omission of the Noun with the Adjective.

The masculine and neuter Nominative and Accusative plural of adjectives are commonly used to mean men (or persons) or things. Because the gender makes it clear, the Noun may be omitted.

boni, good people (subject)
bonos, good people (direct object)
bona, good things or goods (subject or direct object)
multi, many people (subject)
multos, many people (direct object)
multa, many things (subject or direct object)

Sometimes the Noun is omitted with other cases in the plural: **multorum,** of many people (possession); **multis,** to, for many people (indirect object).

FAMILIAR PHRASES

ad nauseam, to the point of nausea, or disgust. She talked about it **ad nauseam.**

summum bonum, the greatest good, and source of all other benefits. It was the **summum bonum** for all.

ut supra, as above.

ut infra, as below. These phrases are used to refer to something mentioned in writing, either above or below. **ut supra,** see above. **ut infra,** see below.

Practice Exercises

No. 25. Give the English for the following.

1. **amicus meus natat**
2. **ad casas tuas**
3. **ex fossis altis**
4. **in via longa**
5. **cum viris claris**
6. **ante castra Romana**
7. **post agros meos**
8. **de aqua bona**
9. **per silvam magnam**
10. **mali amici**

No. 26. Add the correct ending to the adjectives.

1. **virorum mult**...........
2. **filiae me**...........
3. **frumento bon**...........
4. **equis tu**...........
5. **me**........... **filiis**
6. **pueros aegr**...........
7. **puellae miser**...........
8. **soci liber**...........
9. **feminam miser**...........
10. **agris pulchr**...........

No. 27. Match the Latin adjective in Column II with the English adjective in Column I.

Column I	*Column II*
1. many **viros**	**pulchrum**
2. sick **pueri**	**multorum**
3. pretty **oppidum**	**multos**
4. many **servorum**	**laetam**
5. happy **puellam**	**aegri**
6. good **fili**	**boni**
7. bad **famam**	**laetus**
8. wretched **equis**	**malam**
9. Roman **terrae**	**miseris**
10. happy **agricola**	**Romanae**

No. 28. Complete the Verbs with the correct endings.

1. **cura**........... (we)
2. **libera**........... (you s.)
3. **labora**........... (you pl.)
4. **lauda**........... (they)
5. **porta**........... (he)
6. **ar**........... (I)
7. **neca**........... (they)
8. **nuntia**........... (she)
9. **occupa**........... (we)
10. **sta**........... (you pl.)

No. 29. Give the English for the following.

1. **sunt liberi.**
2. **dominarum laetarum**
3. **in aquam altam**
4. **de curis magnis**
5. **in agris latis**
6. **de dominis bonis**
7. **cur estis laeti?**
8. **sunt multi.**
9. **sumus aegri.**
10. **cum amicis bonis**
11. **in terris liberis**
12. **est pulchra.**
13. **sunt pulchrae**
14. **est miser.**
15. **multa**

CHAPTER 9

READING

Dei Antiqui

1. **Romani deos multos et deas multas adorant et ad templa saepe eunt.**
2. **Iuppiter in caelo habitat et est bonus et magnus.**
3. **Mercurius est nuntius deorum. Per terram et aquam it et nuntios ad viros et deos portat.**
4. **Nautae Neptunum adorant quod deus oceani est.**
5. **In aqua habitat et amicus nautarum est.**
6. **Mars viros in proeliis et in bellis curat.**
7. **Vulcanus est deus et deis arma dat.**
8. **In patria nostra et in vestra deas et deos non adoramus.**
9. **Hodie in Italia deos multos non adorant.**

The Ancient Gods

1. The Romans worship many gods and many goddesses and often go to the temples.
2. Jupiter lives in the sky and is good and great.
3. Mercury is the messenger of the gods. He goes across land and water and carries messages to men and gods.
4. The sailors worship Neptune because he is the god of the ocean.
5. He lives in the water and is the sailors' friend.
6. Mars takes care of men in battles and in wars.
7. Vulcan is a god and he gives weapons to the gods.
8. In our native country and in yours we do not worship goddesses and gods.
9. Today in Italy they do not worship many gods.

Deae Antiquae

1. **Multas fabulas de deabus[1] Romanis narrant.**
2. **Feminae Romanae deas in templis et in casis suis saepe adorant.**
3. **Iuno regina dearum est.**
4. **Clara et bona est et deas regnat.**
5. **Vesta casas curat.**

The Ancient Goddesses

1. They tell many stories about the Roman goddesses.
2. Roman women often worship the goddesses in the temples and in their homes.
3. Juno is the queen of the goddesses.
4. She is famous and good and she rules the goddesses.
5. Vesta takes care of houses.

6. **Diana puellas curat. Nautae non timent quod nautis fortunam bonam et auxilium dat.**
7. **Dea lunae etiam est et silvas bene amat.**
8. **Venus pulchra est. Feminae multae ad templum eunt.**
9. **Agricolae bene arant quod Ceres agricolas iuvat et frumentum curat.**
10. **Etiam hodie magna est fama dearum Romanarum.**

6. Diana cares for girls. Sailors are not afraid because she gives good fortune and help to sailors.
7. She is also the goddess of the moon and likes the forests very much.
8. Venus is beautiful. Many women go to her temple.
9. Farmers plough well because Ceres helps farmers and cares for the grain.
10. Even today the fame of the Roman goddesses is great.

[1] Notice the spelling of **deabus.** The Dative and Ablative Plural of **dea is deabus** to distinguish them from **deis** (the Dative and Ablative Plural of **deus**).

Vocabulary

Nouns

deus, dei, *m.*, (deity)
dea, deae, *f.*, goddess
caelum, caeli, *n.*, sky, heaven (celestial)
regina, reginae, *f.*, queen (regal)
sapientia, sapientiae, *f.*, wisdom
templum, templi, *n.*, temple
luna, lunae, *f.*, moon (lunar)
fortuna, fortunae, *f.*, fortune, fate, luck (fortunate)

Adjectives

suus, sua, suum, his, her, its, their (own)
noster, nostra, nostrum, our, ours
vester, vestra, vestrum, your, yours

Verbs

adoro, adorare, worship, adore (adorable)
habeo, habere, have, hold (habit)
timeo, timere, fear, be afraid of (timid)
video, videre, see (vision, video)
regno, regnare, rule
eo, ire, go

POSSESSIVE ADJECTIVES

Possessive adjectives are like other adjectives and must, therefore, agree with their nouns in *gender*, *number* and *case*.

Singular	1st person	**meus, mea, meum,** my, mine
	2nd person	**tuus, tua, tuum,** your, yours
	3rd person	**suus, sua, suum,** his (own), her (own), its (own)
Plural	1st person	**noster, nostra, nostrum,** our, ours
	2nd person	**vester, vestra, vestrum,** your, yours
	3rd person	**suus, sua, suum,** their (own), theirs

Note that the 3rd person possessive Adjective is reflexive. By this is meant that it may only be used when the subject of the verb is the possessor. Thus, the word 'own' may always be added for clarity.

e.g. **Suum servum laudat**	He praises his (own) slave	Correct
Suum servum laudo	I praise his slave.	Incorrect

(The correct form of this sentence is—**Eius servum laudo.** See pages 111 and 164.)

Note also that the Vocative Masculine Singular of **meus** is **mi.**

THE VERB: SECOND CONJUGATION

2nd conjugation Verbs have an **-e-** in the Present Infinitive.

hab-e-re, to have **tim-e-re,** to fear **vid-e-re,** to see

2nd conjugation Verbs form the Present Tense in the same way as the **a-conjugation** Verbs, but there is an **-e-** in each form.

Singular	1. **habeo**	I have, do have, am having
	2. **habes**	you have
	3. **habet**	he, she, it has
Plural	1. **habemus**	we have
	2. **habetis**	you have
	3. **habent**	they have

IRREGULAR VERB: EO, IRE

The verb, **eo, ire,** 'to go', is irregular. Its Present Tense is formed as follows.

Singular	1. **eo**	I go, I do go, I am going
	2. **is**	you go
	3. **it**	he, she, it goes
Plural	1. **imus**	we go
	2. **itis**	you go
	3. **eunt**	they go

LATIN ON TOMBSTONES AND MONUMENTS

Latin often appears on tombstones and monuments. The following are some of the abbreviations and phrases frequently used.

c., standing for **circa** or **circum,** meaning about, used with dates

in aeternum, for ever

in perpetuum, for ever

ae.; aet.; aetat., standing for **aetatis,** of age

anno aetatis suae, in the year of his (her) age

ob., standing for **obiit,** meaning he (she) died

hic iacet, here lies

R.I.P., standing for **requiescat in pace,** meaning may he (she) rest in peace

in memoriam, in memory, to the memory of

A.D., standing for **Anno Domini,** meaning: In the year of (our) Lord

Practice Exercises

No. 30. Complete the following sentences by adding the correct form of the Possessive Adjective.

1. *Our* **reginam amamus.**
2. *Your* (*sing.*) **deas laudas.**
3. *His own* **fortunam timet.**
4. *My* **deis frumentum do.**
5. *Their own* **templa aedificant.**
6. *Your* (*pl.*) **reginae clarae sunt.**
7. *Our* **patriam amamus.**
8. *His own* **templum deus habet.**
9. *Their own* **filiarum casas feminae laudant.**
10. *My* **sapientiam laudant.**

No. 31. Give the English for the following.

1. **timeo**
2. **videt**
3. **timetis**
4. **adorat**
5. **eunt**
6. **vides**
7. **timent**
8. **imus**
9. **regnamus**
10. **habent**
11. **timet**
12. **videtis**
13. **habeo**
14. **regnas**
15. **adoratis**

No. 32. Give the English for the following.

1. **antiquos deos**
2. **deae Romanae**
3. **meorum amicorum**
4. **vestri nautae**
5. **tuam praedam**
6. **filias nostras**
7. **suum dominum**
8. **suum filium**
9. **sua sapientia**
10. **gloriam nostram**

No. 33. Translate the following sentences into English.

1. **Gloria vestra non est magna.**
2. **Cur inimicum tuum necas?**
3. **Nuntius multa narrat.**
4. **Viri trans agros suos ambulant.**
5. **Feminae in casis suis sunt.**
6. **Filiae tuae hodie sunt aegrae.**
7. **Multi trans oceanum navigant.**
8. **Sunt deae nostrae.**

9. **Sunt dei nostri.**
10. **Femina suas filias curat.**
11. **Ante casas sto.**
12. **Non multa habet.**
13. **De luna narramus.**
14. **Fortuna vestra est bona.**
15. **Servi dominos timent.**
16. **Cur non timetis?**
17. **Templa pulchra videmus.**
18. **Castra ibi habet.**
19. **Pueros post fossam videmus.**
20. **Sapientiam magnam habetis.**

SECOND REVISION (CHAPTERS 6–9)

VOCABULARY REVISION

Nouns

1. **ager**
2. **amicus**
3. **arma**
4. **auxilium**
5. **bellum**
6. **caelum**
7. **castra**
8. **cura**
9. **dea**
10. **deus**
11. **domina**
12. **dominus**
13. **equus**
14. **filius**
15. **fortuna**
16. **fossa**
17. **frumentum**
18. **gladius**
19. **gloria**
20. **Graecia**
21. **Hispania**
22. **inimicus**
23. **luna**
24. **nuntius**
25. **oceanus**
26. **oppidum**
27. **periculum**
28. **praeda**
29. **proelium**
30. **provincia**
31. **puer**
32. **regina**
33. **sapientia**
34. **servus**
35. **socius**
36. **templum**
37. **victoria**
38. **vir**

1. field
2. friend
3. arms, weapons
4. aid, help
5. war
6. sky, heaven
7. camp
8. care
9. goddess
10. god
11. mistress
12. master
13. horse
14. son
15. fortune, fate, luck
16. ditch
17. grain
18. sword
19. glory
20. Greece
21. Spain
22. (personal) enemy
23. moon
24. messenger, message
25. ocean
26. town
27. danger
28. booty, plunder
29. battle
30. province
31. boy
32. queen
33. wisdom
34. slave, servant
35. comrade, ally
36. temple
37. victory
38. man

Adjectives

1. **aeger**
2. **altus**
3. **angustus**
4. **laetus**
5. **liber**
6. **miser**
7. **noster**
8. **suus**
9. **vester**

1. sick, ill
2. high, deep
3. narrow
4. happy
5. free
6. wretched, unhappy
7. our, ours
8. his, her, its, their (own)
9. your, yours

Verbs

1. **adoro**
2. **aedifico**
3. **armo**
4. **aro**
5. **curo**
6. **exspecto**
7. **habeo**
8. **libero**
9. **neco**
10. **nuntio**
11. **occupo**
12. **regno**
13. **sto**
14. **supero**
15. **timeo**
16. **video**

1. I worship, adore
2. I build
3. I arm
4. I plough
5. I care for, cure
6. I await, expect, wait for
7. I have
8. I free, set free
9. I kill
10. I announce, report
11. I seize, take possession of
12. I rule
13. I stand
14. I surpass, overcome
15. I fear, am afraid of
16. I see

Adverbs

1. **etiam**
2. **hic**
3. **hodie**
4. **ibi**
5. **saepe**
6. **ubi**

1. even, also
2. here, in this place
3. today
4. there, in that place
5. often
6. where, when

Prepositions

1. **ante**
2. **de**
3. **per**
4. **post**
5. **trans**

1. before, in front of
2. about, concerning, down from
3. through
4. behind
5. across

Conjunction

1. **sed** 1. but

Practice Exercises

No. 34. Give the Infinitive of each of these Verbs.

1. **aedifico**
2. **nuntio**
3. **exspecto**
4. **supero**
5. **video**
6. **libero**
7. **regno**
8. **aro**
9. **sto**
10. **eo**
11. **neco**
12. **adoro**
13. **timeo**
14. **habeo**
15. **occupo**

No. 35. Give the Genitive and Gender of these Nouns.

1. **dea**
2. **proelium**
3. **provincia**
4. **bellum**
5. **oceanus**
6. **socius**
7. **fortuna**
8. **amicus**
9. **inimicus**
10. **regina**
11. **puer**
12. **ager**
13. **castra**
14. **periculum**
15. **victoria**
16. **vir**
17. **gladius**
18. **cura**
19. **praeda**
20. **equus**

No. 36.

1. Rearrange these sentences in the correct Latin order:

a. **Frumentum cur datis non viris?**
b. **Curam dat insularum bonam incolis**

2. Give the Present Tense with English meanings of **sto** and **timeo.**

No. 37. Put into English:

1. **agricolas nostros**
2. **filiarum laetarum**
3. **caelum altum**
4. **patriae liberae**
5. **vester servus**
6. **suos filios**
7. **miseros**
8. **vias angustas**
9. **tuus nuntius**
10. **fortuna mea**
11. **multi**
12. **parvus puer**
13. **agrorum latorum**
14. **cura bona**
15. **gladi longi**

GAIUS VALERIUS CATULLUS

Catullus was born about 84 B.C. at Verona, in north-eastern Italy, but spent most of his life in Rome. He was a master of lyric poetry, especially love poems, and made use of many of the best features of Greek verse. Catullus died in 54 B.C.

Da mi basia mille, deinde centum,
dein mille altera, dein secunda centum,
deinde usque altera mille, deinde centum.
Dein, cum milia multa fecerimus,
conturbabimus illa, ne sciamus,
aut ne quis malus invidere possit,
cum tantum sciat esse basiorum.

Catullus V

Odi et amo. Quare id faciam, fortasse requiris.
Nescio, sed fieri sentio et excrucior.

Catullus LXXXV

Give me a thousand kisses, then a hundred,
then another thousand, then a second hundred,
then up to a thousand more, then a hundred.
At the last, when we have given many thousands,
we shall mix their count, lest we know,
or lest any wicked person could envy us,
when he learns our kisses are so many.

Catullus 5

I hate and I love. Why I do this, perhaps you ask.
I do not know, but I feel it happen and I am
tortured.

Catullus 85

THE BIBLE

Toward the end of the fourth century, the Bible was translated into Latin by Saint Jerome and others, and this Latin version is called the Vulgate, or commonly accepted, Bible.

In principio erat Verbum et
Verbum erat apud Deum, et Deus erat
Verbum. Hoc erat in principio
apud Deum. Omnia per ipsum facta
sunt, et sine ipso factum est nihil
quod factum est; in ipso vita erat,
et vita erat lux hominum; et lux in
tenebris lucet, et tenebrae eam non

**comprehenderunt. Fuit homo missus
a Deo, cui nomen erat Ioannes. Hic
venit in testimonium, ut
testimonium perhiberet de lumine,
ut omnes crederent per illum. Non
erat ille lux, sed ut testimonium
perhiberet de lumine. Erat lux
vera, quae illuminat omnem hominem
venientem in hunc mundum; in mundo
erat, et mundus per ipsum factus
est et mundus eum non cognovit.**

Evangelium Secundum Ioannem, I, i–x

In the beginning was the Word, and
the Word was with God, and the Word was
God. The same was in the beginning
with God. All things were made by him;
and without him was not anything made
that was made; in him was life,
and the life was the light of men. And the light
shineth in darkness; and the darkness
comprehended it not. There was a man sent
from God, whose name was John. The same
came for a witness, to
bear witness of the Light,
that all men through him might believe. He was
not that Light, but [was sent] to bear witness
of that Light. [That] was the true Light,
which lighteth every man that cometh
into the world. He was in the world,
and the world was made by him,
and the world knew him not.

St. John, 1, 1–10

CHAPTER 10

READING

Populus Romanus — The Roman People

1. **Populus Romanus certe clarus est.** — The Roman people are indeed famous.
2. **Nonne populum Romanum amas? Ita.** — You like the Roman people, don't you? Yes.
3. **Viri Romani populos terrarum multarum superant et in provinciis Romanis habitant.** — The Roman men conquer the peoples of many lands and live in the Roman provinces.
4. **Multae copiae in provinciis manent et incolas bene regnant.** — Many troops stay in the provinces and rule the inhabitants well.
5. **Vias bonas et aedificia magna et templa pulchra ibi aedificant.** — They build good roads and large buildings and beautiful temples there.
6. **Incolis fortunam bonam portant.** — They bring good fortune to the inhabitants.
7. **Incolae provinciarum saepe sunt socii. Romani sunt domini boni.** — The inhabitants of the provinces often are allies. The Roman people are good masters.
8. **Socii populo Romano auxilium dant.** — The allies give aid to the Roman people.

Alba Longa — Alba Longa

1. **Alba Longa est oppidum in Italia antiqua.** — Alba Longa is a town in ancient Italy.
2. **In Latio est et agros latos et bonos habet.** — It is in Latium and has wide and good fields.
3. **Vergilius de Alba Longa in fabula sua narrat.** — Vergil tells about Alba Longa in his story.
4. **Quod populus Graecus Troiam superat, multi viri sunt clari.** — Because the people of Greece conquer Troy, many men are famous.
5. **Aeneas est vero clarus.** — Aeneas is truly famous.
6. **In Troia non manet, sed ad Latium navigat.** — He does not stay in Troy, but sails to Latium.
7. **Latinus in Latio regnat.** — Latinus rules in Latium.

Alba Longa	Alba Longa
8. **Aeneas Latini socius est.**	8. Aeneas is the ally of Latinus.
9. **Populus Lati est Latinus et lingua est Latina.**	9. The people of Latium are Latin and the language is Latin.

Vocabulary

Nouns

populus, populi, *m.*, people (popular)
aedificium, aedificii or aedifici, *n.*, building (edifice)
lingua, linguae, *f.*, language (linguist)
Latinus, Latini,, *m.*, Latinus
Troia, Troiae, *f.*, Troy
Latium, Latii or **Lati,** *n.*, Latium

Adjectives

Latinus, Latina, Latinum, Latin
Graecus, Graeca, Graecum, Greek

Verbs

paro, parare, prepare, get ready (preparation)
maneo, manere, remain, stay
debeo, debere, owe, ought (debit)
propero, properare, hurry, hasten

Adverbs

nonne, expects the answer 'yes'
num, expects the answer 'no'
ita, yes, thus, so
minime, by no means, not at all (minimum)
vero, truly, in truth (verily)
certe, certainly, surely, indeed

When **populus** is a collective Noun (i.e., represents a group), it is in the singular and its Verb is also singular. In the plural, it means peoples.

populus est clarus	the people are famous
populi terrae sunt multi	the peoples of the earth are many

QUESTIONS AND ANSWERS

1. **Questions.** Latin had no question mark nor, as we have seen, could the meaning of a sentence be changed by altering the word order, and so a question had to be shown by a word in the sentence.

   a. A question word like **cur,** why?, asks a direct question.

   Cur manes? Why do you stay?

   b. A simple question is indicated by **-ne** on the end of the first word.

   Suntne boni? Are they good?

c. **Nonne** at the beginning of a sentence asks a question expecting the answer 'yes'.

Nonne sunt boni? They are good, aren't they? or, Surely they are good?

d. **Num** at the beginning of a sentence asks a question expecting the answer 'no'.

Num sunt boni? They are not good, are they? or, Surely they are not good?

2. Answers to questions may be stated in various ways.

a. By a statement, either positive or negative.

Sunt boni. They are good.
Non sunt boni. They are not good.

b. By a positive or affirmative word.

Ita. Yes. **Vero.** Yes, truly. **Certe.** Certainly.

c. By a negative word.

Minime. By no means, not at all, not in the least

FAMILIAR PHRASES

persona grata, an acceptable (or welcome) person.
persona non grata, an unacceptable (or unwelcome) person.
verbatim ac litteratim, word for word and letter for letter.
pro bono publico, for the public good.
ad infinitum, to infinity; with no limit.
sine dubio, without doubt.
vice versa, changed and turned; turned about.
addenda et corrigenda, things to be added and corrected; a supplement, especially to a book.

Practice Exercises

No. 38. Give the English for these questions and answers.

1. **Nonne amicos habetis? Certe.**
2. **Aedificantne casas? Ita. Casas aedificant.**
3. **Nonne vero times? Vero timeo.**
4. **Num populus pugnat? Populus non pugnat.**
5. **Num viae sunt longae? Viae minime sunt longae.**
6. **Cur ad oppidum eunt? Oppidum amant.**
7. **Manetne vir in aedificio? Vir in aedificio manet.**
8. **Estne provincia libera? Provincia vero est libera.**

9. **Num in oceano navigat? In oceano non navigat.**
10. **Estne regina tua magna? Regina mea certe magna est.**

No. 39. Complete these Verbs by filling in the correct vowel.

1. **vid...........tis**	6. **iuv...........t**	11. **par...........nt**
2. **oppugn...........t**	7. **hab...........o**	12. **deb...........mus**
3. **hab...........s**	8. **man...........nt**	13. **proper...........t**
4. **ador...........s**	9. **tim...........t**	14. **aedific...........s**
5. **vid...........o**	10. **st...........tis**	15. **ambul...........tis**

No. 40. Fill in the correct Infinitive.

1. (To walk) **debeo.**
2. (To fight) **parat.**
3. (To kill) **non debent.**
4. (To conquer) **paratis.**
5. (To call) **debemus.**
6. (To swim) **non parant.**
7. (To help) **properatis.**
8. (To go) **non debetis.**
9. (To attack) **parat.**
10. (To stay) **debes.**

No. 41. Translate these sentences into English.

1. **Cur frumentum ibi parat?**
2. **Nonne linguam Latinam amatis?**
3. **Ubi aedificia vestra stant?**
4. **Pueris gladios dare non debetis.**
5. **Dei arma sua etiam habent.**
6. **De bello longo Troiano fabulam narrant.**
7. **Aeneas cum viris suis ad Italiam navigat.**
8. **Deus populum Graecum iuvat.**
9. **Cur Romani socios suos timent?**
10. **In caelo lunam claram videt.**

CHAPTER 11

READING

Romulus et Remus	Romulus and Remus
1. **Quod Romulus et Remus filii erant dei armorum et belli, populus Romanus proelia amabat.**	1. Because Romulus and Remus were the sons of the god of weapons and of war, the Roman people liked battles.
2. **Erant etiam filii Rheae Silviae.**	2. They were also the sons of Rhea Silvia.
3. **Amulius erat avunculus Rheae Silviae et Albam Longam regnabat, sed pueros non amabat.**	3. Amulius was the uncle of Rhea Silvia and ruled Alba Longa, but he did not love the boys.
4. **Amulius filios Rheae Silviae necare parabat, sed servus in aqua in arca pueros locat[1] et vitas puerorum servat[1].**	4. Amulius prepared to kill the sons of Rhea Silvia, but a slave placed the boys in the water in a chest and saved the lives of the boys.
5. **Mars filios suos ad ripam Tiberis portat[1].**	5. Mars carried his sons to the bank of the Tiber.
6. **Lupa pueros ibi curabat. Tum agricola bonus ad casam suam Romulum et Remum portat[1].**	6. A wolf took care of the boys there. Then a good farmer carried Romulus and Remus to his cottage.

[1] Note that Latin sometimes uses the Present Tense where English would use a Past Tense. This use in Latin is called the Historic Present. Its purpose is to make the narrative vivid.

Sabini	The Sabines
1. **Romulus et Remus cum amicis suis Romam aedificabant, sed oppidum erat parvum et viri erant miseri quod feminae non erant.**	1. Romulus and Remus were building Rome with their friends, but the town was small and the men were unhappy because there were no women.
2. **Romulus ad ludos magnos Sabinos vocat. Sabini ad ludos eunt et feminas et filias suas portant.**	2. Romulus called the Sabines to great games. The Sabines went to the games and brought their women and daughters.
3. **Viri Romani ad casas suas puellas portant. Sabini ad arma properant.**	3. The Roman men carried the girls to their cottages. The Sabines hastened to arms.

Sabini	The Sabines
4. **In Foro Romano tum pugnabant, sed feminae erant miserae quod Sabini multos necabant.**	4. They fought then in the Roman Forum, but the women were unhappy because the Sabines were killing many people.
5. **Sabini vitas virorum suorum servabant, sed Romani praemium victoriae habebant.**	5. The Sabines saved the lives of their men, but the Romans had the reward of victory.
6. **Sabini ad patriam suam sine feminis et puellis eunt.**	6. The Sabines went to their country without their women and daughters.
7. **Feminae et filiae Sabinorum cum Romanis nunc habitabant.**	7. The women and daughters of the Sabines now lived with the Romans.

Vocabulary

Nouns

avunculus, avunculi, *m.*, uncle (avuncular)
arca, arcae, *f.*, chest, box (ark)
vita, vitae, *f.*, life (vital)
ripa, ripae, *f.*, bank (of a river)
lupa, lupae, *f.*, wolf (lupine)
praemium, praemii or **praemi,** *n.*, reward (premium)
ludus, ludi, *m.*, game (ludicrous)
forum, fori, *n.*, forum, market place (forensic)
Roma, Romae, *f.*, Rome
Sabini, Sabinorum, *m.*, the Sabines
Romanus, Romani, *m.*, a Roman

Verbs

servo, servare, save, preserve (preservation)
loco, locare, place, put (locate)

Adverbs

nunc, now
tum, then

Preposition

sine (with the Ablative Case) without (sinecure)

THE VERB: IMPERFECT TENSE

1. The Imperfect Tense is used to show action going on in the past over a period of time. It may be translated 'was', 'used to', or 'did'.
2. Imperfect Tense of **1st conjugation** Verbs.

Singular		*Plural*	
1. **amabam**	I was loving; I loved	1. **amabamus**	we were loving; we loved
2. **amabas**	you were loving; you loved	2. **amabatis**	you were loving; you loved
3. **amabat**	he, she, it was loving; he, she, it loved	3. **amabant**	they were loving; they loved

3. Imperfect Tense of **2nd conjugation** Verbs.

Singular		*Plural*	
1. **habebam**	I was having; I had	1. **habebamus**	we were having; we had
2. **habebas**	you were having; you had	2. **habebatis**	you were having; you had
3. **habebat**	he, she, it was having; he, she, it had	3. **habebant**	they were having; they had

4. The Imperfect Tense of **sum** is irregular, but may be recognized easily by the Stem, **era-**.

Singular		*Plural*	
1. **eram**	I was	1. **eramus**	we were
2. **eras**	you were	2. **eratis**	you were
3. **erat**	he, she, it was	3. **erant**	they were

5. The Imperfect Tense of **eo** is:

Singular		*Plural*	
1. **ibam**	I was going	1. **ibamus**	we were going
2. **ibas**	you were going	2. **ibatis**	you were going
3. **ibat**	he, she, it was going	3. **ibant**	they were going

SCHOOL MOTTOES

Labor omnia vincit, Work overcomes all things. *Cheltenham*
Ex cultu robur, Strength from cultivation. *Cranleigh*
Studio sapientia crescit, Wisdom grows with study. *Framlingham*
Donorum Dei dispensatio fidelis, Faithful stewardship of the gifts of God. *Harrow School*

Non solum ingenii verum etiam virtutis, Not only for character but also for virtue. *Liverpool College*

Sapiens qui prospicit, Wise is he that looks ahead. *Malvern College*

Practice Exercises

No. 42. Fill in the blanks with the correct forms of the Imperfect Tense.

1. **deb............mus**	8. **ador............mus**	15. **vid............mus**
2. **par............m**	9. **loc............s**	16. **hab............s**
3. **proper............nt**	10. **d............tis**	17. **port............tis**
4. **man............nt**	11. **hab............tis**	18. **iuv............t**
5. **tim............t**	12. **st............t**	19. **voc............t**
6. **vid............s**	13. **laud............m**	20. **tim............mus**
7. **cur............m**	14. **man............s**	

No. 43. Give the English for the following.

1. **monstrabat**	6. **timetis**	11. **laudabatis**	16. **servabat**
2. **voco**	7. **erat**	12. **portatis**	17. **ibam**
3. **paramus**	8. **pugnatis**	13. **superabatis**	18. **oppugnabas**
4. **regnabatis**	9. **properabam**	14. **narrant**	19. **habebatis**
5. **debebas**	10. **videbant**	15. **manemus**	20. **eratis**

No. 44. Change the verbs in the following sentences into the Imperfect Tense.

1. **Sabini ad arma properant.**
2. **Mars filios suos ad ripam Tiberis portat.**
3. **Romulus et Remus oppidum aedificant.**
4. **In oppido manemus.**
5. **Amicus bonus es.**
6. **Cur in proelium is?**
7. **Proelia et bella timeo.**
8. **Fabulam longam laudatis.**
9. **Romani deos multos et deas multas adorant.**
10. **Mercurius est nuntius deorum.**

No. 45. Translate the following into English.

1. **Num viros in castris habet?**
2. **Hodie navigare parabamus.**
3. **Amicus tuus in oppido nostro famam bonam habet.**
4. **Cum puellis manere parabam.**
5. **Nonne in silvis multas lupas saepe necat?**

6. **Romani gladios Sabinorum timere non debent.**
7. **Templa et aedificia in oppido locant.**
8. **Cur servis suis praemia dant?**
9. **Agricola cum amico suo in agro stabat.**
10. **Nonne ad templum is?**

CHAPTER 12

READING

Graecia	Greece
1. **Gloria Graeciae et fama incolarum sunt clarae.**	1. The glory of Greece and the fame of her inhabitants are well-known.
2. **Graecia est paeninsula. Agri et silvae populo bonam fortunam et vitam laetam dabant.**	2. Greece is a peninsula. The fields and forests gave good fortune and a happy life to the people.
3. **Nautae trans oceanum ad terras multas navigabant et multa ad fora oppidorum Graecorum portabant.**	3. The sailors sailed across the ocean to many lands and brought many things to the market places of the towns of Greece.
4. **Graecia est propinqua Italiae, sed non est finitima.**	4. Greece is near to Italy, but it is not neighbouring.
5. **Proelia et bella non erant grata incolis, sed cum populis finitimis pugnare saepe parabant.**	5. Battles and wars were not pleasing to the inhabitants, but they often got ready to fight with the neighbouring peoples.
6. **Bellum populo non idoneum erat. Populus multis amicus erat.**	6. War was not suitable to the people. The people were friendly to many.
7. **Roma erat inimica Graeciae et terram occupabat.**	7. Rome was unfriendly to Greece and seized the land.
8. **Tum populus Graecus erat socius populi Romani. Populus Romanus linguam et templa et aedificia Graeciae laudabat.**	8. Then the people of Greece were allies of the people of Rome. The Roman people praised the language and temples and buildings of Greece.
9. **Linguam et templa Graecorum semper laudabimus.**	9. We shall always praise the language and temples of the Greeks.

Barbari	The Barbarians
1. **Romani multos finitimos barbaros habebant.**	1. The Romans had many uncivilized neighbours.
2. **Barbari ob praedam bella et proelia saepe incitabant.**	2. The barbarians often stirred up wars and battles on account of booty.

3. **Nonne nuntii de periculo monebant?**	3. The messengers warned about the danger, didn't they?
4. **Si nuntium portabant, socii auxilium portare atque copias suas armare debebant.**	4. If they brought the message, the allies had to bring aid and arm their troops.
5. **Romani non timebant et ad terras barbaras saepe ibant.**	5. The Romans were not afraid, and they often went to barbarian lands.
6. **Oppida multa ibi oppugnabant et superabant.**	6. They used to attack many towns there and conquer them.
7. **Victoriae copiarum Romanarum erant clarae et magnae.**	7. The victories of the Roman troops were famous and great.
8. **Copiis praemia dabant, si nuntii famas bonas de gloria in provinciis narrabant.**	8. They gave the troops rewards, if the messengers related good reports about their glory in the provinces.
9. **Multi fabulas de gloria Romanorum narrabunt.**	9. Many people will tell stories about the glory of the Romans.

Vocabulary

Adjectives

propinquus, propinqua, propinquum, near (propinquity)
finitimus, finitima, finitimum, neighbouring (affinity)
idoneus, idonea, idoneum, fit, suitable
amicus, amica, amicum, friendly (amicable)
gratus, grata, gratum, pleasing (grateful)
inimicus, inimica, inimicum, unfriendly (inimical)
barbarus, barbara, barbarum, savage, uncivilized, barbarian (barbarous)

Verbs

moneo, monere, warn, advise (monitor, admonition)
incito, incitare, arouse, stir up, incite

Adverbs

cras, tomorrow (procrastinate)
semper, always

Preposition

ob (with the Accusative case), on account of, because of

Conjunctions

atque or **ac,** and also, also. (**ac** is used only before consonants)
si, if

ADJECTIVES

Some adjectives are followed by the Dative case. They are translated with the preposition *to* or *for* in English. Some of these adjectives are **propinquus** (near), **idoneus** (fit), **amicus** (friendly), **inimicus** (unfriendly), **gratus** (pleasing), and **finitimus** (neighbouring).

Est propinquus agro.	He is near to the field.
Est idoneum bello.	It is fit for war.
Est amicus puero.	He is friendly to the boy.
Est inimicus populo.	He is unfriendly to the people.
Est gratus viris.	He is pleasing to the men.
Est finitimum oppido.	It is neighbouring to the town.

THE VERB: FUTURE TENSE

1. The future Tense shows action going on in the future and is translated 'shall' or 'will'. All but the first and last persons have **-bi-** to show the future tense. In the 1st person, **-bo,** and in 3rd person plural, **-bu-** show the future tense.

2. Future Tense of **1st conjugation** Verbs.

Singular		*Plural*	
1. **amabo**	I shall love, like	1. **amabimus**	we shall love, like
2. **amabis**	you will love, like	2. **amabitis**	you will love, like
3. **amabit**	he, she, it will love, like	3. **amabunt**	they will love, like

3. Future Tense of **2nd conjugation** Verbs.

Singular		*Plural*	
1. **habebo**	I shall have, hold	1. **habebimus**	we shall have, hold
2. **habebis**	you will have, hold	2. **habebitis**	you will have, hold
3. **habebit**	he, she, it will have, hold	3. **habebunt**	they will have, hold

4. The Future Tense of sum is irregular, but is recognized by the Stem, **eri-**.

Singular		*Plural*	
1. **ero**	I shall be	1. **erimus**	we shall be
2. **eris**	you will be	2. **eritis**	you will be
3. **erit**	he, she, it will be	3. **erunt**	they will be

5. The Future Tense of **eo** is:

Singular		*Plural*	
1. **ibo**	I shall go	1. **ibimus**	we shall go
2. **ibis**	you will go	2. **ibitis**	you will go
3. **ibit**	he, she, it will go	3. **ibunt**	they will go

LEGAL TERMS

Latin is used extensively in legal phrases and terminology. Some of the more common Latin legal terms are given below.

ius civile, civil law, referring to the laws of legal systems modelled after the Roman law.

ius gentium, the law of nations, referring to International Law.

lex scripta, written law. Written laws are those passed and put into effect by a legislative body or corporation.

lex non scripta, unwritten law. Unwritten law develops out of common practice, custom, and usage. It is sometimes called common law.

sub iudice, before the judge, referring to a case under consideration by the judge or court, but not yet decided.

corpus iuris, the body of law, comprising all the laws of a sovereign power or legislative body collectively.

subpoena, under penalty or punishment. A **subpoena** is a writ naming a person and ordering him to appear in court, under penalty for failure to do so.

corpus delicti, the body of the crime or offence. The **corpus delicti** refers to the circumstances necessary to a crime. In murder, the **corpus delicti** is the fact of a criminal agent or of the death of the victim. It does not refer to the victim's body.

onus probandi, the burden of proof. The burden of proving its case rests with the side that makes the affirmation in a suit.

prima facie, on or at first appearance. **Prima facie** evidence is evidence that, at first presentation, is adequate enough to establish a fact.

Practice Exercises

No. 46. Give the English for these verb forms.

1. **oppugnat**
2. **liberabant**
3. **videbo**
4. **manebit**
5. **erant**
6. **sunt**
7. **debent**
8. **amare**
9. **habebitis**
10. **pugnabas**
11. **dabant**
12. **erit**
13. **incitabunt**
14. **monebit**
15. **portare**
16. **timebit**
17. **ibis**
18. **superabimus**
19. **parabamus**
20. **erunt**
21. **ibunt**
22. **incitabat**
23. **monebatis**
24. **sumus**
25. **oppugnabamus**
26. **incitabit**
27. **natabant**
28. **locabatis**
29. **servabis**
30. **iuvabitis**

No. 47. Give the English for these phrases.

1. **de caelo claro**
2. **finitimus patriae meae**
3. **propinquum insulis**
4. **cum amico nostro**
5. **ad aedificia alta**
6. **in fossis latis**
7. **gratus socio suo**
8. **ante agros**
9. **amicus servis**
10. **post bellum**
11. **inimici reginae**
12. **de victoria tua**
13. **per proelia multa**
14. **idoneus viro**
15. **sine praeda**

No. 48. Give the tense of the following verbs.

1. **sum**
2. **monebunt**
3. **manebat**
4. **debet**
5. **erat**
6. **dabat**
7. **narrabit**
8. **oppugnant**
9. **pugnabis**
10. **erit**
11. **iuvabis**
12. **natabas**
13. **amabunt**
14. **timebat**
15. **incitabis**
16. **liberabam**
17. **debebit**
18. **narrabant**
19. **ibamus**
20. **erunt**

No. 49. Translate the following into English.

1. **Ad vias angustas ambulabit.**
2. **Ante templa stabant.**
3. **In oceano natabatis.**
4. **In aqua pugnabunt.**
5. **Feminis grata est.**
6. **Patriam liberam habere debebunt.**
7. **Puellae natabunt.**
8. **Finitimos suos amabat.**
9. **Avunculos tuos servabis.**
10. **Reginam laudabunt.**
11. **Ubi esse debetis?**
12. **Puerum vocabas.**
13. **Erit inimicus nuntio.**
14. **Non est provinciae propinquum.**
15. **Gladios tuos non timebimus.**
16. **Servi vestri iuvant.**
17. **Vir ibi manebit.**
18. **Fossam altam parabamus.**
19. **Dominus fabulam narrabit.**
20. **Agrum arabimus.**

CHAPTER 13

READING

Gallia	Gaul
1. **Gallia, patria Gallorum, erat Germaniae et Hispaniae finitima.**	1. Gaul, the native country of the Gauls, was neighbouring to Germany and Spain.
2. **Galli proelia et bella non amabant, sed bellum non timebant.**	2. The Gauls did not like battles and wars, but they did not fear war.
3. **Romani contra Gallos saepe pugnabant. Galli pro patria sua tum bene pugnabant.**	3. The Romans often fought against the Gauls. The Gauls then fought hard for their native country.
4. **Romani in Gallia legatos habebant quod Galli Romanis amici non erant.**	4. The Romans had lieutenants in Gaul because the Gauls were not friendly to the Romans.
5. **Legati cum Gallis pugnare saepe parabant.**	5. The lieutenants often got ready to fight with the Gauls.
6. **Caesar, vir clarus, in Gallia pugnabat et ob victorias suas gloriam magnam habebat.**	6. Caesar, a famous man, fought in Gaul and had great glory because of his victories.
7. **Oppida Galliae erant clara.**	7. The towns of Gaul were famous.
8. **Ibi erant oppida multa et pulchra ac silvae multae et agri boni.**	8. There were many and beautiful towns there, and also many forests and good fields.
9. **Ob periculum belli Romani in multis terris finitimis legatos habebant.**	9. On account of the danger of war the Romans had lieutenants in many neighbouring lands.
10. **Romani pro patria etiam sine praemiis magnis et praeda pugnabant.**	10. The Romans fought for their country even without large rewards and booty.
11. **Erant in Gallia multi agri lati. Agricolis idonea erat.**	11. There were many wide fields in Gaul. It was suitable for farmers.
12. **In Gallia Romani linguam Latinam semper memoria tenebant.**	12. In Gaul, the Romans always remembered the Latin language.

Vocabulary

Nouns

memoria, memoriae, *f.*, memory (memorize)
legatus, legati, *m.*, lieutenant, legate, ambassador (legation)
Gallia, Galliae, *f.*, Gaul (the country) (Gallic)
Gallus, Galli, *m.*, a Gaul (person)
Germanus, Germani, *m.*, a German (person) (Germanic)

Verbs

teneo, tenere, hold, keep, have (tenable)
memoria tenere, to remember (literally, to keep by memory)

Prepositions

contra (with the Accusative case), against (contradict)
pro (with the Ablative case), for, on behalf of

NOUNS IN APPOSITION

A noun is said to be in apposition to another noun when it is being used, like an adjective, to describe. For this reason, it must be in the same case as the noun it is in apposition to.

Julia, mea filia, natat. Julia, my daughter, is swimming.

In this sentence, **filia** is in apposition to **Julia.** Since **Julia,** as the subject of the sentence, is in the Nominative case, **filia** must also be in the Nominative case.

VERBS: THE IMPERATIVE MOOD

The Imperative of a verb is used to express a direct command. It is singular or plural according to the number of people being addressed.

1. **1st conjugation** Verbs form the Imperative:

Singular	*Plural*
ama love, like!	**amate** love, like!

2. **2nd conjugation** Verbs form the Imperative:

Singular	*Plural*
habe have, hold!	**habete** have, hold!

3. The Imperative of **sum** is:

Singular	*Plural*
es be!	**este** be!

4. The Imperative of **eo** is:

Singular		*Plural*	
i	go!	**ite**	go!

FAMILIAR QUOTATIONS

Virginibus puerisque, For girls and boys. *Horace*

Non scholae sed vitae discimus, We learn not for school but for life. *Seneca*

Parvum parva decent, Small things become the small. *Horace*

Eheu fugaces anni, Alas the fleeting years. *Horace*

Vera amicitia est inter bonos, There is true friendship only among good men. *Cicero*

Ave atque vale, Hail and farewell. *Catullus*

Da dextram misero, Give your right hand to the wretched. *Virgil*

Practice Exercises

No. 50. Complete the following sentences with the correct form of the Imperative. Choose your answers from the words in brackets.

1. ...., **puella (Ambula, Ambulate)**
2. .... **in aqua, pueri (Nata, Natate)**
3. ...., **vir (Pugna, Pugnate)**
4. .... **insulam, nautae (Occupa, Occupate)**
5. .... **puellae equum, agricola (Da, Date)**
6. .... **in agris, agricolae (Mane, Manete)**
7. .... **arma, viri (Tene, Tenete)**
8. .... **ad insulam, nautae (Naviga, Navigate)**
9. .... **sapientiam, puella (Ama, Amate)**
10. .... **socios, nauta. (Mone, Monete)**

No. 51. Translate these nouns in Apposition.

1. **vir, agricola**
2. **viri, nautae**
3. **patria, Britannia**
4. **puer, amicus**
5. **regina, puella**
6. **Galli, socii nostri**
7. **nuntius, puer**
8. **Gallos, amicos vestros**
9. **dominum, amicum**
10. **filiorum, puerorum**

No. 52. Translate these sentences into English.

1. **Puer aeger, filius tuus, in oppido manebit.**
2. **In proelium properate et patriam vestram servate.**
3. **Contra bellum, popule Romane, viros tuos incita.**
4. **Monete incolas Galliae, nuntii.**
5. **Sabinos, finitimos nostros, ad ludos vocabo.**

6. **Puellae, videte templa, aedificia pulchra.**
7. **Roma, oppidum in Italia, clara erit.**
8. **Mi fili, Galliam memoria tene.**
9. **Videbatisne forum, Romae gloriam?**
10. **Avunculos meos, nuntios, exspectabo.**

THIRD REVISION (CHAPTERS 10–13)

Vocabulary

Nouns

1. **aedificium**
2. **arca**
3. **avunculus**
4. **barbarus**
5. **finitimus**
6. **forum**
7. **Gallia**
8. **Gallus**
9. **Germanus**
10. **caelum**
11. **Latium**
12. **legatus**
13. **lingua**
14. **ludus**
15. **lupa**
16. **memoria**
17. **populus**
18. **praemium**
19. **ripa**
20. **Roma**
21. **Romanus**
22. **Sabini**
23. **Troia**
24. **vita**

1. building
2. chest, box
3. uncle
4. barbarian
5. neighbour
6. forum, market place
7. Gaul
8. a Gaul
9. a German
10. sky, heaven
11. Latium
12. lieutenant, legate
13. language
14. game
15. wolf
16. memory
17. people
18. reward
19. river bank
20. Rome
21. a Roman
22. the Sabines
23. Troy
24. life

Adjectives

1. **amicus**
2. **barbarus**
3. **finitimus**
4. **gratus**
5. **idoneus**
6. **inimicus**
7. **Latinus**
8. **propinquus**

1. friendly
2. savage, uncivilized, barbarian
3. neighbouring
4. pleasing
5. fit, suitable
6. unfriendly
7. Latin
8. near

Verbs

1. **debeo**
2. **incito**
3. **loco**
4. **maneo**
5. **moneo**
6. **paro**
7. **propero**
8. **servo**
9. **teneo**
10. **memoria teneo**

1. I owe, ought
2. I arouse, stir up, incite
3. I place, put
4. I remain, stay
5. I warn, advise
6. I prepare, get ready
7. I hurry, hasten
8. I save, preserve
9. I hold, keep, have
10. I remember

Adverbs

1. **certe**
2. **cras**
3. **ita**
4. **minime**
5. **nonne**
6. **num**
7. **nunc**
8. **tum**
9. **vero**

1. certainly, indeed, surely
2. tomorrow
3. thus, so, yes
4. not at all, by no means
5. expects the answer 'yes'
6. expects the answer 'no'
7. now
8. then
9. truly, in truth

Prepositions

1. contra — 1. against
2. ob — 2. on account of, because of
3. pro — 3. for, in behalf of
4. sine — 4. without

Conjunction

1. atque, ac — 1. and also, also

Practice Exercises

No. 53. Say whether these questions are simple questions, expect the answer yes, or expect the answer no.

1. **Estne aeger?**
2. **Ubi est puer?**
3. **Cur times?**
4. **Nonne Romanos memoria tenent?**
5. **Num manebat?**
6. **Nonne amici sunt?**
7. **Num manetis?**
8. **Properatne?**
9. **Cur debent?**
10. **Ubi arcam locat?**

No. 54. Change these verbs to the Imperfect tense.

1. **debeo**
2. **locas**
3. **incitat**
4. **properant**
5. **paratis**
6. **tenemus**
7. **is**
8. **teneo**
9. **manemus**
10. **monet**

No. 55. Change these verbs to the Future tense.

1. **videbam**
2. **stabant**
3. **timebas**
4. **regnabat**
5. **necabatis**
6. **habebamus**
7. **aedificabam**
8. **superabas**
9. **curabamus**
10. **ibant**

No. 56. Give the Singular and Plural Imperatives of these verbs.

1. **servare**
2. **monere**
3. **incitare**
4. **manere**
5. **navigare**
6. **parare**
7. **tenere**
8. **properare**
9. **necare**
10. **pugnare**
11. **ire**
12. **esse**

THE BIBLE

In principio creavit Deus caelum et terram. Terra autem erat inanis et vacua, et tenebrae erant super faciem abyssi, et spiritus Dei ferebatur super aquas.

Dixitque Deus: Fiat lux. Et facta est lux. Et vidit Deus lucem quod esset bona et divisit lucem a tenebris. Appellavitque lucem diem et tenebras noctem. Factumque est vespere et mane, dies unus.

Dixit quoque Deus: Fiat firmamentum in medio aquarum et dividat aquas ab aquis. Et fecit Deus firmamentum, divisitque aquas, quae erant sub firmamento, ab his quae erant super firmamentum. Et factum est ita. Vocavitque Deus firmamentum caelum. Et factum est vespere et mane, dies secundus.

Dixit vero Deus: Congregentur aquae, quae sub caelo sunt, in locum unum, et appareat arida. Et factum est ita. Et vocavit Deus aridam terram congregationesque aquarum appellavit maria. Et vidit Deus quod esset bonum. Et ait: Germinet terra herbam virentem et facientem semen et lignum pomiferum faciens fructum iuxta genus suum, cuius semen in semetipso sit super terram. Et factum est ita. Et protulit terra herbam virentem et facientem semen iuxta genus suum lignumque faciens fructum et habens unumquodque sementem secundum speciem suam. Et vidit Deus quod esset bonum. Et factum est vespere et mane, dies tertius.

Liber Genesis I, i–xiii

In the beginning God created the heaven and the earth. And the earth was without form, and void; and darkness was upon the face of the deep. And the Spirit of God moved upon the face of the waters.

And God said: Let there be light. And there was light. And God saw the light, that it was good; and God divided the light from the darkness. And God called the light Day, and the darkness he called Night. And the evening and the morning were the first day.

And God said: Let there be a firmament in the midst of the waters, and let it divide the waters from the waters. And God made the firmament, and divided the waters which were under the firmament from the waters which were above the firmament. And it was so. And God called the firmament Heaven. And the evening and the morning were the second day.

And God said: Let the waters under the heaven be gathered together unto one place, and let the dry land appear. And it was so. And God called the dry land Earth; and the gathering together of the waters called the Seas. And God saw that it was good. And God said: Let the earth bring forth grass, the herb yielding seed, and the fruit tree yielding fruit after his kind, whose seed is in itself, upon the earth. And it was so. And the earth brought forth grass, and herb yielding seed after his kind, and the tree yielding fruit, whose seed was in itself, after his kind. And God saw that it was good. And the evening and the morning were the third day.

Genesis I, 1–13

CHAPTER 14

READING

Germani	The Germans
1. **Germania Galliae finitima erat et Italiae propinqua.**	1. Germany was neighbouring to Gaul and near Italy.
2. **Incolae Germaniae, terrae magnae, non in oppidis magnis et pulchris, sed in silvis aut in casis parvis habitabant, quod barbari erant.**	2. The inhabitants of Germany, a big country, did not live in large and beautiful towns, but in the forests or in small cottages, because they were uncivilized.
3. **Inter Germanos erant multi sagittarii boni. In silvis lupae multae sagittis Germanorum necabantur.**	3. Among the Germans there were many good archers. In the forests many wolves used to be killed by the arrows of the Germans.
4. **Multae terrae et patriae a Vandaliis oppugnabantur atque superabantur.**	4. Many lands and native countries used to be attacked by the Vandals and conquered.
5. **Germani populis finitimis non erant amici.**	5. The Germans were not friendly to the neighbouring peoples.
6. **Vandalii robusti Italiam oppugnabant et populus certe terrebatur quod pro vita sua timebat.**	6. The strong Vandals attacked Italy and the people were indeed frightened because they feared for their lives.
7. **Ubi Vandalii populum superabant, multi vero erant miseri.**	7. When the Vandals conquered the people, many were truly wretched.

Vocabulary

Nouns

pecunia, pecuniae, *f.*, money (pecuniary)

donum, doni, *n.*, gift, present (donation)

sagitta, sagittae, *f.*, arrow

sagittarius, sagittarii or **sagittari,** *m.*, archer (Sagittarius)

littera, litterae, *f.*, letter (of the alphabet). In the plural, a letter or epistle (literal, literature)

Adjective

robustus, robusta, robustum, strong, robust

Adverb

mox, soon, presently

Verbs

moveo, movere, move
castra movere, to break camp
doleo, dolere, grieve, be sorry (dolorous)
terreo, terrere, frighten, scare, terrify

Preposition

inter (with the Accusative case), between, among (interrupt)

Conjunction

aut, or

THE VERB: PASSIVE VOICE

The Passive Voice of a verb is used when the subject is the receiver of the action.

Puer amatur. The boy is loved.

The forms of the Present, Imperfect and Future tenses in the Passive Voice are easily remembered, since they are formed in the same way as the Active tenses.

1. Present Passive tense

1st conjugation

amor	I am loved, being loved
amaris	you are loved, being loved
amatur	he, she, it is loved, being loved
amamur	we are loved, being loved
amamini	you are loved, being loved
amantur	they are loved, being loved

2nd conjugation

habeor	I am held, being held
haberis	you are held, being held
habetur	he, she, it is held, being held
habemur	we are held, being held
habemini	you are held, being held
habentur	they are held, being held

2. Imperfect Passive tense

1st conjugation

amabar	I was being loved, was loved
amabaris	you were being loved, etc.
amabatur	he, she, it was being loved, etc.
amabamur	we were being loved, etc.
amabamini	you were being loved, etc.
amabantur	they were being loved, etc.

2nd conjugation

habebar	I was being held, was held
habebaris	you were being held, etc.
habebatur	he, she, it was being held, etc.
habebamur	we were being held, etc.
habebamini	you were being held, etc.
habebantur	they were being held, etc.

3. Future Passive tense

1st conjugation

amabor	I shall be loved
amaberis	you will be loved
amabitur	he, she, it will be loved
amabimur	we shall be loved
amabimini	you will be loved
amabuntur	they will be loved

2nd conjugation

habebor	I shall be held
habeberis	you will be held
habebitur	he, she, it will be held
habebimur	we shall be held
habebimini	you will be held
habebuntur	they will be held

The only irregularities are in the Future tense: **amaberis, habeberis.** The Passive Voice of **video** often means 'seem'.

AGENTS AND INSTRUMENTS

Passive verbs are often accompanied by a prepositional phrase introduced by the preposition 'by' and indicating who or what is performing the action.

The girl is praised **by the woman**
The man is killed **by an arrow**

In these cases, Latin makes an important distinction between an *agent* of an action (i.e., a person) and an *instrument* by which an action is performed (i.e., usually a thing). The former is expressed by using the preposition **a, ab** with the Ablative; the latter is expressed by using the Ablative *alone*. Thus:

The girl is praised by the woman	**Puella** *a femina* **laudatur**
The man is killed by an arrow	**Vir** *sagitta* **necatur**

FAMILIAR PHRASES

vi et armis, by force and arms.
pax vobiscum, peace be with you.
tempus fugit, time flies.
agenda, things that have to be done.
multum in parvo, much in little.
senatus populusque Romanus, the Senate and the Roman people. Abbr. S.P.Q.R.
res gestae, things done; acts or deeds.
alter idem, another self, referring to a close friend.
apparatus criticus, critical apparatus or material; reference material used in the critical study of a piece of literature.

Practice Exercises

No. 57. Complete the following sentences by inserting the appropriate form of the verb. Choose your answer from the word in brackets.

1. **A puellis...............(videbis, videberis)**
2. **Agricola sagitta............... (necatur, necat)**
3. **Agri .... (arabantur, arabunt)**
4. **Feminae pecuniam filiis .... (dant, dantur)**
5. **Legati ad Galliam .... (eunt, it)**
6. **A viro .... (vocabor, vocabo)**
7. **A sociis nostris .... (iuvamur, iuvamus)**
8. **Templa Romani .... (aedificabant, aedificabantur)**
9. **Num vir gladio .... (superabit, superabitur)**
10. **Oppidumne viri armis .... (occupabuntur, occupabunt)**

No. 58. Change these verbs to the Passive Voice.

1. **exspectabam**
2. **tenent**
3. **monebit**
4. **videbat**
5. **amabit**
6. **habet**
7. **videbatis**
8. **portabit**
9. **movebitis**
10. **parant**
11. **laudabunt**
12. **locatis**
13. **servabunt**
14. **videmus**
15. **incito**
16. **monebas**
17. **servas**
18. **debebat**
19. **vident**
20. **monebant**

No. 59. Give the English for these Ablative phrases.

1. **cum legato**
2. **gladio**
3. **a pueris**
4. **fossis**
5. **ab amicis**
6. **a nuntio**
7. **cum avunculis**
8. **bellis**
9. **ab dominis**
10. **cum socio**
11. **equis**
12. **sagittis**
13. **a sagittario**
14. **a dea**
15. **cum servo**
16. **sapientia**
17. **a populo**
18. **cum inimicis**
19. **aqua**
20. **ab viro**

No. 60. Translate the following into English.

1. **Pecunia viro atque puellae dabitur quod puer aeger est.**
2. **Ad oppidum finitimum ibam sed ab amicis memoria tenebar.**
3. **Dolere videntur sed mox laeti erunt.**
4. **Ob pericula viri proelia timebant.**
5. **Bene pugnate pro Britannia, patria vestra.**
6. **Multi ad templa deorum ambulabant.**
7. **Cur ludus ab amico vestro dabitur?**
8. **In casa ubi puellas videtis habitabamus.**
9. **Num vir gladio oppugnabitur?**
10. **Nonne populus castra movere parabat?**

CHAPTER 15

READING

Cincinnatus

1. **Roma saepe pacem non habebat, sed in periculo erat et contra finitimos suos pugnabat.**
2. **Roma copias bonas atque arma habebat, sed oppugnabatur. Populus timebat quod ducem non habebat.**
3. **Nuntii ad Cincinnatum eunt et ubi Cincinnatum, agricolam Romanum, in agro vident, de bello et magno periculo narrant.**
4. **Cincinnatus agros suos bene amabat, sed Romam quoque bene amabat et ab nuntiis movebatur.**
5. **Populo Romano magnum auxilium dabat quod dictator erat et Romam servabat.**
6. **Copiae Romanae a periculo patriam suam liberant. Cincinnatus a Romanis semper memoria tenebatur.**

Cincinnatus

1. Often Rome did not have peace, but was in danger and fought against her neighbours.
2. Rome had good troops and weapons, but she was being attacked. The people were frightened because they did not have a leader.
3. Messengers go to Cincinnatus and when they see Cincinnatus, a Roman farmer, in the field they tell about the war and great danger.
4. Cincinnatus loved his fields well, but he loved Rome well also and was moved by the messengers.
5. He gave great help to the Roman people because he was dictator and he saved Rome.
6. The Roman troops free their country from danger. Cincinnatus was always remembered by the Romans.

Horatius

1. **Magnae copiae hostium Romam oppugnabant.**
2. **Pars urbis Romae erat in periculo quod hostes pontem ibi occupare parabant.**
3. **Homines Romani ab Horatio, milite bono, contra hostes incitabantur sed pontem non tenebant.**

Horatius

1. Large forces of the enemy were attacking Rome.
2. Part of the city of Rome was in danger because the enemy was preparing to seize the bridge there.
3. The men of Rome were being stirred up against the enemy by Horatius, a good soldier, but they did not hold the bridge.

Horatius

4. **Tum Horatius in ponte sine auxilio stat. Pro vita sua non timebat.**
5. **Mox gladio suo multos milites hostium necat et pontem tenet. Magna erat caedes.**
6. **Post Horatium milites Romani laborabant. Mox pons non stabat.**
7. **Romani victoriam habent et Roma servatur quod aqua inter Romam et hostes stabat.**
8. **Horatius trans aquam ad ripam ubi erant socii natat.**
9. **Horatius inter Romanos laudabatur. Multi agri Horatio dantur.**

Horatius

4. Then Horatius stood on the bridge without aid. He did not fear for his life.
5. Soon he killed many of the enemy's soldiers with his sword and held the bridge. The slaughter was great.
6. Behind Horatius the Roman soldiers were working. Soon the bridge was not standing.
7. The Romans had the victory and Rome was saved because the water stood between Rome and the enemy.
8. Horatius swam across the water to the river bank where his comrades were.
9. Horatius was praised among the Romans. Many fields were given to Horatius.

Vocabulary

Nouns

miles, militis, *m.*, soldier (military)
pax, pacis, *f.*, peace (pacific)
caput, capitis, *n.*, head (capital)
dictator, dictatoris, *m.*, dictator
homo, hominis, *m.*, man (homicide)
Cincinnatus, Cincinnati, *m.*, Cincinnatus
hostis,[1] **hostis,** *m.*, enemy **(hostium)** (hostile)
pars, partis, *f.*, part **(partium)** (partake, particle)
dux, ducis, *m.*, leader (duke)
mare, maris, *n.*, sea **(marium)** (marine)
urbs, urbis, *f.*, city **(urbium)** (suburb)
caedes, caedis, *f.*, slaughter, murder **(caedium)**
pons, pontis, *m.*, bridge **(pontium)** (pontoon)
Horatius, Horati, *m.*, Horatius

Conjunction

quoque, also

[1] **hostis** in the singular means an individual enemy in war; in the plural, it is a collective noun, the enemy, and its verb must also be plural.

THE NOUN: THIRD DECLENSION

More nouns belong to the 3rd declension than to any other declension.

Gender

The 3rd declension contains nouns of all genders—masculine, feminine and neuter. The endings of these nouns give no indication of their gender (although the neuter nouns do differ from the others in some cases), so that the genders must be memorized. The meaning is often helpful here.

Inflection

There is a wide variation in the spellings of 3rd declension nouns in the Nominative singular:

homo pax dictator miles caput

The Genitive case, however, always ends in **-is** and provides us with the stem which enables us to form the other cases. Thus:

Nominative Singular				
homo	**pax**	**dictator**	**miles**	**caput**
Genitive Singular				
hominis	**pacis**	**dictatoris**	**militis**	**capitis**
Stem				
homin-	**pac-**	**dictator-**	**milit-**	**capit-**

Once we know the *Genitive Singular* and, therefore, the stem of a 3rd declension noun and its *gender*, we can form the other cases on the following pattern:

	MASCULINE AND FEMININE NOUNS		NEUTER NOUNS	
	Singular	*Plural*	*Singular*	*Plural*
Nominative	**homo**	**homin-es**	**caput**	**capit-a**
Vocative	**homo**	**homin-es**	**caput**	**capit-a**
Accusative	**homin-em**	**homin-es**	**caput**	**capit-a**
Genitive	**homin-is**	**homin-um**	**capit-is**	**capit-um**
Dative	**homin-i**	**homin-ibus**	**capit-i**	**capit-ibus**
Ablative	**homin-e**	**homin-ibus**	**capit-e**	**capit-ibus**

Note that with masculine and feminine nouns the Vocative Singular is the same as the Nominative Singular, and that with neuter nouns the Nominative, Vocative and Accusative Singular have the same form.

Exceptions

1. Some nouns have **-ium,** instead of **-um,** in the Genitive Plural. The rule governing this is that if a noun increases its number of syllables in the Genitive Singular, it does not further increase them in the Genitive Plural (i.e., Genitive Plural **-um**). Conversely, if it does not increase in the Genitive Singular, it does increase in the Genitive Plural (i.e., Genitive Plural **-ium**). Thus:

Nominative Singular	*Genitive Singular*	*Genitive Plural*
homo (2 syllables)	**hominis** (3)	**hominum** (3)
hostis (2)	**hostis** (2)	**hostium** (3)

There are, however, a number of exceptions to this rule on both sides, so that from now on those nouns that have **-ium** in the Genitive Plural will be indicated in the vocabularies.

2. If a noun having **-ium** in the Genitive Plural is of the neuter gender, other changes of ending occur.

   a. The Ablative Singular ending becomes **-i.** (Some masculine and feminine nouns can also have this form of Ablative Singular.)
   b. The Nominative, Vocative and Accusative Plural endings become **-ia**

Thus **mare, maris,** *n.*, the sea is declined:

	Singular	*Plural*
Nominative	**mare**	**mar*ia***
Vocative	**mare**	**mar*ia***
Accusative	**mare**	**mar*ia***
Genitive	**maris**	**mar*ium***
Dative	**mari**	**maribus**
Ablative	**mar*i***	**maribus**

SUFFIXES

Suffixes are applied to the stems of nouns and adjectives to give a certain meaning to both Latin and English words or to form one part of speech from another. These are some of the more common suffixes that are added to Latin words to give them a special meaning:

-tor (*masc.*), **-trix** (fem.) denote the doer or agent. English, -er, -or.

victor, conqueror
genitor, father
genetrix, mother

-or denotes an action or state. English, -or.

terror, fear, terror

-tio denotes an action. English, -tion.

oratio, oration
(from the verb **oro, orare,** to plead)

-ia, -tia, -tudo, -tas denote a quality or state.

-ia becomes -y in English.

miseria, misery
iniuria, injury
victoria, victory

-tia becomes -ce, -cy in English.

diligentia, diligence
potentia, potency
clementia, clemency

-tudo becomes -tude in English.

longitudo, longitude
latitudo, latitude
altitudo, altitude
magnitudo, magnitude

-tas becomes -ty in English.

gravitas, gravity
dignitas, dignity

Practice Exercises

No. 61. Give the English for the following phrases.

1. **pacis longae**
2. **pro milite**
3. **milites clari**
4. **pax Romana**
5. **capita vestra**
6. **dictatoribus suis**
7. **caput tuum**
8. **ab hominibus laetis**
9. **pars idonea**
10. **in urbe antiqua**
11. **maris nostri**
12. **milites robustos**
13. **homines boni**
14. **pacem longam**
15. **in capitibus suis**
16. **contra dictatores**
17. **cum hominibus**
18. **sine militibus tuis**
19. **de pace longa**
20. **homo amicus**

No. 62. Complete the following sentences by adding the appropriate form of the adjective. Choose your answer from the words in brackets.

1. **Arma militum .... videmus (robustum, robustorum)**
2. **Horatius in ponte .... stabat (angusto, angusta)**
3. **Caput .... habet (magnum, magnam)**
4. **In urbibus .... viae longae erant (antiquus, antiquis)**
5. **Gladium militi .... do (boni, bono)**
6. **Fabulas de caede .... narramus (magna, magno)**
7. **Mare .... est (latus, latum)**
8. **.............. pars hostium oppidum oppugnat (magnas, magna)**
9. **Pax militibus .... non est (idonea, idoneae)**
10. **Homines .... esse debent (amicos, amici)**

No. 63. Change each of the following to the plural, and give the English.

1. **dux**
2. **militem**
3. **capiti**
4. **partem**
5. **hosti**
6. **urbis**
7. **caedem**
8. **pons**
9. **homo**
10. **caput**
11. **militis**
12. **partis**
13. **hominem**
14. **ducis**
15. **dictatorem**
16. **ponti**
17. **maris**
18. **pontis**
19. **hostem**
20. **urbe**

No. 64. Translate the following into English.

1. **Cincinnatus ex agro suo vocatur et auxilium dat.**
2. **Homines in terra regnant sed dei in caelo atque in terra regnant.**

3. **Praemia homini magno ab populo Romano dabuntur.**
4. **Lingua Latina semper servabitur.**
5. **Cras non arabit sed patriam nostram mox servabit.**
6. **Ad ripam natabat quod pons non stabat.**
7. **Bene pugna gladio, Horati, pro patria tua.**
8. **Milites, filii mei, gladiis armabuntur.**
9. **Ob pericula tuam aquam servare debes.**
10. **Nauta mare amat sed agricola agros suos amat.**

CHAPTER 16

READING

Daedalus et Icarus

1. **Daedalus hominem necat et cum filio suo, Icaro, ex Graecia ad Cretam properat.**
2. **Pater filiusque parva in insula diu manebant. Nunc ad Graeciam volare parant.**
3. **Bene laborant et alas parant.**
4. **Pater puerum monet: ‘Per caelum, sed non ad solem volabimus.’**
5. **Sol erat clarus. Icarus ob alas suas erat laetus.**
6. **Consilium patris sui non diu memoria tenebat.**
7. **Cum patre suo non manet, sed summo in caelo ante solem volat.**
8. **Cera in alis pueri non manet.**
9. **Pater filium suum medio in mari mox videbat.**
10. **Icarus non servatur. Daedalus vero dolebat quod puer consilio patris non monebatur.**

Daedalus and Icarus

1. Daedalus kills a man and with his son, Icarus, hurries from Greece to Crete.
2. The father and son stayed for a long time on the small island. Now they prepare to fly towards Greece.
3. They work hard and get wings ready.
4. The father warns the boy: ‘We shall fly through the sky, but not towards the sun.’
5. The sun was bright. Icarus was happy because of his wings.
6. He did not remember the advice of his father for long.
7. He did not stay with his father, but flew very high in the sky in front of the sun.
8. The wax did not stay on the boy’s wings.
9. The father soon saw his son in the middle of the sea.
10. Icarus was not saved. Daedalus was truly grieved because the boy was not warned by his father’s advice.

Vocabulary

Nouns

Daedalus, Daedali, *m.*, Daedalus
Icarus, Icari, *m.*, Icarus
Creta, Cretae, *f.*, Crete
labor, laboris, *m.*, work, toil, labour (laboratory)
virtus, virtutis, *f.*, courage, valour (virtue)
natio, nationis, *f.*, nation
consilium, consilii or **consili,** *n.*, plan, advice (counsel)

magnitudo, magnitudinis, *f.*, size, great size (magnitude)
celeritas, celeritatis, *f.*, speed, swiftness (celerity, accelerator)
pater, patris, *m.*, father (paternal)
cera, cerae, *f.*, wax (ceramics)
ala, alae, *f.*, wing
sol, solis, *m.*, sun (solar)

Adjectives

medius, media, medium, middle, middle of (medium)
summus, summa, summum, greatest, highest, top of (summit, sum)

Verb

volo, volare, fly (volatile)

Adverb

diu, long, for a long time

Conjunctions

-que, and
et . . . et, both . . . and

Preposition

circum (with the Accusative case), around, about (circumnavigate)

GRAMMAR

A. As you noticed in the reading, the preposition **in** (in, on) may stand after the adjective and before the noun.

parva in insula,	on a small island
medio in caelo,	in the middle of the sky

B. The conjunction **-que** (and) never stands alone, but is added to the second of two similarly used words. **-que** at the end of a word is the same as **et** in front of a word.

vir feminaque,	the man and the woman
pueris puellisque,	to the boys and girls

C. The 'of' in 'in the middle of' or 'top of' is part of the adjective and therefore does not affect the case of the noun. The noun has whatever case it would have anyway and the adjective simply agrees with the noun.

in caelo,	in the sky
medio in caelo,	in the middle of the sky
in terra,	on the land
in summa terra,	on the top of the land

D. These rules are helpful in remembering the gender of some **3rd declension** Nouns.

1. Nouns in **-or** are usually masculine. **labor**
2. Nouns in **-io** are usually feminine, **natio**
3. Nouns in **-tudo, -tus,** or **-tas** are feminine. **magnitudo, virtus, celeritas**

CHEMICAL ELEMENTS

The following are some of the Chemical Elements, with their Latin derivations.

Calcium Ca from **calx, calcis,** lime.
Carbon C from **carbo,** coal.
Copper Cu from **cuprum,** derived from the island of Cyprus, anciently renowned for its copper mines.
Gold Au from **aurum,** gold.
Iron Fe from **ferrum,** iron.
Lead Pb from **plumbum,** lead.
Radium Ra from **radius,** ray, because of the alpha, beta, and gamma rays.
Silicon Si from **silex, silicis,** flint.
Silver Ag from **argentum,** silver.
Tellurium Te from **tellus, telluris,** earth.

Practice Exercises

No. 65. Give the English for the following.

1. **dei et deae**
2. **deus deaque**
3. **habemus et damus**
4. **habebat dabatque**
5. **hominem et feminas**
6. **hominum feminarumque**
7. **ad solem et lunam**
8. **ad solem lunamque**
9. **ex mari et terra**
10. **ex terra marique**

No. 66. Translate these phrases.

1. **in mediis viis**
2. **multis in oppidis**
3. **bello in magno**
4. **in summis aedificiis**
5. **parte in bona**
6. **in oceanis latis**
7. **multis in terris**
8. **medio in caelo**
9. **summo in mari**
10. **medio in oceano**

No. 67. Translate these phrases.

1. **ad mare**
2. **ex urbibus**
3. **cum patribus suis**
4. **ante forum**
5. **post templum**
6. **de arca**
7. **sine consilio**
8. **trans oceanum**
9. **per maria**
10. **ob alas**
11. **pro regina tua**
12. **contra populum**
13. **inter hostes**
14. **ab viris**
15. **ab oppidis**
16. **ante castra**
17. **per pericula**
18. **ad dominum**
19. **trans agrum**
20. **de pace**

No. 68. Give the English for these verbs.

1. **erit**
2. **terrebitur**
3. **volabat**
4. **natabit**
5. **dolent**
6. **portamur**
7. **tenebatur**
8. **amabimur**
9. **movebo**
10. **laudabantur**
11. **pugnabat**
12. **locabis**
13. **vocabor**
14. **monebamur**
15. **laborabunt**
16. **incitantur**
17. **debebit**
18. **imus**
19. **curabantur**
20. **liberaberis**

No. 69. Translate the following.

1. **Daedalus cum filio suo, Icaro, alas parabat.**
2. **Icarus cum patre medio in caelo volabat.**
3. **Icarus non servatur quod consiliun patris non diu memoria tenet.**
4. **Hostes media in urbe videmus.**
5. **Pueri puellaeque medio in mari natabant.**
6. **Ob magna pericula Cincinnatus ex agris ad urbem it.**
7. **Et Horatius et Cincinnatus Romam bene amabant.**
8. **Romani virtutem ducum semper laudabant.**
9. **Laudamusne virtutem ducum?**
10. **Cur Ceres, mater Proserpinae, dolebat?**

CHAPTER 17

READING

Proserpina

1. **Ceres, dea frumenti, filiam, Proserpinam, habebat.**
2. **Pluto, deus Inferorum, Proserpinam in agro videt et ad Inferos Proserpinam portat.**
3. **Quod filiam suam non videbat, Ceres, mater, dolebat.**
4. **Quod Ceres misera erat, frumentum in agris agricolarum non erat.**
5. **Iuppiter agricolis auxilium dare parat. Mercurium vocat.**
6. **Mercurius pro Iove ad Plutonem nuntium portat.**
7. **Tum Proserpina cum Plutone non semper manebat, sed in terra partem anni habitabat.**
8. **Si Proserpina in terra erat, Ceres laeta erat et agricolis copiam magnam frumenti dabat. Sed si Proserpina sub terra erat frumentum non erat quod Ceres misera erat.**

Proserpina

1. Ceres, the goddess of grain, had a daughter, Proserpina.
2. Pluto, god of the dead, saw Proserpina in a field and carried Proserpina to the dead.
3. Because she did not see her daughter, Ceres, the mother, grieved.
4. Because Ceres was unhappy, there was not grain in the farmers' fields.
5. Jupiter prepares to give help to the farmers. He calls Mercury.
6. Mercury carried a message for Jupiter to Pluto.
7. Then Proserpina did not always stay with Pluto, but lived for part of the year on earth.
8. If Proserpina was on the earth, Ceres was happy and gave a great plenty of grain to the farmers. But if Proserpina was under the earth there was not grain because Ceres was unhappy.

Colosseum

1. **Romani in urbe sua aedificia multa habebant.**
2. **Colosseum bene amabant quod ludos ibi spectabant.**
3. **Colosseum erat magnum amphitheatrum et etiam nunc stat.**

The Colosseum

1. The Romans had many buildings in their city.
2. They liked the Colosseum well because they watched the games there.
3. The Colosseum was a large amphitheatre and is standing even now.

Colosseum

4. **Milites Romani bello servos captivosque obtinebant.**
5. **Captivi gladiatores erant et gladiis suis contra homines aut contra animalia in Colosseo pugnabant.**
6. **Multi captivi virtutem magnam habebant et liberabantur quod bene pugnabant.**

The Colosseum

4. The Roman soldiers secured slaves and captives in war.
5. The captives were gladiators and fought in the Colosseum with their swords against men or against animals.
6. Many captives had great courage and were freed because they fought well.

Vocabulary

Verbs

specto, spectare, spectavi, spectatus, look at, watch (spectacle)

obtineo, obtinere, obtinui, obtentus, secure, obtain

Preposition

sub, under, below, at the foot of (submarine)
1. With the Accusative case after Verbs showing motion —to the foot of.
2. With the Ablative case after verbs showing rest.

Nouns

annus, anni, *m.*, year (annual)
mater, matris, *f.*, mother (maternal)
Inferi, Inferorum, *m.*, *pl.*, Those Below, the shades of Hades, the dead
Ceres, Cereris, *f.*, Ceres (cereal)
Proserpina, Proserpinae, *f.*, Proserpina
Mercurius, Mercuri, *m.*, Mercury (mercurial)
Iuppiter, Iovis, *m.*, Jupiter (jovial)
Pluto, Plutonis, *m.*, Pluto (plutonium)
animal, animalis, *n.*, animal (**animalium)**
captivus, captivi, *m.*, captive
amphitheatrum, amphitheatri, *n.*, amphitheatre
gladiator, gladiatoris, *m.*, gladiator
Colosseum, Colossei, *n.*, the Colosseum (colossal)

THE VERB: PRINCIPAL PARTS

In order to be able to form all the tenses of any Latin verb, it is necessary to know four things about it—First Person Singular Present Active Tense, Present Active Infinitive, First Person Singular Perfect Active Tense, Perfect Passive Participle. These four parts of the verb are called its **Principal Parts** and from them all its other parts can be formed with complete accuracy.

A. The first two Principal Parts taken together show the conjugation to which the verb belongs and can, therefore, be used to form the tenses you have had so far:

1. Present Tense, Active and Passive
2. Imperfect Tense, Active and Passive
3. Future Tense, Active and Passive

B. The third Principal Part is the First Person Singular Perfect Active Tense.

amavi, 1st conjugation	I have loved
	I have liked
habui, 2nd conjugation	I have had
	I have held

From this the Perfect, Pluperfect and Future Perfect Active Tenses can be formed. (See pages 93–95.)

C. The fourth Principal Part is the Perfect Passive Participle.

amatus, 1st conjugation	having been loved
	having been liked
habitus, 2nd conjugation	having been had
	having been held

From this the Perfect, Pluperfect and Future Perfect Passive Tenses can be formed. (See pages 99–100.)

D. Most of the **1st conjugation** Verbs form their Principal Parts like **amo:**

amo, amare, amavi, amatus

Those you have met so far that do not are:

do, dare, dedi, datus	give
iuvo, iuvare, iuvi, iutus	help, aid
sto, stare, steti, staturus	stand

Note that some verbs (e.g. **sto**) do not have a Perfect Passive Participle. In these cases, the Future Active Participle (e.g. **staturus**) is given as the fourth Principal Part.[1]

Many of the **2rd conjugation** Verbs form their Principal Parts like **habeo.**

habeo, habere, habui, habitus

[1] You will find that some text-books and dictionaries give the *Supine* (e.g. **amatum**) as the fourth Principal Part. From this both the Future Active Participle and, where relevant, the Perfect Passive Participle can be formed.

Of those you have met so far, these do not:

maneo, manere, mansi, mansus	remain, stay
moveo, movere, movi, motus	move
video, videre, vidi, visus	see

The Principal Parts of **sum** are: **sum, esse, fui, futurus**

The Principal Parts of **eo** are:

eo, ire, ii or **ivi, iturus**

PREFIXES

These Latin Prepositions are commonly used as prefixes.

e, ex, out. **exspecto,** look out for, wait for, expect.

per, through. **perduco,** lead through.

inter, between. **interpono,** put between.

in, in, on; into. **invenio,** discover (come upon).

trans, across. **transmitto,** send across.

Practice Exercises

No. 70. Give the Present Active Infinitive of these verbs and the English translation.

1. **voco**	5. **sum**	9. **curo**	13. **terreo**	17. **servo**
2. **debeo**	6. **moneo**	10. **doleo**	14. **adoro**	18. **eo**
3. **ambulo**	7. **timeo**	11. **nuntio**	15. **moveo**	19. **do**
4. **sto**	8. **narro**	12. **volo**	16. **paro**	20. **video**

No. 71. Give the third Principal Part, the First Person Singular Perfect Active Tense, and the translation.

1. **paro**	5. **libero**	9. **habito**	13. **do**	17. **timeo**
2. **incito**	6. **loco**	10. **moneo**	14. **teneo**	18. **eo**
3. **aro**	7. **terreo**	11. **sum**	15. **servo**	19. **moveo**
4. **debeo**	8. **aedifico**	12. **habeo**	16. **monstro**	20. **maneo**

No. 72. Give the fourth Principal Part, the Perfect Passive Participle, and the translation.

1. **amo**	5. **moneo**	9. **occupo**	13. **servo**	17. **moveo**
2. **habeo**	6. **exspecto**	10. **porto**	14. **iuvo**	18. **specto**
3. **libero**	7. **narro**	11. **do**	15. **video**	19. **obtineo**
4. **neco**	8. **terreo**	12. **nuntio**	16. **adoro**	20. **loco**

No. 73. Translate the following into English.

1. **Et mater tua et pater tuus de virtute consilium dabant.**
2. **Medio in oppido erant aedificia multa.**
3. **Fama ad nationem meam ab nuntiis portabitur.**
4. **Puella puerque sub aqua natant.**
5. **Circum urbem ambulare et multa videre debemus.**
6. **Nonne multa mala memoria tenes?**
7. **Sol summa in aqua esse videbatur.**
8. **Nationes Europae non semper pugnabunt.**
9. **Nautae in maribus oceanisque navigant.**
10. **Milites Romani virtutem magnam habent.**

FOURTH REVISION (CHAPTERS 14–17)

VOCABULARY REVISION

Nouns

1. ala
2. amphitheatrum
3. animal
4. annus
5. caedes
6. captivus
7. caput
8. celeritas
9. cera
10. Ceres
11. Cincinnatus
12. Colosseum
13. consilium
14. Creta
15. Daedalus
16. dictator
17. donum
18. gladiator
19. homo
20. Horatius
21. hostis
22. Icarus
23. Inferi
24. Iuppiter
25. labor
26. littera
27. magnitudo
28. mare
29. mater
30. Mercurius
31. miles
32. natio
33. pars
34. pater
35. pax
36. pecunia
37. Pluto
38. pons
39. Proserpina
40. sagitta
41. sagittarius
42. sol
43. stella
44. urbs
45. virtus

1. wing
2. amphitheatre
3. animal
4. year
5. slaughter
6. captive
7. head
8. speed, swiftness
9. wax
10. Ceres
11. Cincinnatus
12. the Colosseum
13. plan, advice
14. Crete
15. Daedalus
16. dictator
17. gift
18. gladiator
19. man
20. Horatius
21. enemy
22. Icarus
23. Those below, the dead
24. Jupiter
25. work, toil, labour
26. letter
27. size, great size
28. sea
29. mother
30. Mercury
31. soldier
32. nation
33. part
32. father
35. peace
36. money
37. Pluto
38. bridge
39. Proserpina
40. arrow
41. archer
42. sun
43. star
44. city
45. courage, valour

Adjectives

1. medius
2. robustus
3. summus

1. middle, middle of
2. strong, robust
3. greatest, highest, top of

Verbs

1. doleo
2. moveo
3. obtineo
4. specto
5. terreo
6. volo

1. I grieve
2. I move
3. I secure, obtain
4. I look at, watch
5. I frighten, terrify, scare
6. I fly

Adverbs

1. diu	**2. mox**	**3. semper**
1. long, for a long time	2. soon, presently	3. always

Prepositions

1. a, ab	**2. circum**	**3. inter**	**4. sub**
1. by; away from, from	2. around, about	3. among, between	4. under

Conjunctions

1. aut	**2. et . . . et**	**3. -que**
1. or	2. both . . . and	3. and

Practice Exercises

No. 74. Complete these Infinitives by filling in the correct vowel.

1. **dol...........re**
2. **terr...........re**
3. **mov...........re**
4. **voc...........re**
5. **obtin...........re**
6. **d...........re**
7. **spect...........re**
8. **vol...........re**
9. **laud...........re**
10. **man...........re**
11. **deb...........re**
12. **tim...........re**
13. **hab...........re**
14. **vid...........re**
15. **nec...........re**
16. **par...........re**
17. **occup...........re**
18. **st...........re**
19. **iuv...........re**
20. **mon...........re**

No. 75. Fill in the missing principal part.

1. **specto, spectare, ..., spectatus**
2. **curo, ..., curavi, curatus**
3. **.............., monere, monui, monitus**
4. **do, dare, ..., datus**
5. **moveo, movere, movi, ...**
6. **paro, parare, ..., paratus**
7. **servo, servare, servavi, ...**
8. **terreo, terrere, terrui, ...**
9. **.............., habitare, habitavi, habitatus**
10. **laudo, ..., laudavi, laudatus**

No. 76. Translate these phrases.

1. **animalium hominumque**
2. **ab patre**
3. **a matribus**
4. **mare stellaque**
5. **patres matresque**
6. **celeritas magnitudoque**
7. **a Mercurio**
8. **ab militibus**
9. **a Plutone**
10. **bellum paxque**

No. 77. Translate these verb forms.

1. **laudabatur**	8. **iuvabatis**	15. **servaris**
2. **dolebunt**	9. **habebo**	16. **parabamur**
3. **monebamur**	10. **moveberis**	17. **debebitur**
4. **necantur**	11. **occupantur**	18. **curabaris**
5. **vocamini**	12. **timebant**	19. **spectabamur**
6. **obtinebimus**	13. **parabitur**	20. **terrebunt**
7. **videris**	14. **dabis**	

EUTROPIUS

Very little is known about Eutropius except that he held official positions in Rome and the provinces, and may have been a secretary to the Emperor Constantine. Of his works, the only one extant is the **Breviarium**, a brief history of Rome from the founding of the city in 753 B.C. to 364 A.D.

Hic quoque ingens bellum civile commovit cogente uxore Cleopatra, regina Aegypti, dum cupiditate muliebri optat etiam in urbe regnare. Victus est ab Augusto navali pugna clara et inlustri apud Actium, qui locus in Epiro est, ex qua fugit in Aegyptum et desperatis rebus, cum omnes ad Augustum transirent, ipse se interemit. Cleopatra sibi aspidem admisit et veneno eius exstincta est. Aegyptus per Octavianum Augustum imperio Romano adiecta est praepositusque ei C. Cornelius Gallus. Hunc primum Aegyptus Romanum iudicem habuit.

Breviarii, Liber VII, vii

He (Antony) also stirred up a great Civil War, with his wife Cleopatra, queen of Egypt, urging it, since she hoped, with a womanly desire, to rule also in the City (Rome). He was defeated by Augustus in a famous and glorious naval battle near Actium, which is a place in Epirus, from which he escaped to Egypt and, because his future was without hope, since everyone was going over to the side of Augustus, he killed himself. Cleopatra let a snake bite her and died from its poison. Egypt was added to the Roman Empire by Octavius Augustus and Gaius Cornelius Gallus was put in command of it. Egypt had him as its first Roman judge.

Breviarium, Book 7, 7

THE BIBLE

Psalmus David, cum fugeret a facie Absalom filii sui	*A Psalm of David, when he fled from the face of Absalom his son*
Domine, quid multiplicati sunt qui tribulant me?	Lord, how are they increased that trouble me!

Multi insurgunt adversum me;	Many are they that rise up against me;
multi dicunt animae meae:	many there be which say of my soul:
Non est salus ipsi in Deo eius.	There is no help for him in God.
Tu autem, Domine, susceptor meus es,	But thou, O Lord, art a shield for me;
gloria mea et exaltans caput meum.	my glory, and the lifter up of mine head.
Voce mea ad Dominum clamavi,	I cried unto the Lord with my voice,
et exaudivit me de monte sancto suo.	and he heard me out of his holy hill.
Ergo dormivi et soporatus sum	I laid me down and slept;
et exsurrexi, quia Dominus suscepit me.	I awaked; for the Lord sustained me.
Non timebo milia populi circumdantis me.	I will not be afraid of ten thousands of people, that have set themselves against me round about.
Exsurge, Domine, salvum me fac, Deus meus;	Arise, O Lord; save me, O my God;
quoniam tu percussisti omnes adversantes mihi sine causa,	for thou hast smitten all mine enemies upon the cheek bone;
dentes peccatorum contrivisti.	thou hast broken the teeth of the ungodly.
Domini est salus, et super populum tuum benedictio tua.	Salvation belongeth unto the Lord; thy blessing is upon thy people.
Liber Psalmorum iii	*Psalm 3*

CHAPTER 18

READING

Libri Sibyllini	The Sibylline Books
1. Inter antiquos erat fabula de libris Sibyllinis.	1. Among the ancients there was a story about the Sibylline books.
2. Tarquinius Superbus urbem Romam regnabat.	2. Tarquin the Proud was ruling the city of Rome.
3. Femina ad Tarquinium libros novem portavit et pro libris pecuniam rogavit.	3. A woman brought nine books to Tarquin and asked for money for the books.
4. Tarquinius feminae pecuniam non dedit.	4. Tarquin did not give the money to the woman.
5. Femina in igni libros tres locavit.	5. The woman put three books in the fire.
6. Pro sex libris pretium librorum novem rogavit.	6. For the six books she asked the price of the nine books.
7. Tarquinius feminae pecuniam non dedit.	7. Tarquin did not give the money to the woman.
8. Postquam[1] femina in igni libros sex locavit, Tarquinius feminae pro libris pecuniam dedit quod audacia feminae movebatur.	8. After the woman had placed six books in the fire, Tarquin gave the money to the woman for the books because he was moved by the woman's boldness.
9. Libri erant libri Sibyllini.	9. The books were the Sibylline books.
10. Populus Romanus ad libros ibat, si periculo incitabatur aut si Roma oppugnabatur.	10. If the Roman people were aroused by danger or if Rome was being attacked they used to go to the books.
11. Libri Romanis auxilium multum semper dabant.	11. The books always gave much help to the Romans.
12. Erantne libri deorum?	12. Were they the books of the gods?

[1] Note that **postquam**, 'after', is followed by a Perfect Tense in Latin and not a Pluperfect Tense as in English.

Vocabulary

Nouns

liber, libri, *m.*, book (library)
ignis, ignis, *m.*, fire **(ignium)** (ignite)
pretium, pretii or **preti,** *n.*, price (precious)
audacia, audaciae, *f.*, boldness, daring (audacity)
Tarquinius, Tarquini, *m.*, Tarquin

Adjectives

Sibyllinus, Sibyllina, Sibyllinum, Sibylline
superbus, superba, superbum, proud (superb)
sex, six (sextet)
novem, nine (November)

Verb

rogo, rogare, rogavi, rogatus, ask, ask for (interrogate)

Conjunction

postquam, after, when

THE VERB: PERFECT ACTIVE TENSES

The three Perfect Active tenses (Perfect, Pluperfect, and Future Perfect) are based on the third principal part.

A. The Perfect tense shows action completed in the past—*I have loved, I loved*, whereas the Imperfect tense expresses a continuous action. The third principal part is the first person singular of the Perfect tense.

1st conjugation

amavi	I have loved; I loved
amavisti	you have loved; you loved
amavit	he, she, it has loved; he, she, it loved
amavimus	we have loved; we loved
amavistis	you have loved; you loved
amaverunt	they have loved; they loved

2nd conjugation

habui	I have had; I had
habuisti	you have had; you had
habuit	he, she, it has had; he, she, it had
habuimus	we have had; we had
habuistis	you have had; you had
habuerunt	they have had; they had

B. The Pluperfect tense shows action completed at a definite point of time in the past—*I had loved*——.

1st conjugation

amaveram	I had loved
amaveras	you had loved
amaverat	he, she, it had loved
amaveramus	we had loved
amaveratis	you had loved
amaverant	they had loved

2nd conjugation

habueram	I had had
habueras	you had had
habuerat	he, she, it had had
habueramus	we had had
habueratis	you had had
habuerant	they had had

C. The Future Perfect tense shows action to be completed before a definite point of time in the future—*I shall have loved*——.

1st conjugation

amavero	I shall have loved
amaveris	you will have loved
amaverit	he, she, it will have loved
amaverimus	we shall have loved.
amaveritis	you will have loved
amaverint	they will have loved

2nd conjugation

habuero	I shall have had
habueris	you will have had
habuerit	he, she, it will have had
habuerimus	we shall have had
habueritis	you will have had
habuerint	they will have had

D. The verb **sum** is regular in the Perfect tenses.

Perfect Tense

fui	I have been, I was
fuisti	you have been, you were
fuit	he, she, it has been, he, she, it was
fuimus	we have been, we were
fuistis	you have been, you were
fuerunt	they have been, they were

Pluperfect Tense

fueram	I had been
fueras	you had been
fuerat	he, she, it had been
fueramus	we had been
fueratis	you had been
fuerant	they had been

Future Perfect Tense

fuero	I shall have been
fueris	you will have been
fuerit	he, she, it will have been
fuerimus	we shall have been
fueritis	you will have been
fuerint	they will have been

FAMILIAR ABBREVIATIONS

fl. or **flor., floruit,** he (she) flourished. Used with the date at which an artist produced his work.

I.H.S., In hoc signo, In this sign. or **Iesus Hominum Salvator,** Jesus Saviour of Men.

I.N.R.I., Iesus Nazarenus, Rex Iudaeorum, Jesus of Nazareth, King of the Jews.

pinx., pinxit, he (she) painted it.

sculp., sculpsit, he (she) carved it.

op. cit., opere citato, in the work cited. Used in footnotes instead of repeating the title of the book referred to.

ibid. or **ib., ibidem,** in the same place. Used in footnotes, if the reference is the same as one made just previously.

Practice Exercises

No. 78. Complete these principal parts.

1. **paro, parare,** ...., **paratus**
2. **laudo, laudare,** ...., **laudatus**
3. **moneo, monere,** ...., **monitus**
4. **debeo, debere,** ...., **debitus**
5. **porto, portare,** ...., **portatus**
6. **servo, servare,** ...., **servatus**
7. **voco, vocare,** ...., **vocatus**
8. **moveo, movere,** ...., **motus**
9. **do, dare,** ...., **datus**
10. **rogo, rogare,** ...., **rogatus**

No. 79. Translate the following pairs of sentences, being especially careful to show the correct tense of the verb.

1. **Agricola in agris laborabat.**
   Filia aquam portavit.
2. **Dux hostes spectabat.**
   Hostes castra oppugnaverunt.
3. **Femina pro libris pecuniam rogabat.**
   Tarquinius pecuniam non dedit.

4. **Feminae in templum ierunt.**
   Feminas spectabamus.
5. **Milites oppidum occupaverunt.**
   Populus timebat.
6. **Roma in periculo magno erat.**
   Cincinnatus Romam servavit.
7. **Horatius in ponte sine auxilio stabat.**
   Militem hostium necavit.
8. **Germani in silvis habitabant, quod barbari erant.**
   Romani in silvas ierunt et Germanos oppugnaverunt.
9. **Gladiator in amphitheatro stabat et animal magnum spectabat.**
   Ibi mansit et animal gladio suo necavit.
10. **Ceres dolebat quod Pluto Proserpinam ad Inferos portaverat.**
    Ad Iovem iit et auxilium rogavit.

No. 80. Translate these Pluperfect tenses.

1. **ambulaveram**	8. **dederas**	15. **nataveram**
2. **adoraverant**	9. **tenueratis**	16. **dolueramus**
3. **araverat**	10. **steteram**	17. **rogaverat**
4. **moverant**	11. **paraverat**	18. **ierant**
5. **manseramus**	12. **fuerant**	19. **viderat**
6. **videratis**	13. **incitaveras**	20. **vocaveratis**
7. **paraveras**	14. **curaveratis**	

No. 81. Translate these Future Perfect tenses.

1. **amaveris**	8. **dederint**	15. **nuntiaveris**
2. **curaverit**	9. **steteris**	16. **ierimus**
3. **laudavero**	10. **tenuerit**	17. **habueritis**
4. **locaverimus**	11. **fuerimus**	18. **debuerit**
5. **habuerint**	12. **servavero**	19. **adoraverint**
6. **terruerit**	13. **portaverit**	20. **ambulaveris**
7. **moverit**	14. **paraverint**	

CHAPTER 19

READING

Reges Romani	The Kings of Rome
1. Urbis Romae septem reges erant. Romulus urbem parvam in monte Palatino aedificavit.	1. There were seven kings of the city of Rome. Romulus built a small city on the Palatine mount.
2. Urbi nomen Romam dedit. Romulus ob sapientiam urbem bene regnabat.	2. To the city he gave the name Rome. Romulus ruled the city well because of his wisdom.
3. Populo consilium bonum dabat.	3. He gave good advice to the people.
4. Quod in urbe non erant mulieres Romani finitimos suos ad ludos vocaverunt.	4. Because there were not women in the city, the Romans called their neighbours to games.
5. Tum feminas puellasque armis obtinuerunt.	5. Then they got women and girls by arms.
6. Et Sabini et socii contra Romanos pugnaverunt, sed copiae Romanae hostes superaverunt.	6. Both the Sabines and their allies fought against the Romans, but the Roman forces conquered the enemy.
7. Postea Numa Pompilius erat rex Romanorum.	7. Afterwards, Numa Pompilius was king of the Romans.
8. Pacem amabat et populo erat gratus quod Romanis leges multas bonasque dedit.	8. He liked peace and he was pleasing to the people because he gave many good laws to the Romans.
9. Aedificia templaque etiam aedificavit.	9. He also built buildings and temples.
10. Deinde Romani ab Anco Marcio regnabantur.	10. Then the Romans were ruled by Ancus Marcius.
11. Multos bello superavit et murum circum montem Caelium aedificavit.	11. He defeated many people in war and he built a wall around the Caelian mount.
12. Postea Roma a Prisco Tarquinio regnabatur.	12. Afterwards, Rome was ruled by Tarquinius Priscus.
13. Circus Maximus, ubi Romani ludos habebant, aedificatus est.	13. The Circus Maximus, where the Romans held their games, was built.

14. **Contra Sabinos pugnavit et agris finitimis et monte Capitolio fines urbis auxit.**	14. He fought against the Sabines and increased the territory of the city by neighbouring fields and the Capitoline mount.
15. **A proximo rege, Servio Tullio, Sabini superati sunt.**	15. By the next king, Servius Tullius, the Sabines were overcome.
16. **Romae collem septimum addidit. Circum colles murum et circum murum fossas aedificavit.**	16. He added the seventh hill to Rome. Around the hills he built a wall and around the wall ditches.
17. **Multi in urbe habitabant. Multi erant agricolae et post colles et post flumen agros arabant.**	17. Many people lived in the city. Many were farmers and ploughed the fields both behind the hills and behind the river.
18. **Tarquinius Superbus erat ultimus rex Romanus, sed bene diuque regnavit.**	18. Tarquin the Proud was the last king of Rome, but he ruled well and for a long time.
19. **Copiae Tarquini Superbi bene pugnabant et nationes proximas Romae superaverunt.**	19. The troops of Tarquin the Proud fought well and defeated the nations next to Rome.

Vocabulary

Nouns

collis, collis, *m.*, hill **(collium)**
flumen, fluminis, *n.*, river, stream
finis, finis, *m.*, end, border **(finium)** In the plural, territory, boundaries. (finish)
rex, regis, *m.*, king (regal)
nomen, nominis, *n.*, name (nominative)
mulier, mulieris, *f.*, woman
mons, montis, *m.*, mountain, mount **(montium)**
lex, legis, *f.*, law (legal)
murus, muri, *m.*, wall (mural)

Adjectives

proximus, proxima, proximum, next, nearest (approximate)
ultimus, ultima, ultimum, last, farthest (ultimate)
septem, seven (September)
septimus, septima, septimum, seventh

Verb

addo, addere, addidi, additus, add
augeo, augere, auxi, auctus, increase, enlarge (augment)

Adverb

postea, afterwards **deinde,** then, next

THE VERB: PERFECT PASSIVE TENSES

A. The Perfect Passive Participle is an adjective and therefore must agree with the word it modifies in *gender*, *number*, and *case*. When it is used with the verb **sum** to form the Perfect Passive tenses, it is always in the Nominative case, but must agree with the subject in gender and number.

mulier amata est, the woman has been loved
mulieres amatae sunt, the women have been loved
vir amatus est, the man has been loved
viri amati sunt, the men have been loved
oppidum liberatum est, the town has been freed
oppida liberata sunt, the towns have been freed

B. The Perfect Passive tense is formed by the fourth principal part, the Perfect Passive Participle, with the *Present tense* of **sum.**

1st conjugation

amatus, a, um sum	I have been loved, was loved
amatus, a, um es	you have been loved, were loved
amatus, a, um est	he, she, it has been loved, etc.
amati, ae, a sumus	we have been loved, etc.
amati, ae, a estis	you have been loved, etc.
amati, ae, a sunt	they have been loved, etc.

2nd conjugation

habitus, a, um sum	I have been held, was held
habitus, a, um es	you have been held, were held
habitus, a, um est	he, she, it has been held, etc.
habiti, ae, a sumus	we have been held, etc.
habiti, ae, a estis	you have been held, etc.
habiti, ae, a sunt	they have been held, etc.

C. The Pluperfect Passive tense is formed by the Perfect Passive Participle with the *Imperfect tense of* **sum.**

1st conjugation

amatus, a, um eram	I had been loved
amatus, a, um eras	you had been loved
amatus, a, um erat	he, she, it had been loved
amati, ae, a eramus	we had been loved

amati, ae, a eratis	you had been loved
amati, ae, a erant	they had been loved

2nd conjugation

habitus, a, um eram	I had been held
habitus, a, um eras	you had been held
habitus, a, um erat	he, she, it had been held
habiti, ae, a eramus	we had been held
habiti, ae, a eratis	you had been held
habiti, ae, a erant	they had been held

D. The Future Perfect Passive tense is formed by the Perfect Passive Participle with the *Future tense* of **sum.**

1st conjugation

amatus, a, um ero	I shall have been loved
amatus, a, um eris	you will have been loved
amatus, a, um erit	he, she, it will have been loved
amati, ae, a erimus	we shall have been loved
amati, ae, a eritis	you will have been loved
amati, ae, a erunt	they will have been loved

2nd conjugation

habitus, a, um ero	I shall have been held
habitus, a, um eris	you will have been held
habitus, a, um erit	he, she, it will have been held
habiti, ae, a erimus	we shall have been held
habiti, ae, a eritis	you will have been held
habiti, ae, a erunt	they will have been held

FAMILIAR PHRASES

carpe diem, seize the opportunity (lit. pluck the day).

cave canem, beware the dog.

ex libris, from the library of. Used often on bookplates.

ex officio, because of an office.

in toto, in the whole; completely.

per capita, by heads; per person or individual.

post mortem, after death.

exeunt omnes, all go out. Used as a stage direction.

ultimatum, the last thing; the farthest thing. Used for the final terms offered by one party to another.

Practice Exercises

No. 82. Give the English for these Perfect tenses.

1. **fuerunt**
2. **ambulavit**
3. **portatus est**
4. **amati sunt**
5. **curata es**
6. **laudatae sunt**
7. **monitus sum**
8. **debuimus**
9. **stetistis**
10. **narratum est**
11. **vocati sumus**
12. **natavi**
13. **servatae estis**
14. **nuntiatum est**
15. **moti sunt**
16. **timuisti**
17. **paratus est**
18. **locata sunt**
19. **laudaverunt**
20. **movistis**

No. 83. Give the English for these Pluperfect tenses.

1. **dederant**
2. **moverat**
3. **territus erat**
4. **manseratis**
5. **tenueras**
6. **pugnaverat**
7. **laudata eram**
8. **curati erant**
9. **amata eras**
10. **incitati eratis**
11. **parati erant**
12. **occupaveras**
13. **liberati eratis**
14. **necatus erat**
15. **servati eramus**
16. **monuerat**
17. **habueratis**
18. **tenueras**
19. **iuti eramus**
20. **adoraverant**

No. 84. Give the English for these Future Perfect tenses.

1. **monuero**
2. **fuerit**
3. **portatum erit**
4. **moniti erunt**
5. **habuerint**
6. **terrueris**
7. **moverimus**
8. **visi eritis**
9. **timuerit**
10. **mota erit**
11. **dederimus**
12. **steterint**
13. **fuerimus**
14. **necati eritis**
15. **laudatae erimus**
16. **armatus eris**
17. **curati erunt**
18. **locatum erit**
19. **fuerint**
20. **servata erit**

No. 85. Complete the following sentences by adding the appropriate form of the Perfect Participle Passive. Choose your answer from the words in parentheses.

1. **Frumentum ab agricolis .... erit (portatum, portatus)**
2. **Urbs ab hostibus .... est (oppugnatas, oppugnata)**
3. **Castra ad urbem .... erant (motum, mota)**
4. **............... estis, feminae (Servatae, Servati)**
5. **Fabulae puellis et pueris .... sunt (narrata, narratae)**
6. **Milites ad bellum .... erant (incitati, incitatos)**
7. **Collis armis .... erit (occupatus, occupata)**
8. **Hostes in collibus .... sunt (visos, visi)**
9. **Puer a feminis .... est (laudata, laudatus)**
10. **Gladii Nautis .... erunt (datae, dati)**

CHAPTER 20

READING

Labores Herculis	The Labours of Hercules
1. **Pythia ab Apolline docebatur et populo consilium dei dabat.**	1. Pythia was taught by Apollo and gave the advice of the god to the people.
2. **Hercules a Pythia amorem suum Apollinis demonstrare iussus est.**	2. Hercules was ordered by Pythia to show his love for Apollo.
3. **Hercules ad urbem regis, Eurysthei, iit. Ibi Eurystheus Herculi labores duodecim dedit.**	3. Hercules went to the city of the king, Eurystheus. There Eurystheus gave Hercules twelve labours.
4. **Sunt multae fabulae de laboribus Herculis.**	4. There are many stories about the labours of Hercules.
5. **Duodecim annos laborabat quod erat servus regis, sed Hercules de laboribus suis minime dolebat.**	5. He laboured for twelve years because he was the servant of the king, but Hercules grieved very little about his labours.
6. **Corpus robustum habebat, neque regem neque laborem timebat.**	6. He had a strong body and did not fear the king or the work.
7. **A rege diu tenebatur, sed post duodecim annos liberatus est quod regem bene iuverat.**	7. He was held for a long time by the king, but after twelve years he was freed because he had helped the king well.
8. **Deo Apollini amorem suum demonstraverat.**	8. He had shown the god, Apollo, his love.

Poma Aurea Hesperidum	The Golden Apples of the Hesperides
1. **Hercules pro rege, Eurystheo, bene laboraverat, sed non liber erat neque domi manebat.**	1. Hercules had worked well for the king, Eurystheus, but he was not free and did not stay at home.
2. **Rex Herculem poma aurea ex horto Hesperidum obtinere iussit.**	2. The king ordered Hercules to get the golden apples from the garden of the Hesperides.
3. **Hesperides erant filiae pulchrae Atlantis et in loco ultimo terrae ruri habitabant.**	3. The Hesperides were the beautiful daughters of Atlas and lived in the country in the farthest place of the earth.

4. **Pro Iunone poma aurea ibi curabant.**
5. **Multi praemio pomorum moti erant, sed Hesperides poma semper bene servabant.**
6. **Erat murus magnus altusque circum hortum ubi erant poma, atque ante hortum erat serpens.**
7. **Serpens capita multa habebat.**
8. **Hercules multa milia passuum ambulavit. Post annum ad hortum venit.**
9. **Erat in fini ultimo terrae et proximus Oceano.**
10. **Hercules Atlantem, virum robustum et amicum, ibi vidit.**
11. **Auxilium rogavit.**

4. They took care of the golden apples there for Juno.
5. Many people had been moved by the reward of the apples, but the Hesperides always preserved the apples well.
6. There was a large high wall around the garden where the apples were, and in front of the garden was a serpent.
7. The serpent had many heads.
8. Hercules walked many miles. After a year he came to the garden.
9. It was on the farthest end of the earth and next to the Ocean.
10. Hercules saw Atlas there, a strong friendly man.
11. He asked for help.

Vocabulary

Nouns

corpus, corporis, *n.*, body (corporal)
hora, horae, *f.*, hour (horology)
amor, amoris, *m.*, love (amorous)
Apollo, Apollinis, *m.*, Apollo
Eurystheus, Eurysthei, *m.*, Eurystheus
mille passus, a mile, **milia passuum,** miles
Hesperides, Hesperidum, *f.*, the Hesperides
Atlas, Atlantis, *m.*, Atlas
Iuno, Iunonis, *f.*, Juno
Pythia, Pythiae, *f.*, Pythia
Hercules, Herculis, *m.*, Hercules
locus, loci, *m.*, place, position. Sometimes neuter in the plural. (location, local)
serpens, serpentis, *f.*, snake, serpent **(serpentium)** (serpentine)
hortus, horti, *m.*, garden (horticulture)

Adjectives

primus, prima, primum, first (prime)
duodecim, twelve (duodecimal)
aureus, aurea, aureum, golden, of gold

Verbs

doceo, docere, docui, doctus, teach, show (doctrine)
iubeo, iubere, iussi, iussus, order, command (jussive)
demonstro, demonstrare, demonstravi, demonstratus, point out, show (demonstrate)

Adverbs

domi, at home (domicile) **quam diu,** how long?
ruri, in the country (rural)

Conjunction

neque, and .... not
neque .... **neque,** neither .... nor

TIME AND PLACE

A. TIME

Both the Accusative and Ablative cases are used to show time.

1. Duration of Time

The Accusative case shows *how long* something goes on.

multos annos, for many years
duodecim horas, for twelve hours

2. Point of Time

The Ablative case shows *when* something happens.

prima hora, at the first hour
proximo anno, in the next year

3. Time within which

The Ablative case is also used to show the time *within which* something happens.

anno, in (within) a year
duodecim horis, in (within) twelve hours

Note that Latin does not use prepositions in these expressions.

B. PLACE

Both the Accusative and Ablative cases are used to show place.

1. The Accusative case, used with a preposition, shows *to* or *into* what place motion is directed.
Without a preposition, it indicates *how far.*

ad urbem, to the city
in oppidum, into the town
multa milia passuum, many miles, for many miles

2. The Ablative case shows *where* the place is, or *from where* the motion is directed.

in oppido, in the town
ab oppido, away from the town
de muro, down from the wall
in mari, on the sea
ex urbe, out of the city

C. With the names of cities, towns, and small islands, and with the words **ruri** (in the country) and **domi** (at home), no Preposition is used.

Romam, to Rome **Roma,** from Rome

ACADEMIC DEGREES AND TERMS

cum laude, with praise. Given with a diploma that has been earned with a grade of work higher than ordinary.
magna cum laude, with great praise.
summa cum laude, with highest praise.
Alumnus, pl. **Alumni,** male graduate or graduates.
Alumna, pl. **Alumnae,** female graduate or graduates.
Alma Mater, Foster Mother. Refers to one's school or college.
A.M. or **M.A., Artium Magister,** Master of Arts.
B.A. or **A.B., Baccalaureus Artium,** Bachelor of Arts.
B.Sc., Baccalaureus Scientiae, Bachelor of Science.
D.D., Divinitatis Doctor, Doctor of Divinity.
D.Litt. or **Litt.D., Doctor Litterarum,** Doctor of Literature or Letters.
M.D., Medicinae Doctor, Doctor of Medicine.
Ph.D., Philosophiae Doctor, Doctor of Philosophy.
LL.D., Legum Doctor, Doctor of Laws.
D.M.D., Dentariae Medicinae Doctor, Doctor of Dental Medicine.

Practice Exercises

No. 86. Give the English for these expressions of time.

1. **multos annos**
2. **proximo anno**
3. **multas horas**
4. **proxima hora**
5. **septem horas**
6. **medio anno**
7. **sex horis**
8. **annos longos**
9. **duodecim horis**
10. **duodecim horas**

No. 87. Complete the following sentences by inserting a noun in the appropriate case. Choose your answers from the words in brackets.

1. **Hostes ad .... eunt (urbe, urbem)**
2. **Populus ex .... properavit (oppidum, oppido)**
3. **Pueri et puellae .... manebant (domo, domi)**
4. **Milites ante .... stabant (forum, foro)**
5. **Pueri in .... natant (aqua, aquam)**
6. **Agricolae in .... properaverunt (agri, agros)**
7. **Fabulae de .... narrantur (Proserpinam, Proserpina)**
8. **Filiae a .... laudantur (matribus, matris)**
9. **Hostes castra post .... locaverunt (colle, collem)**
10. **Agricolae agros .... arant (ruri, rurem)**

No. 88. Translate these verbs.

1. **videbo**	6. **obtinebunt**	11. **movebitur**
2. **pugnaverat**	7. **natabamus**	12. **aedificata erant**
3. **stabatis**	8. **erit**	13. **fuisti**
4. **laborabimus**	9. **videmus**	14. **oppugnabamur**
5. **fuerat**	10. **spectatum est**	15. **manserunt**

No. 89. Translate these sentences.

1. **Proximo anno Romam ibimus.**
2. **Sex horas in urbe manebant.**
3. **Summo in colle oppugnati erant.**
4. **Multas horas in Italia manebam.**
5. **Natabit unam horam.**
6. **Nonne multos annos laborabunt?**
7. **Ad oppidum multas horas longas ambulabat.**
8. **Ab rege non liberatus est.**
9. **Suntne in horto cum pueris?**
10. **Septem milia passuum ab urbe ambulavi.**

CHAPTER 21

READING

Poma Aurea Hesperidum (concluded)	The Golden Apples of the Hesperides (concluded)
1. **Postquam Hercules auxilium petivit, causam itineris sui Atlantem docuit.**	1. After Hercules had sought help, he showed Atlas the cause of his journey.
2. **Atlas erat pater Hesperidum et Herculi de loco ubi erant ea poma aurea narravit.**	2. Atlas was the father of the Hesperides and he told Hercules about the place where those golden apples were.
3. **Atlas quod caelum in umeris suis tenebat, Herculi caelum dedit et eum in umeris caelum tenere iussit.**	3. Atlas, because he was holding the sky on his shoulders, gave the sky to Hercules and he ordered him to hold the sky on his shoulders.
4. **Atlas ad hortum Hesperidum properavit.**	4. Atlas hurried to the garden of the Hesperides.
5. **Diu Hercules in umeris suis caelum tenebat. Diu Atlantem non viderat.**	5. For a long time Hercules held the sky on his shoulders. He had not seen Atlas for a long time.
6. **Et timebat et dolebat.**	6. He was both afraid and anxious.
7. **Pretium eorum pomorum magnum erat.**	7. The price of those apples was great.
8. **Post multas noctes Atlantem vidit et laetus erat.**	8. After many nights he saw Atlas and he was happy.
9. **Mox poma aurea habuit. Deinde Atlas caelum in umeris suis locavit. Hercules erat liber.**	9. Soon he had the golden apples. Then Atlas placed the sky on his own shoulders. Hercules was free.
10. **Ad Graeciam cum pomis properavit.**	10. He hurried to Greece with the apples.

Atalanta	Atalanta
1. **Atalanta erat puella Graecia et vero pulchra.**	1. Atalanta was a Greek girl and truly beautiful.
2. **Multi viri contra eam cucur-**	2. Many men had raced against

Atalanta	Atalanta
rerant, sed magna celeritate currebat nec superata erat.	her, but she ran with great speed and had not been surpassed.
3. **Venus consilium habebat. Puella erat praemium victoriae et pedibus eos currere iussit.**	3. Venus had a plan. The girl was the reward of victory and she ordered them to run on foot.
4. **Hippomenes contra eam currere paratus erat.**	4. Hippomenes was prepared to run against her.
5. **Multi spectabant et eum incitabant.**	5. Many were watching and urging him on.
6. **Signum datum est.**	6. The signal was given.
7. **Atalanta celeritatem suam demonstrabat. Paene volabat.**	7. Atalanta was showing her speed. She was almost flying.
8. **Quam longe ante eum currit!**	8. How far in front of him she runs!
9. **Sed Venus Hippomeni viam ad victoriam docuerat. Ei poma aurea dederat.**	9. But Venus had shown Hippomenes the way to victory. She had given him golden apples.
10. **Hippomenes pomum ad terram misit.**	10. Hippomenes threw an apple to the ground.
11. **Atalanta destitit currere.**	11. Atalanta ceased running.
12. **Hippomenes celeritatem suam auxit.**	12. Hippomenes increased his speed.
13. **Venus, dea amoris, eum bene iuverat.**	13. Venus, goddess of love, had helped him well.
14. **Hippomenes consilio donoque deae puellam superaverat.**	14. Hippomenes had defeated the girl by the plan and gift of the goddess.

Vocabulary

Nouns

mora, morae, *f.*, delay (moratorium)

nox, noctis, *f.*, night **(noctium)** (nocturnal)

causa, causae, *f.*, cause, reason (because)

iter, itineris, *n.*, journey, march, way (itinerary)

umerus, umeri, *m.*, shoulder (humerus)

pes, pedis, *m.*, foot (pedal)

signum, signi, *n.*, signal, standard

Atalanta, Atalantae, *f.*, Atalanta

Hippomenes, Hippomenis, *m.*, Hippomenes

Verbs

duco, ducere, duxi, ductus, lead (conduct, aqueduct)

mitto, mittere, misi, missus, send (mission)

peto, petere, petivi, petitus, seek, ask (petition)

curro, currere, cucurri, cursus, run (current)

dico, dicere, dixi, dictus, say, speak (diction)

desisto, desistere, destiti, destitus, cease (desist)

Adverb

paene, almost, nearly

Pronoun and Adjective

is, ea, id, he, she, it; that

Conjunction

nec, and not

THE VERB: THIRD CONJUGATION

3rd conjugation verbs follow the same principles as those you have met so far, except in the Future tense. The predominant vowels are **e** and **i.**

1. Principal Parts: **duco, ducere, duxi, ductus,** lead
2. Present Tense:

Active		*Passive*	
I lead, am leading, do lead		I am being led, am led	
duco	**ducimus**	**ducor**	**ducimur**
ducis	**ducitis**	**duceris**	**ducimini**
ducit	**ducunt**	**ducitur**	**ducuntur**

3. Imperfect Tense:

Active		*Passive*	
I was leading, led		I was being led, was led	
ducebam	**ducebamus**	**ducebar**	**ducebamur**
ducebas	**ducebatis**	**ducebaris**	**ducebamini**
ducebat	**ducebant**	**ducebatur**	**ducebantur**

4. Future Tense:

Active		*Passive*	
I shall lead		I shall be led	
ducam	**ducemus**	**ducar**	**ducemur**
duces	**ducetis**	**duceris**	**ducemini**
ducet	**ducent**	**ducetur**	**ducentur**

5. Perfect Tense:

Active	*Passive*
I have led, led	I have been led, was led
duxi	**ductus, a, um sum**
duxisti, etc.	**ductus, a, um es**, etc.

6. Pluperfect Tense:

Active	*Passive*
I had led	I had been led
duxeram	**ductus, a, um eram**
duxeras, etc.	**ductus, a, um eras**, etc.

7. Future Perfect Tense:

Active	*Passive*
I shall have led	I shall have been led
duxero	**ductus, a, um ero**
duxeris, etc.	**ductus, a, um eris**, etc.

Note that in the Perfect tense there are no differences between the conjugations. We only need to know the third and fourth principal parts to use a verb in these tenses.

PRONOUNS AND PRONOMINAL ADJECTIVES

is, ea, id is used as either a pronoun or an adjective.

1. **As a Pronoun:** As a Pronoun, in the singular it means *he*, *she*, or *it* and in the plural it means *they*.

Nom.	**is**	he	**ea**	she	**id**	it
Acc.	**eum**	him	**eam**	her	**id**	it
Gen.	**eius**	his	**eius**	her, hers	**eius**	its
Dat.	**ei**	to, for him	**ei**	to, for her	**ei**	to, for it
Abl.	**eo**	from, with, by, in him	**ea**	from, with, by, in her	**eo**	from, with, by, in it

Nom.	**ei or ii**	**eae**	**ea**	they
Acc.	**eos**	**eas**	**ea**	them
Gen.	**eorum**	**earum**	**eorum**	their
Dat.	**eis or iis**	**eis or iis**	**eis or iis**	to, for them
Abl.	**eis or iis**	**eis or iis**	**eis or iis**	from, with, by, in them

As a pronoun, it has the same gender and number as the noun it replaces, but its case is determined by its use in the sentence.

Puer natat; Eum video. The boy is swimming; I see him.
Ea in casa est. She is in the house.

The possessive form of the pronoun, the Genitive case, **eius, eorum** or **earum,** is used only when it does not refer to the subject of the sentence. When the possessor is also the subject of the sentence, the Possessive Adjective, **suus,** is used. (See page 40.)

Pomum eius videmus. We see his apple.
Pomum suum habet. He has his (own) apple.

2. **As an Adjective:** As an adjective, in the singular it means 'that' and in the plural 'those'.

As an adjective, it must be in the same gender, number and case as the noun it modifies.

is puer, that boy **ea puella,** that girl
id bellum, that war

ASSIMILATION

Some prefixes take on the first letter of the word to which they are attached. This process is called assimilation. Assimilation occurs with these prefixes:

ad	**ad** and **pono** become **appono,** put to, put near
con	**con** and **mitto** become **committo,** send together
in	**in** and **mortalis** become **immortalis,** immortal

Sometimes there is a change to a different letter:

in and **porto** become **importo,** carry in, bring in
con and **pono** become **compono,** put together

You will notice that assimilation is a natural process leading to more ease in pronunciation.

Practice Exercises

No. 90. Translate these verb forms.

1. **mittunt**	8. **liberavisti**	15. **ducebas**
2. **doctus sum**	9. **adorabam**	16. **mittet**
3. **petimur**	10. **miserit**	17. **servavi**
4. **debet**	11. **iubebit**	18. **timueras**
5. **moniti eratis**	12. **spectabamur**	19. **petiveratis**
6. **parati erunt**	13. **demonstratis**	20. **manserunt**
7. **duxit**	14. **rogabunt**	

No. 91. Translate these phrases.

1. **ob iniuriam**
2. **ex proeliis**
3. **sex horas**
4. **in itinere**
5. **e finibus**
6. **ad Galliam**
7. **ab colle**
8. **in litteris**
9. **ab hominibus**
10. **in ripam**

No. 92. Complete the following sentences by adding the appropriate form of **is, ea, id.** Choose your answer from the words in parentheses.

1. .... **in horto vidisti (eum, is)**
2. .... **arma militibus dedi (eos, ea)**
3. **Populus ex** .... **urbe ductus est (eam, ea)**
4. **Ab** .... **mittebantur (ei, eo)**
5. .... **mulieri poma dabimus (ei, eae)**
6. **Ad urbem cum** .... **ibo (eis, eos)**
7. .... **iter longum est (eum, id)**
8. **Rex** .... **terrae clarus est (eae, eius)**
9. .... **hora Romam properabamus (ea, eam)**
10. **Gladios** .... **obtinuimus (eorum, eas)**

No. 93. Change these verb forms to the Active or Passive.

1. **ducit**
2. **duxi**
3. **ducebar**
4. **ducti sunt**
5. **ducam**
6. **misisti**
7. **mittebantur**
8. **mittemini**
9. **missus es**
10. **miserat**
11. **petiverunt**
12. **petiti erimus**
13. **petet**
14. **petitur**
15. **petebaris**

FIFTH REVISION (CHAPTERS 18–21)

VOCABULARY REVISION

Nouns

1. amor
2. Apollo
3. Atalanta
4. Atlas
5. audacia
6. causa
7. collis
8. corpus
9. Eurystheus
10. finis
11. fines
12. flumen
13. Hercules
14. Hesperides
15. Hippomenes
16. hora
17. hortus
18. ignis
19. iter
20. Iuno
21. lex
22. liber
23. locus
24. mille passus
25. milia passuum
26. mons
27. mora
28. mulier
29. murus
30. nomen
31. nox
32. pes
33. pomum
34. pretium
35. pugna
36. Pythia
37. rex
38. serpens
39. signum
40. Tarquinius
41. umerus
42. Venus

1. love
2. Apollo
3. Atalanta
4. Atlas
5. boldness, daring
6. cause, reason
7. hill
8. body
9. Eurystheus
10. end, border
11. territory
12. river
13. Hercules
14. the Hesperides
15. Hippomenes
16. hour
17. garden
18. fire
19. journey, march
20. Juno
21. law
22. book
23. place
24. a mile
25. miles
26. mountain, mount
27. delay
28. woman
29. wall
30. name
31. night
32. foot
33. apple
34. price
35. fight
36. Pythia
37. king
38. snake, serpent
39. signal, standard
40. Tarquin
41. shoulder
42. Venus

Adjectives

1. aureus
2. duodecim
3. novem
4. proximus
5. septem
6. sex
7. Sibyllinus
8. superbus
9. ultimus
10. is, ea, id

1. golden
2. twelve
3. nine
4. next, nearest
5. seven
6. six
7. Sibylline
8. proud, haughty
9. last, farthest
10. that

Verbs

1. **augeo**
2. **curro**
3. **demonstro**
4. **dico**
5. **doceo**
6. **duco**
7. **iubeo**
8. **mitto**
9. **peto**
10. **rogo**

1. I increase, enlarge
2. I run
3. I point out, show
4. I speak, say
5. I teach, show
6. I lead
7. I order, command
8. I send
9. I seek
10. I ask, ask for

Adverbs

1. **domi**
2. **paene**
3. **postea**
4. **quam diu**
5. **ruri**

1. at home
2. almost, nearly
3. afterwards
4. how long
5. in the country

Pronouns

1. **is** 2. **ea** 3. **id**

1. he 2. she 3. it

Preposition

1. **in** 1. into, onto; in, on

Conjunction

1. **postquam** 1. after, when

Practice Exercises

No. 94. Give the English for these phrases.

1. **in pedibus**
2. **ab colle**
3. **ad flumina**
4. **ex agris**
5. **in ignem**
6. **in muris**
7. **de corpore**
8. **ruri**
9. **Roma**
10. **Romam**
11. **domi**
12. **ex urbe**

No. 95. Translate the following.

1. **fuerat**
2. **regnavimus**
3. **rogatus est**
4. **portaveris**
5. **dederunt**
6. **locaverunt**
7. **data sunt**
8. **misistis**
9. **petitum erit**
10. **auctum erat**
11. **movimus**
12. **fuimus**
13. **incitati erant**
14. **properaveratis**
15. **fuerint**
16. **rogatus sum**
17. **stetit**
18. **iisti**
19. **laudati erimus**
20. **habuerat**

No. 96. Give the English for these phrases.

1. **proximo anno**
2. **horas septem**
3. **proximis horis**
4. **primo anno**
5. **sex annos**
6. **ea nocte**
7. **eas noctes**
8. **eos annos**
9. **eo anno**
10. **ea hora**

No. 97. Give the English for these pronouns.

1. **eius**	4. **ei**	7. **ea**	10. **eum**
2. **eos**	5. **id**	8. **eorum**	11. **ii**
3. **eae**	6. **eas**	9. **eis**	12. **eo**

No. 98. Translate these phrases.

1. **eum amorem**	6. **eorum itinerum**	11. **ei regi**
2. **eius audaciae**	7. **ea poma**	12. **eam noctem**
3. **ea nomina**	8. **ei mulieri**	13. **eas leges**
4. **eas causas**	9. **id corpus**	14. **eo monte**
5. **eis finibus**	10. **eius loci**	15. **eius signi**

MARCUS VALERIUS MARTIALIS

Martial was born in Spain about 40 A.D. and went to Rome as a young man. He was a master of the epigram, and his poems, depicting scenes of everyday life, are full of wit, freshness, and satire. Martial died about 103 A.D., after returning to Spain.

Non amo te, Sabidi, nec possum dicere quare;	I do not love thee, Sabidius, nor can I tell you why;
hoc tantum possum dicere: non amo te.	this only I can say: I do not love thee.
Epigrammaton Liber I, xxxii	*Epigrams, 1, 32*
Cras te victurum, cras dicis, Postume, semper.	Tomorrow you will live, tomorrow you always say, Postumus.
Dic mihi, cras istud, Postume, quando venit?	Tell me, when, Postumus, is that tomorrow coming?
Quam longe cras istud, ubi est? aut unde petendum?	How far away is your tomorrow, where is it? or where must it be sought?
Numquid apud Parthos Armeniosque latet?	It doesn't lie hidden among the Parthians and Armenians, does it?
Iam cras istud habet Priami vel Nestoris annos.	Already that tomorrow of yours has the years of Priam or Nestor.
Cras istud quanti, dic mihi, posset emi?	Tell me, for how much could that tomorrow of yours be bought?
Cras vives? Hodie iam vivere, Postume, serum est;	You will live tomorrow? Today it is already too late to live, Postumus;
ille sapit, quisquis, Postume, vixit heri.	he is wise, whoever has lived yesterday, Postumus.
Epigrammaton Liber V, lviii	*Epigrams, 5, 58*

THE BIBLE

Omnia tempus habent, et suis spatiis transeunt universa sub caelo.	To every thing there is a season and a time to every purpose under the heaven:
Tempus nascendi et tempus moriendi,	A time to be born, and a time to die;
tempus plantandi et tempus evellendi quod plantatum est,	a time to plant, and a time to pluck that which is planted;
tempus occidendi et tempus sanandi,	A time to kill, and a time to heal;
tempus destruendi et tempus aedificandi,	a time to break down, and a time to build up;
tempus flendi et tempus ridendi,	A time to weep, and a time to laugh;
tempus plangendi et tempus saltandi,	a time to mourn, and a time to dance;
tempus spargendi lapides et tempus colligendi,	A time to cast away stones, and a time to gather stones together;
tempus amplexandi et tempus longe fieri ab amplexibus,	a time to embrace, and a time to refrain from embracing;
tempus adquirendi et tempus perdendi,	A time to get, and a time to lose;
tempus custodiendi et tempus abiciendi,	a time to keep, and a time to cast away;
tempus scindendi et tempus consuendi,	A time to rend, and a time to sew;
tempus tacendi et tempus loquendi,	a time to keep silence, and a time to speak;
tempus dilectionis et tempus odii,	A time to love, and a time to hate;
tempus belli et tempus pacis.	a time of war, and a time of peace.
Quid habet amplius homo de labore suo?	What profit hath he that worketh in that wherein he laboureth?
Liber Ecclesiastes III, i–ix	*Ecclesiastes 3, 1–9*

CHAPTER 22

READING

Midas et Aurum	Midas and the Gold
1. **Temporibus antiquis erat rex, Midas.**	1. In ancient times there was a king, Midas.
2. **Nomen regis erat clarum quod amicus Bacchi erat.**	2. The name of the king was famous because he was a friend of Bacchus.
3. **Bacchus ab hostibus captus erat.**	3. Silenus had been captured by the enemy.
4. **A Mida liberatus erat. Bacchus vero fuit laetus.**	4. He had been freed by Midas. Bacchus was indeed happy.
5. **Bacchus ei nuntiavit: 'Donum dabo.'**	5. Bacchus told him: 'I shall give a gift.'
6. **Hoc regi gratum erat.**	6. This was pleasing to the king.
7. **Donum accepit. Postea multa in aurum vertebantur, si ea tangebat.**	7. He received this gift. Afterwards many things were turned into gold, if he touched them.
8. **Rex donum dei bene amabat.**	8. The king liked well the gift of the god.
9. **Midas multum aurum facere vult.**	9. Midas wishes to make much gold.
10. **In aurum arbores altas atque terram aquamque vertebat.**	10. He turned into gold the high trees and also the land and water.
11. **Ob donum suum deum laudavit. Aurum potius quam sapientiam habere mavult.**	11. He praised the god because of his gift. He prefers to have gold rather than wisdom.
12. **Rex superbus auro suo factus erat.**	12. The king had been made proud by his gold.
13. **Nunc Midas domi est. Magno cum studio multa in aurum vertit.**	13. Now Midas is at home. With great eagerness he turns many things into gold.
14. **Tum edere volebat. Cibus aquaque ante eum a servo suo posita sunt.**	14. Then he wished to eat. Food and water were placed in front of him by his servant.
15. **Ea petivit, sed sine mora in**	15. He sought these things, but

Midas et Aurum	Midas and the Gold
aurum versa sunt. Aurum edere nolebat.	without delay they were turned into gold. He did not wish to eat gold.
16. **Tum Midas timore magno captus est. Suam mortem vero timebat.**	16. Then Midas was seized with great fear. He indeed feared his death.
17. **In locis ultimis proximisque aurum videbat.**	17. He saw gold in the farthest and nearest places.
18. **Ad Bacchum iit. 'Id donum rogavi, sed non est donum bonum. Est poena magna malaque. Nunc auxilium peto.'**	18. He went to Bacchus: 'I asked for that gift, but it is not a good gift. It is a great and evil punishment. Now I seek help.'
19. **Deus ei auxilium mox dedit.**	19. The god soon gave him help.
20. **Corpus caputque in flumine ponere eum iussit.**	20. He ordered him to place his body and head in a river.
21. **Midas magna cum diligentia id fecit. Mox liberatus est, sed flumini suum donum dederat.**	21. Midas did that with great care. Soon he was freed, but he had given his own gift to the river.
22. **Post id tempus arenae fluminis erant aureae.**	22. After that time the sands of the river were golden.

Vocabulary

Nouns

studium, studii or **studi,** *n.*, zeal, eagerness (study)
diligentia, diligentiae, *f.*, diligence, care
timor, timoris, *m.*, fear, dread (timorous)
mors, mortis, *f.*, death **(mortium)** (mortality)
poena, poenae, *f.*, punishment, fine (penal)
arena, arenae, *f.*, sand (arena)
cibus, cibi, *m.*, food
tempus, temporis, *n.*, time (temporary, ex tempore)
aurum, auri, *n.*, gold
arbor, arboris, *f.*, tree (arboreal)
Bacchus, Bacchi, *m.*, Bacchus (bacchanalian)
Midas, Midae, *m.*, Midas

Verbs

pono, ponere, posui, positus, put, place (position, postpone)
capio, capere, cepi, captus, take, seize, capture
accipio, accipere, accepi, acceptus, receive, accept
verto, vertere, verti, versus, turn (subvert)
tango, tangere, tetigi, tactus, touch (tangent)
facio, facere, feci, factus, make, do (factory)
edo, edere (or **esse**), **edi, esus,** eat (edible)
volo, velle, volui, be willing, wish (volition)
nolo, nolle, nolui, be unwilling, not wish
malo, malle, malui, prefer

Adverbs

potius, rather

potius quam, rather than

Prepositions

propter (with the Accusative case), because of, on account of

ob (with the Accusative case), because of, on account of

THE VERB: THIRD CONJUGATION

Some **3rd conjugation** verbs have **-io** in the first principal part. These also have an **-i-** in most forms of the Present, Imperfect, and Future tenses.

Present tense of **capio,** compared with that of **duco**

Active		*Passive*	
I lead; I seize		I am led; I am seized	
duco	**capio**	**ducor**	**capior**
ducis	**capis**	**duceris**	**caperis**
ducit	**capit**	**ducitur**	**capitur**
ducimus	**capimus**	**ducimur**	**capimur**
ducitis	**capitis**	**ducimini**	**capimini**
ducunt	**capiunt**	**ducuntur**	**capiuntur**

Imperfect tense:

Active		*Passive*	
I was leading; I was seizing		I was led; I was seized	
ducebam	**capiebam**	**ducebar**	**capiebar**
ducebas	**capiebas**	**ducebaris**	**capiebaris**
ducebat	**capiebat**	**ducebatur**	**capiebatur**
ducebamus	**capiebamus**	**ducebamur**	**capiebamur**
ducebatis	**capiebatis**	**ducebamini**	**capiebamini**
ducebant	**capiebant**	**ducebantur**	**capiebantur**

Future tense:

Active		*Passive*	
I shall lead; I shall seize		I shall be led; I shall be seized	
ducam	**capiam**	**ducar**	**capiar**
duces	**capies**	**duceris**	**capieris**
ducet	**capiet**	**ducetur**	**capietur**
ducemus	**capiemus**	**ducemur**	**capiemur**
ducetis	**capietis**	**ducemini**	**capiemini**
ducent	**capient**	**ducentur**	**capientur**

The Perfect tenses are all regular.

IRREGULAR VERBS: VOLO, NOLO, MALO

Present tense:

I wish, I am willing	I do not wish, I am unwilling	I prefer
volo	**nolo**	**malo**
vis	**non vis**	**mavis**
vult	**non vult**	**mavult**
volumus	**nolumus**	**malumus**
vultis	**non vultis**	**mavultis**
volunt	**nolunt**	**malunt**

Imperfect tense:

volebam	**nolebam**	**malebam**
volebas	**nolebas**	**malebas**
volebat, etc.	**nolebat,** etc.	**malebat,** etc.

Future tense:

volam	**nolam**	**malam**
voles	**noles**	**males**
volet, etc.	**nolet,** etc.	**malet,** etc.

The Perfect tenses are all regular.

ORDER OF WORDS—CUM

When **cum** is used to show how something was done, it often follows the adjective.

Cum diligentia laborat.	He works with diligence.
Magna cum diligentia laborat.	He works with great diligence.

CAUSE

The cause of an action may be shown by either the Ablative case alone or by **ob** or **propter** and the Accusative case.

timore,	because of (on account of) fear
ob timorem,	because of (on account of) fear
propter timorem,	because of (on account of) fear

LATIN ON BRITISH COINS

Rex, king
Regina, queen

DG., or **Dei Gratia,** by the grace of God.
F.D., or **Fid. Def., Fidei Defensor,** defender of the faith.
Britt. Omn., Brittaniae Omnis, of all Britain
Ind. Imp., Indiae Imperator, Commander of India (only on coins minted before 1948)

Practice Exercises

No. 99. Translate these phrases, showing cause or reason.

1. **ob moram**
2. **cura mea**
3. **propter pericula**
4. **propter timorem**
5. **ob mortem**
6. **per diligentiam**
7. **celeritate**
8. **ob audaciam**
9. **propter moras**
10. **tempore**

No. 100. Translate these phrases, showing manner.

1. **cum studio**
2. **magna cura**
3. **magna cum diligentia**
4. **magno cum timore**
5. **cum celeritate**
6. **studio multo**
7. **magno cum studio**
8. **cum mora**
9. **magna celeritate**
10. **magna cum mora**

No. 101. Complete these principal parts.

1. **pono, ponere,** . . . ., **positus**
2. **supero,** . . . ., **superavi, superatus**
3. **do, dare,** . . . ., **datus**
4. **capio,** . . . ., **cepi, captus**
5. **servo, servare, servavi,** . . . .
6. . . . ., **facere, feci, factus**
7. **verto, vertere,** . . . ., **versus**
8. **terreo, terrere,** . . . ., **territus**
9. . . . ., **ducere, duxi, ductus**
10. **paro, parare, paravi,** . . . .

No. 102. Translate these verb forms.

1. **iussit**
2. **duxisti**
3. **demonstraverunt**
4. **vult**
5. **fecimus**
6. **docetur**
7. **mitteris**
8. **capimini**
9. **mavis**
10. **augebimus**
11. **petent**
12. **volabant**
13. **mavultis**
14. **vertebatur**
15. **terruerat**
16. **petiveratis**
17. **ceperant**
18. **moti erunt**
19. **ducti eramus**
20. **nolunt**

No. 103. Translate these prepositional phrases.

1. **ob horam**
2. **propter telum**
3. **ante castra**
4. **ab urbe**
5. **de arbore**
6. **ab rege**
7. **ex arboribus**
8. **in eum locum**
9. **cum patre**
10. **magna cum cura**
11. **in aqua**
12. **sub oceano**
13. **circum muros**
14. **contra eum**
15. **inter oppida**
16. **per agrum**
17. **post castra**
18. **sine eis**
19. **trans mare**
20. **de viris**

CHAPTER 23

READING

Hannibal

1. **Hannibal adulescens erat inimicus Romanis quod pater eos non amabat.**
2. **In Africa habitabant, sed mox Hannibal cum suis trans mare in navibus multis ad Hispaniam navigavit.**
3. **Ipse multas copias et classem bonam habebat.**
4. **In Hispania multa oppida oppugnavit et praedam captivosque cepit.**
5. **Deinde ad Italiam viros suos duxit, sed inter Hispaniam Italiamque erant montes.**
6. **Hi montes pedites equitesque eius maxime impediebant. Multa impedimenta portabantur.**
7. **Ad imperatorem Romanum nuntius portatus est.**
8. **Romani contra hostes ierunt.**
9. **In Italia Romani proelio hostes non vicerunt, sed ubi in Africa pugnaverunt ad victoriam ab imperatore suo ducti sunt.**

Hannibal

1. As a youth, Hannibal was unfriendly to the Romans because his father did not like them.
2. They lived in Africa, but soon Hannibal with his men sailed across the sea in many ships to Spain.
3. He himself had many troops and a good fleet.
4. In Spain he attacked many towns and took booty and captives.
5. Then he led his men to Italy, but between Spain and Italy there were mountains.
6. These mountains greatly hindered his foot-soldiers and horsemen. Much baggage was being carried.
7. The news was carried to the Roman general.
8. The Romans went against the enemy.
9. The Romans did not conquer the enemy in battle in Italy, but when they fought in Africa they were led to victory by their general.

Theseus et Minotaurus

1. **Populus Graecus contra populum insulae Cretae multos annos bellum gesserat.**

Theseus and the Minotaur

1. The people of Greece had waged war against the people of the island of Crete for many years.

Theseus et Minotaurus	Theseus and the Minotaur
2. **Graeci magno cum animo diu contendebant, sed ab copiis Minois, regis Cretae, victi erant.**	2. The Greeks fought for a long time with great spirit, but they had been conquered by the forces of Minos, the king of Crete.
3. **Haec fuerat causa belli: Filius Minois a Graecis interfectus erat. Itaque rex ob iniuriam illam ab eis poenam petebat.**	3. This had been the cause of the war: The son of Minos had been killed by the Greeks. And so the king sought punishment from them because of that injury.
4. **Septem puellas et septem pueros rogavit.**	4. He asked for seven girls and seven boys.
5. **Graeci erant miseri, sed eos miserunt.**	5. The Greeks were unhappy, but they sent them.
6. **Minos, rex, labyrinthum habebat. In labyrintho animal barbarum, Minotaurum, tenebat.**	6. Minos, the king, had a labyrinth. In the labyrinth he kept a savage animal, the Minotaur.
7. **In labyrinthum puellas puerosque duxit.**	7. He led the girls and boys into the labyrinth.
8. **In eo loco terrebantur quod contra Minotaurum sine armis pugnare non poterant et mortem acceperunt.**	8. In that place they were terrified because they were not able to fight against the Minotaur without weapons and they accepted death.

Vocabulary

Nouns

animus, animi, *m.*, mind, spirit (animosity)

labyrinthus, labyrinthi, *m.*, labyrinth

iniuria, iniuriae, *f.*, injury, harm

adulescens, adulescentis, *m.*, youth **(adulescentium)** (adolescent)

classis, classis, *f.*, fleet **(classium)**

imperator, imperatoris, *m.*, general, commander, emperor (imperative)

impedimentum, impedimenti, *n.*, hindrance. In the plural, baggage (impediment)

eques, equitis, *m.*, horseman, knight (equestrian)

pedes, peditis, *m.*, foot soldier

navis, navis, *f.*, ship **(navium)** (navy)

Minotaurus, Minotauri, *m.*, the Minotaur

Minos, Minois, *m.*, Minos (a Greek noun)

Hannibal, Hannibalis, *m.*, Hannibal

Africa, Africae, *f.*, Africa

Adjectives

hic, haec, hoc, this
ille, illa, illud, that
idem, eadem, idem, the same (identical)
ipse, ipsa, ipsum, himself, herself, itself; very

Verbs

vinco, vincere, vici, victus, conquer (victory)
contendo, contendere, contendi, contentus, hasten, strive, contend
interficio, interficere, interfeci, interfectus, kill
gero, gerere, gessi, gestus, carry on, wage
impedio, impedire, impedivi, impeditus, hinder, impede

Pronouns

hic, haec, hoc, he, she, it
ille, illa, illud, he, she, it
idem, eadem, idem, he, she, it
ipse, ipsa, ipsum, he (himself), she (herself), it (itself)

Conjunction

itaque, and so, therefore

PRONOUNS AND PRONOMINAL ADJECTIVES

These words are used as both pronouns and adjectives in the same way as **is, ea, id.**

	Pronoun	*Adjective*
hic, haec, hoc	he, she, it (here)	this
ille, illa, illud	he, she, it (there)	that
idem, eadem, idem	he, she, it (the same)	the same
ipse, ipsa, ipsum	he, she, it (-self)	himself, herself, itself; very

hic vir, this man — **hic,** he
ille homo, that man — **ille,** he
idem homo, the same man — **idem,** he
vir ipse, the man himself — **ipse,** he

The declension of these words is very much the same as **is, ea, id:**

Singular

Nom.	**hic**	he	**haec**	she	**hoc**	it	this
Acc.	**hunc**	him	**hanc**	her	**hoc**	it	this
Gen.	**huius**	his	**huius**	her	**huius**	its	of this
Dat.	**huic**	to him	**huic**	to her	**huic**	to it	to this
Abl.	**hoc**	by him	**hac**	by her	**hoc**	by it	by this

Plural

Nom.	**hi**	**hae**	**haec**	they	these
Acc.	**hos**	**has**	**haec**	them	these
Gen.	**horum**	**harum**	**horum**	their	of these
Dat.	**his**	**his**	**his**	to them	to these
Abl.	**his**	**his**	**his**	by them	by these

	Singular			*Plural*		
Nom.	**ille**	**illa**	**illud**	**illi**	**illae**	**illa**
Acc.	**illum**	**illam**	**illud**	**illos**	**illas**	**illa**
Gen.	**illius**	**illius**	**illius**	**illorum**	**illarum**	**illorum**
Dat.	**illi**	**illi**	**illi**	**illis**	**illis**	**illis**
Abl.	**illo**	**illa**	**illo**	**illis**	**illis**	**illis**

ille, illa, illud has the same meanings (he, she, it) as **is, ea, id** or **hic, haec, hoc** when used as a Pronoun. As an adjective, **ille, illa, illud** means *that*.

ipse, ipsa, ipsum is declined just like **is, ea, id** or **ille, illa, illud** after the first few forms:

Singular

Nom.	**ipse**	**ipsa**	**ipsum**
Acc.	**ipsum**	**ipsam**	**ipsum**
Gen.	**ipsius**	**ipsius**	**ipsius**
Dat.	**ipsi**	**ipsi**	**ipsi**
Abl.	**ipso**	**ipsa**	**ipso**

As a pronoun, **ipse, ipsa, ipsum** means **he** (himself), *she* (herself), *it* (itself). As an adjective, it means *himself, herself, itself, very.*

Plural

As for **bonus**

idem, eadem, idem is based on **is, ea, id** and declined in much the same way:

Nom.	**idem**	**eadem**	**idem**	**eidem, iidem**	**eaedem**	**eadem**
Acc.	**eundem**	**eandem**	**idem**	**eosdem**	**easdem**	**eadem**
Gen.	**eiusdem**	**eiusdem**	**eiusdem**	**eorundem**	**earundem**	**eorundem**
Dat.	**eidem**	**eidem**	**eidem**	**eisdem, iisdem**	in all genders	
Abl.	**eodem**	**eadem**	**eodem**	**eisdem, iisdem**	in all genders	

As a pronoun, **idem, eadem, idem** means (the same) *he*, (the same) *she*, (the same) *it*. As an adjective it means *same.*

Note that because Latin has several words which mean *he*, *she*, *it*, it can avoid confusion without recourse to words like *the former* and *the latter* which are necessary in English.

IRREGULAR VERB: POSSUM

possum, posse, potui, *to be able, can,* is based on **sum, esse, fui.**

Present tense:

possum	I am able, can	**possumus**	we are able, can
potes	you are able, can	**potestis**	you are able, can
potest	he, she, it is able, can	**possunt**	they are able, can

Imperfect tense:

poteram I was able, could
poteras you were able, could
etc.

Future tense:

potero I shall be able
poteris you will be able
etc.

Note that where the appropriate part of **sum** begins with an 's' the prefix is **pos-**; where it begins with an **'e'**, the prefix is **pot-**.

The Perfect tenses are formed in a regular way from the third principal part.

Perfect tense:

potui I have been able, could
potuisti you have been able, could, etc.

Pluperfect tense:

potueram I had been able, could
potueras you had been able, could
etc.

Future Perfect tense:

potuero I shall have been able, could
potueris you will have been able, could
etc.

THE PRONUNCIATION OF CHURCH LATIN

The pronunciation of Church Latin may follow the classical Latin pronunciation or the general pattern of the Italian pronunciation. The rules are by no means fixed and standardized, but, with widened oral communication, the Italian pronunciation of liturgical Latin has increased in the Roman Catholic Church, as it has also in the singing of all Church Latin.

1. Vowels.
   The vowels have the same pronunciation, except that **u** becomes **ou.** meus, **meous**
2. Consonants.
   The most noticeable difference is that **c** before **e** or **i** is not k, but **ch.** cibus, **chi**bous
   ti between two vowels is **tsi.** nationem, **natsi**onem
   ti after a consonant (except s, t, or x) is **ci.** amanti, aman**ci**

g before **e** or **i** is soft, like **j.** gens, jens
All double consonants are pronounced definitely, with equal stress on each. anno, an-no

Practice Exercises

No. 104. Translate these phrases which use **hic and ille.**

1. **hic murus**
2. **illam urbem**
3. **in illo loco**
4. **hi duces**
5. **illis militibus**
6. **illi legato**
7. **hos imperatores**
8. **illa consilia**
9. **illius oceani**
10. **horum hominum**
11. **in illo horto**
12. **illa dea**
13. **illius peditis**
14. **de hoc domino**
15. **ex illa arbore**
16. **hoc impedimentum**
17. **his patribus**
18. **has naves**
19. **ille liber**
20. **illi puellae**
21. **haec arma**
22. **harum partium**
23. **de illa pace**
24. **illarum arenarum**
25. **his annis**
26. **illam horam**
27. **illud signum**
28. **huius equi**
29. **ad has feminas**
30. **illos nuntios**

No. 105. Translate these pronouns.

1. **huius**
2. **ille**
3. **illi**
4. **hos**
5. **illis**
6. **harum**
7. **hoc**
8. **huic**
9. **illa**
10. **hi**
11. **haec**
12. **hanc**
13. **has**
14. **illum**
15. **illos**

No. 106. Translate these phrases which use **idem** and **ipse.**

1. **dea ipsa**
2. **ex templis ipsis**
3. **urbem eandem**
4. **homines ipsos**
5. **ab eodem adulescente**
6. **idem nomen**
7. **eiusdem nationis**
8. **cum eisdem equitibus**
9. **eadem itinera**
10. **iisdem viris**
11. **ex agro ipso**
12. **annis ipsis**
13. **pueri ipsi**
14. **legati ipsius**
15. **eadem hora**
16. **lex ipsa**
17. **mons ipse**
18. **puellae ipsae**
19. **idem iter**
20. **ab mulieribus ipsis**
21. **eodem tempore**
22. **eorundem imperatorum**
23. **eadem oppida**
24. **in urbibus ipsis**
25. **eiusdem populi**
26. **iidem homines**
27. **ex iisdem locis**
28. **iisdem annis**
29. **nocte ipsa**
30. **pax ipsa**

No. 107. Complete these sentences by adding the appropriate form of 'hic', 'ille', 'idem' or 'ipse'. Choose your answer from the words in parentheses.

1. **Romani .... bellum saepe gerebant (ipsi, ipsa)**
2. **.............. anno Theseus Minotaurum interfecit (idem, eodem)**
3. **Trans .... montes Hannibal copias duxit (hos, has)**

4. **Huic aurum dabo, ... sapientiam (illam, illi)**
5. **Filiae .... feminarum in aqua natabant (earundem, eisdem)**
6. **Populum .... patriae vicimus (huius, hanc)**
7. **Regem .... in urbe vidimus (ipsa, ipsum)**
8. **.............. bellum, ... pacem amant (hi, hic) (illam, illi)**
9. **.............. dona ad deas mittemus (hae, haec)**
10. **Filius .... legati sagitta interfectus est (eiusdem, eidem)**

No. 108. Translate these sentences.

1. **ducere poterant**
2. **manere vis**
3. **adorare non vult**
4. **liberare poterit**
5. **curare possunt**
6. **necare malumus**
7. **iubere potueram**
8. **docere potes**
9. **rogare volemus**
10. **augere nolui**
11. **iuvare poterimus**
12. **pugnare nolebas**
13. **vocare non potuerunt**
14. **laborare noluerant**
15. **manere potuistis**

CHAPTER 24

READING

Theseus et Minotaurus
(concluded)

Theseus and the Minotaur
(concluded)

1. **Interea Theseus fortuna misera puerorum puellarumque Graecorum incitatus est.**

1. Meanwhile Theseus was aroused by the unhappy fortune of the Greek boys and girls.

2. **Rogavit: 'Estne nullum auxilium his filiis civium nostrorum?'**

2. He asked: 'Is there no help for these children of our citizens?'

3. **Itaque ad Cretam cum sociis suis navi contendit.**

3. And so he hurried to Crete by ship with his comrades.

4. **Ariadne, filia regis, eum vidit et ob virtutem eius amavit.**

4. Ariadne, the daughter of the king, saw him and loved him because of his courage.

5. **Sine mora illa de labyrintho eum docuit.**

5. Without delay she explained to him about the labyrinth.

6. **Deinde Theseus solus ad labyrinthum iit. Arma portabat et bonum consilium Ariadnes memoria tenebat.**

6. Then Theseus alone went to the labyrinth. He carried weapons and he remembered the good advice of Ariadne.

7. **Mox Minotaurum vidit. Cum eo animali diu pugnabat. Tandem id interficere potuit.**

7. Soon he saw the Minotaur. He fought with that animal for a long time. At last he was able to kill it.

8. **Minotaurus necatus erat. Pueri puellaeque liberati erant.**

8. The Minotaur had been killed. The boys and girls had been freed.

9. **Omnes annos postea populus Graecus laetus erat quod regi malo Cretae nullas poenas dabat.**

9. For all the years afterwards the people of Greece were happy because they paid no penalties to the evil king of Crete.

Ulixes et Cyclops

Ulysses and the Cyclops

1. **Homerus, poeta antiquus, de bello inter viros Graecos Troi-**

1. Homer, an ancient poet, wrote in his great work about the

anosque in suo magno opere scripsit.	war between the men of Greece and Troy.
2. **Post multos annos longos Troia ab Graecis capta erat.**	2. After many long years Troy had been captured by the Greeks.
3. **Graeci ab illo loco navigabant. Apud eos erat Ulixes, homo audax, sed brevi tempore navis eius tempestate ad aliam partem maris portata est.**	3. The Greeks were sailing away from that place. Among them was Ulysses, a bold man, but in a short time his ship was carried by a storm to another part of the sea.
4. **Ex navi ad terram cum sociis suis Ulixes contendit.**	4. Ulysses hurried from his ship to the land with his comrades.
5. **Non longe ab eo loco ubi stabant corpus magnum Polyphemi, Cyclopis, mox viderunt. Ille in colle habitabat.**	5. Not far from that place where they were standing they soon saw the large body of Polyphemus, the Cyclops. He lived on a hill.
6. **Graeci iniuriam timebant.**	6. The Greeks feared injury.
7. **Polyphemus eos a mari ad antrum suum duxit.**	7. Polyphemus led them away from the sea to his cave.
8. **Viri cibum exspectabant, sed Cyclops unum hominem, deinde alterum, et alium edit.**	8. The men waited for food, but the Cyclops ate one man, then another, and another.
9. **Omnes pro sociis suis dolebant.**	9. They all grieved for their comrades.
10. **Poteruntne ab Polyphemo fugere?**	10. Will they be able to flee from Polyphemus?

Vocabulary

Nouns

civis, civis, *m.* or *f.*, citizen **(civium)** (civic)

Theseus, Thesei, *m.*, Theseus

Ariadne, Ariadnes, *f.*, Ariadne (a Greek noun)

opus, operis, *n.*, work (opera)

tempestas, tempestatis, *f.*, storm, bad weather (tempest)

poeta, poetae, *m.*, poet

Polyphemus, Polyphemi, *m.*, Polyphemus

Cyclops, Cyclopis, *m.*, Cyclops

Homerus, Homeri, *m.*, Homer

Ulixes, Ulixis, *m.*, Ulysses

antrum, antri, *n.*, cave

Verbs

scribo, scribere, scripsi, scriptus, write (scribe)

fugio, fugere, fugi, fugiturus, flee, run away, escape (fugitive)

Adverb

interea, meanwhile

Adjectives

celer, celeris, celere, quick, swift (celerity)

acer, acris, acre, sharp, active, keen (acrid)

omnis, omne, all, every (omnibus)

audax, audacis, bold; **audacis** is the Gen. Case (audacious)

brevis, breve, short, brief (brevity)

alius, alia, aliud, other, another (alien)

unus, una, unum, one (unit)

alter, altera, alterum, the one, the other of two (alternate)

nullus, nulla, nullum, no, none (null)

solus, sola, solum, alone, only (sole)

totus, tota, totum, all, whole (total)

Prepositions

apud (with the Acc. case), among, in the presence of

pro (with the Abl. case), in front of, for, instead of

ADJECTIVES

Some adjectives that belong to the **1st** and **2nd declensions** have the Genitive singular ending in **-ius** and the Dative singular ending in **-i.** Otherwise, they are regular.

Nominative	**unus**	**una**	**unum**
Accusative	**unum**	**unam**	**unum**
Genitive	**unius**	**unius**	**unius**
Dative	**uni**	**uni**	**uni**
etc.			

These adjectives are declined like **unus:**

alius, alia, aliud, other, another
alter, altera, alterum, the one, the other
neuter, neutra, neutrum, neither
nullus, nulla, nullum, no, none
solus, sola, solum, alone, only
totus, tota, totum, whole, all
ullus, ulla, ullum, any
uter, utra, utrum, which (of two)

Sometimes **alius** or **alter** may be in pairs:

alius . . . alius, one . . . another **alii . . . alii,** some . . . others
alter . . . alter, the one . . . the other (of two)

Alterum iter longum est, alterum non est.	One road is long, the other is not.
Alii sunt boni, alii sunt mali.	Some are good, some are bad.

3rd Declension Adjectives.

These are of three kinds, according to the number of spellings in the Nominative singular, but all have the **3rd declension** endings. The masculine and feminine genders are declined like **urbs** (except that the Ablative singular always ends in **-i**); the neuter like **mare.** (See page 76.) The three kinds are:

1. One spelling for all genders in the Nominative singular:

	Singular		
	m.	*f.*	*n.*
Nominative	**audax**	**audax**	**audax**
Vocative	**audax**	**audax**	**audax**
Accusative	**audacem**	**audacem**	**audax**
Genitive	**audacis**	all genders	
Dative	**audaci**	all genders	
Ablative	**audaci**	all genders	

	Plural		
	m.	*f.*	*n.*
Nominative	**audaces**	**audaces**	**audacia**
Vocative	**audaces**	**audaces**	**audacia**
Accusative	**audaces**	**audaces**	**audacia**
Genitive	**audacium**	all genders	
Dative	**audacibus**	all genders	
Ablative	**audacibus**	all genders	

2. Two spellings—one for the masculine and feminine, one for the neuter:

	m.	*f.*	*n.*
Nominative	**omnis**	**omnis**	**omne**
Vocative	**omnis**	**omnis**	**omne**
Accusative	**omnem**	**omnem**	**omne**
Genitive	**omnis**	**omnis**	**omnis**
Dative	**omni**	**omni**	**omni**
etc.			

3. Three spellings—one for each gender:

	m.	*f.*	*n.*
Nominative	**celer**	**celeris**	**celere**
Vocative	**celer**	**celeris**	**celere**

Accusative	**celerem**	**celerem**	**celere**
Genitive	**celeris**	**celeris**	**celeris**
Dative	**celeri**	**celeri**	**celeri**
etc.			

Note that, as with **1st** and **2nd declension** adjectives in **-er,** some of these adjectives retain the '**e**' and others lose it (e.g., acer, acris, acre).

SUFFIXES

Some of the more common suffixes used to form adjectives are:

-eus, denoting the material. English, of —**aureus,** of gold

-osus, denoting fullness. English, full of —**periculosus,** full of danger

-bilis, denoting possibility. English, able —**amabilis,** able to be loved, lovable

-anus, -icus, -alis, -inus, denoting connection.

-anus becomes -ane or -an in English. **Romanus,** Roman

-icus becomes -ic in English. **publicus,** public

-alis becomes -al in English. **mortalis,** mortal

-inus becomes -in or -ine in English. **Latinus,** Latin

Practice Exercises

No. 109. Give the English for these phrases.

1. **uno anno**
2. **nullam curam**
3. **utrius doni**
4. **ulli navi**
5. **totos annos**
6. **cum patre solo**
7. **nullarum mortium**
8. **neutri nationi**
9. **in altera via**
10. **alio nomine**
11. **ad utrum flumen**
12. **ullius collis**
13. **uni libro**
14. **ob nullas causas**
15. **ab neutro homine**

No. 110. Translate these verb forms.

1. **timuerant**
2. **fuistis**
3. **mittent**
4. **cepit**
5. **timebit**
6. **spectabant**
7. **tenebuntur**
8. **mittar**
9. **laudati sunt**
10. **factum erat**
11. **navigabas**
12. **dabantur**
13. **gerit**
14. **fuerant**
15. **habuerunt**

No. 111. Give the English for the following:

1. **alter magnus, alter parvus est**
2. **nullo tempore**
3. **ullius belli**
4. **ad utra castra**
5. **mulieres ipsae solae**
6. **neutrius adulescentis**
7. **alias urbes**
8. **unam partem**
9. **de neutra puella**
10. **aliud iter**

No. 112. Give the English for these phrases.

1. **hora brevi**
2. **servi audacis**
3. **eques celer**
4. **in flumine celeri**
5. **ab viris audacibus**
6. **tempora omnia**
7. **a legato acri**
8. **vita brevis**
9. **omnibus horis**
10. **in navi celeri**
11. **opus audax**
12. **brevi tempore**
13. **copiae acres**
14. **equi celeris**
15. **acres feminae**
16. **mortem celerem**
17. **itinera brevia**
18. **audaci homini**
19. **brevem annum**
20. **omni in loco**

CHAPTER 25

READING

Ulixes et Cyclops (concluded)	Ulysses and the Cyclops (concluded)
1. **Postquam Cyclops haec fecit, Graeci fortes mortem exspectabant, sed Ulixes Polyphemum interficere malebat.**	1. After the Cyclops had done these things, the brave Greeks waited for death, but Ulysses preferred to kill Polyphemus.
2. **Ob magnitudinem viri facile non erat ex periculo fugere, sed consilium parabant et animos bonos tenebant.**	2. Because of the great size of the man it was not easy to escape from their danger, but they prepared a plan and kept their good spirits.
3. **Ante hoc tempus alia pericula gravia superaverant et hoc periculum novum superare in animo habebant.**	3. Before this time they had overcome other serious dangers and they had in mind to overcome this new danger.
4. **Uterque Cyclopem timebat, sed Polyphemus inimicus omnibus erat.**	4. Each feared the Cyclops, but Polyphemus was unfriendly to all.
5. **Eum incitare nolebant. Itaque Ulixes suum consilium eis demonstravit.**	5. They did not wish to arouse him. And so Ulysses showed them his plan.
6. **Partem arboris in igni posuerunt. Post breve tempus ramus acutus erat.**	6. They placed part of a tree in the fire. After a short time the end of the tree was sharp.
7. **Hoc erat telum eorum contra Cyclopem. Id magna cum diligentia paraverant.**	7. This was their weapon against the Cyclops. They had prepared it with great care.
8. **Hoc telo Cyclops poenas dabit.**	8. With this weapon the Cyclops will pay the penalty.
9. **Polyphemus unum oculum solum habebat. Magna cum audacia Ulixes et socii in oculum eius finem arboris posuerunt.**	9. Polyphemus had only one eye. With great boldness Ulysses and his comrades put the end of the tree into his eye.
10. **Iniuria erat gravis. Postea Cyclops videre non poterat.**	10. The injury was serious. The Cyclops was not able to see after that.

11. **Polyphemus etiam multa animalia habebat.**	11. Polyphemus also had many animals.
12. **Ante portam saxum grave et magnum posuerat.**	12. He had put a heavy and large stone in front of the door.
13. **Id a Graecis moveri non poterat, sed Cyclops ab porta saxum movebat, si animalia cibum petebant.**	13. This could not be moved by the Greeks, but the Cyclops used to move the stone away from the door, if the animals sought food.
14. **Ulixes et amici fugam suam noctu paraverunt.**	14. Ulysses and his friends prepared their flight at night.
15. **Cyclops eos videre non poterat.**	15. The Cyclops was not able to see them.
16. **Mane saxum ab porta movit.**	16. In the morning he moved the stone away from the door.
17. **Animalia per portam cucurrerunt. Sub animalibus erant Graeci.**	17. The animals ran through the door. Under the animals were the Greeks.
18. **Polyphemus eos non agnovit.**	18. Polyphemus did not recognize them.
19. **Deinde Ulixes clamavit. Itaque Cyclops fugam eorum cognovit.**	19. Then Ulysses shouted. And so the Cyclops learned of their flight.
20. **Cyclops ad mare properavit. Saxum magnum ad Graecos iecit.**	20. The Cyclops hurried to the sea. He threw a large stone towards the Greeks.
21. **Polyphemus, 'Quis es?' inquit.**	21. Polyphemus said, 'Who are you?'
22. **Ulixes clamavit: 'Ulixes sum.' Graeci in navi erant et laeti erant quod a Polyphemo fugerant et ad Graeciam navigabant.**	22. Ulysses shouted: 'I am Ulysses.' The Greeks were on the ship and were happy because they had escaped from Polyphemus and were sailing to Greece.
23. **Postea de oculo suo Polyphemus 'Ulixes,' inquiebat, 'id fecit.'**	23. Afterwards Polyphemus used to say about his eye, 'Ulysses did it.'

Vocabulary

Nouns

oculus, oculi, *m.*, eye (oculist)
porta, portae, *f.*, gate, door, entrance (portal)
saxum, saxi, *n.*, stone, rock
telum, teli, *n.*, weapon
fuga, fugae, *f.*, flight, escape (fugitive)
ramus, rami, *m.*, branch (ramification)

Adjectives

facilis, facile, easy (facility)
fortis, forte, brave, strong (fortitude)
gravis, grave, heavy, severe, serious (gravity)
novus, nova, novum, new (novel)
uterque, utraque, utrumque, each, every
acutus, acuta, aucutum, sharp (acute)

Pronoun

quis, quid, who?, what?

Verbs

simulo, simulare, simulavi, simulatus, pretend (simulate)
clamo, clamare, clamavi, clamatus, shout, cry (clamour)
iacio, iacere, ieci, iactus, throw (project)
agnosco, agnoscere, agnovi, agnitus, recognize
cognosco, cognoscere, cognovi, cognitus, learn, get to know (cognizance)
inquit, he, she, it says. This verb is defective in many parts, but must always be used with Direct Speech.

Adverbs

noctu, at night (nocturnal)
mane, in the morning

GRAMMAR

A. **uterque, utraque, utrumque** is declined just like **uter, utra, utrum.**

uterque vir, each man
utrique viro, to each man
utriusque viri, of each man
utrumque virum, each man

B. The declension of **quis, quid,** who?, what?, is quite similar to that of **is, ea, id.**

	Singular			*Plural*		
	m.	*f.*	*n.*	*m.*	*f.*	*n.*
Nom.	**quis**	**quis**	**quid**	**qui**	**quae**	**quae**
	who? what?					
Acc.	**quem**	**quem**	**quid**	**quos**	**quas**	**quae**
	whom? what?					
Gen.	**cuius**	**cuius**	**cuius**	**quorum**	**quarum**	**quorum**
	of whom?, whose?, of what?					

Dat.	**cui**	**cui**	**cui**	**quibus**	**quibus**	**quibus**
			to, for whom?, to, for what?			
Abl.	**quo**	**qua**	**quo**	**quibus**	**quibus**	**quibus**
			from, with, by, whom?, what?			

Quis est? Who is it?
Cuius est? Whose is it?
Quem vides? Whom do you see?

Qui sunt? Who are they?
Quorum est? Whose is it?
Quid vides? What do you see?

When **cum** is used with the Ablative case of **quis,** it is generally added to the end.

quocum, with whom **quibuscum,** with whom

C. The Present Passive Infinitive of the **1st** and **2nd conjugations** is like the Present Active Infinitive except that it ends in **-i.**

amare, to love **amari,** to be loved
habere, to have **haberi,** to be had

In the **3rd conjugation,** the **-i** is added directly to the stem.

ducere, to lead **duci,** to be led
capere, to take **capi,** to be taken

FAMILIAR QUOTATIONS

Nil homini certum est, Nothing is certain for man. *Ovid*

Virtus praemium est optimum, Virtue is the best reward. *Plautus*

Omnia praeclara rara, All the best things are rare. *Cicero*

Possunt quia posse videntur, They can because they think they can. *Virgil*

Alea iacta est, The die is cast. *Caesar*

Mens sana in corpore sano, A sound mind in a sound body. *Juvenal*

Carmina morte carent, Songs do not die. *Ovid*

Practice Exercises

No. 113. Translate these phrases.

1. **solis aurei**
2. **ex neutro loco**
3. **summo in monte**
4. **itineris facilis**
5. **ullae horae**
6. **poenas graves**
7. **nationum proximarum**
8. **civem audacem**
9. **corpus robustum**
10. **fluminum celerium**
11. **libros Latinos**
12. **homines alii**
13. **navis vestra**
14. **patrum multorum**
15. **utriusque regis**

No. 114. Give the English for the following.

1. **Qui estis?**
2. **Cui ea dedit?**
3. **Quos videbo?**
4. **Cuius oculi?**
5. **Quae cognoscit?**
6. **Quocum ambulat?**
7. **A quo captus est?**
8. **Quis clamat?**
9. **Quis pugnat?**
10. **Quorum tela?**
11. **Quid habes?**
12. **Quem necavit?**
13. **Quibus id dabo?**
14. **Quid rogatum est?**
15. **Cui donum dedisti?**
16. **Quem amas?**
17. **Quis fugit?**
18. **Quid facile est?**
19. **Cuius est?**
20. **Quibuscum?**
21. **Quos mittet?**
22. **Quid facit?**
23. **Qui contendunt?**
24. **A quo bellum gestum est?**
25. **Quis vocat?**

No. 115. Give the Active form of these Present Passive Infinitives.

1. **portari**
2. **mitti**
3. **regi**
4. **dari**
5. **laudari**
6. **rogari**
7. **scribi**
8. **videri**
9. **cognosci**
10. **necari**
11. **capi**
12. **iuberi**
13. **haberi**
14. **moveri**
15. **parari**
16. **duci**
17. **augeri**
18. **servari**
19. **vinci**
20. **terreri**

No. 116. Give the Passive form of these Present Active Infinitives.

1. **demonstrare**
2. **ducere**
3. **movere**
4. **iubere**
5. **vertere**
6. **armare**
7. **amare**
8. **capere**
9. **docere**
10. **occupare**
11. **mittere**
12. **gerere**
13. **accipere**
14. **terrere**
15. **vocare**
16. **interficere**
17. **iuvare**
18. **tenere**
19. **cognoscere**
20. **simulare**

SIXTH REVISION (CHAPTERS 22–25)

VOCABULARY REVISION

Nouns

1. **adulescens**
2. **Africa**
3. **animus**
4. **arbor**
5. **arena**
6. **Ariadne**
7. **aurum**
8. **Bacchus**
9. **cibus**
10. **civis**
11. **classis**
12. **Cyclops**
13. **diligentia**
14. **eques**
15. **fuga**
16. **Hannibal**
17. **Homerus**
18. **impedimentum**
19. **imperator**
20. **iniuria**
21. **labyrinthus**
22. **Midas**
23. **Minos**
24. **Minotaurus**
25. **mors**
26. **navis**
27. **oculus**
28. **opus**
29. **pedes**
30. **poena**
31. **poeta**
32. **Polyphemus**
33. **porta**
34. **saxum**
35. **Silenus**
36. **studium**
37. **telum**
38. **tempestas**
39. **tempus**
40. **Theseus**
41. **timor**
42. **Ulixes**

1. youth
2. Africa
3. mind, spirit
4. tree
5. sand
6. Ariadne
7. gold
8. Bacchus
9. food
10. citizen
11. fleet
12. Cyclops
13. diligence, care
14. horseman, knight
15. flight, escape
16. Hannibal
17. Homer
18. hindrance
19. commander, general, emperor
20. injury, harm
21. labyrinth
22. Midas
23. Minos
24. the Minotaur
25. death
26. ship
27. eye
28. work
29. foot soldier
30. punishment
31. poet
32. Polyphemus
33. gate, door
34. stone, rock
35. Silenus
36. zeal, eagerness
37. weapon
38. storm, bad weather
39. time
40. Theseus
41. fear, dread
42. Ulysses

Pronouns

1. **hic, haec, hoc**
2. **idem, eadem, idem**
3. **ille, illa, illud**
4. **ipse, ipsa, ipsum**
5. **quis, quid**

1. he, she, it
2. he, she, it
3. he, she, it
4. he himself, she herself, it itself
5. who?, what?

Adjectives

1. **acer**
2. **alius**
3. **alter**
4. **audax**
5. **brevis**
6. **celer**
7. **facilis**
8. **fortis**
9. **gravis**
10. **hic**
11. **idem**
12. **ille**
13. **ipse**
14. **novus**
15. **nullus**
16. **omnis**
17. **solus**
18. **totus**
19. **unus**
20. **uterque**

1. sharp, active, keen
2. other, another
3. the one, the other
4. bold
5. short, brief
6. quick, swift
7. easy
8. brave, strong
9. heavy, severe, serious
10. this
11. the same
12. that
13. very, himself, herself, itself
14. new
15. no, none
16. all, every
17. alone, only
18. all, whole
19. one
20. each, every

Verbs

1. **capio**
2. **clamo**
3. **cognosco**
4. **contendo**
5. **facio**
6. **fugio**
7. **gero**
8. **iacio**
9. **interficio**
10. **pono**
11. **scribo**
12. **simulo**
13. **verto**
14. **vinco**

1. I take, seize, capture
2. I shout, cry
3. I learn, recognize, know
4. I hasten, strive, contend
5. I make, do
6. I flee, run away
7. I carry on, wage
8. I throw
9. I kill
10. I put, place
11. I write
12. I pretend
13. I turn
14. I conquer

Adverbs

1. **interea**
2. **noctu**
3. **mane**

1. meanwhile
2. at night
3. in the morning

Prepositions

1. **apud**
2. **pro**
3. **propter**

1. among, in the presence of
2. in front of, for, instead of
3. because of, on account of

Conjunction

1. **itaque** 1. and so, therefore

Practice Exercises

No. 117. Translate these verbs.

1. **capiunt**
2. **cognitum erat**
3. **victi sunt**
4. **vertent**
5. **interficiebamus**
6. **fecerunt**
7. **ceperas**
8. **fugiebat**
9. **ponetur**
10. **gesserint**
11. **scribit**
12. **iacis**
13. **contendent**
14. **positi sunt**
15. **gestum est**

No. 118. Translate these phrases.

1. **propter mortem**
2. **ob iniuriam**
3. **diligentia magna**
4. **ob imperatorem**
5. **propter cibum**
6. **ob classes**
7. **parva cum poena**
8. **magno cum studio**
9. **ob impedimentum**
10. **propter arenam**

No. 119. Translate these pronouns.

1. **hunc**	4. **illud**	7. **eadem**	10. **ipsorum**	13. **cuius**
2. **huius**	5. **ipse**	8. **eiusdem**	11. **quem**	14. **cui**
3. **illos**	6. **illorum**	9. **hic**	12. **quid**	15. **quocum**

No. 120. Translate these sentences.

1. **clamare voluit**	6. **contendere poterit**
2. **capere nolebant**	7. **scribere maluerunt**
3. **facere potes**	8. **cognoscere poteramus**
4. **ponere nolumus**	9. **vertere noles**
5. **vincere potuistis**	10. **gerere possunt**

No. 121. Translate these phrases.

1. **unius operis**	5. **brevi tempore**	9. **audaces equites**
2. **omnium civium**	6. **acri saxo**	10. **celeris poena**
3. **aliud impedimentum**	7. **nullius peditis**	
4. **nova tela**	8. **ullam iniuriam**	

MARCUS TULLIUS CICERO

Cicero was born near Arpinum, in Latium, the province in which Rome was located, in 106 B.C., of an upper middle-class family. He studied law, philosophy and rhetoric in Rome, Athens and Rhodes, and became consul in 63 B.C. It was in this office that he disclosed Catiline's conspiracy to overthrow the government and, in four orations delivered in the Senate, persuaded the Senators to decree the death penalty for the conspirators. After Caesar's assassination in 44 B.C. and the formation of the Second Triumvirate, Cicero was murdered in 43 B.C., while trying to escape from his political enemies.

O tempora! O mores! Senatus haec intellegit, consul videt; hic tamen vivit. Vivit? Immo vero etiam in senatum venit, fit publici consili particeps, notat et designat oculis ad caedem unum quemque nostrum. Nos autem, fortes viri, satis facere rei publicae videmur, si istius furorem ac tela vitamus. Ad mortem te, Catilina, duci iussu consulis iam pridem oportebat; in te conferri pestem, quam tu in nos machinaris.

In Catilinam Oratio Prima, ii

Oh what times these are! Oh what habits we have! The Senate knows these things, the consul sees them; this man, however, lives. Does he live? Indeed, he even comes into the Senate, he becomes a participant in the public plans, he notes and designates with his eyes each single one of us for murder. We, however, brave men, seem to do enough for the Republic, if we avoid the fury and weapons of this man. You,

Catiline, should have been led to your death by the order of the consul long ago; the destruction that you are plotting against us should have been brought against you.

First Oration Against Catiline, 2

ODO DE CERINTON

These two stories were written by Odo de Cerinton, who lived in the twelfth century and composed a work called *Narrationes*, which drew stories from various fables and other sources, giving a mystical interpretation to tales about animals.

De Hydro

Quoddam animal dicitur hydrus, cuius natura est se involvere luto, ut melius posset labi. Tandem in os crocodili, quando dormit, intrat et sic, ventrem eius ingrediens, cor eius mordet et sic crodilum interimit.

Mistice: Hydrus significat filium Dei, qui assumpsit lutum nostrae carnis ut facilius laberetur in os diaboli, et sic, ventrem eius ingrediens et cor eius mordens, ipsum interficit.

About the Hydra

There is a certain animal called the hydra, whose nature it is to bury itself in the mud so that it might be better able to glide. Finally it enters the mouth of a crocodile, when it is sleeping, and thus, entering its stomach, it eats its heart and thus kills the crocodile.

Mystical interpretation: The hydra signifies the son of God, who has assumed the mud of our flesh so that he might slip more easily into the mouth of the devil, and thus, entering his stomach and eating his heart, he kills him.

De Antilope

Quoddam animal est quod vocatur antilops; quod cum virgultis ludit cum cornibus, tandem cornua eius implicantur cum virgultis quod non potest ea extrahere et tunc incipit clamare; quo audito veniunt venatores et interficiunt eum.

Mistice: Sic contigit quod plerique delectati sunt et ludunt cum negotiis huius mundi et sic in eisdem implicantur quod evelli non possunt et sic a venatoribus, id est a daemonibus, capiuntur et interficiuntur.

About the Antelope

There is a certain animal that is called the antelope; when this animal plays in a thicket with its horns, finally its horns are entangled with the thicket because it is not able to extricate them and then it begins to cry aloud; when this is heard, hunters come and kill him.

Mystical interpretation: Thus it happens that many people are delighted and play with the occupations of this world and thus are entangled in these things because they can not be torn away and thus by hunters, that is by demons, they are taken and killed.

CHAPTER 26

READING

Orpheus et Eurydice	Orpheus and Eurydice
1. Orpheus erat vir fortis, sed dolebat quod Eurydice mortua erat et eum solum miserumque reliquerat.	1. Orpheus was a brave man, but he grieved because Eurydice had been taken by death and had left him alone and wretched.
2. Orpheus animalia omnia et naturam magnopere amabat et laetus esse videbatur, sed Eurydicen semper petebat.	2. Orpheus greatly loved all animals and nature and he seemed to be happy, but he always looked for Eurydice.
3. Tandem Orpheus auxilium ab deis petivit.	3. Finally Orpheus sought help from the gods.
4. Nihil ab Iove fieri poterat. Eurydice ab terra discesserat et apud Inferos nunc habitabat.	4. Nothing could be done by Jupiter. Eurydice had departed from the earth and was now living among the dead.
5. Iter facere ad regnum Plutonis difficile erat.	5. It was difficult to journey to the kingdom of Pluto.
6. Pluto suos non saepe tradit, sed Orpheus audax erat neque timebat.	6. Pluto does not often give up his own, but Orpheus was bold and was not afraid.
7. Sub terram magna cum celeritate contendit. Ante regem, Plutonem, mox stabat.	7. He hurried below the earth with great speed. Soon he was standing before the king, Pluto.
8. Orpheus ab Plutone petivit: 'Cur Eurydicen hic tenes? Non solum eam semper maxime amabam sed etiam mors ei non est idonea. Nihil ab Eurydice ipsa facta est.'	8. Orpheus asked Pluto: 'Why do you keep Eurydice here? Not only did I always have the greatest love for her, but also death is not suitable to her. Nothing was done by Eurydice herself.'
9. Deinde Pluto ipse misericordiam magnam habebat, sed Orpheum iussit: 'Eam tradam,	9. Then Pluto himself felt great pity, but he instructed Orpheus: 'I shall give her up, but

sed iter facere ex regno Inferorum difficile est. Eurydice ad terram tuam reduci poterit, sed eam spectare non debes. Si eam spectabis, mortua iterum fiet. Cum eam ad terram eduxeris, tum eam spectare poteris.'	it is difficult to journey out of the kingdom of the dead. Eurydice can be led back to your land, but you ought not to look at her. If you look at her, she will again become dead. When you lead her back to earth, then you can look at her.'
10. **Ab Plutone grate discesserunt et iter ab illo loco malo celeriter faciebant.**	10. They departed from Pluto gratefully and quickly made the journey away from that evil place.
11. **Primo Orpheus fortiter ambulabat, sed amore regebatur. Mox ad eam oculos suos vertit.**	11. At first Orpheus walked bravely, but he was ruled by love. Soon he turned his eyes towards her.
12. **Ob eam causam Pluto magna cum celeritate eam cepit et ad Inferos reduxit.**	12. For that reason Pluto seized her with great speed and led her back to the dead.
13. **Postea in terra non visa est.**	13. Afterwards she was not seen on the earth.

Vocabulary

Nouns

misericordia, misericordiae, *f.*, pity
regnum, regni, *n.*, kingdom (interregnum)
natura, naturae, *f.*, nature
nihil, *n.*, nothing **nihil** has the same spelling in all Cases. (nihilist)
Orpheus, Orphei, *m.*, Orpheus
Eurydice, Eurydices, *f.*, Eurydice (a Greek noun)

Adjectives

difficilis, difficile, difficult, hard
mortuus, mortua, mortuum, dead (mortuary)

Adverbs

tandem, at length, finally
parum, too little, not enough
magnopere, greatly
iterum, again

Verbs

relinquo, relinquere, reliqui, relictus, leave, leave behind (relinquish)
rego, regere, rexi, rectus, rule (regent)

F

discedo, discedere, discessi, discessus, withdraw, go away, leave
trado, tradere, tradidi, traditus, give up, surrender (tradition)
educo, educere, eduxi, eductus, lead out
reduco, reducere, reduxi, reductus, lead back (reduce)
fio, fieri, factus sum, become, be made, be done

FORMATION OF ADVERBS

Adverbs are generally formed from adjectives.

1. Adverbs based on **1st** and **2nd declension** adjectives end in **-e.**

altus, high	**alte,** high, on high
latus, wide	**late,** widely
longus, long	**longe,** far, distant
miser, wretched	**misere,** wretchedly
pulcher, beautiful	**pulchre,** beautifully

2. Adverbs based on **3rd declension** adjectives end in **-ter.**

acer, keen	**acriter,** keenly
audax, bold	**audacter,** boldly
celer, swift	**celeriter,** swiftly
fortis, brave	**fortiter,** bravely

3. Some adverbs are irregular.

bonus, good	**bene,** well
facilis, easy	**facile,** easily
magnus, great	**magnopere,** greatly
primus, first	**primum,** first, or **primo,** at first
solus, alone	**solum,** alone, only

4. Other adverbs are not based on any adjective, e.g., **nunc, semper, non,** etc.

THE VERB: FOURTH CONJUGATION

4th conjugation verbs have **i** as the predominant vowel.
Principal parts: **audio, audire, audivi, auditus,** hear
Present tense:

Active	*Passive*
I hear, do hear, am hearing	I am being heard, am heard
audio	**audior**
audis	**audiris**

audit	**auditur**
audimus	**audimur**
auditis	**audimini**
audiunt	**audiuntur**

Imperfect tense:

Active	*Passive*
I was hearing, heard	I was being heard, was heard
audiebam	**audiebar**
audiebas	**audiebaris**
audiebat	**audiebatur**
audiebamus	**audiebamur**
audiebatis	**audiebamini**
audiebant	**audiebantur**

Future tense:

Active	*Passive*
I shall hear	I shall be heard
audiam	**audiar**
audies	**audieris**
audiet	**audietur**
audiemus	**audiemur**
audietis	**audiemini**
audient	**audientur**

The Perfect tenses are formed in the usual way from the principal parts.

IRREGULAR VERB: FIO

Present Tense:	Imperfect Tense:	Future Tense:
I become, am made	I was becoming, was made	I shall become, shall be made
fio	**fiebam**	**fiam**
fis	**fiebas**	**fies**
fit	**fiebat**, etc.	**fiet**, etc.
—		
—		
fiunt		

Note that the Present tense is defective in the 1st and 2nd Persons Plural.

Note also that in these tenses **fio** must always be used for the Passive Tenses of **facio.**

For the Perfect tenses the Passive of **facio** is used.

Perfect Tense:	Pluperfect Tense:	Future Perfect Tense:
factus sum	**factus eram**	**factus ero**
factus es	**factus eras**	**factus eris**
factus est, etc.	**factus erat,** etc.	**factus erit,** etc.

FAMILIAR PHRASES

status quo or **status in quo,** the state in which. That is, the existing conditions.

mirabile dictu, wonderful to tell, relate.

per se, by itself, of itself; by its own force.

cum grano salis, with a grain of salt.

modus vivendi, manner of living (often temporary).

post scriptum, written after. Abbreviated, **P.S.** or **p.s.**

inter nos, among us, among ourselves.

sine qua non, something indispensable or necessary. Literally, without which not.

Practice Exercises

No. 122. Give the adverbs formed from the following adjectives and their English meanings.

1. **pulcher**	4. **bonus**	7. **brevis**	10. **audax**	13. **fortis**
2. **longus**	5. **acer**	8. **altus**	11. **miser**	14. **celer**
3. **magnus**	6. **gravis**	9. **gratus**	12. **proximus**	15. **liber**

No. 123. Translate these verb forms.

1. **portas**	8. **auditi sunt**	15. **audiunt**	22. **fecit**
2. **habeo**	9. **acceptus es**	16. **fient**	23. **rogabunt**
3. **ducunt**	10. **auditus eram**	17. **audiebamur**	24. **audivimus**
4. **iacit**	11. **fiebant**	18. **vertebamus**	25. **facti erant**
5. **audivistis**	12. **paratus erit**	19. **capientur**	
6. **liberatus est**	13. **audiet**	20. **audieris**	
7. **visi erant**	14. **petiverunt**	21. **audiris**	

No. 124. Give the English for the following.

1. **fortiter pugnant**	5. **bene docemur**	9. **magnopere amabat**
2. **proxime vidimus**	6. **longe ambulat**	10. **parum acriter**
3. **bellum fortiter gessit**	7. **bene stant**	
4. **late accipientur**	8. **facile cognovit**	

No. 125. Translate these sentences.

1. **Locus facile defendetur.**
2. **Primo nihil parari poterat.**
3. **Ob timorem non fortiter contendistis.**
4. **Utramque portam amas?**
5. **Omnia fiunt.**
6. **Non solum rex sed etiam regina id audiverunt.**
7. **De quo audacter scripsit?**
8. **Illo anno multa parabamus.**
9. **Eurydice sub terra misere habitabat.**
10. **Longe ab hoc loco eos duxit.**

F

CHAPTER 27

READING

Hero et Leander	Hero and Leander
1. **Sunt multae fabulae de amore Leandri Herusque.**	1. There are many stories about the love of Hero and Leander.
2. **Hero fuit puella pulchra, quae in Graecia habitabat et omnia in templo, quod erat in oppido, curabat.**	2. Hero was a beautiful girl, who used to live in Greece and took care of everything in the temple, that was in her town.
3. **Ille in altera regione, quae erat trans Hellespontum, mare Graecum, habitabat, sed, si eam videre volebat, trans mare quod non erat latum natabat.**	3. He lived in another region, which was across the Hellespont, the sea of Greece, but, if he wished to see her, he used to swim across the sea, which was not wide.
4. **Ob leges templi cum ea videri non poterat, sed illa lex eum non impediebat. Itaque ad eam semper noctu veniebat.**	4. Because of the laws of the temple he could not be seen with her, but that law did not hinder him. And so he used to come to her always at night.
5. **Etiam iter longum et difficile ab puella eum non prohibebat.**	5. Even the long and difficult journey did not keep him from the girl.
6. **Hero mare de alta turri omnibus noctibus spectabat.**	6. Hero used to watch the sea every night from a high tower.
7. **Leander sine periculo ullo saepe veniebat. Tum Hero ipsa vero laeta erat, quod eum bene amabat.**	7. Leander often came without any danger. Then Hero herself was truly happy, because she loved him well.
8. **Diu Leander bonam fortunam habebat et omnibus noctibus ad Graeciam facile natabat atque ad illam terram sine ullo periculo perveniebat.**	8. For a long time Leander had good fortune and swam easily to Greece every night and came to that land without any danger.
9. **Neque celeritate neque studio carebat. Ut accidit tamen uno tempore tempestate magna victus est.**	9. He lacked neither speed nor eagerness. As it happened, however, one time he was overcome by a great storm.

10. **Primo turris Herus ab eo videri poterat, sed iam iter erat difficile. Mox tempestate sub mare mittebatur.**	10. At first Hero's tower could be seen by him, but already the way was difficult. Soon he was sent under the sea by the storm.
11. **Hero totam noctem eum misere exspectabat.**	11. Hero waited for him unhappily all night.
12. **Deinde ad mare contendit et corpus eius petebat. Id primo non conspexit.**	12. Then she hurried to the sea and sought his body. She did not see it at first.
13. **Deinde non longe ab mari corpus Leandri repperit.**	13. Then not far from the sea she found the body of Leander.
14. **Misera Hero ipsa in mare cucurrit et mortua est.**	14. The unhappy Hero herself ran into the sea and died.

Vocabulary

Nouns

turris, turris, *f.*, tower **(turrium)** (turret)

regio, regionis, *f.*, region, boundary

Hero, Herus, *f.*, Hero (a Greek noun)

Leander, Leandri, *m.*, Leander

Hellespontus, Hellesponti, *m.*, Hellespont

inopia, inopiae, *f.*, want, scarcity

Relative Pronoun

qui, quae, quod, who, which, that; which, what

Adverbs

tamen, however, nevertheless

iam, already, now

Conjunction

ut, as

Verbs

impedio, impedire, impedivi, impeditus, hinder (impede)

prohibeo, prohibere, prohibui, prohibitus, keep off, hinder, prohibit, prevent

venio, venire, veni, ventus, come (advent)

pervenio, pervenire, perveni, perventus, arrive

careo, carere, carui, caritus, be without, lack

accido, accidere, accidi, happen (accident)

conspicio, conspicere, conspexi, conspectus, observe

reperio, reperire, repperi, repertus, find, discover

THE RELATIVE PRONOUN

Inflection

The relative pronoun, **qui, quae, quod,** is declined as follows:

	Singular			*Plural*		
	m.	*f.*	*n.*	*m.*	*f.*	*n.*
Nom.	**qui**	**quae**	**quod**	**qui**	**quae**	**quae**
Acc.	**quem**	**quam**	**quod**	**quos**	**quas**	**quae**
Gen.		**cuius**		**quorum**	**quarum**	**quorum**
Dat.		**cui**			**quibus**	
Abl.	**quo**	**qua**	**quo**		**quibus**	

Use

The relative pronoun is used to introduce a relative clause. A relative clause is an adjectival clause which describes a noun, its *antecedent*. The relative pronoun, therefore, agrees with the antecedent in *gender* and *number*.

vir qui	the man who ....
puellae quae	the girls who ....
bellum quod	the war which ....

The *case* of a relative pronoun, however, is determined by its use in its own clause.

vir quem video.	The man whom I see.
puella cui aquam do.	The girl to whom I give water.

When the Ablative is used with **cum, cum** is added to the end of the Ablative: **quocum, quacum, quibuscum.**

INTERROGATIVE ADJECTIVES

An interrogative adjective modifies a noun and asks a question. It is therefore in the same gender, number, and case as the noun it modifies.

qui vir? which man? **quae puella?** which girl?

quod bellum? what war?

The interrogative adjective **qui, quae, quod,** in Latin is spelled the same as the relative pronoun. Only its use is different.

PREFIXES

prae, before. **praepono,** put before.
re, again, back. **remitto,** send back.
con, together, with; very, thoroughly. **convoco,** call together. **conficio,** finish (do thoroughly).
pro, out, forth. **provoco,** call forth (provoke).

Practice Exercises

No. 126. In the following sentences translate (1) the relative clause, and (2) the whole sentence.

1. **Homines qui cum copiis suis iter faciunt sunt fortes.**
2. **Turris quam aedificavit barbaros ex oppido prohibebat.**
3. **Femina quacum ambulabam mater mea est.**
4. **Navis cuius nomen conspicere non possumus ad Italiam navigat.**
5. **Puer cui litteras dedi celeriter veniet.**
6. **Mox timor quem habebitis non memoria tenebitur.**
7. **Flumen ad quod fugiebant erat altum latumque.**
8. **Locus de quo scripsit urbs pulcherrima est.**
9. **Omnia quae habebat nunc mea sunt.**
10. **Viri quorum filios vides sunt amici.**

No. 127. Translate these phrases containing interrogative adjectives.

1. **in quibus locis?**
2. **qui homo?**
3. **quod oppidum?**
4. **quae praeda?**
5. **quos viros?**
6. **qua celeritate?**
7. **quo anno?**
8. **cuius nominis?**
9. **qua hora?**
10. **quo tempore?**
11. **quibuscum militibus?**
12. **quorum civium?**
13. **quae impedimenta?**
14. **cuius magnitudinis?**
15. **quo consilio?**

No. 128. Give the English for these verb forms.

1. **faciunt**
2. **iubebit**
3. **impedivisti**
4. **perveniet**
5. **haberi**
6. **malebat**
7. **fuerat**
8. **cepit**
9. **conspexerunt**
10. **accidebat**
11. **auditis**
12. **pervenisti**
13. **contendebat**
14. **dederant**
15. **videri**
16. **prohibuerunt**
17. **erunt**
18. **videbor**
19. **rogari**
20. **fiam**

No. 129. Translate the following:

1. **non potuit**
2. **illius loci**
3. **filios tuos**
4. **alii veniunt**
5. **venire vult**
6. **fortis populus**
7. **ob tempestatem**
8. **magno studio**
9. **domi mansit**
10. **eius nationis**
11. **proximo anno**
12. **mi amice**
13. **omnes homines**
14. **nihil timet**
15. **non solum mater tua**

CHAPTER 28

READING

Equus Troianus

1. **Graeci novem annos Troiam oppugnaverant et iam domum redire volebant.**
2. **Bellum diu et fortiter gesserant, sed neque urbem ceperant neque eum locum relinquere potuerant.**
3. **Itaque consilium ceperunt. Magno studio laboreque equum magnum fecerunt. Multi milites Graeci, qui bene pugnare poterant, a sociis suis in equo ipso noctu locati sunt.**
4. **Exercitus urbis Troianae, qui post muros urbis erat, equum ea nocte non vidit.**
5. **Cives Troiani tamen, adventu solis equum viderunt et eum in urbem duxerunt, sed mox Graeci, qui in equo positi erant, in cives exercitumque Troianum impetum fecerunt.**
6. **Populus maxime timebat.**
7. **Graeci telis suis et igni urbem ceperunt. Deinde Graeci ad mare, ubi alii Graeci naves instruxerant, cucurrerunt.**
8. **Post breve tempus, manus Graecorum cum captivis multis a Troia navigavit.**

The Trojan Horse

1. The Greeks had attacked Troy for nine years and now they wanted to return home.
2. They had carried on war for a long time and bravely, but they had neither captured the city nor had they been able to leave that place.
3. And so they decided on a plan. With great zeal and work they made a large horse. Many Greek soldiers, who were able to fight well, were placed in the horse itself by their comrades at night.
4. The army of the city of Troy, which was behind the walls of the city, did not see the horse that night.
5. The citizens of Troy, however, at the arrival of the sun saw the horse and led it into the city, but soon the Greeks, who had been placed in the horse, made an attack on the citizens and army of Troy.
6. The people were very afraid.
7. With their weapons and fire the Greeks took the city. Then the Greeks ran to the sea, where the other Greeks had drawn up their ships.
8. After a short time, the band of Greeks sailed from Troy with many captives.

Proelium Marathonium	The Battle of Marathon
1. **Anno XD Ante Christum, Graecia ab exercitu Persarum graviter oppugnabatur.**	1. In the year 490 B.C., Greece was heavily attacked by the army of the Persians.
2. **Persae trans mare ad Graeciam navigaverant et multa oppida occupaverant.**	2. The Persians had sailed across the sea to Greece and had seized many towns.
3. **Hostes ad locum, qui non multa milia passuum Athenis aberat, iam iter fecerant. Quam[1] ob rem cives qui Athenas et alias urbes propinquas habitabant adventum hostium timebant.**	3. The enemy had already made the journey to a place, which was not many miles from Athens. For this reason the citizens who lived in Athens and in other neighbouring cities feared the arrival of the enemy.
4. **Athenienses Spartam virum miserunt.**	4. The Athenians sent a man to Sparta.
5. **Ille totum iter cucurrit et ab populo auxilium petivit, sed legem habebat, qua sine luna in caelo bellum gerere non poterant. Eo tempore luna non aderat.**	5. He ran the whole way and sought help from the people, but they had a law, by which they were not able to carry on war without a moon in the sky. At that time there was no moon.
6. **Itaque milites Athenienses aciem suam soli instruxerunt et sagittis ac telis gravibus hostes vicerunt. Eo die Athenienses spem victoriae magnae videbant.**	6. And so the soldiers of Athens drew up their battle line alone and conquered the enemy with arrows and heavy weapons. On that day the Athenians saw the hope of a great victory.
7. **Postea ob virtutem viri, qui Athenis Spartam cucurrerat, ludos habebant. His ludis nomen proeli, quod in agro Marathonio fuerat, dederunt.**	7. Afterwards because of the courage of the man, who had run from Athens to Sparta, they held games. To these games they gave the name of the battle, that had been on the field of Marathon.
8. **Hodie etiam cursum Marathonium in ludis habemus.**	8. Even today we have a Marathon race at the games.

[1]Note that the relative pronoun is used at the beginning of a sentence instead of a demonstrative pronoun to make a closer connection between the sentence and the one that precedes it—'for *which* reason' rather than 'for this reason'.

Vocabulary

Nouns

domus, domus, *f.*, house, home (domicile)
exercitus, exercitus, *m.*, army (exercise)
cornu, cornus, *n.*, horn, wing (of an army) (cornucopia)
adventus, adventus, *m.*, arrival, approach (advent, adventure)
impetus, impetus, *m.*, attack (impetuous)
manus, manus, *f.*, hand, group (manual)
passus, passus, *m.*, pace (passage)
dies, diei, *m.* or *f.*, day
res, rei, *f.*, thing
spes, spei, *f.*, hope
acies, aciei, *f.*, line of battle
Persae, Persarum, *m.*, the Persians
Athenae, Athenarum, *f. pl.*, Athens
Sparta, Spartae, *f.*, Sparta

Adjectives

Marathonius, Marathonia, Marathonium, of Marathon
Atheniensis, Atheniense, Athenian

Verbs

instruo, instruere, instruxi, instructus, draw up, form, train (instruct)
redeo, redire, redii, reditus, return, go back

THE NOUN: FOURTH AND FIFTH DECLENSIONS

A. FOURTH DECLENSION

Nouns that end in **-us** in the Genitive singular are **4th declension.** Those that end in **-us** in the Nominative singular are masculine, with a few exceptions; those in **-u** are neuter.

Nominative	**exercitus**	**cornu**
Vocative	**exercitus**	**cornu**
Accusative	**exercitum**	**cornu**
Genitive	**exercitus**	**cornus**
Dative	**exercitui**	**cornu**
Ablative	**exercitu**	**cornu**
Nominative	**exercitus**	**cornua**
Vocative	**exercitus**	**cornua**
Accusative	**exercitus**	**cornua**
Genitive	**exercituum**	**cornuum**
Dative	**exercitibus**	**cornibus**
Ablative	**exercitibus**	**cornibus**

Domus (house, home) has endings in both the **2nd declension** and the **4th declension.**

Nominative	**domus**	**domus**
Vocative	**domus**	**domus**
Accusative	**domum**	**domos, domus**
Genitive	**domus, domi**	**domuum, domorum**
Dative	**domui, domo**	**domibus**
Ablative	**domo, domu**	**domibus**

Remember that **domus** has a Locative case **(domi)** and that no preposition is used in the expressions 'to home' **(domum)** and 'from home' **(domo)** (see page 105).

B. FIFTH DECLENSION

Nouns that end in **-ei** in the Genitive singular are **5th declension.** They are all feminine, except **dies** (day), which is generally masculine.

Nominative	**res**	**res**
Vocative	**res**	**res**
Accusative	**rem**	**res**
Genitive	**rei**	**rerum**
Dative	**rei**	**rebus**
Ablative	**re**	**rebus**

FAMILIAR ABBREVIATIONS

A.D., Anno Domini, in the year of (our) Lord.
a.m., ante meridiem, before noon.
p.m., post meridiem, after noon.
cf., confer, compare.
et al., et alibi, and elsewhere; **et alii,** and others.
vs., versus, against.
c., circ., circa, circum, about. Used with dates.

Practice Exercises

No. 130. Give the English for these phrases.

1. **multos passus**
2. **vestra manus**
3. **longum impetum**
4. **ob adventum eius**
5. **utrumque cornu**
6. **exercituum nostrorum**
7. **in cornu tuo**
8. **ex exercitu**
9. **in domum**
10. **sex milia passuum**
11. **contra exercitus**
12. **ob adventum tuum**
13. **impetus hostium**
14. **manus militum**
15. **ab exercitu**

No. 131. Give the English for these phrases.

1. **acies suas**
2. **eo die**
3. **proximo die**
4. **ob has res**
5. **ullius spei**
6. **totam rem**
7. **unam diem**
8. **quarum rerum?**
9. **nostrae acies**
10. **quas res?**
11. **in qua acie?**
12. **utriusque diei**
13. **ob eam rem**
14. **in his aciebus**
15. **multam spem**

No. 132. Translate these verb forms.

1. **ambulavit**
2. **videmur**
3. **erant**
4. **fecerat**
5. **fugiebat**
6. **impedit**
7. **datum erat**
8. **potest**
9. **instructum est**
10. **videri**
11. **relicti sunt**
12. **fiemus**
13. **instruxit**
14. **iter facit**
15. **audientur**

No. 133. Translate these sentences.

1. **Omnes res faciles esse videntur.**
2. **Post sex dies neuter miles ullam spem habebat.**
3. **Captivi quos reduxisti ex exercitu eorum venerunt.**
4. **Quis fortem impetum magnopere impedivit?**
5. **Una hora homines domum venient.**
6. **Quam ob rem aciem suam in colle instruebat?**
7. **Inter has res quas habemus parva copia aquae est.**
8. **Milites equos suos ab illo cornu ad hostes vertunt.**
9. **Neque cornu neque acies spem videbat.**
10. **Qui inter hos populos regnum tenent?**

CHAPTER 29

READING

Proelium Thermopylarum

1. **Post decem annos Persae ad Graeciam suos reduxerunt.**
2. **Anno XD Ante Christum Athenienses Persas in agro Marathonio vicerant.**
3. **Hic annus erat XXD Ante Christum et hoc proelium appellatur Proelium Thermopylarum.**
4. **Persae magnam copiam et cibi et frumenti, quam trans mare portare in animo habebant, decem annos paraverant atque exercitum fortem acremque habebant.**
5. **In hoc impetu omnem spem posuerant, sed illo tempore apud Graecos pax non erat. Alia civitas contra aliam contendebat.**
6. **Athenienses Lacedaimoniique Graeciam totam defendere non poterant.**
7. **Exercitus hostium ad partem montium quae Thermopylae appellatur pervenit.**
8. **Hic locus natura fortis est quod via angusta quae inter montes et mare iacet ab paucis militibus teneri poterat.**
9. **In eo loco manus parva Graecorum conlocata erat et adventum hostium exspectabat.**

The Battle of Thermopylae

1. After ten years the Persians led their men back to Greece.
2. It was in the year 490 B.C. that the Athenians had conquered the Persians on the field of Marathon.
3. This year was 480 B.C. and this battle is called the Battle of Thermopylae.
4. The Persians for ten years had prepared a great supply both of food and grain, which they intended to carry across the sea, and they also had a brave and keen army.
5. They had placed all their hope in this attack, but at that time there was no peace among the Greeks. One state was fighting against another.
6. The Athenians and Spartans were unable to defend all Greece.
7. The army of the enemy came to the part of the mountains which is called Thermopylae.
8. This place is strong by nature because the narrow road which lies between the mountains and the sea could be held by a few soldiers.
9. In that place a small group of Greeks had been stationed and was waiting for the arrival of the enemy.

Proelium Thermopylarum	The Battle of Thermopylae
10. **Graeci in montibus facile pugnare poterant.**	10. The Greeks were able to fight easily in the mountains.
11. **Via et difficilis et angusta erat. Itaque Graeci praesidium ibi conlocaverant.**	11. The road was both difficult and narrow. And so the Greeks had stationed a garrison there.
12. **Contra milites fortes hostium, qui spem iam relinquebant, diu et fortiter contenderunt, sed erat unus homo, qui Persis auxilium dedit.**	12. They fought for a long time and bravely against the brave soldiers of the enemy, who were already giving up hope, but there was one man, who gave help to the Persians.
13. **Hic hostes post locum ubi praesidium Graecum instructum erat, trans montes duxit.**	13. This man led the enemy across the mountains behind the place where the Greek guard had been drawn up.
14. **Exercitus hostium post aciem Graecam noctu iter fecit.**	14. The army of the enemy made its way at night behind the Greek battle line.
15. **Alii Graeci fugere potuerunt, sed neque militei Lacedaimonii neque socii timebant.**	15. Some Greeks were able to escape, but neither the soldiers of Sparta nor their allies were afraid.
16. **Hi gladiis et aliis telis fortiter pugnabant, sed brevi tempore Graeci omnes ab hostibus interfecti sunt. Persae Athenas iter fecerunt.**	16. These men fought bravely with swords and other weapons, but in a short time all the Greeks were killed by the enemy. The Persians made their way to Athens.

Vocabulary

Nouns

civitas, civitatis, *f.*, state

Thermopylae, Thermopylarum, *f. pl.*, Thermopylae

praesidium, praesidii or **praesidi,** *n.*, guard, garrison

Pronouns

ego, mei, I (egotist)

nos, nostrum, we

tu, tui, you (sing.)

vos, vestrum, you (pl.)

Verbs

appello, appellare, appellavi, apellatus, address, call, name (appellation)

iaceo, iacere, iacui, —, lie, be situated (adjacent)

conloco, conlocare, conlocavi, conlocatus, place, station

Adjectives

decem, ten (decimal)

Lacedaimonius, Lacedaimonia, Lacedaimonium, Spartan

pauci, paucae, pauca, few, little (paucity)

Conjunction

enim, for (never the first word in a Latin sentence)

PERSONAL PRONOUNS

1. Personal pronouns of the First Person.

	Singular		*Plural*	
Nominative	**ego**	I	**nos**	we
Accusative	**me**	me	**nos**	us
Genitive	**mei**	of me	**nostrum** or **nostri**	of us
Dative	**mihi**	to, for me	**nobis**	to, for us
Ablative	**me**	from, with, by me	**nobis**	from, with, by us

2. Personal pronouns of the Second Person.

	Singular		*Plural*	
Nominative	**tu**	you	**vos**	you
Accusative	**te**	you	**vos**	you
Genitive	**tui**	of you	**vestrum** or **vestri**	of you
Dative	**tibi**	to, for you	**vobis**	to, for you
Ablative	**te**	from, with, by, you	**vobis**	from, with, by, you

3. You have already met the personal pronouns of the Third Person.

Singular		*Plural*	
is, ea, id	he, she, it	**ei, eae, ea**	they
ille, illa, illud	he, she, it	**illi, illae, illa,**	they
hic, haec, hoc	he, she, it	**hi, hae, haec**	they

NOTE:

(a) Personal pronouns are only used in the Nominative case to give emphasis or to make a clear distinction.

Emphasis: **ego scio,** I (myself) know.
Clarity: **ego et tu scimus,** You and I know.

(b) Possessive adjectives are more commonly used to show possession than is the Genitive case of the personal pronouns. (See page 40.)

1st Person	**meus, mea, meum**	my, mine
	noster, nostra, nostrum	our, ours
2nd Person	**tuus, tua, tuum**	your, yours
	vester, vestra, vestrum	your, yours
3rd Person	**suus, sua, suum**	his, her, its, their (own)

But remember that **suus, sua, suum** can only be used reflexively, i.e., to refer back to the subject of the sentence. When it does not refer to the subject, a Genitive must be used. (See pages 40 and 111.)

	eius, eius, eius	his, her, its
	eorum, earum, eorum	their
or		
	illius, illius, illius	his, her, its
	illorum, illarum, illorum	their
or		
	huius, huius, huius	his, her, its
	horum, harum, horum	their

(c) When **cum** is used with a personal pronoun, it is added to the end.

mecum, with me — **nobiscum,** with us
tecum, with you — **vobiscum,** with you

(d) Personal pronouns of the First and Second Person can be used reflexively, i.e., to refer back to the subject of the sentence.

Me video, I see myself. **Te vides,** you see yourself.

The Third Person, however, has a special reflexive pronoun.

	Singular	
Accusative	**se**	himself, herself, itself
Genitive	**sui**	of himself, herself, itself
Dative	**sibi**	to, for himself, herself, itself
Ablative	**se**	from, with, by, himself, herself, itself

In the plural, the Latin is the same—**se, sui, sibi, se**—but the meaning is plural—themselves.

LEGAL TERMS

a vinculo matrimoni, from the bond of marriage. Used in a decree of absolute divorce.

caveat emptor, let the buyer beware. The buyer buys at his own risk.

inter vivos, between the living. Used to indicate a gift from a living person to another living person.

compos mentis, sound or sane of mind. **non compos mentis** or **non compos,** not sound or sane of mind.

nolo contendere, I do not wish to contend. A plea by which a defendant is subject to conviction, but does not admit his guilt.

nolle prosequi, to be unwilling to prosecute. Abbr. **nol pros.** A court record stating that the prosecutor will not carry his suit further.

non prosequitur, he does not prosecute. Abbr. **non pros.** Used to indicate a decision against a plaintiff who does not appear in court to prosecute.

obiter dictum, something said along the way. Used of remarks made by a judge that are not part of the legal decision, but are his personal comments and observations on matters relating to the case and decision.

nisi, if not, unless. Used to indicate that an order or decree will go into effect at a specified time unless modified by further evidence or cause presented before that time.

sui iuris or **suo iure,** of one's own right or in one's own right. Used of a person who has full capacity and ability to act for himself in legal proceedings.

Practice Exercises

No. 134. Give the English for these personal pronouns.

1. **vos**	7. **te**	13. **vobis**	19. **illorum**	25. **illis**
2. **nos**	8. **ego**	14. **eos**	20. **ad vos**	26. **de his**
3. **a te**	9. **eum**	15. **illud**	21. **tibi**	27. **illa**
4. **eorum**	10. **mihi**	16. **huic**	22. **vestrum**	28. **cum ea**
5. **ea**	11. **nobiscum**	17. **eius**	23. **nostri**	29. **horum**
6. **ei**	12. **tu**	18. **tecum**	24. **de me**	30. **illos**

No. 135. Give the English for these reflexive pronouns.

1. **sibi**	3. **a me**	5. **se**	7. **mihi**	9. **me**
2. **te**	4. **vos**	6. **vobis**	8. **nobis**	10. **nos**

No. 136. Translate these sentences.

1. **Homo ipse nos videt.**
2. **Ego ad te auxilium misi.**
3. **Nos in hoc loco te repperimus.**
4. **Vosne venietis mecum?**
5. **Tu nobis libros das.**
6. **Vos eum non auditis.**
7. **Illi ad nos fugiebant.**
8. **Is ad me haec misit.**
9. **Tecum domum ambulare non poterit.**
10. **Haec est patria nostra.**
11. **Tu id illis narrabis.**
12. **Nos hunc domum reducemus.**
13. **Illi ab his pacem petebant.**
14. **Ego a te et tuo gladio terrebar.**
15. **Nos illo tempore nos servaveramus.**
16. **Nonne tu nos iuvare potes?**
17. **Ille urbem eorum vidit.**
18. **Nos ipsi eos venire iubebimus.**
19. **Vos nobis ea demonstrabitis.**
20. **Animus eius me non diu terrebat.**

SEVENTH REVISION (CHAPTERS 26–29)

VOCABULARY REVISION

Nouns

1. acies
2. adventus
3. Athenae
4. civitas
5. cornu
6. dies
7. domus
8. Eurydice
9. exercitus
10. Hellespontus
11. Hero
12. impetus
13. inopia
14. Leander
15. manus
16. natura
17. nihil, nil
18. Orpheus
19. passus
20. Persae
21. praesidium
22. regio
23. regnum
24. res
25. Sparta
26. spes
27. Thermopylae
28. turris

1. line of battle
2. arrival, approach
3. Athens
4. state
5. horn, wing
6. day
7. house, home
8. Eurydice
9. army
10. Hellespont
11. Hero
12. attack
13. want, scarcity
14. Leander
15. hand, group
16. nature
17. nothing
18. Orpheus
19. pace
20. the Persians
21. guard, garrison
22. region, boundary
23. kingdom
24. thing
25. Sparta
26. hope
27. Thermopylae
28. tower

Adjectives

1. decem
2. difficilis
3. pauci
4. Marathonius
5. primus
6. Atheniensis

1. ten
2. difficult, hard
3. few, little
4. of Marathon
5. first
6. Athenian

Pronouns

1. ego
2. nos
3. qui
4. tu
5. vos

1. I
2. we
3. who, which, that; which, what?
4. you (s.)
5. you (pl.)

Verbs

1. accido
2. appello
3. conloco
4. conspicio
5. cupio
6. discedo
7. educo
8. impedio
9. instruo
10. pervenio
11. prohibeo
12. reduco
13. rego
14. relinquo
15. reperio
16. scribo
17. trado
18. venio

1. I happen
2. I address, call, name
3. I place, station
4. I observe
5. I desire, wish, want
6. I withdraw, go away, leave
7. I lead out
8. I hinder
9. I draw up, form, train
10. I arrive
11. I keep off, hinder, prohibit, prevent
12. I lead back
13. I rule
14. I leave, leave behind
15. I find, discover
16. I write
17. I give up, surrender
18. I come

Adverbs

1. **iam**
2. **magnopere**
3. **parum**
4. **primum, primo**
5. **solum**
6. **tamen**

1. now, already
2. greatly
3. too little, not enough
4. first, at first
5. alone, only
6. however, nevertheless

Conjunctions

1. **enim**
2. **neque**
3. **neque . . . neque**
4. **ut**

1. for
2. and not
3. neither . . . nor
4. as

Practice Exercises

No. 137. Give the adverbs of these adjectives, with their meanings.

1. **latus**
2. **acer**
3. **facilis**
4. **miser**
5. **longus**
6. **magnus**
7. **laetus**
8. **liber**
9. **bonus**
10. **angustus**

No. 138. Translate these verbs.

1. **veniam**
2. **sciebat**
3. **auditus est**
4. **perveniebamus**
5. **impedientur**
6. **reperiunt**
7. **audiebaris**
8. **scitum erat**
9. **cupiverunt**
10. **audieris**

No. 139. Translate these pronouns.

1. **cuius**
2. **quem**
3. **quae**
4. **qui**
5. **quibuscum**
6. **nos**
7. **mihi**
8. **me**
9. **vestrum**
10. **tibi**
11. **tecum**
12. **eius**
13. **eorum**
14. **illum**
15. **hanc**

No. 140. Translate these nouns.

1. **exercitui**
2. **res**
3. **cornus**
4. **aciem**
5. **spem**
6. **manuum**
7. **die**
8. **impetibus**
9. **adventum**
10. **domum**
11. **rebus**
12. **cornua**
12. **exercituum**
14. **manui**
15. **spei**

PUBLIUS VERGILIUS MARO

Virgil was born in 70 B.C. near Mantua, in the north of Italy, and was educated in Milan, Rome and Naples, where he studied philosophy and rhetoric. During the latter part of his life, he lived near Naples, where he composed his epic poem, **The Aeneid.** Virgil died in 19 B.C. at Brundisium, while returning from Greece.

Ibant obscuri, sola sub nocte, per umbram	They walked obscured by darkness, in the lonely night, through the shadows
perque domos Ditis vacuas, et inania regna;	and through the vacant homes of Pluto, and the empty kingdoms;
quale per incertam lunam sub luce maligna	just as under the dim light of a wavering moon
est iter in silvis, ubi caelum condidit umbra	is a journey in the woods, when Jupiter has hidden the sky in shadows
Iuppiter, et rebus nox abstulit atra colorem.	and black night has taken away the colour from things.
Vestibulum ante ipsum primisque in faucibus Orci	Before the very entrance and in the very jaws of Orcus
Luctus et ultrices posuere cubilia Curae,	Grief and avenging Cares have placed their couches,
pallentesque habitant Morbi, tristisque Senectus,	and pale Diseases dwell, and sad Old Age,
et Metus, et malesuada Fames, ac turpis Egestas,	and Fear, and Hunger persuading-evil, also base Want,
terribiles visu formae, Letumque Labosque,	forms terrible to see, both Death and Toil,
tum consanguineus Leti Sopor, et mala mentis	then Sleep the kinsman of Death, and evil Pleasures
Gaudia, mortiferumque adverso in limine Bellum,	of the mind, and death-bearing War on the threshold opposite,
ferreique Eumenidum thalami, et Discordia demens,	and the iron chambers of the Furies, and mad Discord,
vipereum crinem vittis innexa cruentis.	entwining her snaky hair with bloody fillets.
Aeneidos VI, 268–281	*Aeneid 6, 268–281*

JAMES OF VITRY

These two stories are found in the sermons of James of Vitry, who was the Cardinal Bishop of Tusculum and died in 1240 A.D. The stories were used to illustrate a point as well as to entertain the listeners.

De Arbore In Qua Se Suspendebant Mulieres

De quodam alio audivi, qui habebat arborem in horto suo, in qua duae eius uxores suspenderant semetipsas. Cui quidam eius vicinus ait: 'Valde

fortunata est arbor illa et bonum omen habet. Habeo autem uxorem pessimam; rogo te, da mihi surculum ex ea, ut plantem in horto meo.'

About a Tree on Which Women Were Hanging

I have heard about a certain other man, who had a tree in his garden, on which two of his wives had hung themselves. A certain one of his neighbours said to him: 'Certainly that tree is lucky and holds a good omen. I, however, have a very bad wife; I ask you, give me a young shoot from it, so that I may plant it in my garden.'

De Bachone Qui Pendebat In Quadam Villa

Aliquando transivi per quandam villam in Francia, ubi suspenderant pernam seu bachonem in platea hac condicione ut, qui vellet iuramento firmare quod uno integro anno post contractum matrimonium permansisset cum uxore ita quod de matrimonio non paenituisset, bachonem haberet. Et cum per decem annos ibi pependisset non est unus solus inventus qui bachonem lucraretur, omnibus infra annum de matrimonio contracto paenitentibus.

About a Side of Bacon Which was Hanging in a Certain Town

Once I passed through a certain town in France, where they had hung a ham or side of bacon in the street with this condition that, whoever might wish to swear on oath that he had lived one whole year with his wife after the marriage had been contracted in such a way that he had not regretted the marriage, might have the side of bacon. And although it had hung there for ten years not one single man was found who might win the side of bacon, because all inside of a year from the contract of marriage regretted it.

CHAPTER 30

READING

Aeneas in Igni Troiae	Aeneas in the Fire of Troy
1. **Aeneas in vias Troiae nocte cucurrit et multitudinem militum Graecorum, qui vero laeti erant, quod urbem vicerant, ibi vidit.**	1. Aeneas ran into the streets of Troy at night and he saw there a great number of Greek soldiers, who were truly happy, because they had conquered the city.
2. **Aeneas cum parva manu sociorum suorum contra hostes primo contendebat, sed nihil facere poterant.**	2. Aeneas with a small band of his comrades at first struggled against the enemy, but they could do nothing.
3. **Deinde domum properavit, ubi pater et filius manebant.**	3. Then he hurried home, where his father and son were remaining.
4. **Troia eo tempore acriter ardebat. Populus Troianus se dediderat.**	4. Troy at that time was burning fiercely. The people of Troy had surrendered.
5. **Aeneas patrem suum secum venire coegit et in umeris suis totum onus corporis eius ferebat. Itaque Aeneas atque pater atque filius parvus, ex igni contendebant.**	5. Aeneas forced his father to come with him and he carried the whole burden of his body on his shoulders. And so, Aeneas and his father and his small son, hurried from the fire.
6. **Ob victoriam hostium magnopere dolebant.**	6. Because of the victory of the enemy they grieved greatly.
7. **Creusa, autem, uxor eius, in urbe erat. Itaque in urbem celeriter se tulit.**	7. However, Creusa, his wife, was in the city. And so he rushed quickly into the city.
8. **Centiens eam appellabat, sed non inveniebat. A Morte educta erat.**	8. He called her a hundred times, but did not find her. She had been carried off by Death.

Iter Ulixis	The Journey of Ulysses
1. **Decem annos Ulixes ab portu Troiae ad patriam suam navigabat. Ipse et socii ad multa loca ferebantur.**	1. Ulysses sailed for ten years from the harbour of Troy to his native country. He and his comrades were carried to many places.
2. **Primus locus erat eis gratus idoneusque.**	2. The first place was pleasing and suitable to them.
3. **Secundus locus erat terra in qua Polyphemus habitabat.**	3. The second place was the land in which Polyphemus lived.
4. **Tertio in loco, venti eis ab rege ventorum dati sunt.**	4. In the third place, winds were given to them by the king of the winds.
5. **Quarto in loco, multi viri ab illo, quem ibi reppererunt, necati sunt.**	5. In the fourth place, many of the men were killed by him, whom they found there.
6. **Ob feminam pulchram ab quinto loco vix se recipere potuerunt.**	6. They were able to depart from the fifth place with difficulty because of a beautiful woman.
7. **Sexto in loco, omnes qui apud Inferos convenerant viderunt.**	7. In the sixth place, they saw all those who had come together among the dead.
8. **Septimo in loco, multas res pulchras audiverunt et ibi manere cupiverunt.**	8. In the seventh place, they heard many beautiful things and wished to stay there.
9. **Ab octavo loco celeriter effugerunt. Nam duo animalia ibi habitabant. Unum ex his erat serpens et alterum erat magnum saxum.**	9. They escaped from the eighth place quickly. For two animals lived there. One of these was a serpent and the other was a large rock.
10. **Nono in loco animalia dei solis tenebantur.**	10. In the ninth place the animals of the god of the sun were kept.
11. **Deinde omnes socii eius in mari necati sunt. Itaque ille solus ad decimum locum pervenit.**	11. Then all his comrades were killed on the sea. And so he arrived alone at the tenth place.
12. **Iter difficile susceperat, sed post decem aestates atque decem hiemes servatus erat et domum venit.**	12. He had undertaken a difficult journey, but after ten summers and ten winters he had been saved and he came home.

Vocabulary

Nouns

multitudo, multitudinis, *f.*, great number, multitude
onus, oneris, *n.*, burden, weight (onerous)
Creusa, Creusae, *f.*, Creusa
uxor, uxoris, *f.*, wife (uxorial)
aestas, aestatis, *f.*, summer
ventus, venti, *m.*, wind (vent)
hiems, hiemis, *f.*, winter
portus, portus, *m.*, harbour, port

Adverbs

centiens, a hundred times
vix, scarcely, with difficulty

Conjunctions

autem, but, however (never the first word in a Latin sentence)
nam, for

Verbs

ardeo, ardere, arsi, arsus, be on fire, burn (ardent)
dedo, dedere, dedidi, deditus, give up, surrender
cogo, cogere, coegi, coactus, collect, drive, compel (cogent)
fero, ferre, tuli, latus, bear, carry
me fero, move, hasten, rush
recipio, recipere, recepi, receptus, take back, receive (reception)
me recipio, withdraw, retreat, depart
convenio, convenire, conveni, conventus, come together, assemble (convention)
cupio, cupere, cupivi, cupitus, desire, wish (cupidity)
effugio, effugere, effugi —, flee away, escape
suscipio, suscipere, suscepi, susceptus, take up, undertake (susceptible)

NUMERALS

A. The Cardinal Numbers—one to twenty, one hundred, and one thousand:

1—**unus, una, unum**
2—**duo, duae, duo**
3—**tres, tria**
4—**quattuor**
5—**quinque**
6—**sex**
7—**septem**
8—**octo**
9—**novem**
10—**decem**
11—**undecim**
12—**duodecim**
13—**tredecim**
14—**quattuordecim**
15—**quindecim**
16—**sedecim**
17—**septendecim**
18—**duodeviginti, octodecim**
19—**undeviginti, novendecim**
20—**viginti**

100—**centum**
1000—**mille**

These Cardinal Numbers are declined:

1—

	m.	*f.*	*n.*
Nominative	**unus**	**una**	**unum**
Accusative	**unum**	**unam**	**unum**
Genitive	**unius**	**unius**	**unius**
Dative	**uni**	**uni**	**uni**
Ablative	**uno**	**una**	**uno**

2—

	m.	*f.*	*n.*
Nominative	**duo**	**duae**	**duo**
Accusative	**duos, duo**	**duas**	**duo**
Genitive	**duorum**	**duarum**	**duorum**
Dative	**duobus**	**duabus**	**duobus**
Ablative	**duobus**	**duabus**	**duobus**

3—

	m and *f.*	*n.*
Nominative	**tres**	**tria**
Accusative	**tres**	**tria**
Genitive	**trium**	**trium**
Dative	**tribus**	**tribus**
Ablative	**tribus**	**tribus**

1000—

	Singular	*Plural*
Nominative	**mille**	**milia**
Accusative	**mille**	**milia**
Genitive	**mille**	**milium**
Dative	**mille**	**milibus**
Ablative	**mille**	**milibus**

Note that **mille** is an adjective in the singular and a noun in the plural.

mille homines, a thousand men
milia hominum, thousands of men

B. The Ordinal Numbers—first to tenth:

first—**primus, prima, primum**
second—**secundus, secunda, secundum**
third—**tertius, tertia, tertium**
fourth—**quartus, quarta, quartum**

fifth—**quintus, quinta, quintum**
sixth—**sextus, sexta, sextum**
seventh—**septimus, septima, septimum**
eighth—**octavus, octava, octavum**
ninth—**nonus, nona, nonum**
tenth—**decimus, decima, decimum**

All Ordinal Numbers are **1st** and **2nd declension** adjectives.

sexto die, on the sixth day
quartum annum, for the fourth year

IRREGULAR VERB: FERO

Present tense:

Active	*Passive*
fero	**feror**
fers	**ferris**
fert	**fertur**
ferimus	**ferimur**
fertis	**ferimini**
ferunt	**feruntur**

Future tense:

Active	*Passive*
feram	**ferar**
feres	**fereris**
feret, etc.	**feretur,** etc.

Imperfect tense:

Active	*Passive*
ferebam	**ferebar**
ferebas	**ferebaris**
ferebat, etc.	**ferebatur,** etc.

The Perfect tenses of **fero** are regular, e.g., **tuli, tulero, tuleram, latus sum, ero, eram.**

SCHOOL MOTTOES

Detur gloria soli Deo. Let glory be given to God alone. *Dulwich College and Alleyn's School*
Sapere aude. Dare to be wise. *Manchester Grammar School*
Homo plantat, homo irrigat sed Deus dat incrementum. Man plants, man waters but it is God who gives increase. *Merchant Taylors' School*
Dura virum nutrix. Hard nurse of men. *Sedbergh School*

Fons vitae sapientia. Wisdom is the fount of life. *Trent College*
Vincit qui patitur. He that endures conquers. *Whitgift School*
Aut vincere aut mori. Either to conquer or to die. *Wrekin College*

Practice Exercises

No. 141. Give the meanings of these Cardinal Numbers.

1. **quindecim**
2. **novem**
3. **viginti**
4. **quinque**
5. **sedecim**
6. **decem**
7. **tres**
8. **septendecim**
9. **quattuor**
10. **undecim**
11. **centum**
12. **quattuordecim**
13. **octo**
14. **undeviginti**
15. **duo**
16. **tredecim**
17. **septem**
18. **unus**
19. **duodeviginti**
20. **mille**
21. **duodecim**
22. **sex**

No. 142. Give the meanings of these Ordinal Numbers.

1. **quartus**
2. **octavus**
3. **decimus**
4. **tertius**
5. **septimus**
6. **secundus**
7. **quintus**
8. **nonus**
9. **primus**
10. **sextus**

No. 143. Translate these phrases which contain Cardinal Numbers.

1. **mille naves**
2. **tres homines**
3. **milia militum**
4. **quattuordecim dies**
5. **unius viri**
6. **viginti milia passuum**
7. **centum pueros**
8. **quinque annos**
9. **sex de militibus**
10. **septem horis**
11. **centum annis**
12. **octo ex pueris**
13. **duos dies**
14. **decem legum**
15. **tria loca**
16. **duae de provinciis**
17. **duodecim diebus**
18. **sex animalium**
19. **duodeviginti ex regibus**
20. **tribus annis**

No. 144. Translate these phrases which contain Ordinal Numbers.

1. **decimae puellae**
2. **octavo die**
3. **sexta hora**
4. **septima navis**
5. **quinta aestate**
6. **tertium diem**
7. **decima hieme**
8. **septimus impetus**
9. **nonae horae**
10. **primo anno**

CHAPTER 31

READING

Cupido et Psyche	Cupid and Psyche
1. Erant olim tres sorores pulchrae, quae erant filiae regis reginaeque. Harum Psyche erat clarissima. Itaque fama eius in regionibus, quae finitimae erant domui suae, erat aequa illi Veneris.	1. There were once three beautiful sisters, who were daughters of the king and queen. Of these Psyche was the most famous. And so her reputation in the regions, that were neighbouring to her home, was equal to that of Venus.
2. Venus non solum immortalis sed etiam superbissima erat. Itaque de puella, quae neque dea neque immortalis erat, poenas sumere constituit.	2. Venus was not only immortal but also very proud. And so she decided to exact punishment from the girl, who was neither a goddess nor immortal.
3. Itaque filium suum, Cupidem, deum amoris, ad se vocavit.	3. And so she called her son, Cupid, the god of love, to her.
4. Ei difficultatem suam demonstravit et 'Omnes Psychen petunt', inquit, 'neque me adorant. Ob iniurias, quas matri tuae fecit, poenas dare debet. Hoc opus tibi idoneum est.'	4. To him she pointed out her difficulty and said: 'All seek Psyche and they do not worship me. Because of the injuries, which she has done to your mother, she ought to pay the penalty. This work is suitable for you.'
5. Cupido matrem suam iuvare celeriter parabat.	5. Cupid quickly prepared to help his mother.
6. Ad hortum Veneris, in quo erant duo fontes, quorum alter dulcis erat alterque acerbus se tulit.	6. He hastened to the garden of Venus, in which there were two fountains, one of which was sweet and the other bitter.
7. Postquam ex utroque fonte aquam obtinuit, Psychem, quae domi dormiebat, petivit.	7. After he had obtained water from each fountain, he sought Psyche, who was asleep at home.
8. Ipse, ubi eam vidit, magnopere motus est quod pulcherrima	8. He himself, when he saw her, was greatly moved because

erat, sed deus matrem memoria tenebat et puellam aqua acerba et sagitta sua tetigit.

she was very beautiful, but the god remembered his mother and touched the girl with the bitter water and with his arrow.

9. **Psyche incitata est, sed Cupidinem videre non poterat. Ille territus est et in ea aquam dulcem posuit.**

9. Psyche was aroused, but she was not able to see Cupid. He was frightened and placed the sweet water on her.

10. **Postea Psyche, quamquam pulchra erat, miserrima fiebat. Quod a Venere non amabatur nemo eam in matrimonium ducere volebat.**

10. Afterwards Psyche, although she was beautiful, became very unhappy. Because she was not loved by Venus, no one was willing to marry her.

11. **Itaque Psyche domi manebat. Pater materque puellae miserrimi quoque erant.**

11. And so Psyche remained at home. The father and mother of the girl were also very unhappy.

12. **Hoc ab oraculo dictum erat: 'Non a viro, sed ab eo contra quem nemo stare potest tu in matrimonium duceris.'**

12. This had been said by the oracle: 'You will be married not by a man, but by him against whom no one can stand.'

Vocabulary

Nouns

Psyche, Psyches, *f.*, Psyche (a Greek noun) (psychic)
soror, sororis, *f.*, sister (sorority)
Cupido, Cupidinis, *m.*, Cupid (cupidity)
difficultas, difficultatis, *f.*, difficulty
fons, fontis, *m.*, spring, fountain **(fontium)** (font)
matrimonium, matrimonii or **matrimoni,** *n.*, marriage (matrimony) **in matrimonium ducere,** marry
oraculum, oraculi, *n.*, oracle

Adjectives

similis, simile, like, similar (similarity)
dulcis, dulce, sweet (dulcet)
acerbus, acerba, acerbum, harsh, bitter (acerbity)
aequus, aequa, aequum, equal, level, fair
immortalis, immortale, immortal

Verbs

dormio, dormire, dormivi, dormiturus, sleep (dormant, dormitory)
constituo, constituere, constitui, constitutus, decide, establish (constitution)
poenas sumo, sumere, sumpsi, sumptus, punish

Adverbs

olim, formerly, once upon a time
quoque, also

Conjunction

quamquam, although

COMPARISON OF ADJECTIVES

Adjectives have three degrees of comparison—positive, comparative and superlative.

1. The Positive degree is always the simple form of the adjective.

longus, longa, longum, long
fortis, forte, brave
miser, misera, miserum, wretched
pulcher, pulchra, pulchrum, pretty
acer, acris, acre, keen
facilis, facile, easy

2. The Comparative degree of all adjectives ends in **-ior.**

longior, longius, longer, rather long, too long, quite long
fortior, fortius, braver, rather brave, too brave, quite brave
miserior, miserius, more wretched, rather wretched, too wretched, quite wretched
pulchrior, pulchrius, prettier, rather pretty, too pretty, quite pretty
acrior, acrius, keener, rather keen, too keen, quite keen
facilior, facilius, easier, rather easy, too easy, quite easy

3. The Superlative degree endings are:

a. for those adjectives that end in **-er,**

miserrimus, a, um, very wretched, most wretched
pulcherrimus, a, um, very pretty, most pretty, prettiest
acerrimus, a, um, very keen, most keen, keenest

b. for **facilis, difficilis,** and **similis,**

facillimus, a, um, very easy, most easy, easiest
difficillimus, a, um, very difficult, most difficult
simillimus, a, um, very similar, most similar

c. for all other adjectives, the ending is **-issimus, a, um**

longissimus, a, um, very long, most long, longest
fortissimus, a, um, very brave, bravest, most brave

DECLENSION

The Positive degree of an adjective is declined regularly in the **1st** and **2nd declensions** or in the **3rd declension.**

1. The Comparative degree is declined:

	Singular		*Plural*	
	m. and f.	*n.*	*m. and f.*	*n.*
Nominative	**longior**	**longius**	**longiores**	**longiora**
Accusative	**longiorem**	**longius**	**longiores**	**longiora**
Genitive	**longioris**	**longioris**	**longiorum**	**longiorum**
Dative	**longiori**	**longiori**	**longioribus**	**longioribus**
Ablative	**longiore**	**longiore**	**longioribus**	**longioribus**

2. The Superlative degree is declined regularly as a **1st** and **2nd declension** adjective.

FAMILIAR QUOTATIONS

Laudator temporis acti. A praiser of past times. *Horace*

Abeunt studia in mores. Pursuits pass over into habits. *Ovid*

Factum fieri infectum non potest. What is done can not be undone. *Terence*

O tempora! O mores! Oh the times! Oh the customs! *Cicero*

Tu ne cede malis. Do not yield to misfortunes. *Virgil*

Docendo discitur. We learn by teaching. *Seneca*

In hoc signo vinces. By this sign thou shalt conquer. *Constantine*

Non datur ad Musas currere lata via. It is not granted to run to the Muses on a wide road. *Propertius*

Est modus in rebus. There is a middle course in things. *Horace*

Forsan et haec olim meminisse iuvabit. Perhaps some time it will be pleasant to remember even these things. *Virgil*

Practice Exercises

No. 145. Translate these Positive adjectives.

1. **iter difficile**
2. **domum miseram**
3. **virorum liberorum**
4. **timores acres**
5. **exercitus similes**
6. **diem longum**
7. **in monte alto**
8. **flumina celeria**
9. **vias latas**
10. **puellarum pulchrarum**

No. 146. Translate these Comparative adjectives.

1. **viae angustiores**
2. **puer altior**
3. **puellarum laetiorum**
4. **populus amicior**
5. **iter longius**
6. **in locis gratioribus**
7. **sororum clariorum**
8. **hiemem longiorem**
9. **flumina latiora**
10. **virum audaciorem**

No. 147. Translate these Superlative adjectives.

1. **fontis dulcissimi**
2. **ex hortis pulcherrimis**
3. **templum angustissimum**
4. **ob memorias miserrimas**
5. **oracula clarissima**
6. **civis laetissimus**
7. **ex agro latissimo**
8. **cum matribus pulcherrimis**
9. **in navi novissima**
10. **nomina brevissima**

No. 148. Translate these sentences.

1. **Is est locus miserrimus.**
2. **Fortissimi homines ad insulam pervenerunt.**
3. **Acerrimi equi celeriter currebant.**
4. **Hoc est iter facilius.**
5. **Populus Italiae est liberrimus.**
6. **Haec est angustior pars fluminis.**
7. **Hae res sunt quoque simillimae.**
8. **Flumen altissimum et latius vidimus.**
9. **Nostri viam breviorem delegerunt.**
10. **Aedificium altum ab hoc loco videre potestis.**

CHAPTER 32

READING

Cupido et Psyche (continued)

1. **Locus in quo hic maritus eam exspectabat, summo in monte erat.**
2. **Ipsa etiam miserior aut patre aut matre erat. Itaque suae fortunae malae se dedere constituit.**
3. **Mox puella, cum matre patreque atque multis ex amicis suis, ad montem a civibus oppidi, in quo habitabat, ducta est.**
4. **Hi eam solam ibi reliquerunt, quamquam eam magnopere dolebant, et se receperunt.**
5. **Psyche, quae summo in monte diu steterat et omnia in eo loco timebat, ab uno ex ventis, Zephyro, a monte ad terram pulcherrimam celeriter lata est.**
6. **Postquam breve tempus dormivit, circumspexit et silvam, quae propinqua erat agro, in quo a Zephyro relicta erat, audacter iniit.**
7. **In silva domum, quae pulchrior erat ulla quam antea viderat, repperit. Ad eam cucurrit.**
8. **Omnia quae in domo videbat**

Cupid and Psyche (continued)

1. The place in which this husband was waiting for her, was on the top of a mountain.
2. She herself was more unhappy than either her father or mother. And so she decided to surrender herself to her bad fortune.
3. Soon the girl, with her mother and father and many of her friends, was led to the mountain by the citizens of the town, in which she lived.
4. They left her there alone, although they felt very sorry for her, and departed.
5. Psyche, who had stood on the top of the mountain for a long time and was afraid of everything in that place, was carried quickly from the mountain to a very beautiful land by one of the winds, Zephyr.
6. After she had slept for a short time, she looked around her and boldly entered the forest, which was near the field, in which she had been left by Zephyr.
7. In the forest she found a house, which was prettier than any that she had seen before. She ran towards it.
8. All the things which she saw

Cupido et Psyche (continued)

ei gratissima erant et ipsa laetissima fiebat.

9. **Mox vocem audivit, sed neque virum neque mulierem vidit. Vox 'Haec domus,' inquit, 'tua est et nos servi tui erimus. Omnia quae rogabis fient.'**

10. **Postea in domo habitabat et laetior erat quam ulla puella. Nil carebat.**

11. **Domum, servos, omnia bona, et maritum habebat, sed hunc non videbat. Noctu veniebat et ab ea ante diem abibat.**

12. **Quam ob rem maxime dolebat, sed maritum suum bene amabat. Ipse 'Me nunc amas,' inquit, 'quod aequi sumus. Hoc optimum est.'**

13. **Diu tamen laetissima erat, sed posteriore tempore matrem patremque sororesque quoque cupiebat et dolebat quod non aderant.**

14. **Postera nocte, ubi maritus venit, ei omnia narravit.**

Cupid and Psyche (continued)

in the house pleased her very much and she herself became very happy.

9. Soon she heard a voice, but she saw neither man nor woman. The voice said: 'This house is yours and we shall be your servants. Everything that you ask will be done.'

10. Afterwards she lived in the house and she was happier than any girl. She lacked nothing.

11. She had a house, servants, all good things, and a husband, but she did not see him. He came at night and went away from her before day.

12. For this reason she grieved greatly, but she loved her husband well. He said: 'You love me now because we are equal. This is best.'

13. For a long time, however, she was very happy, but at a later time she longed for her mother and father and also her sisters and was sad because they were not there.

14. On the next night, when her husband came, she told him everything.

Vocabulary

Nouns

maritus, mariti, *m.*, husband (marital)

Zephyrus, Zephyri, *m.*, Zephyr, west wind

vox, vocis, *f.*, voice (vocal)

Adjective

posterus, postera, posterum, next, following (posterior)

Verbs

circumspicio, circumspicere, circumspexi, circumspectus, look around, observe, see (circumspect)

ineo, inire, inii, initus, go in, enter

abeo, abire, abii, abitus, go away

Adverbs

quam, than

antea, before

multo, much, by much

magis, more

maxime, most, especially (maximum)

Conjunction

aut . . . aut, either . . . or

COMPARISON OF ADJECTIVES

A. There are two ways to show a comparison between two things.

1. **quam,** with the same case for the two things being compared.

   Ego altior sum quam tu, I am taller than you
   amicior illi quam huic, more friendly to that one than this

2. the Ablative Case after the Comparative degree, *without* **quam.**

   Ego altior sum te, I am taller than you

   This construction is only used where the case of the noun or pronoun would be Nominative or Accusative.

B. Some adjectives have an irregular comparison.

bonus, a, um good	**melior, melius** better	**optimus, a, um** best
magnus, a um large	**maior, maius** larger	**maximus, a, um** largest
malus, a, um bad	**peior, peius** worse	**pessimus, a, um** worst
parvus, a, um small	**minor, minus** smaller	**minimus, a, um** smallest
multus, a um much	**—, plus** more	**plurimus, a, um** most

The Superlative degree of **posterus** is **postremus, a, um,** or **postumus, a, um.**

C. Most adjectives ending in a *vowel* and **-us** are compared in this way:

idoneus, a, um suitable	**magis idoneus, a, um** more suitable	**maxime idoneus, a, um** most suitable

D. **Plus** is a neuter noun in the singular; an adjective in the plural.

	Singular	*Plural* *m. and f.*	*n.*
Nominative	**plus**	**plures**	**plura**
Accusative	**plus**	**plures**	**plura**
Genitive	**pluris**	**plurium**	**plurium**
Dative	—	**pluribus**	**pluribus**
Ablative	**plure**	**pluribus**	**pluribus**

MATHEMATICAL TERMS BASED ON LATIN

plus, more, increased by.
minus, less, diminished by.
multiplication, from **multiplicare,** to make manifold or many fold.
division, from **dividere,** divide.
subtraction, from **subtrahere,** withdraw, draw from beneath.
addition, from **addere,** add to, or **additio,** adding.
ratio, from **ratio,** reason.
quotient, from **quotiens,** how often, how many times.
sum, from **summa,** sum or total, or **summus,** highest.
number and numeral, from **numerus,** number.
integer, from **integer,** whole, untouched.
fraction, from **frangere,** break.
per cent, from **per centum,** by the hundred, in the hundred.

Practice Exercises

No. 149. Translate these sentences.

1. **Hae turres altiores sunt quam illae.**
2. **Es altior patre tuo.**
3. **Illa itinera aliis faciliora non sunt.**
4. **Patri tuo quam matri similior es.**
5. **Homines multo fortiores mulieribus sunt.**
6. **Domus eius novior est mea.**
7. **Puer laetior est quam soror.**
8. **Barbari multo audaciores sunt finitimis suis.**
9. **Ille amicior vobis quam mihi erit.**
10. **Estne manus celerior quam oculus?**

No. 150. Give the English for these verb forms.

1. **erunt**
2. **latum est**
3. **constituit**
4. **parabitur**
5. **ducebant**
6. **relictus est**
7. **mittetur**
8. **ferris**
9. **videbamus**
10. **ambulavit**

No. 151. Give the English for these adjectives.

1. **plura**
2. **melior**
3. **pessimorum**
4. **maioris**
5. **minorum**
6. **plurimorum**
7. **pluribus**
8. **posteros**
9. **magis idonei**
10. **maxime idoneum**

No. 152. Translate the following phrases.

1. **in pluribus urbibus**
2. **ex fontibus minoribus**
3. **virtutem maximam**
4. **vox optima**
5. **de muris altioribus**
6. **plus aquae**
7. **tempus magis idoneum**
8. **rei pessimae**
9. **ad partem meliorem**
10. **cum maiore exercitu**
11. **die longiore**
12. **plurimas civitates**
13. **finem peiorem**
14. **annos optimos**
15. **soror minima**
16. **plurium difficultatum**
17. **iter melius**
18. **aestatis pessimae**
19. **dona plurima**
20. **navis minoris**

CHAPTER 33

READING

Cupido et Psyche (continued)

1. **Postridie ad Zephyrum quam celerrime contendit et ei narravit id quod maritus suus dixerat.**
2. **Imperia Psyches facillime confecit. Brevi tempore duae sorores domum eius a Zephyro celeriter latae sunt.**
3. **Psyche adventu earum laetissima fiebat et illis omnia sua demonstravit. Illae tamen postquam domum atque servos eius viderunt bonam fortunam cognoverunt.**
4. **Multa rogabant: 'Esne uxor laeta?' 'Quis est maritus tuus?'**
5. **Magno cum studio verba eius audiebant. Vita eius melior quam vita earum esse videbatur.**
6. **Eam miserrime conspiciebant. Eodem tempore spem maiorem videbant: 'Num tu maritum tuum umquam vidisti? Maritus quem uxor numquam vidit optimus maritus esse non potest. Nonne verba oraculi memoria tenes? Ille aut serpens aut animal est.'**
7. **Itaque consilium ceperunt. Psyche consilium sororum suarum accepit quod ab eis semper facillime ducebatur.**

Cupid and Psyche (continued)

1. On the next day she hurried as quickly as possible to Zephyr and told him what her husband had said.
2. He very easily carried out the commands of Psyche. In a short time her two sisters were carried quickly to her house by Zephyr.
3. Psyche became very happy at their arrival and showed them all her possessions. They, however, after thay had seen her house and servants, recognized her good fortune.
4. They asked many things: 'Are you a happy wife?' 'Who is your husband?'
5. They listened to her words with great eagerness. Her life seemed to be better than their life.
6. They looked at her most unhappily. At the same time they saw a greater hope: 'You haven't ever seen your husband, have you? A husband whom his wife has never seen can not be the best husband. You remember the words of the oracle, don't you? He is either a serpent or an animal.'
7. And so they formed a plan. Psyche accepted the plan of her sisters because she was always very easily influenced

Itaque lucem ac gladium cepit et haec in loco idoneo conlocavit.

by them. And so she took a light and a sword and placed these things in a suitable place.

8. **Psyche consilium sororum suarum minime amabat, sed verba earum plurimum poterant. Facilius quam ipsa dicere poterant.**

8. Psyche did not like her sister's plan at all, but their words were very powerful. They were able to talk more easily than she.

9. **Itaque lucem gladiumque paravit. Ubi maritus noctu venit, ipsa maxime timebat, sed ei timorem suum non demonstrabat.**

9. And so she got the light and the sword ready. When her husband came at night, she was very much afraid, but she did not show her fear to him.

10. **Dum ille dormit, lucem cepit et supra eum tenebat. Quid vidit? Neque serpentem neque animal ante se conspexit. Erat deus pulcherrimus atque gratissimus.**

10. While he slept, she took the light and held it above him. What did she see? She saw in front of her neither a serpent nor an animal. He was a most handsome and pleasing god.

11. **A timore liberata erat. Eum non diutius timebat, sed magis amabat.**

11. She had been freed from fear. She no longer feared him, but loved him more.

12. **Ut accidit autem, ubi umerum eius luce tetigit, ille excitatus est. Nullum verbum dixit, sed oculis suis eam monuit et alis celeribus eam reliquit.**

12. As it happened, however, when she touched his shoulder with the light, he was aroused. He said no word, but warned her with his eyes and left her on swift wings.

13. **Psyche ad terram cecidit. Cupido supra eam breve tempus volabat et 'Contra imperia matris meae,' inquit, 'te amavi. Immortales mortales non saepe amant, sed quamquam te in matrimonium duxi nunc vis me interficere. Amor tuus minus fortis meo est.'**

13. Psyche fell to the ground. Cupid flew above her for a short time and said: 'I have loved you against the commands of my mother. Immortals do not often love mortals, but although I married you, now you want to kill me. Your love is less strong than mine.'

14. **His verbis puellam miserrimam reliquit et ad caelum volavit.**

14. With these words he left the very unhappy girl and flew to the sky.

Vocabulary

Nouns

imperium, imperii or **imperi,** *n.*, command (imperial)

verbum, verbi, *n.*, word (verb)

lux, lucis, *f.*, light (lucent)

Adjective

mortalis, mortale, mortal

Conjunction

dum, while. With the Present tense.

Verbs

excito, excitare, excitavi, excitatus, arouse, stir up (excite)

cado, cadere, cecidi, casurus, fall (cadence)

conficio, conficere, confeci, confectus, finish, complete, carry out (confection)

plus posse, be more powerful

plurimum posse, be most powerful

Adverbs

supra, over, above. Also a preposition with the Accusative case.

quam, as possible. With the Superlative degree.

numquam, never

umquam, ever

postridie, on the next day

COMPARISON OF ADVERBS

1. Comparison of adverbs that are formed from adjectives.

The comparative adverb is usually the Accusative Singular neuter of the comparative adjective.

Adverb	*Adjective*	*Comparative Adjective*	*Comparative Adverb*
longe	**longus**	**longior**	**longius**
acriter	**acer**	**acrior**	**acrius**

The superlative adverb is formed by replacing the **-us** ending of the superlative adjective with an **-e.**

Superlative Adjective	*Superlative Adverb*
longissimus	**longissime**
acerrimus	**acerrime**

Thus:

longe far	**longius** farther	**longissime** farthest
misere unhappily	**miserius** more unhappily	**miserrime** most unhappily
pulchre beautifully	**pulchrius** more beautifully	**pulcherrime** most beautifully
acriter keenly	**acrius** more keenly	**acerrime** most keenly
fortiter bravely	**fortius** more bravely	**fortissime** most bravely
facile easily	**facilius** more easily	**facillime** most easily
bene well	**melius** better	**optime** best
male badly	**peius** worse	**pessime** worst
paullum little	**minus** less	**minime** least

2. Some adverbs have irregular forms.

magnopere greatly	**magis** more	**maxime** most
multum much	**plus** more	**plurimum** most

3. Some adverbs not formed from adjectives are compared as follows:

diu long (time)	**diutius** longer	**diutissime** longest
saepe often	**saepius** more often	**saepissime** most often

When **quam** is used with the superlative degree of an adjective or adverb it means *as . . . as possible*.

quam pulcherrimus, as pretty as possible
quam pulcherrime, as beautifully as possible

GEOMETRICAL TERMS BASED ON LATIN

perpendicular, from **per,** through, and **pendere,** hang.
circumference, from **circum,** around, and **ferre,** carry.
circle, from **circus,** circle.
radius, from **radius,** staff, rod, ray.
arc, from **arcus,** bow, arc.
tangent, from **tangere,** touch.
angle, from **angulus,** angle, corner.
obtuse, from **obtundere,** blunt.
acute, from **acuere,** sharpen.
triangle, from **tres,** three, and **angulus,** angle.
rectangle, from **rectus,** right, and **angulus,** angle.
Q.E.D., abbreviation of **quod erat demonstrandum,** which was to be demonstrated.

Practice Exercises

No. 153. Give the English for these adjectives and adverbs.

1. **latus**
2. **late**
3. **latior**
4. **latius**
5. **latissimus**
6. **latissime**
7. **liber**
8. **libere**
9. **liberior**
10. **liberrimus**
11. **liberius**
12. **liberrime**
13. **pulcher**
14. **pulchrior**
15. **pulcherrimus**
16. **pulchre**
17. **pulchrius**
18. **pulcherrime**
19. **celer**
20. **celeriter**
21. **celerior**
22. **celerius**
23. **celerrimus**
24. **celerrime**
25. **acer**
26. **acriter**
27. **acrior**
28. **acrius**
29. **acerrimus**
30. **acerrime**

No. 154. Translate these sentences.

1. **Diutissime oppugnabantur.**
2. **Fortius pugnat.**
3. **Celeriter incensi sunt.**
4. **Multo brevius dicent.**
5. **Audacissime monebitur.**
6. **Celerrime aciem instruxerunt.**
7. **Acrius bellum gessit.**
8. **Superbe ambulant.**
9. **Liberius dabat.**
10. **Maxime laudatur.**
11. **Latius missi sunt.**
12. **Liberrime dedit.**
13. **Longissime navigat.**
14. **Celerius currit.**
15. **Clarius videbantur.**
16. **Diutius manent.**
17. **Acerrime timebit.**
18. **Audacter capti sunt.**
19. **Brevissime dicebat.**
20. **Fortiter pugnant.**

No. 155. Give the English for these adverbs.

1. **bene**
2. **magnopere**
3. **male**
4. **multum**
5. **parum**
6. **diu**
7. **saepe**
8. **diutius**
9. **plus**
10. **magis**
11. **melius**
12. **peius**
13. **minus**
14. **saepius**
15. **maxime**
16. **plurimum**
17. **diutissime**
18. **saepissime**
19. **optime**
20. **pessime**
21. **minime**

No. 156. Translate these sentences, containing adverbs.

1. **Saepius perveniunt.**
2. **Quam diutissime pugnavit.**
3. **Magis excitatus est.**
4. **Plus impediebatur.**
5. **Optime rexisti.**
6. **Id saepissime auditum est.**
7. **Facillime ambulat.**
8. **Apud nos plurimum possunt.**
9. **Celerius volat.**
10. **Multo diutius manebit.**

EIGHTH REVISION (CHAPTERS 30–33)

VOCABULARY REVISION

Nouns

1. aestas
2. Creusa
3. Cupido
4. difficultas
5. fons
6. hiems
7. imperium
8. lux
9. maritus
10. matrimonium
11. multitudo
12. onus
13. oraculum
14. acies
15. portus
16. Psyche
17. soror
18. uxor
19. ventus
20. verbum
21. vox
22. Zephyrus

1. summer
2. Creusa
3. Cupid
4. difficulty
5. spring, fountain
6. winter
7. command
8. light
9. husband
10. marriage
11. great number, multitude
12. burden, weight
13. oracle
14. battle line
15. harbour, port
16. Psyche
17. sister
18. wife
19. wind
20. word
21. voice
22. Zephyr, west wind

Adjectives

1. aequus
2. dulcis
3. immortalis
4. maior
5. maximus
6. melior
7. minimus
8. minor
9. mortalis
10. optimus
11. peior
12. pessimus
13. plurimus
14. posterus
15. postumus
16. similis

1. equal, level, fair
2. sweet
3. immortal
4. larger
5. largest
6. better
7. smallest
8. smaller
9. mortal
10. best
11. worse
12. worst
13. most
14. next, following
15. next, following
16. like, similar

Verbs

1. cado
2. cogo
3. conficio
4. constituo
5. convenio
6. dedo
7. deligo
8. dormio
9. excito
10. incendo
11. opprimo
12. plurimum posse
13. plus posse
14. recipio
15. suscipio
16. tango

1. I fall
2. I collect, drive, compel
3. I finish, complete, carry out
4. I decide, establish
5. I come together, assemble
6. I give up, surrender
7. I choose, select
8. I sleep
9. I arouse, stir up
10. I set fire to, burn
11. I overcome, crush
12. To be most powerful
13. To be more powerful
14. I take back, receive
15. I take up, undertake
16. I touch

Adverbs

1. **antea**
2. **centiens**
3. **magis**
4. **maxime**
5. **multo**
6. **numquam**
7. **olim**
8. **postridie**
9. **quam**
10. **supra**
11. **umquam**

1. before
2. a hundred times
3. more
4. most, especially
5. much, by much
6. never
7. formerly, once upon a time
8. on the next day
9. as possible; than
10. over, above
11. ever

Conjunctions

1. **aut . . . aut**
2. **dum**
3. **nam**
4. **quamquam**
5. **quoque**

1. either . . . or
2. while
3. for
4. although
5. also

Practice Exercises

No. 157. Translate these phrases.

1. **una ex sororibus**
2. **tria flumina**
3. **duos annos**
4. **mille anni**
5. **duas uxores**
6. **centum verba**
7. **unius vocis**
8. **viginti fontes**
9. **quarta hora**
10. **quinto die**
11. **secundo anno**
12. **septimum verbum**
16. **primum oraculum**
14. **in quarto portu**
15. **ex sexta porta**

No. 158. Translate these phrases.

1. **longiorem hiemem**
2. **pulcherrima aestas**
3. **longissimorum annorum**
4. **dulcius verbum**
5. **onus simillimum**
6. **vocis immortalis**
7. **iter facilius**
8. **luces clariores**
9. **difficultatis maximae**
10. **maritorum fortiorum**

No. 159. Give the English for these adjectives.

1. **dulcis, dulcior, dulcissimus**
2. **acer, acrior, acerrimus**
3. **longus, longior, longissimus**
4. **similis, similior, simillimus**
5. **altus, altior, altissimus**
6. **liber, liberior, liberrimus**
7. **celer, celerior, celerrimus**
8. **latus, latior, latissimus**
9. **clarus, clarior, clarissimus**
10. **audax, audacior, audacissimus**

No. 160. Give the English for these adjectives.

1. **magnus, maior, maximus**
2. **parvus, minor, minimus**
3. **bonus, melior, optimus**
4. **malus, peior, pessimus**
5. **multus, plus, plurimus**
6. **multi, plures, plurimi**
7. **idoneus, magis idoneus, maxime idoneus**

No. 161. Translate into English.

1. **celerius ambulabat**
2. **misere oppressus est**
3. **parum dormit**
4. **diutissime ardebit**
5. **maxime excitati sunt**
6. **magis tangebant**
7. **se facilius dediderunt**
8. **plurimum possunt**
9. **plus poterit**
10. **minus facile cogentur**

PHAEDRUS

Phaedrus was a freedman of Augustus, who lived in the first half of the first century A.D. Five books of his *Fables* are extant. These are based on early folk tales and on the Greek fables of Aesop. Phaedrus, in turn, furnished the material for the French fabulist, La Fontaine.

Qui se laudari gaudet verbis subdolis,	He who rejoices that he is praised by words of flattery,
sera dat poenas turpes paenitentia.	pays his shameful penalty with late repentance.
Cum de fenestra corvus raptum caseum	When a crow wished to eat the cheese
comesse vellet, celsa residens arbore,	he snatched from a window, perching in a lofty tree,
vulpes hunc vidit; deinde sic coepit loqui:	a wolf saw him; then he began to speak thus:
'O qui tuarum, corve, pinnarum est nitor.	'Oh what a brightness, crow, your feathers have.
Quantum decoris corpore et vultu geris.	What grace of body, what charm of looks you possess.
Si vocem haberes, nulla prior ales foret.'	If you should have a voice, no bird would be above you.'
At ille stultus, dum vult vocem ostendere,	Then he, foolish one, while he wished to show off his voice,
emisit ore caseum, quem celeriter	dropped the cheese from his mouth. This quickly
dolosa vulpes avidis rapuit dentibus.	the cunning fox snatched in his greedy teeth.
Tum demum ingemuit corvi deceptus stupor.	Then the crow, deceived by his stupidity, groaned, but too late.
Phaedrus I, xiii	*Phaedrus I, 13*

STABAT MATER

The *Stabat Mater* was composed by an unknown author, although Saint Bonaventure is sometimes given the credit for its composition, probably in the thirteenth century, and has been set to music by many musicians since the eighteenth century.

Stabat mater dolorosa	At the Cross her station keeping,
iuxta crucem lacrimosa,	Stood the mournful Mother weeping,
dum pendebat filius,	Close to Jesus at the last.
cuius animam gementem,	Through her soul, of joy bereaved,
contristantem et dolentem	Bowed with anguish, deeply grieved,
pertransivit gladius.	Now at length the sword hath passed.
O quam tristis et afflicta	Oh how sad and sore distressed
fuit illa benedicta	Was that Mother, highly blest,
mater unigenti,	Of the sole begotten One!
quae maerebat et dolebat	Oh that silent, ceaseless mourning,
et tremebat, dum videbat	Oh those dim eyes, never turning
nati poenas incliti!	From that wondrous suffering Son!
Quis est homo qui non fleret,	Who on Christ's dear Mother gazing,
matrem Christi si videret	In her trouble so amazing,
in tanto supplicio?	Born of woman, would not weep?
Quis non posset contristari	Who on Christ's dear Mother thinking,
piam matrem contemplari	Such a cup of sorrow drinking,
dolentem cum filio?	Would not share her sorrow deep?
Pro peccatis suae gentis	For the sins of his own nation,
vidit Iesum in tormentis	Saw him hang in desolation
et flagellis subditum;	Till his Spirit forth he sent;
vidit suum dulcem natum	Bruised, derided, cursed, defiled,
morientem, desolatum,	She beheld her tender Child,
dum emisit spiritum.	All with bloody scourges rent.
Eia mater, fons amoris!	O, thou Mother, fount of love!
Me sentire vim doloris	Touch my spirit from above,
fac, ut tecum lugeam.	Make my heart with thine accord.
Fac ut ardeat cor meum	Make me feel as thou hast felt;
in amando Christum Deum,	Make my soul to glow and melt
ut sibi complaceam.	With the love of Christ my Lord.
Sancta mater, istud agas,	Holy Mother, pierce me through.
crucifixi fige plagas	In my heart each wound renew
cordi meo valide;	Of my Saviour crucified;

tui nati vulnerati, **tam dignati pro me pati,** **poenas mecum divide.**	Let me share with thee his pain, Who for all my sins was slain, Who for me in torment died.
Fac me vere tecum flere, **crucifixo condolere,** **donec ego vixero;** **iuxta crucem tecum stare,** **meque tibi sociare** **in planctu desidero.**	Let me mingle tears with thee, Mourning him who mourned for me, All the days that I may live. By the cross with thee to stay, There with thee to weep and pray, Is all I ask of thee to give.
Virgo virginum praeclara, **mihi iam non sis amara,** **fac me tecum plangere;** **fac ut portem Christi mortem,** **passionis fac consortem** **et plagas recolere.**	Virgin of all virgins blest, Listen to my fond request: Let me share thy grief divine. Let me to my latest breath, In my body bear the death Of that dying Son of thine.
Fac me plagis vulnerari, **cruce hac inebriari,** **et cruore filii;** **per te, Virgo, sim defensus** **inflammatus et accensus,** **in die iudicii.**	Wounded with his every wound, Steep my soul till it hath swooned In his very blood away. Be to me, O Virgin, nigh, Lest in flames I burn and die In his awful judgment day.
Fac me cruce custodiri **morte Christi praemuniri,** **confoveri gratia.** **Quando corpus morietur,** **fac ut animae donetur** **paradisi gloria.**	Christ, when thou shalt call me hence, Be thy Mother my defence, Be thy cross my victory. While my body here decays May my soul thy goodness praise Safe in Paradise with thee.

CHAPTER 34

READING

Cupido et Psyche (continued)	Cupid and Psyche (continued)
1. **Postquam Cupido uxorem tam celeriter reliquit, ea circumspexit. Nunc omnem spem amisit, quia horti pulchri ac domus magna non iam manebant.**	1. After Cupid had left his wife so quickly, she looked around her. Now she lost all hope, because the beautiful gardens and large house no longer remained.
2. **Prope urbem, ubi antea habitaverat, sola stabat. Stultitiae eam pudebat et paenitebat.**	2. She was standing alone near the city, where she had lived before. She was ashamed of and repented her foolishness.
3. **Sorores fabulam eius magno cum studio audiverunt. 'Cupido unam ex nobis,' inquiunt, 'nunc certe deliget.'**	3. Her sisters heard her story with great eagerness. They said 'Cupid will now certainly choose one of us.'
4. **Postridie prima luce ad montem ierunt et Zephyrum audacissime appellaverunt. Utraque tamen ad terram sub monte cecidit et interfecta est, quod deo venti eas iuvare non libebat.**	4. At dawn the next day they went to the mountain and very boldly called Zephyr by name. Each, however, fell to the ground at the foot of the mountain and was killed, because it did not please the god of the wind to help them.
5. **Psyche interea maritum suum noctu dieque petebat. Montem altissimum, in quo templum magnum erat, conspexit. Eratne templum Cupidinis? Templum intravit.**	5. Psyche meanwhile sought her husband night and day. She saw a very high mountain, on which there was a large temple. Was it the temple of Cupid? She entered the temple.
6. **Ceres, dea frumenti, in templum venit, quia templum Cereris erat. Cererem puellae miserrimae miserebat. Eam iuvare volebat.**	6. Ceres, the goddess of grain, came into the temple, since it was the temple of Ceres. Ceres pitied the very unhappy girl. She wished to help her.
7. **'Veneri,' inquit, 'auxilium tibi dare non libet. Dea bona est,**	7. She said: 'It does not please Venus to give help to you.

sed filium suum, maritum tuum, maxime amat et eum tibi dedere non vult.'

The goddess is good, but she loves her son, your husband, very much and does not want to give him up to you.'

8. **Psyche nullam spem habebat, sed domum deae pulcherrimae iit.**

8. Psyche had no hope, but she went to the house of the very beautiful goddess.

9. **Ibi Venerem superbam invenit, quae 'Nonne tu,' inquit, 'me memoria tenes? Maritus tuus nunc curat vulnus quod tu luce ei dedisti. Postquam hunc laborem confecisti tibi eum dare volo.'**

9. There she found the proud Venus, who said: 'You remember me, don't you? Your husband is now caring for the wound that you gave him with the light. After you have finished this work I am willing to give him to you.'

10. **Hoc opus erat: Magnam copiam et multa genera frumenti sine ordine ante se videbat. Hunc frumenti acervum ordinare eam oportuit.**

10. This was the task: She saw in front of her a great amount and many kinds of grain without order. She had to put this pile of grain in order.

11. **Mors melior quam hoc opus esse videbatur. Eam laboris mox taedebat, sed Cupido uxorem vidit et ad eam auxilium misit.**

11. Death seemed to be better than this task. Soon she was tired of the work, but Cupid saw his wife and sent help to her.

12. **Parva formica cum sociis amicisque ad eam venit.**

12. A small ant with his comrades and friends came to her.

13. **Hae formicae brevissimo tempore frumentum in ordine conlocaverunt. Postquam hoc fecerunt omnes fugerunt.**

13. These ants placed the grain in order in a very short time. After they had done this, they all fled.

Vocabulary

Nouns

stultitia, stultitiae, *f.*, foolishness, stupidity

vulnus, vulneris, *n.*, wound (vulnerable)

genus, generis, *n.*, kind, class (genus)

ordo, ordinis, *m.*, rank, order

acervus, acervi, *m.*, pile

formica, formicae, *f.*, ant

Verbs

amitto, amittere, amisi, amissus, lose

intro, intrare, intravi, intratus, enter

ordino, ordinare, ordinavi, ordinatus, arrange, set in order

invenio, invenire, inveni, inventus, find, come upon (invent)

pudet, pudere, puduit, it shames. (Impersonal verb)

paenitet, paenitere, paenituit, it repents. (Impersonal verb)

libet, libere, libuit, it pleases. (Impersonal verb)

miseret, miserere, miseruit, it pities. (Impersonal verb)

oportet, oportere, oportuit, it behoves, is necessary (Impersonal verb)

taedet, taedere, it disgusts, wearies. (Impersonal verb)

Conjunction

quia, because

THE VERB: IMPERSONAL VERBS

Some Latin verbs are called *Impersonal Verbs,* because they are used only, or mainly, in the Third Person Singular. Many of them correspond to impersonal verbs in English, but Latin sometimes uses an impersonal construction where English prefers a personal one.

1. **Verbs describing the weather.** Here the Latin impersonal expression is just like the English equivalent.

pluit	it is raining
ningit	it is snowing
tonat	it is thundering

The subject of these verbs was originally **Iuppiter,** but this is not normally expressed.

2. **Verbs that usually need an Infinitive as subject and an Accusative as object.** Here again Latin is very like English, although English sometimes has an alternative method of expressing the same idea.

oportet	it behoves, it is necessary.
Me venire oportet	It is necessary for me to come. (Coming is necessary for me) I have to come

decet	it is becoming
dedecet	it is unbecoming
Puellam clamare dedecet	Shouting does not become a girl It is unbecoming for a girl to shout

Sometimes **decet** and **dedecet** have a noun as subject.

Virtus militem decet Courage becomes a soldier

3. **Verbs whose object must be in the Dative case.** Again English has a similar construction.

libet	it is pleasing
licet	it is lawful
Nobis abire licet	It is lawful for us to go away We may go away
Militibus dormire libebat	It was pleasing to the soldiers to sleep The soldiers were pleased to sleep

4. **Verbs that need an Accusative and Genitive construction.** These impersonal verbs express an emotion. The *person* who experiences the emotion must be in the Accusative case; the *cause* of the emotion must be in the Genitive case.

Such a construction is needed with the following impersonal verbs:

miseret	it pities
paenitet	it repents
piget	it vexes
pudet	it shames
taedet	it wearies

Me stultitiae meae paenitet	It repents me of my foolishness I repent of my foolishness.
Puellam laboris taedet	It wearies the girl of the work. The girl is weary of the work.

MEDICAL ABBREVIATIONS

The following are some of the more common medical and pharmaceutical abbreviations of Latin terms.

℞, recipe, take
bib., bibe, drink
d., da, give
cap., capsula, capsule
gtt., guttae, drops
gr., granum, grain
quotid., quotidie, every day
alt. dieb., alternis diebus, every other day, on alternate days
t.i.d., ter in die, three times a day
q.i.d., quater in die, four times a day

Lb., libra, pound
mist., mistura, mixture
ol., oleum, oil
ung., unguentum, ointment
pulv., pulvis, powder
aq., aqua, water
c̄, cum, with
no, numero, number
os., os, ora, mouth
p.o., per os, by mouth
Q.s., quantum sufficiat, a sufficient quantity
Q.v., quantum vis, as much as you wish
a.c., ante cibum, before food, before meals
p.c., post cibum, after food, after meals
stat., statim, immediately
H., hora, hour
h.s., hora somni, at the hour of sleep, bedtime
Q.h., quaque hora, every hour **Q.2h.,** every two hours
omn. hor., omni hora, every hour
noct., nocte, at night
omn. noct., omni nocte, every night
t.i.n., ter in nocte, three times a night, **q.i.n., quater in nocte,** four times a night
rep. repetatur, let it be repeated
non rep., non repetatur, do not repeat
p.r.n., pro re nata, as the occasion arises, as needed
Sig., S., signetur, let it be marked (directions to patient)

Practice Exercises

No. 162. Translate the following verbs.

1. **amaris**	6. **tulerat**	11. **piget**	16. **es**
2. **vis**	7. **fis**	12. **nolumus**	17. **licebat**
3. **ferris**	8. **rexero**	13. **audiam**	18. **paenituit**
4. **habitum erat**	9. **oportuit**	14. **dedecebit**	19. **poterat**
5. **mavult**	10. **ierant**	15. **fecimus**	20. **pudebit**

No. 163. Complete the following sentences by inserting the correct word. Choose your answer from the words in parentheses.

1. **Imperatorem .... celeriter paenitebit. (consilium, consilii)**
2. **.............. pugnare non libet (Me, Mihi)**
3. **Paucos dies manere .... oportet. (nos, nobis)**
4. **A proelio fugere .... dedecet (militi, militem)**
5. **Troianos .... taedebat. (bellum, belli)**
6. **Cur .... orationis Ciceronis pigebat? (Antonium, Antonio)**
7. **Licebatne .... filium necare? (patrem Romanum, patri Romano)**
8. **Nos .... qui patriam non amant pudet. (civium, cives)**
9. **.............. milites Romanos decet. (Virtutis, Virtus)**
10. **Brutum .... necare non oportuit. (Caesarem, Caesari)**

No. 164. Translate these sentences.

1. **Milites pro patria quam fortissime pugnare decet.**
2. **Dum pluit puellis exire non licet.**
3. **Miseretne te feminarum Sabinarum quas Romani ceperunt?**
4. **Si ningit nos domi manere oportet.**
5. **Veneri Psychen iuvare non libebat.**
6. **Psychen maritum spectare non oportuit.**
7. **Me Latinae linguae mox taedebit.**
8. **Quid facere nos oportebit?**
9. **Cur sorores Psyches stultitiae non paenitebat?**
10. **Cupido dixit se contra imperia matris Psychen amavisse.**

CHAPTER 35

READING

Cupido et Psyche (continued)

1. **Sub vesperam Venus ad templum suum venit et sine mora properavit ad eam partem templi ubi puellam reliquerat.**
2. **Ubi laborem confectum esse vidit, filium suum id fecisse putabat et puellae cibum minimum dedit.**
3. **Postridie puellam ad se venire iussit. Dea eam currere ad silvam in qua erant multae oves, quarum lana erat aurea, et lanam reportare iussit.**
4. **Ubi Psyche ad flumen pervenit non solum oves sed etiam deum fluminis invenit.**
5. **Ille dixit flumen celerrimum esse atque oves die maxime inimicas esse, sed noctu dulciores futuras esse. Quam ob rem illa noctem exspectavit et oves dormire conspexit.**
6. **Labor eius facillimus erat quod lana ovium in arboribus erat. Oves non etiam tangere necesse erat, sed auxilio dei multam lanam auream ab arboribus obtinuit et eodem die ad Venerem, dominam suam, iit, quod omnia bene facere volebat.**

Cupid and Psyche (continued)

1. Towards evening Venus came to her temple and hurried without delay to that part of the temple where she had left the girl.
2. When she saw that the work had been finished, she thought her son had done it and she gave the girl very little food.
3. On the next day she ordered the girl to come to her. The goddess ordered her to run to the forest in which there were many sheep, whose wool was golden, and to bring back the wool.
4. When Psyche came to the river, she found not only the sheep but also the god of the river.
5. He said that the river was very swift and the sheep were especially unfriendly in the daytime, but that they would be more gentle at night. For this reason she waited for night and saw that the sheep were sleeping.
6. Her work was very easy because the wool of the sheep was on the trees. It was not necessary even to touch the sheep, but with the help of the god she obtained much golden wool from the trees and the same day she went to Venus, her mistress, because she wished to do everything well.

7. **Postquam ad Venerem venit et ei lanam dedit, Psyche deam se liberaturam esse atque se maritum suum recepturam esse sperabat.**

7. After she came to Venus and gave her the wool, Psyche hoped that the goddess would free her and that she would get back her husband.

8. **Domina autem eam sine auxilio alterius lanam obtinuisse negavit.**

8. However, her mistress said that she had not obtained the wool without the help of another.

9. **Puellam esse utilem cupiebat. Itaque eam apud Inferos iter facere iussit. Ei arcam parvam dedit.**

9. She wanted the girl to be useful. And so she ordered her to make a journey among the dead. She gave her a small box.

10. **Psyche misera templum Veneris reliquit et se certe necatum iri putabat. Dea enim partem pulchritudinis Proserpinae ex terra mortis ad se reportari cupiebat.**

10. The unhappy Psyche left the temple of Venus and thought that she would certainly be killed. For the goddess wished a part of Proserpina's beauty to be brought back to her from the land of death.

11. **Psyche tamen fortissima erat et ad turrem altissimam venit. Celerrimum iter ad Inferos petebat, sed vox eam ex turre revocavit et eam eo modo se necare debere negavit.**

11. Psyche, however, was very brave and came to a very high tower. She was seeking the fastest way to the dead, but a voice called her from the tower and said she ought not to kill herself in that manner.

12. **Vox quoque nuntiavit hunc laborem ei postremum futurum esse. Puellae iter facile celereque ad regnum Plutonis demonstravit. Illa timore ab eodem amico qui eam antea servaverat nunc liberata est.**

12. The voice also announced that this would be the last task for her. It pointed out to the girl an easy and quick way to the kingdom of Pluto. She was now freed from fear by the same friend who had saved her before.

Vocabulary

Nouns

vespera, vesperae, *f.*, evening
lana, lanae, *f.*, wool (lanolin)
ovis, ovis, *f.*, sheep **(ovium)** (ovine)
pulchritudo, pulchritudinis, *f.*, beauty (pulchritude)

Adjectives

necesse, necessary (Nom. and Acc. neuter only—used with **esse**)

utilis, utile, useful (utility)

Verbs

puto, putare, putavi, putatus, think, believe (putative)

conspicio, conspicere, conspexi, conspectus, catch sight of, see, perceive, observe

spero, sperare, speravi, speratus, hope (aspire)

nego, negare, negavi, negatus, deny (negative)

reporto, reportare, reportavi, reportatus, carry back, bring back (report)

revoco, revocare, revocavi, revocatus, call back (revoke)

THE VERB: INFINITIVES

A. All Infinitives are formed on the same pattern.

1. The Present Active Infinitive is the second principal part.

amare, to love	**ducere,** to lead	**esse,** to be
habere, to have	**capere,** to take	**ire,** to go
ferre, to carry	**audire,** to hear	**posse,** to be able

2. The Present Passive Infinitive ends in **-i.** Note the **3rd conjugation** drops the **-er-.**

amari, to be loved	**duci,** to be led	**audiri,** to be heard
haberi, to be had	**capi,** to be taken	

3. The Perfect Active Infinitive is the third principal part ending in **-sse.**

amavisse, to have loved	**duxisse,** to have led
habuisse, to have had	**cepisse,** to have taken
tulisse, to have carried	**audivisse,** to have heard

fuisse, to have been
iisse, to have gone
potuisse, to have been able

4. The Perfect Passive Infinitive is the fourth principal part, the Perfect Passive, Participle with **esse.**

amatus, a, um esse, to have been loved
habitus, a, um esse, to have been had
ductus, a, um esse, to have been led
captus, a, um esse, to have been taken
auditus, a, um esse, to have been heard

5. The Future Active Infinitive is the Future Active Participle with **esse.**

    amaturus, a, um esse, to be about to love
    habiturus, a, um esse, to be about to have
    ducturus, a, um esse, to be about to lead
    capturus, a, um esse, to be about to take
    auditurus, a, um esse, to be about to hear
    futurus, a, um esse, to be about to be

6. The Future Passive Infinitive is the Supine[1] (which is the same as the neuter Nominative of the Perfect Passive Participle, e.g., **amatum**) with the Present Passive Infinitive of **eo—iri.**

amatum iri	to be about to be loved
habitum iri	to be about to be had
ductum iri	to be about to be led
captum iri	to be about to be taken
auditum iri	to be about to be heard

Note that the Supine in this usage does not decline.

B. You have already met several uses of the Infinitive.

1. The completing Infinitive.

    Id capere cupit. He wants to take it.

2. The Infinitive as a Subject.

    Me venire oportet { To come behoves me. / It behoves me to come. / I ought to come. }

3. The Infinitive as a Direct Object.

    Natare amat. He likes to swim.

INDIRECT STATEMENTS

However, the most common use of the Infinitive in Latin, especially Infinitives other than the Present Infinitives, is to express an *Indirect Statement*, that is, a statement in *Reported Speech.*

Indirect Statements are expressed in Latin by an *Accusative and Infinitive* construction.

Direct Statement

Puella natat.	The girl is swimming.

Indirect Statement

Dico puellam natare	I say that the girl is swimming. (Literally: I say the girl to be swimming.)

[1] See note on page 85.

There are several important points to remember about this construction.

1. The Participle in the Perfect Passive and Future Active Infinitives must agree with the Accusative in Gender, Number and Case.

Agros aratos esse dicit.	He says that the fields have been ploughed.
Puellam laboraturam esse dicit.	He says that the girl is about to work.

2. The *tense* of the Infinitive is always the tense of the verb in the *original statement.*

Direct Speech

Agricola agros arabit.	The farmer *will plough* the fields.

Indirect Speech

Agricolam agros araturum esse dixit.	He said that the farmer *would plough* the fields.

3. When the subject of the Indirect Statement is *he*, *she*, *it* or *they* and the person (or persons) referred to is also the subject of the introductory verb, then the reflexive pronoun, **se,** is used.

Dixit se agros araturum esse.	He said that he (himself) would plough the fields.

4. When the Indirect Statement is negative and the introductory verb is a verb of saying, the verb, **nego** (I deny), must be used.

Negavit se agros araturum esse.	He said that he would not plough the fields. (Literally: He denied that he would plough the fields)

FAMILIAR ABBREVIATIONS

i.e., id est, that is.
pro and **con, pro et contra,** for and against.
etc., et cetera, and the rest; and so forth.
e.g., exempli gratia, for (the sake of) example.
no., numero, by number.
viz., videlicet, namely, that is to say; introduces further explanation.
d.v. or **D.V., Deo volente,** God willing; if God is willing.
vox pop., vox populi, the voice of the people.

Practice Exercises

No. 165. Give the English for these Infinitives.

1. **monere**
2. **auxisse**
3. **iaci**
4. **positurus esse**
5. **fugisse**
6. **impedire**
7. **natavisse**
8. **territurus esse**
9. **mansisse**
10. **auditurus esse**
11. **scripsisse**
12. **pugnaturus esse**
13. **laudaturus esse**
14. **excitari**
15. **petitus esse**
16. **mittere**
17. **tangi**
18. **oppugnatus esse**
19. **laudatum iri**
20. **gesturus esse**
21. **accipi**
22. **victus esse**
23. **velle**
24. **ambulaturus esse**
25. **timuisse**

No. 166. Change these Infinitives to the Active, and give the English.

1. **peti**
2. **captus esse**
3. **haberi**
4. **rectus esse**
5. **portari**
6. **vocatus esse**
7. **fieri**
8. **datus esse**
9. **instrui**
10. **verti**

No. 167. Change these Infinitives to the Passive, and give the English.

1. **narrare**
2. **defendisse**
3. **videre**
4. **iuvare**
5. **laudavisse**
6. **movisse**
7. **vocaturus esse**
8. **invenire**
9. **necavisse**
10. **relinquere**

No. 168. Give the Future Active Infinitive of these Verbs, and the English.

1. **esse**
2. **iubere**
3. **facere**
4. **defendere**
5. **oppugnare**
6. **properare**
7. **capere**
8. **invenire**
9. **dare**
10. **ponere**

No. 169. Complete the following sentences by adding the appropriate words. Choose your answers from the words in parentheses.

1. **Caesar dixit legatos ab hostibus .... (necatos esse, necare)**
2. **Hannibal sperat se Alpes .... (transiturum esse, transire)**
3. **Galli putabant .... nostros facillime capturos esse (eos, se)**
4. **Nonne negas te Crassum in foro .... (videri, vidisse)**
5. **Psyche vidit maritum deum .... (esse, fuisse)**
6. **Legatus nuntiavit .... ad flumen abiisse. (agricolae, agricolas)**
7. **Aeneas scivit Troiam .... (captam esse, capere)**
8. **Sabini clamabant .... feminas puellasque recepturos esse (se, eos)**
9. **Populus Romanus scivit Caesarem Romam iter .... et tribus diebus .... (facere, fieri) (advenire, adventurum esse)**
10. **Diu putabamus nos a sagittariis .... (impeditum iri, impedituros esse)**

No. 170. Translate these sentences.

1. **Illi milites se viris auxilium daturos esse dixerunt.**
2. **Putatisne opus vestrum factum esse?**
3. **Nos hostes quam celerrime venturos esse sperabamus.**
4. **Puellae laetae esse videntur.**
5. **Hic rex bene regere volebat.**
6. **Ille revocari non volet.**
7. **Oppidum nostrum defendere optimum est.**
8. **Speravisse melius erat quam se recepisse.**
9. **Celeritatem augeri posse nuntiavit.**
10. **Nos locum meliorem invenire iussit.**

CHAPTER 36

READING

Cupido et Psyche (concluded)

1. **Psyche, timida videri nolens, verba vocis magno cum gaudio audivit et hunc laborem non difficillimum futurum esse sperabat.**
2. **Itaque haec omnia, quae ei demonstrata erant, facere contendit. Sine periculo enim ad regnum Inferorum iter facere magnopere volebat.**
3. **Cerberus, canis ante portam Inferorum positus, tria capita habebat, sed Psyche voce monita eum non timebat.**
4. **Deinde Charon eam in regnum Plutonis ituram in scapha minima trans flumen tulit.**
5. **Illa ante Proserpinam, reginam pulcherrimam Inferorum, stans Venerem donum cupire nuntiavit.**
6. **Regina arcam a puella accepit et in eandem arcam partem parvam suae pulchritudinis posuit. Deinde dea arcam dans puellam monuit.**
7. **Eam, in arcam spectantem, in periculum magnum casuram esse dixit, sed Psyche, ex terra Inferorum iter facere volens,**

Cupid and Psyche (concluded)

1. Psyche, who did not wish to seem timid, heard the words of the voice with great joy and hoped this task would not be very difficult.
2. And so she hurried to do all these things, that had been pointed out to her. For she greatly wished to make the journey to the kingdom of the dead without danger.
3. Cerberus, the dog who was placed in front of the door that leads to the land of death, had three heads, but Psyche, because she had been warned by the voice, was not afraid of him.
4. Charon then carried her, as she was about to go into the kingdom of Pluto, across the river in a very small boat.
5. Standing in front of Proserpina, the very beautiful queen of the dead, she reported that Venus wanted a gift.
6. The queen received the box from the girl and put a small part of her own beauty into the same box. Then the goddess warned the girl as she gave her the box.
7. She said that she would fall into great danger, if she looked into the box, but Psyche, who wished to make

Cupido et Psyche (concluded)	Cupid and Psyche (concluded)
verbis reginae ad timorem non excitata est.	the journey out of the land of the dead, was not aroused to fear by the words of the queen.
8. **Ad terram mortalium eadem via iit. Postquam ad lucem pervenit spectare in arcam et videre pulchritudinem atque habere volebat, sed arca aperta nil pulchritudinis ibi invenit.**	8. She went by the same road to the land of mortals. After she had arrived at the light she wished to look into the box and to see and have the beauty, but when the box was opened she found no beauty there.
9. **Psyche dolens pulchritudinem ibi non invenit quia Proserpina in arca somnum altum Inferorum posuerat.**	9. The grieving Psyche did not find beauty there because Proserpina had placed in the box the deep sleep of the dead.
10. **Somno ex carcere liberato, puella celeriter capta est et sine mora, sicut corpus a Morte delectum, media in via cecidit. Nil sciebat nec aliquid faciebat. Solum dormiebat.**	10. When the sleep had been freed from its prison, the girl was quickly overcome by it and without delay, just like a body chosen by Death, she fell in the middle of the road. She knew nothing and she did nothing. She only slept.
11. **Cupido tamen, vulnere curato, magno cum gaudio uxorem suam vidit. Ad locum ubi illa dormiebat quam celerrime volavit.**	11. Cupid, however, when his wound had been healed, saw his wife with great joy. He flew as quickly as possible to the place where she was sleeping.
12. **Supra eam stans, somnum qui eam opprimebat cepit et, hoc in arca posito, una ex sagittis suis uxorem tetigit.**	12. Standing above her, he took the sleep that was oppressing her and, when this had been placed in the box, he touched his wife with one of his arrows.
13. **'Te oportet,' inquit, 'multis temporibus e morte servatam, omnes labores tuos conficere. His factis, omnia reliqua faciam.'**	13. He said: 'You, because you have been saved from death many times, ought to finish all your tasks. When these have been done, I shall do all the other things.'

14. **Illa satis poenae habuerat. Hic ad Iovem properavit et ab eo auxilium petivit. Iuppiter ad Venerem eodem die iter fecit. Illa tandem puellam dedidit.**

14. She had had enough punishment. He hurried to Jupiter and begged aid from him. Jupiter made the journey to Venus the same day. She at last surrendered the girl.

15. **Psyche, ad regnum deorum a Mercurio ducta, immortalis facta est.**

15. Psyche, after she had been led to the kingdom of the gods by Mercury, became immortal.

16. **Itaque ab eo tempore ad finem temporis omnis matrimonium eius laetissimum erat.**

16. And so her marriage from that time to the end of all time was very happy.

17. **Mortales hac fabula docentur animum immortalem esse atque per omnes difficultates se semper laetos futuros esse.**

17. Mortals are taught by this story that the spirit is immortal and that through all difficulties they will always be happy.

Vocabulary

Nouns

gaudium, gaudii or **gaudi,** *n.*, joy (gaudy)
Cerberus, Cerberi, *m.*, Cerberus
canis, canis, *m.* and *f.*, dog (canine)
Charon, Charontis, *m.*, Charon
scapha, scaphae, *f.*, boat
somnus, somni, *m.*, sleep (insomnia)
carcer, carceris, *n.*, prison (incarcerate)

Adjectives

timidus, timida, timidum, timid
apertus, aperta, apertum, open (aperture)
reliquus, reliqua, reliquum, remaining, rest of

Verb

opprimo, opprimere, oppressi, oppressus, weigh down, overwhelm, oppress

Adverb

sicut, just as, like

Pronoun

aliquis, aliqua, aliquid, someone, anyone. (Declined in the other cases like **quis**)

THE VERB PARTICIPLES

A. There are three participles in Latin.

1. The Present *Active* Participle ends in **-ns, -ntis,** and is declined like **audax, audacis** (except that the Ablative Singular ends in **-e**).

amans, amantis, loving
habens, habentis, having
ducens, ducentis, leading
capiens, capientis, seizing
audiens, audientis, hearing
iens, euntis, going
volens, volentis, wishing
nolens, nolentis, being unwilling

Note that **sum** and **malo** have no Present Participle.

2. The Perfect *Passive* Participle is the fourth principal part.

amatus, a, um, having been loved
habitus, a, um, having been had
ductus, a, um, having been led
captus, a, um, having been seized
auditus, a, um, having been heard

3. The Future *Active* Participle is the fourth principal part ending in **-urus.**

amaturus, a, um, about to love
habiturus, a, um, about to have
ducturus, a, um, about to lead
capturus, a, um, about to seize
auditurus, a, um, about to hear
futurus, a, um, about to be
iturus, a, um, about to go

B. Participles are adjectives and must agree with their nouns in gender, number, and case.

C. Participles are best translated by a clause in English, beginning with *when, who, because, if* or *although.*

Miles captus non timebat.	The soldier, although he was captured, was not afraid.
Miles captus timebat.	The soldier, because he was captured, was afraid.
Miles pugnans necatus est.	The soldier, when he was fighting, was killed.
	or The soldier, who was fighting, was killed.

THE ABLATIVE ABSOLUTE

A participle with a noun or pronoun, both in the Ablative case, may be used as a clause.

Note:

1. The noun or pronoun that is the subject of the clause must have no place in the main part of the sentence, i.e., it must be *absolute.*
2. The clause may be translated with *because, when, after, although,* or *if.*

3. The participle may be replaced by a noun or an adjective, in which case the verb 'to be' must be supplied in English.

Oppidis captis, cives pacem petebant.	When the towns had been captured, the citizens sought peace.
Hoc viro duce, vincemur.	If this man is leader, we shall be conquered.
Navibus gravibus, celerius navigabamus.	Although the ships were heavy, we were sailing quite quickly.

FAMILIAR QUOTATIONS

Veni, vidi, vici, I came, I saw, I conquered. *Caesar*

Vae victis, Woe to the vanquished. *Livy*

In medias res, Into the midst of things. *Horace*

Finis coronat opus, The end crowns the work. *Ovid*

Non omnia possumus omnes, We can't all do everything. *Virgil*

Diem perdidi, I have lost a day. *Titus*

Pares cum paribus facillime congregantur, Equals very easily congregate with equals. *Cicero*

Practice Exercises

No. 171. Translate these participles.

1. **vocans**
2. **motus**
3. **missurus**
4. **accipiens**
5. **venturus**
6. **spectatus**
7. **perveniens**
8. **capturus**
9. **ponens**
10. **nuntiatus**
11. **monitus**
12. **timens**
13. **dicturus**
14. **excitatus**
15. **iens**

No. 172. Translate these participial phrases.

1. **naves navigantes**
2. **ducem iussurum**
3. **illi oppugnati**
4. **viros perventuros**
5. **petentes pacem**
6. **canem currentem**
7. **urbes captae**
8. **templa aedificata**
9. **portus inventos**
10. **flumina currentia**

No. 173. Translate these sentences.

1. **Populus urbium captarum fortissimus erat.**
2. **Viri perventuri iter quam celerrime faciebant.**
3. **Rex patriam vestram nunc regens timidus esse videtur.**
4. **Mulier difficultatem tuam videns auxilium dabit.**
5. **Psyche ad regnum Inferorum iter factura multa timebat.**
6. **Pater filios suos visurus magnum gaudium habebat.**
7. **Ei nostros timentes quam celerrime currebant.**
8. **Homines victi maxime timebant.**
9. **Ad oppidum perveniens illa fabulam suam narravit.**
10. **Illi portam defendentes amici non erant.**

No. 174. Complete the following sentences by adding the appropriate participial phrase. Choose your answer from the phrases in parentheses.

1. .... **populus celeriter fugiebat. (Urbe capta, Urbem captam)**
2. .... **populus reliquit. (Urbe capta, Urbem captam)**
3. .... **milites laudabant. (Te duce, Te ducem)**
4. .... **milites fortissimi erant. (Te duce, Te ducem)**
5. .... **equites domum redierunt. (Hostibus oppressis, Hostes oppressos)**
6. .... **equites ad urbem duxerunt. (Hostibus oppressis, Hostes oppressos)**
7. .... **nos laudamus. (Puella natante, Puellam natantem)**
8. .... **nos dormiebamus. (Puella natante, Puellam natantem)**
9. .... **cepimus. (Militibus mare spectantibus, Milites mare spectantes)**
10. .... **nos recepimus. (Militibus mare spectantibus, Milites mare spectantes)**

No. 175. Translate these adverbs.

1. **fortiter**
2. **quam celerrime**
3. **minime**
4. **diutissime**
5. **acrius**
6. **optime**
7. **facillime**
8. **melius**
9. **male**
10. **magnopere**
11. **saepius**
12. **miserrime**

Practice Exercises

No. 176. Translate these sentences.

1. **Oraculo audito multi ad terram nostram venire constituerunt.**
2. **Signo dato, in agrum impetum fecerunt.**
3. **Armis amissis homines fortiter pugnaverunt.**
4. **Militibus multis interfectis, pacem petiverunt.**
5. **Bello confecto milites magno cum gaudio domi accipientur.**
6. **Hac re gesta pueri domum venient.**
7. **Illo duce id sine difficultate faciemus.**
8. **His nuntiatis ex urbe iter facere volebam.**
9. **His necatis, populus melius regetur.**
10. **Die dicto, omnia quam celerrime paraverunt.**
11. **Porta aperta, in casam venire potuit.**
12. **Oppido capto nullam spem habebat.**
13. **His rebus factis, rex plus poterat.**
14. **Reliquis visis, ad silvam curremus.**
15. **Patre eius duce omnia audacter faciunt.**
16. **Pace facta ab insula navigabit.**
17. **Multis timidis flumina invenire non poterimus.**
18. **Sociis victis nullum auxilium perveniet.**
19. **Loco idoneo hic diutius manere vis.**
20. **Auxilio dato gaudium magnum erat.**

NINTH REVISION (CHAPTERS 34–36)

VOCABULARY REVISION

Nouns

1. canis
2. carcer
3. Cerberus
4. Charon
5. dux
6. formica
7. gaudium
8. genus
9. lana
10. modus
11. numerus
12. ordo
13. ovis
14. pulchritudo
15. satis
16. somnus
17. vulnus

1. dog
2. prison
3. Cerberus
4. Charon
5. leader
6. ant
7. joy
8. kind, class
9. wool
10. manner, way
11. number
12. rank, order
13. sheep
14. beauty
15. enough
16. sleep
17. wound

Adjectives

1. acerbus **2. reliquus** **3. timidus** **4. utilis**

1. bitter 2. remaining, rest of 3. timid 4. useful

Verbs

1. invenio **2. puto** **3. reporto** **4. spero**

1. I find, come upon 2. I think, believe 3. I carry back, bring back 4. I hope

Adverbs

1. satis **2. tam** **3. tandem**

1. enough 2. so 3. finally

Practice Exercises

No. 177. Translate these infinitives.

1. **esse**
2. **fuisse**
3. **inventurus esse**
4. **inventum iri**
5. **putatus esse**
6. **putavisse**
7. **reportare**
8. **reportaturus esse**
9. **speravisse**
10. **speraturus esse**
11. **duci**
12. **duxisse**
13. **habitus esse**
14. **habere**
15. **cupere**
16. **cupi**
17. **potuisse**
18. **posse**
19. **pugnavisse**
20. **laudatus esse**
21. **moneri**
22. **monuisse**
23. **dixisse**
24. **dici**
25. **voluisse**
26. **timuisse**
27. **factus esse**
28. **facturus esse**
29. **videri**
30. **visum iri**

·H

No. 178. Translate these participles.

1. **ducens**	11. **sperantia**	21. **mittens**
2. **ducturus**	12. **speraturam**	22. **missus**
3. **habentes**	13. **moturos**	23. **visuris**
4. **habitos**	14. **moventes**	24. **videntium**
5. **putata**	15. **venientium**	25. **dicturos**
6. **putaturus**	16. **ventura**	26. **dicens**
7. **invenientem**	17. **timenti**	27. **monentes**
8. **inventa**	18. **territus**	28. **moniti**
9. **reportantium**	19. **ituri**	29. **positos**
10. **reportaturus**	20. **euntis**	30. **ponens**

No. 179. Translate these Ablative Absolutes.

1. **eis visis**	6. **puella ambulante**	11. **urbe capta**
2. **illo capto**	7. **ducibus timidis**	12. **reliquis dicentibus**
3. **his dictis**	8. **armis amissis**	13. **verbo audito**
4. **bello facto**	9. **somno veniente**	14. **spe inventa**
5. **viris timentibus**	10. **militibus pugnantibus**	15. **multis necatis**

QUINTUS HORATIUS FLACCUS

Horace was born in 65 B.C. at Venusia, in southern Italy, the son of a freedman, and studied in Rome and Athens. He was a friend of Virgil and of Augustus, through his literary patron, Maecenas. Before his death in 8 B.C. he had gained enduring popularity from the quality and universality of his poetry and philosophy.

Integer vitae scelerisque purus	He who is upright of life and free from crime
non eget Mauris iaculis neque arcu	needs neither Moorish javelins nor a bow
nec venenatis gravida sagittis, Fusce, pharetra,	nor a quiver heavy with poisoned arrows, Fuscus,
sive per Syrtis iter aestuosos	whether he is going to journey through the hot Quicksands
sive facturus per inhospitalem	or through the inhospitable
Caucasum vel quae loca fabulosus lambit Hydaspes.	Caucasus or the places which the storied Hydaspes laps.
Carminum Liber Primus, xxii	*First Book of Odes, 22*

CARMINA BURANA

In the early nineteenth century, a manuscript from the thirteenth century was found in the monastery of Benedictbeuren in Bavaria, from which it gets its name, *Carmina Burana*. These *carmina*, or songs, were mostly poems, chiefly in Latin or German, or a combination of both, composed by the goliards, or wandering students and monks, on a wide variety of topics. By the Middle Ages the classical pronunciation and meter had changed and the use of rhyme had been introduced in poetry. These poems provided both inspiration and the text for the contemporary German composer Carl Orff's famous 'Carmina Burana'.

Omnia sol temperat	The sun, pure and clear,
purus et subtilis,	Tempers everything,
nova mundo reserat	A new world resows
facies Aprilis,	The appearance of April;
ad amorem properat	The sweetheart's spirit
animus erilis,	Hurries to love,
et iucundis imperat	And over pleasant things rules
deus puerilis.	The boyish god. [Cupid]
Rerum tanta novitas	So much newness of nature
in sollemni vere	In the festive springtime
et veris auctoritas	And the power of the spring
iubet nos gaudere,	Order us to rejoice,
vias praebet solitas,	Shows us the accustomed ways,
et in tuo vere	And in your own springtime
fides est et probitas	There is trust and the right
tuum retinere.	To cling to your loved one.
Ama me fideliter,	Love me faithfully,
fidem meam nota,	Mark my trust,
de corde totaliter	In my heart completely,
et ex mente tota,	And with my whole mind
sum praesentialiter	I am in your presence,
absens in remota;	Even when absent at a distance;
quisquis amat taliter,	Whoever loves in such a way,
volvitur in rota.	Is turned on a wheel of torture.
Ecce gratum	Behold, pleasing
et optatum	And longed for,
ver reducit gaudia,	The spring brings back our joys;
purpuratum	Clad in purple
floret pratum,	The meadow is in flower,
sol serenat omnia,	The sun makes all serene,
iam iam cedunt tristia.	Now, now, sorrows depart,
aestas redit,	Summer returns,
nunc recedit	Now retreats
hiemis saevitia.	The severity of winter.
Iam liquescit	Now there melts
et decrescit	And disappears
grando, nix, et cetera,	All hail, snow, and such,

bruma fugit,	Winter flees,
et iam sugit	And now the spring
ver aestatis ubera;	Sucks in the richness of summer;
illi mens est misera,	His heart is wretched,
qui nec vivit,	Who neither lives,
nec lascivit	Nor plays
sub aestatis dextera.	Under the propitious hand of summer.
Gloriantur	They glory
et laetantur	And delight
in melle dulcedinis	In the honey of sweetness
qui conantur	Who try
ut utantur	To use
praemio Cupidinis;	The favour of Cupid;
simus iussu Cypridis	Let us be, at the command of Venus,
gloriantes	Boasting
et laetantes	And rejoicing
pares esse Paridis.	To be the equals of Paris.

CHAPTER 37

READING

MARCUS TULLIUS CICERO

You have already read one extract from Cicero's speeches against Catalina (see pages 143–4). Here is a passage from the first speech in which he urges all Catalina's fellow conspirators to give up their attempts on the state and promises that the conspiracy will be stopped.

Quare secedant improbi, secernant se a bonis, unum in locum congregentur, muro denique, quod saepe iam dixi, secernantur a nobis;

Therefore let the wicked ones withdraw, let them set themselves apart from good men, let them be gathered together into one place, finally let them be set apart from us by a wall, as I have often said already;

desinant insidiari domi suae consuli, circumstare tribunal praetoris urbani, obsidere cum gladiis curiam:

let them cease to lay ambush to the consul at his home, to surround the platform of the city praetor, to lay siege to the senate-house with swords:

sit denique inscriptum in fronte unius cuiusque, quid de re publica sentiat.

and finally let it be written on the forehead of each one of them, what he feels for the state.

Polliceor hoc vobis, patres conscripti, tantam in nobis consulibus fore diligentiam, tantam in vobis auctoritatem, tantam in equitibus Romanis virtutem, tantam in omnibus bonis consensionem, ut Catalinae profectione omnia patefacta illustrata oppressa vindicata esse videatis.

(Adapted from *Cicero—In Catalinam I 32.*)

I promise you this, conscript fathers, there will be such great diligence in us, the consuls, such great power in you, such great valour in the Roman knights, such great agreement among all good men, that you will see that by the departure of Catalina everything has been revealed, disclosed, crushed and avenged.

Vocabulary

Nouns

tribunal, tribunalis, *n.*, platform tribunal
praetor, praetoris, *m.*, praetor
curia, curiae, *f.*, the senate house
res publica, rei publicae, *f.*, the state (republic)
diligentia, diligentiae, *f.*, diligence, industry
auctoritas, auctoritatis, *f.*, power authority
consensio, consensionis, *f.*, agreement, unanimity, (consent)
profectio, profectionis, *f.*, departure

Adjectives

improbus, a, um, bad, wicked
urbanus, a, um, of the city
tantus, a, um, so great

Adverbs

quare, by what means? how? wherefore, therefore
denique, finally, at last

Verbs

secedo, secedere, secessi, secessus, go away, withdraw (secede)
secerno, secernere, secrevi, secretus, divide, separate, set apart (secret)
congrego, congregare, congregavi, congregatus, assemble, gather together
desino, desinere, desii, desitus, cease, desist
insidior, insidiari, insidiatus sum, (Deponent verb) lie in ambush (insidious)
circumsto, circumstare, circumsteti —, stand around, surround.
obsideo, obsidere, obsedi, obsessus, besiege (obsession)
inscribo, inscribere, inscripsi, inscriptus, write on
sentio, sentire, sensi, sensus, feel, perceive (sense)
polliceor, polliceri, pollicitus sum, (Deponent verb) promise
fore, to be about to be (an alternative form of the Future Infinitive of **esse**)
patefacio, patefacere, patefeci, patefactus, open, reveal
illustro, illustrare, illustravi, illustratus, make clear, disclose (illustrate)
vindico, vindicare, vindicavi, vindicatus, save, avenge (vindicate)

THE SUBJUNCTIVE MOOD

1. Formation of the Present Subjunctive tense.

THE PRESENT SUBJUNCTIVE

1st *Conjugation*		2nd *Conjugation*	
Active	*Passive*	*Active*	*Passive*
amem	**amer**	**habeam**	**habear**
ames	**ameris**	**habeas**	**habearis**
amet	**ametur**	**habeat**	**habeatur**
amemus	**amemur**	**habeamus**	**habeamur**
ametis	**amemini**	**habeatis**	**habeamini**
ament	**amentur**	**habeant**	**habeantur**

3rd *Conjugation*

Active	*Passive*	*Active*	*Passive*
ducam	**ducar**	**capiam**	**capiar**
ducas	**ducaris**	**capias**	**capiaris**
ducat, etc.	**ducatur**, etc.	**capiat**, etc.	**capiatur**, etc.

4th *Conjugation*

Active	*Passive*
audiam	**audiar**
audias	**audiaris**
audiat, etc.	**audiatur**, etc.

IRREGULAR VERBS

IRE	FIERI	FERRE
eam	**fiam**	**feram**
eas	**fias**	**feras**
eat, etc.	**fiat**, etc.	**ferat**, etc.

ESSE	POSSE	VELLE	NOLLE	MALLE
sim	**possim**	**velim**	**nolim**	**malim**
sis	**possis**	**velis**	**nolis**	**malis**
sit	**possit**	**velit**	**nolit**	**malit**
simus	**possimus**	**velimus**	**nolimus**	**malimus**
sitis	**possitis**	**velitis**	**nolitis**	**malitis**
sint	**possint**	**velint**	**nolint**	**malint**

2. The Use of the Subjunctive mood

THE JUSSIVE SUBJUNCTIVE

When a Subjunctive verb is the main verb of a sentence, it usually has the force of a command. This is called the Jussive use of the Subjunctive (**iubeo,** I order).

eamus	let us go
urbem capiant	let them capture the town
secedant improbi	let the wicked withdraw

The negative used with the Subjunctive in this sense is **ne.**

ne eamus let us not go

However, as the name suggests, verbs in the Subjunctive Mood are more often found in subordinate clauses, i.e., clauses which are 'subjoined' to the main clause. Not all subordinate clauses need a verb in the Subjunctive mood, but in the next chapters we will be looking at some of those that do. The first example of such clauses is the Consecutive or Result Clause.

CONSECUTIVE OR RESULT CLAUSES

Clauses indicating a result are expressed in Latin by the conjunction, **ut,** and a Subjunctive verb.

Tantum est mare ut natare non possit
The sea is so great that he cannot swim

DEPONENT VERBS

Some Latin verbs are Passive in form, but they have a normal Active meaning. Such verbs are called Deponent verbs. They can be used quite normally but must always have a passive ending.

The commonest of these verbs are:

conor, conari, conatus sum, I try
hortor, hortari, hortatus sum, I encourage (exhort)
vereor, vereri, veritus sum, I fear
sequor, sequi, secutus sum, I follow (consecutive)
loquor, loqui, locutus sum, I speak (loquacious)
proficiscor, proficisci, profectus sum, I set out
aggredior, aggredi, aggressus sum, I attack (aggression)
morior, mori, mortuus sum, I die (mortuary)
patior, pati, passus sum, I suffer, allow (passive)
ordior, ordiri, orsus sum, I begin
orior, oriri, ortus sum, I rise (orient)
potior, potiri, potitus sum, I gain mastery of (potent)

ROMAN MAGISTRATES—CONSULS AND PRAETORS

The Consuls. When the Romans expelled Tarquin, their last king, in 510 B.C. and established a republican government, they decided that the supreme authority **(imperium)** in the republic would always be shared by two men, so that no individual could be in a position to overthrow the republic and re-establish a monarchy. These two magistrates who shared the supreme authority were called consuls.

Their main duties were to command the armies, to conduct the assemblies of the people that would be called for elections or for the passing of laws, and to convene the senate.

They held office for one year and at the end of that year, they were given proconsular power **(imperium pro consule)** and responsibility for a major area of administration. This would in most cases mean the governorship of a Roman province.

During his year of office, each consul was attended by twelve official attendants, known as lictors, who walked in single file before him bearing **fasces,** a bundle of rods with an axe, symbolizing the consul's power to beat and to execute criminals.

The Praetors. The praetorship was instituted to relieve the consuls of their responsibility for the administration of justice. Originally there was only one praetor and it was his duty to administer justice in Rome. Later a second praetorship was created to deal with law suits between Roman citizens and foreign residents **(peregrini).** This praetor was called the **Praetor Peregrinus** and the other praetor then became known as the **Praetor Urbanus** (the City Praetor). The number of praetors was later increased further and was finally fixed at 12 by Augustus.

The praetors held office for one year and could then be given power **pro praetore.** They were attended by two lictors each within the city boundary and by six outside it.

No. 180. Give the first person singular of the Present Subjunctive Active of the following verbs.

1. **laudo**	6. **sum**	11. **sequor**	16. **malo**
2. **video**	7. **eo**	12. **aggredior**	17. **possum**
3. **dico**	8. **fero**	13. **ordior**	18. **fio**
4. **facio**	9. **conor**	14. **volo**	19. **inscribo**
5. **venio**	10. **vereor**	15. **nolo**	20. **vindico**

Practice Exercises

No. 181. Complete the following sentences by replacing the English words in italics by the appropriate Latin verb. Choose your answer from the words in parentheses.

1. *Let us go* **ad Galliam (eamus, imus)**
2. **Unum in locum** *let them be gathered together* **(congregentur, congregantur)**
3. **Tam lata via est ut transire non** *we are able* **(possumus, possimus)**
4. **Haec est puella quam videre** *I wish* **(volo, velim)**
5. **Vivamus atque** *let us love*, **mea Lesbia (amamus, amemus)**
6. **Milites hostes sex milia passum** *having followed* **impetum fecerunt (secuti, sequentes)**
7. **Proelium tam longum fuit ut vix stare** *I can* **(possum, possim)**
8. **Tot pueri aderunt ut filium tuum non** *you will find* **(invenies, invenias)**
9. **Aggrediamur aut** *let us die* **(moriamur, moriemur)**
10. **Ab insula** *after we had set out*, **Romam celeriter pervenimus (profecti, profecti sumus)**

No. 182. Translate the following sentences.

1. **Hostes tam celeriter current ut eos aggredi difficile sit.**
2. **Talis oratio est ut omnes Ciceronem laudent.**
3. **Milites hortatus Caesar in castra hostium impetum facere iussit.**
4. **Ciceronem sequamur; Catalinam Romam opprimere ne patiamur.**
5. **Troia decem annos obsessa Graeci equum magnum aedificaverunt.**
6. **Rempublicam amare atque servare semper velimus.**
7. **Tanti sunt di ut eos vereamur et adoremus.**
8. **Leandro mortuo Hero vivere non vult.**
9. **Venus negavit Psychen ipsam frumentum ordinavisse.**
10. **Tot Persae impetum faciunt ut vincere non possimus.**

CHAPTER 38

READING

In this extract from his third speech against Catalina, Cicero tells how he has been constantly on the watch for evidence against the other conspirators.

Quae quoniam in senatu illustrata, patefacta, comperta sunt per me, vobis iam exponam breviter, Quirites, ut et quanta et quam manifesta et qua ratione investigata et comprehensa sint, vos, qui et ignoratis et exspectatis, scire possitis.

Since these things have been disclosed, revealed and discovered through me in the senate, I shall now explain them to you briefly, citizens, in order that you, who both are in ignorance and are waiting [to hear], may be able to know how great and how evident they are and in what manner they have been investigated and discovered.

Principio, cum sceleris sui socios Romae reliquisset, semper vigilavi et providi, Quirites, quem ad modum in tantis insidiis salvi esse possemus.

At the beginning, when he had left the associates of his crime at Rome, I always kept watch and took precautions how amid such a great snare we could be safe.

Atque ego ut vidi, quos maximo furore et scelere esse inflammatos sciebam, eos nobiscum esse et Romae remansisse, in eo omnes dies noctesque consumpsi, ut, quid agerent, quid molirentur, sentirem ac viderem.

And when I saw that those whom I knew had been inflamed by the greatest passion and wickedness were with us and had stayed in Rome, I spent every day and night in that pursuit, that I might perceive and see what they were doing, what they were attempting.

(Adapted from *Cicero—In Catalinam III, 3.*)

Vocabulary

Nouns

ratio, rationis, *f.*, account, affair, method (rational)

insidiae, insidiarum, *f.*, trap, snare, ambush (insidious)

scelus, sceleris, *n.*, crime, wickedness

Quiris, Quiritis (Quiritium), a Roman citizen, Quirite

furor, furoris, *m.*, rage, fury, passion

Adjectives

quantus, a, um, how much, how great (quantity)

manifestus, a, um, clear, evident, manifest

salvus, a, um, safe (salvage)

Adverbs

principio, in the beginning

quem ad modum, in what manner, how

Verbs

comperio, comperire, comperi, compertus, find out, learn, discover

expono, exponere, exposui, expositus, set forth, exhibit, explain (expose)

investigo, investigare, investigavi, investigatus, search after, discover, investigate

comprehendo, comprehendere, comprehendi, comprehensus, seize, apprehend, discover (comprehend)

ignoro, ignorare, ignoravi, ignoratus, not know, be ignorant

vigilo, vigilare, vigilavi, vigilatus, be awake, keep watch (vigil)

provideo, providere, providi, provisus, foresee, take precautions (provide)

remaneo, remanere, remansi, —, remain, stay behind

consumo, consumere, consumpsi, consumptus, use up, consume, spend

ago, agere, egi, actus, put in motion, carry on, do (agent, action)

molior, moliri, molitus sum, endeavour, struggle, attempt

FINAL OR PURPOSE CLAUSES

Clauses indicating purpose are expressed in Latin, like Consecutive or Result clauses, by **ut** followed by a verb in the Subjunctive mood.

Romam it ut Caesarem videat. He goes to Rome (in order) to see Caesar.

Impetum facimus ut urbem capiamus. We make an attack (in order) to capture the city.

When the Purpose clause is negative, the conjunction, **ne,** is used to introduce it.

Fugit ne capiatur. He flees in order not to be captured (lest he be captured).

INDIRECT QUESTIONS

Indirect Questions, i.e., questions in reported speech, also require a Subjunctive verb. They are normally introduced by the same interrogative adverb or adjective as would be used in the Direct Question.

Rogat cur Romam eam.	He asks why I am going to Rome.
Scit quanta insula sit.	He knows how great the island is.

Where the Direct Question would be introduced by **-ne, nonne** or **num,** the Indirect Question is introduced by **num.**

Rogat num Romam eam.	He asks if I am going to Rome.

Alternative Indirect Questions are introduced by **utrum**............**an....**

Rogat utrum Romam eam an domi maneam.	He asks whether I am going to Rome or staying at home.

Note that 'or not' is expressed by **necne.**

Note also that while Final and Consecutive clauses are *adverbial clauses*, an Indirect Question is a *noun clause*. In the sentence

Currit ut domum perveniat. He runs in order to reach home.

the Purpose clause performs the same function as the Adverb in the sentence

Celeriter currit. He runs quickly.

On the other hand, in the sentence

Video quid faciat. I see what he is doing.

the Indirect Question clause performs the same function as the Noun in the sentence

Pueros video. I see the boys.

THE SEQUENCE OF TENSES

1. **Formation of the other tenses of the Subjunctive mood**

Latin verbs have four Subjunctive tenses, Present, Imperfect, Perfect and Pluperfect.

The Imperfect Subjunctive

The Imperfect Subjunctive of every verb is formed from the Present Infinitive as follows.

Active	*Passive*
amarem	**amarer**
amares	**amareris**

Active	*Passive*
amaret	**amaretur**
amaremus	**amaremur**
amaretis	**amaremini**
amarent	**amarentur**

Thus:

haberem, ducerem, caperem, audirem, irem, fierem, ferrem, essem, possem, vellem, nollem, mallem.

The Perfect and Pluperfect Subjunctive

The Perfect and Pluperfect Subjunctives are formed as follows.

PERFECT SUBJUNCTIVE		PLUPERFECT SUBJUNCTIVE	
Active	*Passive*	*Active*	*Passive*
amaverim	**amatus sim**	**amavissem**	**amatus essem**
amaveris	**amatus sis**	**amavisses**	**amatus esses**
amaverit	**amatus sit**	**amavisset**	**amatus esset**
amaverimus	**amati simus**	**amavissemus**	**amati essemus**
amaveritis	**amati sitis**	**amavissetis**	**amati essetis**
amaverint	**amati sint**	**amavissent**	**amati essent**

2. The Use of the other tenses of the Subjunctive

The tense of the Subjunctive verb in a subordinate clause in Latin depends on:

(a) the tense of the main verb
(b) the particular meaning of the clause

(a) The tense of the main verb—Sequence of Tenses

PRIMARY SEQUENCE

Main Verb	*Subjunctive*
Present	Present
Future	*or*
True Perfect ('have')	Perfect
Future Perfect	

HISTORIC SEQUENCE

Main Verb	*Subjunctive*
Imperfect	Imperfect
Perfect (without 'have')	*or*
Pluperfect	Pluperfect

Primary Sequence

Rogat cur Romam eam. He asks why I *am* going to Rome.

Historic Sequence

Rogavit cur Romam irem. He asked why I *was* going to Rome.

(b) **The particular meaning of the clause**

Whether in Primary Sequence a Present or a Perfect Subjunctive is used depends on the particular meaning that is required.

Rogat cur Romam eam. He asks why I *am* going to Rome.
Rogat cur Romam ierim. He asks why I *have* gone to Rome.

The same is true of Historic sequence

Rogavit cur Romam irem. He asked why I *was* going to Rome.
Rogavit cur Romam iissem. He asked why I *had* gone to Rome.

ROMAN MAGISTRATES—AEDILES, QUAESTORS, TRIBUNES

The Aediles. Two aediles were appointed in the first instance to superintend the public games. Later they acquired additional duties, including the policing of Rome, protection of the city against fires and superintendence of the markets. They continued to be responsible for the management of the games.

They held office for a year and had no lictors, since they had no **imperium.**

The Quaestors. Originally there were two quaestors who acted as secretaries to the consuls and were nominated by them. Later the office became elective and the number of quaestors was increased to four. Two of these **(quaestores urbani)** took responsibility for the state treasury at Rome; the other two **(quaestores militares)** went with the generals on warlike expeditions and were responsible for the military finances.

As the Roman Empire grew so did the need for financial officers so that gradually the number of quaestors was increased until it was finally fixed at twenty.

Like the other officers, the quaestor held office for a year. He had no lictors since he had no **imperium.**

The Tribunes. The tribunes of the people **(tribuni plebis)** were not magistrates in the usual sense, since they had no clearly defined administrative role. They were originally appointed to protect the plebs (the common people) and in order to do this, they were given great power **(potestas)** but no **imperium.** They were empowered to protect any citizen who was being oppressed by the other magistrates, and in order to be able to do this effectively they were declared inviolate **(sacrosancti).** They could convene meetings of the plebs and carry through legislation at such meetings. They could also convene and consult the Senate. They had the right of veto **(intercessio)** over all acts of the Senate or magistrates. This they exercised by saying 'I forbid', **veto.**

Their power, therefore, was very great and they used it initially to procure equality for the plebs. Once this was secured, most of them worked with the Senate, but, because of their great powers, some of the more unscrupulous tribunes became very useful tools in the hands of politically ambitious men like Caesar and Pompey.

Originally there were probably five tribunes; later the number was raised to ten. Again the office was an annual one.

Practice Exercises

No. 183. Give the first person singular of the Imperfect Subjunctive Active of the following verbs.

1. **nato**	6. **sum**	11. **vereor**	16. **nolo**
2. **video**	7. **eo**	12. **loquor**	17. **malo**
3. **scribo**	8. **fero**	13. **morior**	18. **expono**
4. **fugio**	9. **fio**	14. **orior**	19. **ignoro**
5. **dormio**	10. **hortor**	15. **volo**	20. **ago**

No. 184. Give the first person singular of the Perfect Subjunctive Active of the following verbs.

1. **specto**	6. **sum**	11. **vereor**	16. **nolo**
2. **teneo**	7. **eo**	12. **proficiscor**	17. **malo**
3. **mitto**	8. **fero**	13. **patior**	18. **vigilo**
4. **iacio**	9. **fio**	14. **potior**	19. **consumo**
5. **scio**	10. **conor**	15. **volo**	20. **comprehendo**

No. 185. Give the first person singular of the Pluperfect Subjunctive Active of the following verbs.

1. **ambulo**	6. **sum**	11. **vereor**	16. **nolo**
2. **debeo**	7. **eo**	12. **sequor**	17. **malo**
3. **incendo**	8. **fero**	13. **aggredior**	18. **secedo**
4. **interficio**	9. **fio**	14. **molior**	19. **sentio**
5. **cupio**	10. **insidior**	15. **volo**	20. **circumsto**

No. 186. Complete the following sentences by adding a verb in the appropriate subjunctive tense. Choose your answer from the words in parentheses.

1. **Caesar pontem aedificavit ut flumen .... (transeat, transiret)**
2. **Quantum .... scelus Catalinae exponam (sit, esset)**

3. **Difficile erat videere utrum navis .... necne. (capta esset, capta sit)**
4. **Pater meus semper rogat utrum ad ludos ire an domi manere .... (velim, vellem)**
5. **Nemo rogat cur hoc .... (fecisses, feceris)**
6. **Psyche lucem parabat ut maritum suum .... (videret, videat)**
7. **Nescio utrum .... an .... (veniam, venirem) (eam, irem)**
8. **Totam noctem vigilabimus ne hostes impetum .... (faciant, facerent)**
9. **Tam manifestum erat scelus ut nemo id ignorare .... (possit, posset)**
10. **Orpheus ad Inferos ibat ut Eurydicen .... (recipiat, reciperet)**

No. 187. Translate the following sentences.

1. **Galli nesciebant quid fieret.**
2. **Galli nesciebant quid factum esset.**
3. **Caesar cognoscere conatus est ubi Galli castra posuissent.**
4. **Caesar cognoscere conatus est ubi Galli castra ponerent.**
5. **Dux rogat quot naves amissae sint.**
6. **Dux rogat quot naves amittantur.**
7. **Nescio qualis miles sit.**
8. **Nescio qualis miles fuerit.**
9. **Nunc cognoscamus quid Caesar in Gallia agat.**
10. **Nunc cognoscamus quid Caesar in Gallia egerit.**

CHAPTER 39

READING

GAIUS JULIUS CAESAR

Caesar was born in Rome, of a noble family, in 100 B.C. He was educated as an orator and lawyer, but soon turned to politics and became consul in 59 B.C. For the next seven years he was proconsul in Gaul, where he was successful in subduing and conquering the Gallic tribes. The Commentaries on the Gallic War are a military history of the period. Caesar's refusal to surrender the command of his army led to Civil War, his long dictatorship, and political turmoil, resulting in his assassination in 44 B.C.

One of the first problems that Caesar encountered in Gaul was a movement of the Helvetii tribe, which was inspired by an ambitious nobleman of the tribe, Orgetorix, as the following passage shows.

Apud Helvetios longe nobilissimus fuit et divitissimus Orgetorix.	By far the noblest and richest man among the Helvetii was Orgetorix.
Is, M. Messalla et M. Pupio Pisone consulibus, regni cupiditate inductus coniurationem nobilitatis fecit, et civitati persuasit ut de finibus suis cum omnibus copiis exirent:	In the consulships of Marcus Mesalla and Marcus Pupius Piso, led on by a desire for kingship he made an alliance of the nobility and persuaded the state to withdraw from its territory with all its forces:
perfacile esse, cum virtute omnibus praestarent, totius Galliae imperio potiri.	[he said that] it was very easy, since they excelled all men in bravery, to obtain control of the whole of Gaul.
Auctoritate Orgetorigis permoti, constituerunt ea quae ad proficiscendum pertinerent comparare, iumentorum et carrorum quam maximum numerum coemere, sementes quam maximas facere ut in itinere copia frumenti suppeteret,	Aroused by the prestige of Orgetorix, they decided to get together those things which pertained to the departure, to purchase the greatest possible number of beasts of burden and baggage waggons, to make the greatest possible sow-

cum proximis civitatibus pacem et amicitiam confirmare.

ings, so that the supply of corn would suffice on the journey, to strengthen their peace and friendship with the nearest states.

Ad eas res conficiendas biennium sibi satis esse duxerunt:[1] **in tertium annum profectionem lege confirmant.**

They reckoned that a two year period was sufficient for them to complete those preparations: they confirmed the departure by law for the third year.

Ad eas res conficiendas Orgetorix deligitur.

Orgetorix was chosen to complete these arrangements.

(Adapted from *Caesar—De Bello Gallico I, 2 and 3*)

[1] Note the meaning of **duco** in this context.

Vocabulary

Nouns

cupiditas, cupiditatis, *f.*, desire
conuiratio, coniurationis, *f.*, alliance, plot
nobilitas, nobilitatis, *f.*, fame, nobility
iumentum, i, *n.*, beast of burden, mule, ass
carrus, i, *m.*, baggage waggon
sementis, -is, *f.*, a sowing
biennium, -i, *n.*, a period of two years (biennial)

Verbs

induco, inducere, induxi, inductus, lead in, lead on, induce, excite
praesto, praestare, praestiti, praestitus, stand out, excel
permoveo, permovere, permovi, permotus, move deeply, excite, arouse
pertineo, pertinere, pertinui, —, reach, relate, concern, pertain
comparo, comparare, comparavi, comparatus, bring together, compare
coemo, coemere, coemi, coemptus, purchase, buy up
suppeto, suppetere, suppetivi, suppetitus, be available, suffice
confirmo, confirmare, confirmavi, confirmatus, establish, strengthen, confirm

Adjectives

nobilis, e, famous, noble
dives, divitis, rich
perfacilis, e, very easy

THE VERB: GERUND AND GERUNDIVE

1. Formation

The Gerund is a *verbal noun* and is formed by adding **-ndum** to the stem of the verb. Thus:

amandum	loving	**capiendum**	capturing
habendum	having	**audiendum**	hearing
ducendum	leading	**ferendum**	bearing

The Gerundive is formed in the same way, but since it is a *verbal adjective* it has the same endings as an adjective of the 1st and 2nd declensions.

amandus, a, um	being loved, to be loved
habendus, a, um	being had, to be had
ducendus, a, um	being led, to be led
capiendus, a, um	being captured, to be captured
audiendus, a, um	being heard, to be heard

The Gerund of **eo** is **eundum. Sum, possum, fio, volo** and **malo** have no Gerund.

2. Use

The Gerund is a verbal noun, as the Infinitive often is. The Infinitive can be used only as a Nominative or an Accusative. The Gerund, therefore, is normally used to supply the other cases. It is not used in the Nominative and only in the Accusative when it follows a preposition.

Nominative

natare	**Natare difficile est**	Swimming is difficult

Accusative

natare	**Puer natare amat**	The boy likes swimming
natandum	**Pisces ad natandum nati sunt**	Fish were born for swimming

Genitive

natandi	**Ars natandi**	The art of swimming

Dative

natando	**Puer natando operam dat**	The boy gives attention to swimming

Ablative

natando	**Flumen natando transiit**	He crossed the river by swimming

Like the Infinitive, a Gerund can have its own object.

Spes est urbem capiendi. There is hope of capturing the city.

However, the use of a Gerund with a direct object is usually to be avoided in Latin. Instead the Gerundive is used.

Spes est urbis capiendae. There is hope of the city being taken.

In the Nominative (and occasionally in the Accusative) the Gerundive has a special meaning and expresses obligation or necessity

Urbs capienda est. The city is *to be* captured.

In this kind of expression the person on whom the necessity or obligation falls must be in the Dative case.

Urbs nobis capienda est. The city is to be captured by us. *or* We must capture the city.

The Ablative of **causa**, cause or reason, is often used after a noun in the Genitive case to mean for the sake of, or on account of.

virtutis causa for the sake of courage

It is also used quite often with a Gerund or a Gerundive to express purpose.

oppidi capiendi causa for the sake of capturing the town
in order to capture the town

ROMAN DATES—THE YEARS

The Romans dated their years from the foundation of Rome. Their dates are given therefore **A.U.C. (anno urbis conditae,** in the year of the founding of the city.)

The traditional date for the foundation of Rome was 753 B.C., so that if a date is given A.U.C. we can find its equivalent B.C. by subtracting it from 754, or its equivalent A.D. by subtracting 753 from it. Thus 700 A.U.C. is 54 B.C. and 773 A.U.C. is A.D. 20.

However, most Roman writers give dates by the names of the two men who were consuls for the year. Thus in the passage of Caesar we have just read, the date is fixed by the phrase, **M. Messalla et M. Pupio Pisone consulibus** (61 B.C.).

Practice Exercises

No. 188. Complete the following sentences by adding the appropriate form of the Gerund or the Gerundive. Choose your answer from the words in parentheses

1. .... **ad castra celeriter pervenimus (Currendo, Currendi)**
2. **Hostes nobis .... sunt (vincendi, vincendo)**

3. **Nonne Psyche spem mariti .... habet? (recipiendum, recipiendi)**
4. **Fietne Caesar clarus ad Galliam .... ? (eundam, eundo)**
5. **Ad eas res .... Orgetorix deligitur. (conficiendum, conficiendas)**
6. **Lingua Latina .... sapiens fio. (discendo, discenda)**
7. **Nostri impetu .... castra servaverunt (faciendi, faciendo)**
8. **Duce necato multa nobis .... sunt. (patienda, patiendi)**
9. **Iovis .... causa ad templum iimus (laudandi, laudanda)**
10. **Num Brutum Caesaris .... paenituit? (interficiendum, interficiendi)**

No. 189. Translate the following sentences.

1. **Linguae Latinae discendae causa hic solus sedeo.**
2. **Ut linguam Latinam discam his solus sedeo.**
3. **Nonne linguae Latinae discendae te taedet?**
4. **Legati Caesari nuntiaverunt nullam spem esse exercitus servandi.**
5. **Troiani nesciebant quid in equo esset.**
6. **Athenis captis cives feminas ad insulas portaverunt ne a Persis interficerentur.**
7. **Helvetii dixerunt eas res Oretorigi conficiendas esse.**
8. **Tam latum mare est ut id natando transire non possimus.**
9. **Psychen scire non oportebat qualem maritum haberet.**
10. **Psyche nesciebat utrum sorores audiendae essent necne.**

CHAPTER 40

READING

In the course of attending to the arrangements for the migration, Orgetorix intrigues with the leading men of two other Gallic tribes.

Orgetorix sibi legationem ad civitates suscepit.	Orgetorix himself undertook the embassies to the states.
In eo itinere persuadet Castico Catamantaloedis filio Sequano, cuius pater regnum in Sequanis multos annos obtinuerat et a senatu populi Romani amicus appellatus erat, ut regnum in civitate sua occuparet quod pater ante habuerat;	On that journey he persuaded Casticus, the Sequanian, the son of Catamantaloedes, whose father had held the kingship among the Sequani for many years and had been named a friend of the Roman people by the senate, to seize the kingship in his state which his father had held before him;
itemque Dumnorigi Aeduo fratri Diviciaci, qui eo tempore principatum in civitate obtinebat ac maxime plebi acceptus erat, ut idem conaretur persuadet, eique filiam suam in matrimonium dat.	he also persuaded Dumnorix, the Aeduan, the brother of Diviciacus, who at that time held the sovereignty in the state and was very popular with the people, to attempt the same thing, and he gave him his daughter in marriage.
Perfacile factu esse illis probat conata perficere, propterea quod ipse suae civitatis imperium obtenturus esset:	He convinced them that it was very easy (to do) to carry out those undertakings, because of the fact that he himself intended to hold the power in his own state:
non esse dubium quin totius Galliae plurimum Helvetii possent;	[he said that] there was no doubt that the Helvetii were the most powerful tribe of the whole of Gaul;
se suis copiis suoque exercitu illis regna conciliaturum confirmat.	He asserted that he would win their kingdoms for them with his own forces and his own army.

Hac oratione adducti inter se fidem et ius iurandum dant, et regno occupato per tres potentissimos ac firmissimos populos totius Galliae sese potiri posse sperant.

Led on by this speech they gave a mutual pledge and an oath, and hoped that when the kingdom had been seized they could gain possession of all Gaul through its three most powerful and strongest peoples.

(Adapted from *Caesar—De Bello Gallico I, 3*)

Vocabulary

Nouns

legatio, legationis, *f.*, embassy, legation
frater, fratris (fratrium), *m.*, brother (fraternal)
principatus, principatus, *m.*, leadership, sovereignty
plebs, plebis, *f.*, the common people (plebeian)
fides, fidei, *f.*, faith, pledge (fidelity)
ius iurandum, iuris iurandi, *n.*, oath

Adjectives

dubius, a, um, doubtful, uncertain
potens, potentis, able, mighty, powerful, potent
firmus, a, um, firm, strong

Verbs

probo, probare, probavi, probatus, approve, show, prove (probation)
perficio, perficere, perfeci, perfectus, carry out, accomplish, finish (perfect)
concilio, conciliare, conciliavi, conciliatus, reconcile, win over, win (conciliate)

Adverbs

item, moreover, also
propterea, therefore, on that account

NOUN CLAUSES

We have already seen (page 227) that clauses which express Indirect Questions are noun clauses. A noun clause with its verb in the Subjunctive mood is also used after certain Latin verbs which imply acts of the will, e.g., verbs of 'commanding', 'exhorting', 'warning', 'persuading', 'asking', etc. Such clauses are clauses of *Indirect Command*, and are introduced by **ut** or, if negative, **ne.**

The following verbs are among those that require this construction.

impero (Object in the Dative case) I command
rogo I ask
peto I ask, seek
persuadeo (Object in the Dative case) I persuade
constituo I decide
permitto (Object in the Dative case) I permit, allow
oro I beg
moneo I warn

All of these verbs are followed by a noun clause of Indirect Command introduced by **ut** or, if negative, **ne,** and having a verb in the Subjunctive mood.

Ei impero ut eat.	I order him to go.
Eum rogo ut eat.	I ask him to go.
Ab eo peto ut eat.	I ask him to go.
Ei persuadeo ut eat.	I persuade him to go.
Constituo ut eat.	I decide that he should go.
Ei permitto ut eat	I allow him to go.
Eum oro ut eat.	I beg him to go.
Moneo ut eat.	I warn him to go.

Note, however, that **iubeo,** I command, **veto,** I forbid, I order not, **patior,** I allow, **volo,** I wish, **nolo,** I do not wish, **malo,** I prefer, **cupio,** I desire, require an Accusative and Infinitive construction.

Ei impero ut eat.	I order him to go.
Eum ire iubeo.	I order him to go.

'Hindering, preventing and forbidding'

Verbs of hindering, preventing and forbidding (e.g., **impedio, deterreo)** take a noun clause of Indirect Command introduced by **ne, quominus** or **quin** and having a verb in the Subjunctive mood. If the verb of hindering, preventing or forbidding is itself positive, **ne** or **quominus** is used. If it is negative, **quin** (occasionally **quominus**) is used.

Eum deterreo ne eat.	I forbid him to go.
Eum non impedio quin eat.	I do not hinder him from going.

'Doubting'

Negative expressions of 'doubt' are followed by a noun clause introduced by **quin** and having its verb in the Subjunctive mood.

Non dubito quin eat.	I do not doubt that he is going.
Non erat dubium quin totius Galliae plurimum Helvetii possent.	There was no doubt that the Helvetii were the most powerful tribe of the whole of Gaul.

'Fearing'

Verbs of fearing in Latin are followed by a noun clause introduced by **ne** or, if negative, **ut**.

Timeo ne eat.	I fear 'may he not go'.
	I fear lest he go.
	I fear that he is going.
Timeo ut eat.	I fear 'may he go'.
	I fear that he is not going.

In all of these noun clauses, the usual rules for the sequence of tenses apply.

THE SENATE

The Senate existed as an advisory council during the time of the kings and it survived in this capacity when the monarchy was replaced by the republic. During the monarchy the senators were chosen by the kings; later they were chosen by the consuls and then by the censors, who, as their title suggests, also had the right to withdraw membership from persons guilty of misconduct. However, the main source of recruitment was through the election of magistrates, since any man who had held office as consul, praetor or aedile was entitled to membership of the Senate. Later the office of quaestor also gave entrance to the Senate. In this way, the Senate was recruited indirectly by election.

The main functions of the Senate were to advise the magistrates and to ratify formally the decisions of the popular assemblies. It was also responsible for assigning the various duties of the magistrates and pro-magistrates and for the administration of the public finances. War and foreign policy in general were effectively in its control.

Although it is said that Romulus instituted a Senate of 100 members, the number increased greatly and was finally fixed at 600 by Augustus. Julius Caesar had raised it to 900.

The membership of the Senate included both patricians (noblemen) and plebeians and a distinction was always made between them. The patrician senators were called **patres** and the plebeians **conscripti**. Hence the term used by speakers addressing the whole body was often **patres[et]conscripti.**

Practice Exercises

No. 190. Complete the following sentences by inserting the appropriate adverb or conjunction. Choose your answer from the words in parentheses.

1. **Me rogat .... veniam. (ut, quin)**
2. **Me rogat .... venias. (ut, cur)**

3. **Me deterret .... veniam (ut, ne)**
4. **Me non deterret .... veniam (ne, quin)**
5. **Non dubium est .... veniam (ut, quin)**
6. **Timet .... veniam (ut, ne)**
7. **Orgetorix Castico persuadet .... regnum in civitate sua occuparet. (ut, quin)**
8. **Equites hostes impediverunt .... in aciem nostram impetum facerent. (ne, ut)**
9. **Ventus naves non impedivit .... ad portum ante noctem pervenirent (ne, quin)**
10. **Psyche Venerem rogavit .... sibi auxilium dare vellet necne. (utrum, ut)**

No. 191. Translate the following sentences.

1. **Orgetorix civibus persuasit ut fines suos cum omnibus copiis relinquerent.**
2. **Nostros monere non potuimus ut se reciperent.**
3. **Milites timebant ne hostes se circumstarent et vincerent.**
4. **Non dubium est quin Caesar omnibus virtute praestet.**
5. **Venus Psychen deterruit ne maritum suum spectaret.**
6. **Cupido ad Psychen noctu veniebat ne eum videret.**
7. **Sorores Psychen rogabant quis maritus esset et num eum vidisset.**
8. **Milites a Caesare petiverunt ut contra hostes se duceret.**
9. **Orgetorix plebem rogavit num sibi permittere vellet ut legationem ad civitates susciperet.**
10. **Quid faciet Caesar ut Orgetorigem et Casticum et Dumnorigem impediat ne totius Galliae potiantur.**

CHAPTER 41

READING

The intrigues of Orgetorix are discovered by the Helvetii. He escapes before his trial but dies, possibly by his own hand. The Helvetii, however, continue with the preparations for their migration and begin to move. This brings them into conflict with Caesar and with several other Gallic tribes who appeal to Caesar for help. Caesar is hindered in his attempts to deal with them by the failure of the Aedui, another Gallic tribe, to provide the food supplies for his army which they had promised. He discovers that Dumnorix is responsible for this.

In this passage we hear of Caesar's reluctance to deal with Dumnorix because of his regard for his brother, Diviciacus.

Quibus rebus cognitis, cum ad has suspiciones certissimae res accederent, Caesar satis esse causae arbitrabatur quare in Dumnorigem aut ipse animadverteret aut civitatem animadvertere iuberet.

After these things had been discovered, when most indisputable facts were supporting these suspicions, Caesar thought that there was sufficient reason why either he himself should punish Dumnorix or he should order the state to punish him.

His omnibus rebus unum repugnabat, quod Diviciaci fratris summum in populum Romanum studium, summam in se voluntatem, egregiam fidem, iustitiam, temperantiam cognoverat;

To all of these facts there was one objection, the fact that he knew of the very great zeal of his brother Diviciacus towards the Roman people, his very great goodwill towards Caesar himself, his outstanding loyalty, his sense of justice, his moderation;

nam ne eius supplicio Diviciaci animum offenderet verebatur.

for he was afraid that by the punishment of Dumnorix he might wound the feelings of Diviciacus.

Itaque prius quam quicquam conaretur, Diviciacum ad se vocari iubet et, cotidianis interpretibus remotis, per C. Valerium Procillum, principem Galliae provinciae, familiarem suum, cui sum-

And so before he attempted anything, he ordered Diviciacus to be summoned to him and, after he had sent away the usual interpreters, he spoke with him through Caius Valerius Procillus, a lead-

mam omnium rerum fidem habebat, cum eo colloquitur:	ing man in the province of Gaul, a friend of his, in whom he had the greatest confidence in all matters:
simul commonefacit quae ipso praesente in concilio Gallorum de Dumnorige sint dicta, et ostendit quae separatim quisque de eo apud se dixerit.	he reminded him at the same time of what had been said about Dumnorix in the council of the Gauls when he (Diviciacus) himself had been present, and stated what each had said separately about Dumnorix to him (Caesar).
Petit atque hortatur, ut sine eius offensione animi vel ipse de eo causa cognita statuat, vel civitatem statuere iubeat.	He begged and urged him that without offence to his feelings either Caesar himself should hear the case and pass judgement on him or he should order the state to judge him.

(Adapted from *Caesar—De Bello Gallico I, 19*)

Vocabulary

Nouns

suspicio, suspicionis, *f.*, suspicion
voluntas, voluntatis, *f.*, wish, will, goodwill (voluntary)
iustitia, ae, *f.*, justice
temperantia, ae, *f.*, moderation, self-control, temperance
supplicium, i, *n.*, punishment
interpres, interpretis, *m.* or *f.*, interpreter
princeps, principis, *m.*, leader
familiaris, familiaris, *m.* or *f.*, friend (familiar)
concilium, i, *n.*, council

Adjectives

certus, a, um, certain, sure
egregius, a, um, excellent, outstanding
cotidianus, a, um, daily, usual
praesens, praesentis, present

Verbs

accedo, accedere, accessi, accessurus, approach, be added to, agree, support (accede)
repugno, repugnare, repugnavi, repugnatus, resist, oppose (repugnant)
offendo, offendere, offendi, offensus, wound, offend
colloquor, colloqui, collocutus sum, speak with (colloquial)
commonefacio, commonefacere, commonefeci, commonefactus, remind
ostendo, ostendere, ostendi, ostentus, point out, show (ostentatious)

removeo, removere, removi, remotus, remove, send away

statuo, statuere, statui, statutus, decide, judge, (statute)

Adverbs

prius, before, previously

priusquam, before

separatim, separately

Pronouns

quisquam, any, anyone (**quis** is declined in the usual way, except that the Neuter Nominative and Accusative singular is **quicquam**)

quisque, whoever, each (of more than two) (**quis** declined normally)

TEMPORAL CLAUSES

We have already met some temporal clauses which in Latin have a verb in the Indicative mood, e.g., **postquam,** after, **ubi,** when, **ut,** when, which are followed by a Perfect Indicative.

A. Temporal clauses requiring an Indicative verb

Temporal clauses in Latin (with the exception of those uses of **cum** which are discussed below) normally require a verb in the Indicative mood, provided that their meaning is *purely temporal.* This is always the case with:

ubi, when
ut, when
postquam, after
simul ac, as soon as

cum primum, as soon as
quotiens, as often as
dum, while
quamdiu, as long as

Ubi Romam venit, Caesarem vidit. When he had come to Rome, he saw Caesar.

Several points, however, need to be noted:

1. Where the time is past time (as in the example above), Latin uses a Perfect tense, although English prefers the Pluperfect. Where a Pluperfect is used in Latin, it indicates the repeated occurrence of the action.

   Ubi Romam venerat, Caesarem vidit.
   Whenever he came to Rome, he saw Caesar.

2. **dum** requires a Present tense when it introduces a clause which refers to a long period of time, *in only a part of which* the action of the main clause occurred. Thus:

   Dum hostes impetum faciunt, Crassus necatus est. While the enemy were making an attack, Crassus was killed.

but

Dum vivam, Caesarem laudabo. While I live (i.e., as long as), I shall praise Caesar

B. Temporal clauses which sometimes have a Subjunctive verb

These clauses follow the rule given above and have an Indicative verb if their meaning is purely temporal. However, temporal clauses that refer to the future, e.g., those introduced by **donec,** until, **priusquam,** before, **antequam,** before, sometimes have more than a purely temporal meaning. Frequently they contain the additional idea of *purpose.* Where this is so, they must have a verb in the Subjunctive mood. Again the normal rules for the sequence of tenses apply. Thus:

Priusquam captus sum, laetus eram. Before I was captured, I was happy

but

Priusquam capi possem, effugi. I escaped before I could be captured (i.e., in order not to be captured)

Note that **antequam** and **priusquam** are sometimes used as **ante** .... **quam** .... and **prius** .... **quam** ....

Caesar prius Romam venit quam consul factus est. Caesar came to Rome before he became consul.

CUM

1. When **cum** introduces a clause that refers to a present or future action, the verb is Indicative.

   Cum hoc disces, sapiens eris. When you learn this, you will be wise.
   Cum hoc discis, miser es. When you are learning this, you are unhappy.

2. When **cum** introduces a clause that refers to a past action, the verb is usually Subjunctive. When the action of the **cum** clause is *coextensive* with that of the main clause, an Imperfect Subjunctive is used.

   Cum hoc disceres, miser eras. When you were learning this, you were unhappy.

   When the action of the **cum** clause is *completed before* the action of the main clause, a Pluperfect Subjunctive is used.

   Cum hoc didicisses, sapiens eras. When you had learnt this, you were wise.

   Note that these clauses express not only a temporal relationship but also a *causal* connection. This is why the Subjunctive must be used. Thus:

3. When the significance of the **cum** clause is *purely temporal*, the indicative is used.

Cum tu hoc discebas, tum ego dormiebam.	When you were learning this, at that time I was asleep.

4. When **cum** means 'whenever', an Indicative verb is used. (See A.1, page 244.) When the main verb is Present, the verb in the **cum** clause must be *Perfect*.

Cum te vidi, laetus sum.	Whenever I see you, I am happy.

When the main verb is Past, the verb in the **cum** clause must be *Pluperfect*.

Cum te videram, laetus eram.	Whenever I saw you, I was happy.

ROMAN DATES—THE MONTHS

Mensis Januarius. The month of Janus, the god of gates and doors who had two heads so that he could see inside and outside. As the god of gates and doors, Janus was the god of all beginnings and hence of the New Year.

Mensis Februarius. Februarius is derived from **febris,** fever, and **februa,** purification rites. A festival of purification was celebrated each year on the 15th of February. This was called the Lupercalia and it later became a Christian feast of purification.

Mensis Martius. The month of Mars, god of war. It was the first month of the year, before Caesar's reformed Calendar was introduced in 45 B.C.

Mensis Aprilis. Aprilis may be derived from the verb, **aperire,** to open. If this is so, then the allusion presumably is to the opening of the trees and flowers with the beginning of spring. This month certainly contained a festival of Ceres.

Mensis Maius. Probably the month of the goddess Maia, the mother of Mercury. Sacrifices were made to her on the first day of this month by Roman women.

Mensis Iunius. Possibly the month of Juno, the queen of the gods.

Mensis Iulius. This month was originally called **Quintilis** because it was the fifth month of the old calendar. In 44 B.C., after the assassination of Julius Caesar, it was renamed in his honour.

Mensis Augustus. Originally **Sextilis,** the sixth month of the old calendar, this month was renamed in honour of Rome's first emperor, Augustus Caesar.

The other months are the seventh, eighth, ninth and tenth months of the old calendar, although suggestions were made, and occasionally acted on temporarily, for renaming them after some emperors and their relatives. This prompted the emperor, Tiberius, to say to the Senate when they suggested renaming November after him, 'What will you do, Conscript Fathers, if you have thirteen Caesars?'

Practice Exercises

No. 192. Complete the following sentences by adding to the temporal clause a verb in the appropriate tense and mood. Choose your answer from the words in parentheses.

1. **Hostes celeriter se receperunt antequam aggredi .... (possemus, poteramus)**
2. **Postquam hostes .... oppidum incendimus (vicimus, viceramus)**
3. **Priusquam .... gladium filio suo dedit (abiit, abiret)**
4. **Caesar suos in castris manere iussit donec equites .... (redierint, redirent)**
5. **Cum milites Gallum .... ad Caesarem eum semper ferebant (cepissent, ceperant)**
6. **Dum per Galliam iter ...., multi mortui sunt. (facimus, faciebamus)**
7. **Cum Psyche maritum ...., ille excitatus est (spectaret, spectavisset)**
8. **Cum Psyche maritum ...., ille alis celeribus eam reliquit. (spectaret, spectavisset)**
9. **Cum primum Ceres Psychen ...., ei auxilium dare volebat, (viderat, vidit)**
10. **Britanni prius barbari erant quam Romani ad Britanniam .... (pervenerunt, pervenirent)**

No. 193. Translate the following sentences.

1. **Ubi castra capta sunt ad montes nos recepimus.**
2. **Cum castra capta essent ad montes nos recepimus.**
3. **Castris captis ad montes nos recepimus.**
4. **Postquam castra capta sunt ad montes nos recepimus.**
5. **Hero verita est ne Leander moreretur.**
6. **Dum urbs ardet, Aeneas rediit ut uxorem suam inveniret.**
7. **Pluto Orpheo imperat ne Eurydicen spectet.**
8. **Theseus tam fortis erat ut Minotaurum interficeret.**
9. **Caesar ante de Dumnorige supplicium sumere nolebat quam cum Diviciaco collocutus est.**
10. **Caesar Diviciacum rogavit utrum se ipsum de Dumnorige statuere oporteret an ille civitatem statuere iubere vellet.**

I

Revise IRE, VENIRE passive

conj of pres & past subj,
3 pl. pluperf, pf, impf.

CHAPTER 42

READING

CICERO'S LETTERS

Among the extant works of Cicero is a large number of letters written by him to his friends and relatives. They have been collected under three headings: those written to Atticus, his close friend **(ad Atticum),** those written to his other friends **(ad Familiares)** and those he wrote to his brother, Quintus **(ad Quintum fratrem).** The collection also includes some letters written by others to Cicero and to each other.

The following letter was written in 54 or 55 B.C. (700 or 701 A.U.C.) by Cicero to Marius Tullius Tiro, his freedman, secretary and assistant. It was Tiro who was largely responsible for collecting and preserving Cicero's letters.

M.T.C.S.P.D. Tironi (Marcus Tullius Cicero salutem plurimam dicit Tironi)

Marcus Tullius Cicero offers a very hearty greeting to Tiro.

Aegypta ad me venit pr. Idus Apr.

Aegypta came to me on April 12th.

Is etsi mihi nuntiavit te plane febri carere et belle habere, tamen, quod negavit te potuisse ad me scribere, curam mihi attulit, et eo magis, quod Hermia, quem eodem die venire oportuerat, non venerat.

Although he informed me that you were completely free of your fever and were doing well, nevertheless, because he said that you had not been able to write to me, he brought me anxiety and the more so, because Hermia, who should have arrived on the same day, had not arrived.

Incredibili sum sollicitudine de tua valetudine, qua si me liberaris, ego te omni cura liberabo.

I am in an unbelievable state of anxiety about your health, and if you free me from this, I will free you from all your duties.

Plura scriberem, si iam putarem libenter te legere posse.

I would write more, if I thought you could now read it with pleasure.

Ingenium tuum, quod ego maximi facio, confer ad te mihi tibique conservandum.	Apply your talents, which I hold in the highest esteem, to keeping yourself safe for me and for you.
Cura te etiam atque etiam diligenter.	Look after yourself carefully (again and again I say it).
Vale.	Good-bye.
Scripta iam epistola Hermia venit.	When the letter had already been written, Hermia arrived.
Accepi tuam epistolam vacillantibus litterulis, nec mirum, tam gravi morbo.	I have received your letter with its wavering handwriting, nor is it surprising after so serious an illness.
Ego ad te Aegyptam misi, quod nec inhumanus est et te visus est mihi diligere, ut is tecum esset, et cum eo coquum, quo uterere.	I have sent Aegypta to you, so that he might be with you, because he is not uncultured and he seemed to me to be fond of you, and with him I have sent a cook for you to make use of.
Vale.	Goodbye.

(Cicero—*Epistulae ad Familiares XVI, 15*)

Vocabulary

Nouns

salus, salutis, *f.*, health, safety, greeting (salutary)
Idus, Iduum, *f.*, the Ides
febris, febris, *f.*, fever
sollicitudo, sollicitudinis, *f.*, anxiety, solicitude
valetudo, valetudinis, *f.*, health, state of health
litterula, ae, *f.*, a little letter
morbus, i, *m.*, disease, sickness
coquus, i, *m.*, cook
epistola, ae, *f.*, letter (epistle)

Adjectives

Aprilis, e, of April
incredibilis, e, unbelievable
mirus, a, um, wonderful, surprising (miracle)
inhumanus, a, um, rude, uncultured

Conjunction

etsi, although

Verbs

adfero, adferre, attuli, adlatus, bring

lego, legere, legi, lectus, read (lecture)

confero, conferre, contuli, conlatus, bring together, collect, apply

conservo, conservare, conservavi, conservatus, keep safe, preserve

vacillo, vacillare, vacillavi, vacillatus, stagger, waver, vacillate

diligo, diligere, dilexi, dilectus, value, love

utor, uti, usus sum, use (Object must be in the Ablative case)

Adverbs

plane, plainly, completely

belle, prettily, neatly, well

libenter, gladly, with pleasure

diligenter, carefully

eo, for that reason

CONCESSIVE CLAUSES

Concessive clauses are those clauses that are introduced by 'although' **(quamquam, quamvis)** or 'even if' **(etsi, tametsi, etiamsi).**

A. 'Although'

1. Quamquam

If the clause is introduced by **quamquam,** the verb is in the Indicative mood.

Quamquam audis, non discis. Although you are listening, you are not learning.

The particular force of **quamquam** with an Indicative verb is to admit the statement contained in the clause as a *fact* (e.g., in this example, 'I concede that you are in fact listening, but . . .').

2. Quamvis

If the clause is introduced by **quamvis,** the verb must be in the Subjunctive mood.

Quamvis audias, non discis. Although you are listening, you are not learning.

The particular force of **quamvis** is to imply 'in spite of', and it is because of this shade of meaning that it has a Subjunctive verb (i.e., in this example, 'In spite of the fact that you are listening . . .' *or* 'Let you listen as much as you please. . . .')

3. Etsi

Note that **etsi** is also used to mean 'although', like **quamquam,** as we saw in the extract from Cicero above.

B. 'Even if'

Etsi, tametsi and **etiamsi** are compounds of **si,** if, and the rules governing their use are the same as those which follow for Conditional clauses.

CONDITIONAL CLAUSES

Conditional clauses differ from the other types of clause we have already looked at in that often what is stated in them *affects the mood of the verb in the main clause.*

If I had been listening, I *would have* learnt.

This means that in what follows we must keep *both clauses* in mind.

Conditional clauses may be divided into two main types—those that are quite *open* and *straightforward,* in that they contain no further implication than what is stated, and, therefore, have verbs in the Indicative mood, and those that do contain a further implication and therefore require Subjunctive verbs.

If you listened, you learnt. (Quite open and straightforward—Indicative verbs)

If you had listened, you would have learnt. ('But you did not listen' is clearly implied here, i.e., the condition is *unfulfilled*—Subjunctive verbs)

We may further classify Conditional clauses according to *time,* i.e., whether they are past, present, or future.

We, therefore, have six regular types of conditional clause—past straightforward, past unfulfilled, present straightforward, present unfulfilled, future straightforward, future remote (i.e., unlikely to be fulfilled).

The rules that govern the treatment of these conditions in Latin are as follows:

1. Straightforward or Open Conditions

These conditions have an *Indicative* verb in both clauses.

Past.

Si audivisti, didicisti.	If you listened, you learnt.
Si audiebas, discebas.	If you were listening, you were learning.

Perfect or Imperfect Indicative in both clauses

Present

Si audis, discis. If you listen, you learn.

Present Indicative in both clauses

Future

Si audies, disces. If you [will] listen, you will learn.

Future Indicative in both clauses

Note that the Future condition has a Future tense *in both clauses*, whereas English has a Present tense in the 'if' clause.

Note also that often in Future conditions the 'if' clause has a verb in the Future Perfect, if the action of the 'if' clause is completed before the action of the main clause takes place.

Si Romam ieris, Caesarem videbis. If you go (lit. will have gone) to Rome, you will see Caesar

2. **Conditions that have further implications**
These conditions have a *Subjunctive* verb in *both* clauses.

Past.

Si audivisses, didicisses. If you had listened [but you did not], you would have learnt.

Pluperfect Subjunctive in both clauses

Present.

Si audires, disceres. If you were listening [but you are not], you would be learning.

Imperfect Subjunctive in both clauses

Future.

Si audias, discas. If you were to listen [but you will not], you would learn.

Present Subjunctive in both clauses

3. **Some further points should be noted.**

(a) **Mixed conditions.** Sometimes a conditional sentence may contain an 'if' clause (protasis) of one of the types above with a main clause (apodosis) of another type.

Si audivisses, sapiens iam esses. If you had listened (***Past***), you would now be wise (***Present***)

(b) **Negative conditions.** These are introduced in Latin by **nisi,** 'if not', 'unless', when the whole clause is negative. If only one word is to be negatived, then **si . . . non . . .** is used.

Nisi bene laborabis, non laudaberis.	Unless you work well, you will not be praised.
Si non bene laboras, non laudaris.	If you work badly (not well), you are not praised.

ROMAN DATES: THE DAYS

There were three main days in each month of the Roman calendar. The first day of the month was called the Kalends **(Kalendae),** the fifth was called the Nones **(Nonae)** and the thirteenth the Ides **(Idus).** But,

In March, July, October, May
The Nones fall on the seventh day
and the Ides on the fifteenth.

All the days of the month were numbered according to their relationship with these three days. The day immediately preceding the Kalends, Nones or Ides was **Pridie Kalendas, Nonas** or **Idus.** The other dates were reckoned according to the number of days up to and including the next key day. Thus:

Nonae Ianuariae (Non. Ian.)	January 5th
Pridie Nonas Ianuarias (prid. Non. Ian.)	January 4th
Ante diem tertium Nonas Ianuarias (a.d. III Non. Ian.)	January 3rd
Ante diem quartum Nonas Ianuarias (a.d. IV Non. Ian.)	January 2nd
Kalendae Ianuariae (Kal. Ian.)	January 1st
Pridie Kalendas Ianuarias (prid. Kal. Ian.)	December 31st
Ante diem tertium Kalendas Ianuarias (a.d. III Kal. Ian.)	December 30th
and so on until we come to	
Idus Decembres (Id. Dec.)	December 13th

Practice Exercises

No. 194. Complete the following sentences by adding the appropriate form of the verb. Choose your answers from the words in parentheses.

1. **Si impetum ...., facillime vincemus. (facimus, fecerimus)**
2. **Si Romam ...., Caesarem vidissemus. (iissemus, ieramus)**
3. **Quamvis Tiro aeger ...., epistulam scribere poterat. (erat, esset)**

4. **Etiamsi bene ...., linguam Latinam discere difficile erit (laboramus, laborabimus)**
5. **Si Ulixes Polyphemum vereatur, effugere non .... (possit, posset)**
6. **Quamquam Ulixes Polyphemum ...., mox effugiet (vereatur, veretur).**
7. **Si tum Helvetii oppressi essent, non nunc .... (pugnaremus, pugnavissemus)**
8. **Quamvis Persae exercitum maximum ...., non vicerunt. (habebant, haberent)**
9. **Si Icarus cum patre maneat, ... (servetur, servabitur)**
10. **Nisi Theseus fortis esset, in labyrinthum nunc non .... (intraret, intrat)**

No. 195. Translate the following sentences.

1. **Si Romae essemus, ad Circum Maximum ire possemus.**
2. **Etiamsi Orgetorix non mortuus esset, totius Galliae non potitus esset.**
3. **Quamvis Catalina Romam reliquisset, Cicero sciebat socios et amicos eius in urbe esse.**
4. **Postquam hostes oppidum reliquerunt, incolae rogaverunt utrum redire liceret necne.**
5. **Alia legendo et scribendo discimus, alia faciendo.**
6. **Quamvis Troia arderet, Aeneas rediit ut uxorem peteret.**
7. **Uxoris suae recipiendae causa Orpheus ad Inferos iit.**
8. **Ponte incendendo hostes deterruimus ne flumen transirent.**
9. **Nisi Psyche maritum vidisset, stultitiae eam non paenituisset.**
10. **Quamquam Tironem amamus, nunc cognoscamus quid Caesar in Gallia faciat.**

CHAPTER 43

READING

CAESAR

Dumnorix has been interviewed by both Caesar and Diviciacus. Caesar has contented himself with giving him a strong warning and appointing guards to watch his future behaviour.

After several setbacks, the war against the Helvetii has ended in victory for Caesar. In this passage, envoys from the other tribes come to Caesar to congratulate him on his victory.

Bello Helvetiorum confecto, totius fere Galliae legati, principes civitatum, ad Caesarem gratulatum[1] convenerunt:

When the war with the Helvetii had been completed, envoys of almost the whole of Gaul, the leaders of the states, gathered together to Caesar to congratulate him:

intellegere sese, tametsi pro veteribus Helvetiorum iniuriis populi Romani ab his poenas bello repetisset, tamen eam rem non minus ex usu terrae Galliae quam populi Romani accidisse;

[they said that] they understood that, although by the war he had been exacting punishment from the Helvetii for their old injuries to the Roman people, nevertheless that affair had turned out no less to the advantage of the land of Gaul than to the Roman people;

propterea quod eo consilio florentissimis rebus domos suas Helvetii reliquissent, uti toti Galliae bellum inferrent imperioque potirentur, locumque domicilio ex magna copia deligerent quem ex omni Gallia opportunissimum ac fructuosissimum iudicassent, reliquasque civitates stipendiarias haberent.

because of the fact that the Helvetii had left their homes when their affairs were flourishing with the intention of making war on the whole of Gaul and gaining the supreme power, and were choosing for their abode from a great abundance the place which they had decided was the most suitable and most fertile of all Gaul, and with the intention of having the other states as tributary to them.

[1] Note the use of the Supine after verbs of motion to imply purpose.

Petierunt uti sibi concilium totius Galliae in diem certam indicere idque Caesaris voluntate facere liceret:	They asked that they should be allowed to summon a meeting of the whole of Gaul for a fixed day and to do it with the Caesar's consent:
sese habere quasdam res quas ex communi consensu ab eo petere vellent.	they said that they had certain things which they wished to ask of him by common agreement.
Ea re permissa, diem concilio constituerunt et iure iurando ne quis enuntiaret, nisi quibus communi consilio mandatum esset, inter se sanxerunt.	When this had been allowed, they decided on a day for the meeting and ratified it with an oath among themselves so that no-one should make it known except those to whom orders should be given to do so by common policy.

(*Caesar—De Bello Gallico I, 30*)

Vocabulary

Nouns

usus, usus, *m.*, use, advantage; **ex usu,** of advantage

domicilium, i, *n.*, dwelling, domicile

consensus, us, *m.*, agreement, consensus

Adjectives

vetus, veteris, old (veteran)

opportunus, a, um, suitable, opportune

fructuosus, a, um, fruitful, abundant

stipendiarius, a, um, tributary (stipend)

communis, e, common, general

Verbs

gratulor, gratulari, gratulatus sum, be glad, congratulate

intellego, intellegere, intellexi, intellectus, understand

repeto, repetere, repetivi, repetitus, seek again, demand, exact

floreo, florere, florui, —, bloom, flourish

infero, inferre, intuli, inlatus, bring in, introduce; **bellum infero,** make war

iudico, iudicare, iudicavi, iudicatus, judge, decide (judiciary)

indico, indicere, indixi, indictus, proclaim, appoint, summon

enuntio, enuntiare, enuntiavi, enuntiatus, speak out, disclose, make known (enunciate)

mando, mandare, mandavi, mandatus, commit, entrust, order

sancio, sancire, sanxi, sanctus, make sacred, ratify (sanctify)

SUBORDINATE CLAUSES IN INDIRECT SPEECH

All clauses in Indirect Speech in Latin must have a Subjunctive verb. This means that those clauses (e.g., relative clauses and some temporal and concessive clauses) that normally have a verb in the Indicative mood have a Subjunctive verb when they form part of a speech that is reported. As always, the rules for the sequence of tenses apply.

Direct Speech

Puellam quae natat specto.	I am watching the girl who is swimming.

Indirect Speech

Primary Sequence

Dico me puellam quae natet spectare.	I say that I am watching the girl who is swimming.

Historic Sequence

Dixi me puellam quae nataret spectare.	I said that I was watching the girl who was swimming.

FINAL POINTS

In the last chapters all of the major Latin constructions have been dealt with. To aid understanding, they have been dealt with in their simplest forms. The student will find in his subsequent reading more complex forms of each of them. However, he should by now have sufficient understanding of the basic elements of Latin sentence construction to be able to cope with further modifications when he encounters them. In any case, if he is careful to obtain annotated editions of the texts he wishes to read, complex forms of these constructions will be explained to him there.

A LATIN ACROSTIC

R O T A S
O P E R A
T E N E T
A R E P O
S A T O R

This acrostic can be read in eight different directions. In four of them it makes:

rotas opera tenet arepo sator

In the other four directions it makes the same sentence with the words in reverse order.

If **arepo** is taken as a proper name, the sentence means:

'Arepo the sower carefully guides the wheels'

In 1868 this acrostic was found scratched on a piece of wall plaster in a house in the Roman city of Corinium (Cirencester). It was probably written there as a charm, since it was well known in the Middle Ages, when it was regarded as having magic powers. Similar arrangements of letters and numbers are often accredited with magic qualities by primitive peoples.

Practice Exercises

No. 196. Complete the following sentences by adding a verb in the appropriate tense and mood. Choose your answer from the words in parentheses.

1. **Quod bellum ...., dixit se domum rediturum esse (confectum erat, confectum esset).**
2. **Dixit se quod bellum .... domum rediturum esse (confectum erat, confectum esset)**
3. **Tu es homo quem diu .... (petivi, petiverim)**
4. **Dico te hominem esse quem diu .... (petivi, petiverim)**
5. **Quamquam aeger ...., ad curiam iit (erat, esset)**
6. **Dixit se ad curiam iturum esse, quamquam aeger .... (erat, esset)**
7. **Quia Diviciacus populi Romani amicus ...., Caesar de Dumnorige supplicium sumere nolebat. (erat, esset)**
8. **Caesar dixit se de Dumnorige supplicium sumere nolle quia Diviciacus populi Romani amicus .... (erat, esset)**
9. **Postquam hostes se ...., castra eorum intravimus (receperunt, recipissent)**
10. **Dux nobis imperavit ut castra hostium intraremus postquam hostes se .... (receperunt recepissent)**

No. 197. Translate the following passage.

Dumnorix begins to intrigue again as Caesar is preparing to invade Britain.

Caesar Dumnorigem secum habere in primis constituerat, quod eum cupidum rerum novarum, cupidum imperi, magni animi, magnae inter Gallos auctoritatis cognoverat. Accedebat huc quod in concilio Aeduorum Dumnorix dixerat sibi a Caesare regnum civitatis deferri. Id factum ex suis hospitibus Caesar cognoverat. Ille omnibus primo precibus petere contendit ut in Gallia relinqueretur, partim quod insuetus navigandi mare timeret, partim quod religionibus impediri se diceret. Postea quam id

obstinate sibi negari vidit, principes Galliae sollicitare hortarique coepit ut in continenti remanerent: non sine causa fieri ut Gallia omni nobilitate spoliaretur; id esse consilium Caesaris ut quos in conspectu Galliae interficere vereretur hos omnes in Britanniam traductos necaret; ius iurandum poscere ut quod esse ex usu Galliae intellexissent communi consilio administrarent. Haec a compluribus ad Caesarem deferebantur.

(Adapted from *Caesar—De Bello Gallico V*, 6)

FINAL REVISION (CHAPTERS 37–43)

VOCABULARY REVISION

Nouns

1. **curia**
2. **respublica**
3. **auctoritas**
4. **scelus**
5. **insidiae**
6. **furor**
7. **cupiditas**
8. **coniuratio**
9. **nobilitas**
10. **iumentum**
11. **frater**
12. **plebs**
13. **fides**
14. **iusiurandum**
15. **voluntas**
16. **supplicium**
17. **princeps**
18. **salus**
19. **morbus**
20. **usus**

1. senate house
2. state
3. power, authority
4. crime, wickedness
5. trap, ambush
6. rage, fury, passion
7. desire
8. alliance, plot
9. fame, nobility
10. beast of burden
11. brother
12. the common people
13. faith, pledge
14. oath
15. wish, will, goodwill
16. punishment
17. leader
18. health, safety, greeting
19. disease
20. use, advantage

Adjectives

1. **improbus**
2. **tantus**
3. **quantus**
4. **tot**
5. **quot**
6. **salvus**
7. **dives**
8. **potens**
9. **egregius**
10. **mirus**
11. **vetus**
12. **fructuosus**

1. bad, wicked
2. so great
3. how great
4. so many
5. how many
6. safe
7. rich
8. mighty, powerful
9. excellent, outstanding
10. wonderful
11. old
12. fruitful, abundant

Verbs

1. **obsideo**
2. **sentio**
3. **polliceor**
4. **circumsto**
5. **comperio**
6. **ignoro**
7. **vigilo**
8. **consumo**
9. **ago**
10. **praesto**
11. **comparo**
12. **coemo**
13. **confirmo**
14. **probo**
15. **perficio**
16. **repugno**
17. **colloquor**
18. **adfero**
19. **utor**
20. **intellego**

1. I besiege
2. I feel, perceive
3. I promise
4. I surround
5. I find out, discover
6. I don't know, am ignorant
7. I am awake, keep watch
8. I use up, spend
9. I carry on, do
10. I stand out, excel
11. I bring together, compare
12. I purchase, buy up
13. I establish, strengthen
14. I show, prove
15. I carry out, finish
16. I resist, I oppose
17. I speak with
18. I bring
19. I use
20. I understand

Adverbs

1. denique	**3. item**	**5. separatim**
2. quem ad modum	**4. propterea**	
1. finally, at last	3. moreover, also	5. separately
2. in what manner, how	4. therefore, on that account	

Practice Exercises

No. 198. Give the first person singular of all the Active Subjunctive tenses of the following.

1. **vigilo**	4. **perficio**	7. **vereor**	10. **molior**	13. **fio**
2. **sedeo**	5. **sentio**	8. **utor**	11. **sum**	14. **fero**
3. **ago**	6. **conor**	9. **patior**	12. **eo**	15. **volo**

No. 199. Translate the following sentences.

1. **Galli putabant se nostros facillime victuros esse.**
2. **Proelium tam longum fuit ut vix stare possim.**
3. **Num licebat Dumnorigi in Gallia manere donec Caesar a Britannia redierit?**
4. **Si rogavissemus, incolae eius oppidi nobis nuntiavissent ubi hostes castra posuissent.**
5. **Caesare ad Italiam profecto hostes castra aggressi sunt.**
6. **Quamvis aeger sis, Romam veniemus ut te videamus.**
7. **Imperator Graecis imperavit ut Troiae capiendae causa equum intrarent.**
8. **Libris legendis sapientes fieri possumus.**
9. **Nos sapientes fieri oportet ne stultitiae nos pudeat.**
10. **Si hunc librum diligenter legisti, scis quam difficilis Latina lingua sit.**

No. 200. Translate the following.

The end of Dumnorix

Qua re cognita Caesar coercendum atque deferrendum quibuscumque rebus posset Dumnorigem statuebat. Itaque dies circiter XXV in eo loco commoratus, quod Caurus ventus navigationem impediebat, qui magnam partem omnis temporis in eis locis flare consuevit, dabat operam ut in officio Dumnorigem contineret. Tandem idoneam nactus tempestatem milites equitesque conscendere in naves iubet. At omnium impeditis animis Dumnorix cum equitibus Aeduorum a castris insciente Caesare domum discedere coepit. Qua re nuntiata Caesar, intermissa profectione atque omnibus rebus postpositis, magnam partem equitatus ad eum imsequendum mittit retrahique imperat; si vim faciat neque pareat, interfici iubet. Ille autem revocatus resistere ac se manu defendere suorumque fidem implorare coepit, saepe clamitans liberum se liberaeque

esse civitatis. Illi, ut erat imperatum, circumsistunt hominem atque interficiunt: at equites Aedui ad Caesarem omnes revertuntur.

(Adapted from *Caesar—De Bello Gallico V, 7.*)

PUBLIUS OVIDIUS NASO

Ovid was born in 43 B.C., the year following that in which Julius Caesar had been assassinated, so that for most of his life Rome was under the control of Augustus Caesar, Julius Caesar's adopted son and Rome's first Emperor. At the age of 50, he was banished from Rome by Augustus and he died in exile ten years later in 18 A.D. The reason for his banishment is uncertain.

Although he did play some part in politics, Ovid devoted most of his life to poetry, producing a number of important works, the largest of which is the *Metamorphoses*. This is a collection of Greek myths and was given the name *Metamorphoses*, or *Transformations*, because many of these myths involve the transformation of the hero or heroine into a flower, a tree, a star or something else.

The poem culminates in a eulogy of Julius Caesar and of Augustus. It is from this final section that the following extract is taken. It had been claimed (by Virgil in the *Aeneid*, for example) that the family of the Caesars was descended directly from Aeneas and therefore from the goddess Venus, his mother. Ovid portrays Venus as attempting to protect Julius from his would-be assassins. Jupiter, however, is forced to take a hand and he forbids her to interfere with the workings of fate, but suggests that she should catch up Caesar's soul and transform him into a star.

Vix ea fatus erat, media cum sede senatus	Scarcely had he spoken, when bountiful Venus, visible to no one, stood in the middle of the senate-house,
constitit alma Venus nulli cernenda suique	
Caesaris eripuit membris nec in aera solvi	snatched the newly arisen soul of her Caesar from his body
passa recentem animam caelestibus intulit astris	and, not suffering it to be dissolved into the air, she bore it to the stars of heaven
dumque tulit, lumen capere atque ignescere sensit	and as she bore it she perceived that it acquired a radiance and began to burn
emisitque sinu: luna volat altius illa	and she let it go from her bosom: it flew higher than the moon
flammiferumque trahens spatioso limite crinem	and dragging a fiery tail on its long path

stella micat natique videns bene facta fatetur
it shone as a star and seeing the achievements of his son (Augustus) he confesses

esse suis maiora et vinci gaudet ab illo.
that they are greater than his own and he is glad to be surpassed by him.

hic sua praeferri quamquam vetat acta paternis,
Although the son forbids that his deeds should be set above those of his father

libera fama tamen nullisque obnoxia iussis
nevertheless fame, free and obedient to no commands,

invitum praefert unaque in parte repugnat:
exalts him against his will and opposes him in this one sphere:

sic magnus cedit titulis Agamemnonis Atreus,
so did the great Atreus yield to the glories of Agamemnon,

Aegea sic Theseus, sic Pelea vicit Achilles;
so did Theseus surpass Aegeus, so did Achilles surpass Peleus;

denique, ut exemplis ipsos aequantibus utar,
finally, to use an example that equals those themselves,

sic et Saturnus minor est Iove: Iuppiter arces
so is Saturn too less than Jupiter: Jupiter governs the citadels of

temperat aetherias et mundi regna triformis,
heaven and the kingdoms of the threefold universe,

terra sub Augusto est; pater est et rector uterque.
but the earth is under Augustus; each is father and ruler.

di, precor, Aeneae comites, quibus ensis et ignis
I pray you, O Gods, comrades of Aeneas, to whom sword and fire

cesserunt, dique Indigetes genitorque Quirine
yield, and ye Native gods and Quirinus, founder

urbis et invicti genitor Gradive Quirini
of the city and Gradivus sire of the unconquered Quirinus

Vestaque Caesareos inter sacrata penates,
and Vesta consecrated among the gods of the house of Caesar,

et cum Caesarea tu, Phoebe domestice, Vesta,
and with Caesar's Vesta thou, Phoebus of the household,

quique tenes altus Tarpeias Iuppiter arces,
and lofty Jupiter, thou who holdest the Tarpeian heights,

quosque alios vati fas appellare piumque est:
and all the other gods whom it is right and holy for a poet to name:

tarda sit illa dies et nostro serior aevo,
may that day be slow in coming and later than our own age,

qua caput Augustum, quem temperat, orbe relicto	on which our revered leader Augustus, abandoning the world which he governs,
accedat caelo faveatque precantibus absens!	shall ascend to heaven and listen absent to our prayers.
Iamque opus exegi, quid nec Iovis ira nec ignis	And now I have finished my work, which neither the anger of Jupiter nor fire
nec poterit ferrum nec edax abolere vetustas.	nor the sword nor voracious old age will be able to destroy.
cum volet, illa dies, quae nil nisi corporis huius	When it wishes, let that day, which has no power except
ius habet, incerti spatium mihi finiat aevi:	over this body, end for me the span of my uncertain life:
parte tamen meliore mei super alta perennis	nevertheless in the better part of me I shall be borne undying
astra ferar, nomenque erit indelebile nostrum,	beyond the lofty stars, and my name will be everlasting,
quaque patet domitis Romana potentia terris,	and wherever the power of Rome extends over the conquered lands,
ore legar populi, perque omnia saecula fama,	I shall be on the lips of the people
siquid habent veri vatum praesagia, vivam.	and if the prophecies of bards have any truth, I shall live in fame through every age.

(Ovid—*Metamorphoses XV, 843–879*)

ANSWERS

Practice Exercise No. 1

1. **aquas,** the waters
2. **puellarum,** of the girls
3. **terrae,** the lands
4. **agricolis,** for the farmers
5. **stellis,** by the stars
6. **vocant,** they call
7. **laboratis,** you work
8. **portamus,** we carry
9. **laudamus,** we praise
10. **amant,** they like

Practice Exercise No. 2

1. we 2. he, she, it 3. I 4. you 5. they 6. you

Practice Exercise No. 3

1. direct object
2. prepositional phrase
3. subject
4. indirect object
5. possession

Practice Exercise No. 4

1. **portamus**
2. **amat**
3. **porto**
4. **laudamus**
5. **vocant**
7. **laboratis**
7. **portat**
8. **vocas**
9. **amamus**
10. **laudatis**

Practice Exercise No. 5

1. **Feminae**
2. **Puella**
3. **Agricolae**
4. **Copiae**
5. **Nauta**
6. **Agricola**
7. **Filiae**
8. **Nautae**
9. **Puellae**
10. **Filia**

Practice Exercise No. 6

1. **Puellam**
2. **Insulas**
3. **Aquam**
4. **Britanniam**
5. **Feminas**
6. **Paeninsulam**
7. **Silvas**
8. **Patriam**
9. **Agricolas**
10. **Copias**

Practice Exercise No. 7

1. **puellae**
2. **aquae**
3. **agricolarum**
4. **feminarum**
5. **nautae**
6. **nautae**
7. **agricolae**
8. **nautarum**
9. **stellarum**
10. **feminae**

Practice Exercise No. 8

1. towards the road
2. in the cottage
3. with the woman
4. into the wood
5. out of the cottages
6. away from the land
7. away from the cottages
8. out of the forests
9. into the islands
10. towards the streets
11. into the forests
12. with the girl
13. in or on the water
14. towards the water
15. away from the girls
16. towards the island
17. out of the land
18. with the farmer
19. in the native country
20. with the girls

Practice Exercise No. 9

1. **Feminae,** to the woman
2. **Nautae,** to the sailor
3. **Nautis,** to the sailors
4. **Puellae,** to the girl
5. **Puellis,** to the girls
6. **Feminis,** to the women
7. **Agricolis,** to the farmers
8. **Feminae,** to the woman
9. **Puellis,** to the girls
10. **Agricolae,** to the farmer

Practice Exercise No. 10

1. **Casam parvam**
2. **mearum filiarum**
3. **pulchras stellas**
4. **tua terra**
5. **filiae malae**
6. **casis Romanis**
7. **puellas parvas**
8. **aquam bonam**
9. **feminae parvae**
10. **casarum pulchrarum**

Practice Exercise No. 11

1. you are
2. he, she, it is; there is
3. they are; there are
4. I am
5. you are
6. we are

Practice Exercise No. 12

1. **magna,** big
2. **pulchrae,** pretty
3. **bonae,** good
4. **mea,** mine
5. **Romanae,** Roman
6. **mala,** bad
7. **tua,** yours
8. **parvae,** small
9. **pulchra,** beautiful
10. **bona,** good

Practice Exercise No. 13

1. **agricola,** a farmer
2. **nautae,** sailors
3. **patria mea,** my native country
4. **insula,** an island
5. **casae,** cottages
6. **nauta,** a sailor
7. **feminae,** women
8. **puella,** a girl
9. **agricolae,** farmers
10. **silva,** a forest

Practice Exercise No. 14

1. **antiquam**
2. **pulchrae**
3. **parvis**
4. **claras**
5. **multarum**
6. **Romana**
7. **bonas**
8. **malam**
9. **pulchrae**
10. **multis**

Practice Exercise No. 15

1. **casae,** *f.*
2. **feminae,** *f.*
3. **stellae,** *f.*
4. **aquae,** *f.*
5. **fabulae,** *f.*
6. **insulae,** *f.*
7. **puellae,** *f.*
8. **copiae,** *f.*
9. **filiae,** *f.*
10. **nautae,** *m.*
11. **terrae,** *f.*
12. **Britanniae,** *f.*
13. **famae,** *f.*
14. **Italiae,** *f.*
15. **silvae,** *f.*
16. **patriae,** *f.*
17. **incolae,** *m.* or *f.*
18. **Europae,** *f.*
19. **agricolae,** *m.*
20. **viae,** *f.*

Practice Exercise No. 16

1. **amare**
2. **laudare**
3. **navigare**
4. **esse**
5. **vocare**
6. **oppugnare**
7. **monstrare**
8. **dare**
9. **habitare**
10. **portare**
11. **narrare**
12. **laborare**
13. **natare**
14. **pugnare**
15. **ambulare**

Practice Exercise No. 17

1. Nominative Case, Subject; Predicate Noun or Adjective
Vocative Case, addressing
Accusative Case, Direct Object; Prepositional Phrases
Genitive Case, Possession
Dative Case, Indirect Object
Ablative Case, Prepositional Phrases

2. **insula lata,** wide island
insula lata, o wide island
insulam latam, wide island
insulae latae, of the wide island
insulae latae, to, for the wide island
insula lata, from, with, by the wide island

insulae latae, wide islands
insulae latae, o wide islands
insulas latas, wide islands
insularum latarum, of the wide islands
insulis latis, to, for the wide islands
insulis latis, from, with, by the wide islands

via longa, long road
via longa, o long road
viam longam, long road
viae longae, of the long road
viae longae, to, for the long road
via longa, from, with, by the long road

viae longae, long roads
viae longae, o long roads
vias longas, long roads
viarum longarum, of the long roads
viis longis, to, for the long roads
viis longis, from, with, by the long roads

3. **laboro,** I work; I am working; I do work
laboras, you work; you do work; you are working
laborat, he, she, it works; he, she, it is working; he, she, it does work

laboramus, we work; we are working; we do work
laboratis, you work; you are working; you do work
laborant, they work; they are working; they do work

laudo, I praise; I am praising; I do praise
laudas, you praise; you are praising; you do praise
laudat, he, she, it praises; he, she, it is praising; he, she, it does praise

laudamus, we praise; we are praising; we do praise
laudatis, you praise; you are praising; you do praise
laudant, they praise; they are praising; they do praise

sum, I am
es, you are
est, he, she, it is; there is

sumus, we are
estis, you are
sunt, they are; there are

Practice Exercise No. 18

1. we are
2. they conquer, they are conquering, they do conquer
3. he, she, it stands; he, she, it is standing; he, she, it does stand
4. he, she, it is; there is
5. you wait for; you are waiting for; you do wait for
6. he, she, it builds; he, she, it is building; he, she, it does build
7. they are, there are
8. we swim; we are swimming; we do swim
9. he, she, it overcomes; he, she, it is overcoming; he, she, it does overcome
10. they sail; they are sailing; they do sail
11. you give; you are giving; you do give
12. you call; you are calling; you do call
13. we build; we are building; we do build
14. they walk; they are walking; they do walk
15. you stand; you are standing; you do stand

Practice Exercise No. 19

1. in Italy
2. towards Britain
3. with the women
4. towards Italy
5. in the province
6. with the troops
7. on the peninsula
8. in front of the cottages
9. behind the cottages
10. with the girl
11. in the woods
12. towards the road
13. towards the island
14. into the cottages
15. in front of the ditch

Practice Exercise No. 20

1. of the inhabitant; to, for the inhabitant; the inhabitants
2. Why do they work?
3. You help your native country.
4. He (she, it) is carrying the booty.
5. He (she, it) fights well.
6. They are pretty.
7. The victory is great.
8. a famous native country
9. He, she tells a long story.
10. out of the cottage
11. away from the road
12. Where is he (she, it)?
13. in front of the island
14. after the victory
15. with the troops
16. out of the provinces
17. towards the streets
18. Britain is an island.
19. There are many girls.
20. Where are they?

Practice Exercise No. 21

1. **agro**
2. **Bella**
3. **amicorum**
4. **Pueri**
5. **Viro**
6. **Agros**
7. **Sociis**
8. **oppido**
9. **Periculum**
10. **Viri**

Practice Exercise No. 22

1. **amici,** the friends
2. **puerorum,** of the boys
3. **agris,** to, for, from, with, by the fields
4. **bellorum,** of the wars
5. **oppida,** the towns
6. **viri,** the men
7. **pericula,** dangers
8. **gladiorum,** of the swords
9. **nuntios,** messengers
10. **auxiliis,** to, for, from, with, by the aids
11. **nuntiis,** to, for, from, with, by the messenger, messages
12. **viris,** to, for, from, with, by the men
13. **periculis,** to, for, from, with, by the dangers
14. **agri,** the fields
15. **bella,** the wars

Practice Exercise No. 23

1. of
2. the, an
3. the, a
4. about
5. through
6. of
7. of
8. the
9. the
10. of

Practice Exercise No. 24

1. out of the field
2. they are arming
3. a narrow street
4. friends
5. with the boy
6. He ploughs there.
7. behind the camp
8. of the friends
9. with the man
10. They fight with swords.
11. They point out the towns.
12. They give arms to the man.
13. We tell stories about the war.
14. He likes dangers.
15. The camp is in the field.
16. You walk through the fields.
17. There are towns.
18. You give aid.
19. Swords kill.
20. They live in camp.

Practice Exercise No. 25

1. My friend is swimming.
2. towards your cottages
3. out of the deep ditches
4. in, on the long road
5. with famous men
6. in front of the Roman camp
7. behind my fields
8. about good water
9. through the large forest
10. of the bad friend; the bad friends

Practice Exercise No. 26

1. **virorum mult*orum***
2. **filiae me*ae***
3. **frumento bon*o***
4. **equis tu*is***
5. **me*is* filiis**
6. **pueros aegr*os***
7. **puellae miser*ae***
8. **soci liber*i***
9. **feminam miser*am***
10. **agris pulchr*is***

Practice Exercise No. 27

1. **multos viros**
2. **aegri pueri**
3. **pulchrum oppidum**
4. **multorum servorum**
5. **laetam puellam**
6. **boni fili**
7. **malam famam**
8. **miseris equis**
9. **Romanae terrae**
10. **laetus agricola**

Practice Exercise No. 28

1. **curamus**
2. **liberas**
3. **laboratis**
4. **laudant**
5. **portat**
6. **aro**
7. **necant**
8. **nuntiat**
9. **occupamus**
10. **statis**

Practice Exercise No. 29

1. They are free.
2. of the happy mistresses
3. into deep water
4. concerning great cares
5. in wide fields
6. about good masters, mistresses
7. Why are you happy?
8. There are many people.
9. We are ill.
10. with good friends
11. in free lands
12. She is pretty.
13. they are pretty
14. He is unhappy.
15. many things

Practice Exercise No. 30

1. **nostram**
2. **tuas**
3. **suam**
4. **meis**
5. **sua**
6. **vestrae**
7. **nostram**
8. **suum**
9. **suarum**
10. **meam**

Practice Exercise No. 31

1. I fear; I am fearing; I do fear
2. he, she, it sees; he, she, it is seeing; he, she, it does see
3. you fear; you are fearing; you do fear
4. he, she, it adores; he, she, it is adoring; he, she, it does adore
5. they go; they are going; they do go
6. you see; you are seeing; you do see
7. they fear; they are fearing; they do fear
8. we go; we are going; we do go
9. we rule; we are ruling; we do rule
10. they have; they are having; they do have
11. he, she, it fears; he, she, it is fearing; he, she, it does fear
12. you see; you are seeing; you do see
13. I have; I am having; I do have
14. you rule; you are ruling; you do rule
15. you adore; you are adoring; you do adore

Practice Exercise No. 32

1. ancient gods
2. of, to, for the Roman goddess; Roman goddesses
3. of my friends
4. of your sailor; your sailors
5. your booty
6. our daughters
7. his, her, its, their master
8. his, her, their son
9. his her, its, their wisdom; from, with, by his, her, its, their wisdom
10. our glory

Practice Exercise No. 33

1. Your glory is not great.
2. Why do you kill your enemy?
3. The messenger tells many things.
4. The men are walking across their own fields.
5. The women are in their cottages.
6. Your daughters are sick today.
7. Many people sail across the ocean.
8. They are our goddesses.
9. They are our gods.
10. The woman cares for her daughters.
11. I am standing in front of the cottages.
12. He does not have many things.
13. We are telling about the moon.
14. Your fortune is good.
15. The slaves fear their masters.
16. Why are you not afraid?
17. We see beautiful temples.
18. He has a camp there.
19. We see the boys behind the ditch.
20. You have great wisdom.

Practice Exercise No. 34

1. **aedificare**
2. **nuntiare**
3. **exspectare**
4. **superare**
5. **videre**
6. **liberare**
7. **regnare**
8. **arare**
9. **stare**
10. **ire**
11. **necare**
12. **adorare**
13. **timere**
14. **habere**
15. **occupare**

Practice Exercise No. 35

1. **deae,** *f.*
2. **proelii** or **proeli,** *n.*
3. **provinciae,** *f.*
4. **belli,** *n.*
5. **oceani,** *m.*
6. **socii** or **soci,** *m.*
7. **fortunae,** *f.*
8. **amici,** *m.*
9. **inimici,** *m.*
10. **reginae,** *f.*
11. **pueri,** *m.*
12. **agri,** *m.*
13. **castrorum,** *n.*
14. **periculi,** *n.*
15. **victoriae,** *f.*
16. **viri,** *m.*
17. **gladii** or **gladi,** *m.*
18. **curae,** *f.*
19. **praedae,** *f.*
20. **equi,** *m.*

Practice Exercise No. 36

1. a. **Cur viris frumentum non datis?**
   b. **Incolis insularum curam bonam dat.**

2. **sto** I stand; I am standing; I do stand
   stas you stand; you are standing; you do stand
   stat he, she, it stands; he, she, it is standing; he, she, it does stand

   stamus we stand; we are standing; we do stand
   statis you stand; you are standing; you do stand
   stant they stand; they are standing; they do stand

   timeo I fear; I am fearing; I do fear
   times you fear; you are fearing; you do fear
   timet he, she, it fears; he, she, it is fearing; he, she, it does fear

   timemus we fear; we are fearing; we do fear
   timetis you fear; you are fearing; you do fear
   timent they fear; they are fearing; they do fear

Practice Exercise No. 37

1. our farmers
2. of the happy daughters
3. high sky
4. of, to, for a free country; free countries
5. your slave
6. his, her, their sons
7. wretched people
8. narrow roads
9. your messenger; your message
10. my fortune; from, with, by my fortune
11. many people
12. small boy
13. of the wide fields
14. good care; from, with, by good care
15. of the long sword

Practice Exercise No. 38

1. You have friends, haven't you? Certainly.
2. Are they building cottages? Yes. They are building cottages.
3. You are indeed afraid, aren't you? I am indeed afraid.
4. The people are not fighting, are they? The people are not fighting.
5. The roads are not long, are they? The roads are not at all long.
6. Why are they going towards the town? They like the town.
7. Is the man staying in the building? The man is staying in the building.
8. Is the province free? The province is truly free.
9. He isn't sailing on the ocean, is he? He is not sailing on the ocean.
10. Is your queen great? My queen is certainly great.

Practice Exercise No. 39

1. e	4. a	7. e	10. a	13. a
2. a	5. e	8. e	11. a	14. a
3. e	6. a	9. e	12. e	15. a

Practice Exercise No. 40

1. **Ambulare**	3. **Necare**	5. **Vocare**	7. **Iuvare**	9. **Oppugnare**
2. **Pugnare**	4. **Superare**	6. **Natare**	8. **Ire**	10. **Manere**

Practice Exercise No. 41

1. Why is he preparing grain there?
2. You like the Latin language, don't you?
3. Where do your buildings stand?
4. You ought not to give swords to the boys.
5. The gods also have their own weapons.
6. They tell the story about the long war of Troy.
7. Aeneas is sailing with his men to Italy.
8. The god helps the people of Greece.
9. Why do the Romans fear their allies?
10. He sees the clear moon in the sky.

Practice Exercise No. 42

1. **debebamus**	6. **videbas**	11. **habebatis**	16. **habebas**
2. **parabam**	7. **curabam**	12. **stabat**	17. **portabatis**
3. **properabant**	8. **adorabamus**	13. **laudabam**	18. **iuvabat**
4. **manebant**	9. **locabas**	14. **manebas**	19. **vocabat**
5. **timebat**	10. **dabatis**	15. **videbamus**	20. **timebamus**

Practice Exercise No. 43

1. he, she, it was pointing out, used to point out, did point out, pointed out
2. I call; I am calling; I do call
3. we prepare; we are preparing; we do prepare
4. you were ruling; you used to rule; you did rule; you ruled
5. you ought
6. you fear; you are fearing; you do fear
7. he, she, it was; there was
8. you fight; you are fighting; you do fight
9. I was hurrying; I used to hurry; I did hurry; I hurried
10. they were seeing; they used to see; they did see; they saw
11. you were praising; you used to praise; you did praise; you praised
12. you carry; you are carrying; you do carry
13. you were conquering; you used to conquer; you did conquer; you conquered
14. they tell; they are telling; they do tell
15. we remain; we are remaining; we do remain
16. he, she, it was saving, used to save, did save, saved
17. I was going; I used to go; I did go; I went
18. you were attacking; you used to attack; you did attack; you attacked
19. you were having; you used to have; you did have; you had
20. you were

Practice Exercise No. 44

1. **properabant**
2. **portabat**
3. **aedificabant**
4. **manebamus**
5. **eras**
6. **ibas**
7. **timebam**
8. **laudabatis**
9. **adorabant**
10. **erat**

Practice Exercise No. 45

1. He does not have men in camp, does he?
2. We were preparing today to sail.
3. Your friend has a good reputation in our town.
4. I was preparing to stay with the girls.
5. He often kills many wolves in the forests, doesn't he?
6. The Romans ought not to fear the swords of the Sabines.
7. They place temples and buildings in the town.
8. Why do they give rewards to their slaves?
9. The farmer was standing in the field with his friend.
10. You are going to the temple, aren't you?

Practice Exercise No. 46

1. he, she, it attacks
2. they were setting free
3. I shall see
4. he, she, it will remain
5. they were; there were
6. they are; there are
7. they ought; they owe
8. to love; to like
9. you will have
10. you were fighting
11. they were giving
12. he, she, it will be; there will be
13. they will stir up, arouse
14. he, she, it will warn, advise
15. to carry
16. he, she, it will fear
17. you will go
18. we shall conquer, overcome
19. we were preparing, getting ready
20. they will be; there will be
21. they will go
22. he, she, it was inciting, arousing
23. you were warning
24. we are
25. we were attacking
26. he will stir up, arouse
27. they were swimming
28. you were placing
29. you will save, preserve
30. you will help, aid

Practice Exercise No. 47

1. down from a clear sky
2. neighbouring to my country
3. near to the islands
4. with our friend
5. towards the high buildings
6. in the wide ditches
7. pleasing to his comrade
8. in front of the fields
9. friendly to the slaves
10. after the war
11. unfriendly to the queen
12. concerning your victory
13. through many battles
14. suitable to the man
15. without booty

Practice Exercise No. 48

1. present
2. future
3. imperfect
4. present
5. imperfect
6. imperfect
7. future
8. present
9. future
10. future
11. future
12. imperfect
13. future
14. imperfect
15. future
16. imperfect
17. future
18. imperfect
19. imperfect
20. future

Practice Exercise No. 49

1. He (she) will walk towards the narrow streets.
2. They were standing in front of the temples.
3. You were swimming in the ocean.
4. They will fight in the water.
5. She is pleasing to the women.
6. They ought to have a free country.
7. The girls will swim.
8. He liked his neighbours.
9. You will save your uncles.
10. They will praise the queen.
11. Where ought you to be?
12. You were calling the boy.
13. He will be unfriendly to the messenger.
14. It is not near to the province.
15. We shall not fear your swords.
16. Your slaves are helping.
17. The man will remain there.
18. We were preparing a deep ditch.
19. The master will tell a story.
20. We shall plough the field.

Practice Exercise No. 50

1. **Ambula**
2. **Natate**
3. **Pugna**
4. **Occupate**
5. **Da**
6. **Manete**
7. **Tenete**
8. **Navigate**
9. **ama**
10. **Mone**

Practice Exercise No. 51

1. The man, a farmer.
2. The men, sailors.
3. The native country, Britain.
4. The boy, a friend.
5. The queen, a girl.
6. The Gauls, our allies.
7. The messenger, a boy.
8. The Gauls, your friends.
9. The master, a friend.
10. Of the sons, the boys.

Practice Exercise No. 52

1. The sick boy, your son, will stay in the town.
2. Hasten into battle and save your country.
3. Arouse your men, Roman people, against war.
4. Warn the inhabitants of Gaul, messengers.
5. I shall call the Sabines, our neighbours, to the games.
6. See the temples, girls, beautiful buildings.
7. Rome, a town in Italy, will be famous.
8. Remember Gaul, my son.
9. Did you see the forum, the glory of Rome?
10. I shall wait for my uncles, the messengers.

Practice Exercise No. 53

1. simple question
2. simple question
3. simple question
4. answer yes
5. answer no
6. answer yes
7. answer no
8. simple question
9. simple question
10. simple question

Practice Exercise No. 54

1. **debebam**
2. **locabas**
3. **incitabat**
4. **properabant**
5. **parabatis**
6. **tenebamus**
7. **ibas**
8. **tenebam**
9. **manebamus**
10. **monebat**

Practice Exercise No. 55

1. **videbo**
2. **stabunt**
3. **timebis**
4. **regnabit**
5. **necabitis**
6. **habebimus**
7. **aedificabo**
8. **superabis**
9. **curabimus**
10. **ibunt**

Practice Exercise No. 56

1. **serva, servate**
2. **mone, monete**
3. **incita, incitate**
4. **mane, manete**
5. **naviga, navigate**
6. **para, parate**
7. **tene, tenete**
8. **propera, properate**
9. **neca, necate**
10. **pugna, pugnate**
11. **i, ite**
12. **es, este**

Practice Exercise No. 57

1. **videberis**
2. **necatur**
3. **arabuntur**
4. **dant**
5. **eunt**
6. **vocabor**
7. **iuvamur**
8. **aedificabant**
9. **superabitur**
10. **occupabunt**

Practice Exercise No. 58

1. **exspectabar**
2. **tenentur**
3. **monebitur**
4. **videbatur**
5. **amabitur**
6. **habetur**
7. **videbamini**
8. **portabitur**
9. **movebimini**
10. **parantur**
11. **laudabuntur**
12. **locamini**
13. **servabuntur**
14. **videmur**
15. **incitor**
16. **monebaris**
17. **servaris**
18. **debebatur**
19. **videntur**
20. **monebantur**

Practice Exercise No. 59

1. with the lieutenant
2. with a sword
3. by the boys
4. with ditches
5. by friends
6. by a messenger
7. with uncles
8. by wars
9. by the masters
10. with a comrade
11. with horses
12. by arrows
13. by an archer
14. by a goddess
15. with a slave
16. with wisdom
17. by the people
18. with enemies
19. with water
20. by a man

Practice Exercise No. 60

1. Money will be given to the man and the girl because the boy is ill.
2. I was going to the neighbouring town but I was remembered by my friends.
3. They seem to grieve, but soon they will be happy.
4. On account of the dangers the men were afraid of the battles.
5. Fight well for Britain, your native country.
6. Many people were walking towards the temples of the gods.
7. Why will the game be given by your friend?
8. We were living in the cottage where you see the girls.
9. The man will not be attacked by a sword, will he?
10. The people were preparing to move camp, weren't they?

Practice Exercise No. 61

1. of the long peace
2. for the soldier
3. famous soldiers
4. Roman peace
5. your heads
6. to, for their dictators
7. your head
8. by happy men
9. suitable part
10. in an ancient city
11. of our sea
12. strong soldiers
13. good men
14. long peace
15. on their heads
16. against dictators
17. with the men
18. without your soldiers
19. about the long peace
20. friendly man

Practice Exercise No. 62

1. **robustorum**
2. **angusto**
3. **magnum**
4. **antiquis**
5. **bono**
6. **magna**
7. **latum**
8. **magna**
9. **idonea**
10. **amici**

Practice Exercise No. 63

1. **duces,** the leaders
2. **milites,** the soldiers
3. **capitibus,** to, for the heads
4. **partes,** parts
5. **hostibus,** to, for the enemy
6. **urbium,** of the cities
7. **caedes,** slaughters
8. **pontes,** bridges
9. **homines,** men
10. **capita,** heads
11. **militum,** of the soldiers
12. **partium,** of the parts
13. **homines,** the men
14. **ducum,** of the leaders
15. **dictatores,** the dictators
16. **pontibus,** to, for the bridges
17. **marium,** of the seas
18. **pontium,** of the bridges
19. **hostes,** the enemy
20. **urbibus,** from, with, by the cities

Practice Exercise No. 64

1. **Cincinnatus is called from his field and gives aid.**
2. **Men rule on earth, but the gods rule in heaven and earth.**
3. **Rewards will be given to a great man by the Roman people.**
4. **The Latin language will always be preserved.**
5. **He will not plough tomorrow, but he will soon save our country.**
6. **He was swimming towards the river bank because the bridge was not standing.**
7. **Fight well, Horatius, for your country with your sword.**
8. **The soldiers, my sons, will be armed with swords.**
9. **Because of the dangers you ought to save your water.**
10. **The sailor loves the sea, but the farmer loves his fields.**

Practice Exercise No. 65

1. gods and goddesses
2. the god and the goddess
3. we have and we give
4. he had and he gave
5. a man and women
6. of the men and of the women
7. towards the sun and moon
8. towards the sun and moon
9. from the sea and land
10. from the land and sea

Practice Exercise No. 66

1. in the middle of the roads
2. in many towns
3. in a great war
4. on the tops of the buildings
5. in a good part
6. on (in) wide oceans
7. in many lands
8. in the middle of the sky
9. on the top of the sea
10. in the middle of the ocean

Practice Exercise No. 67

1. towards the sea
2. from the cities
3. with their fathers
4. in front of the forum

5. behind the temple
6. concerning the box
7. without a plan (advice)
8. across the ocean
9. through the seas
10. because of wings
11. for your queen
12. against the people
13. among the enemy
14. by (away from) the men
15. away from the towns
16. in front of the camp
17. through the dangers
18. towards the master
19. across the field
20. concerning peace

Practice Exercise No. 68

1. he, she, it will be; there will be
2. he, she, it will be frightened
3. he, she, it was flying
4. he, she, it will swim
5. they are grieving
6. we are being carried
7. he, she, it was being held
8. we shall be loved, liked
9. I shall move
10. they were being praised
11. he, she, it was fighting
12. you will place
13. I shall be called
14. we were being warned
15. they will work
16. they are being stirred up, aroused
17. he, she, it will owe, ought
18. we are going
19. they were being cared for
20. you will be freed

Practice Exercise No. 69

1. Daedalus was preparing wings with his son, Icarus.
2. Icarus was flying with his father in the middle of the sky.
3. Icarus is not saved because he does not remember for long his father's advice.
4. We see the enemy in the middle of the city.
5. The boys and the girls were swimming in the middle of the sea.
6. Because of the great dangers Cincinnatus goes from his fields to the city.
7. Both Horatius and Cincinnatus loved Rome well.
8. The Romans always praised the courage of their leaders.
9. Do we praise the courage of our leaders?
10. Why was Ceres, the mother of Proserpina, grieving?

Practice Exercise No. 70

1. **vocare,** to call
2. **debere,** to owe
3. **ambulare,** to walk
4. **stare,** to stand
5. **esse,** to be
6. **monere,** to warn
7. **timere,** to fear
8. **narrare,** to tell
9. **curare,** to take care of
10. **dolere,** to grieve
11. **nuntiare,** to announce
12. **volare,** to fly
13. **terrere,** to frighten
14. **adorare,** to worship
15. **movere,** to move
16. **parare,** to prepare
17. **servare,** to preserve, save
18. **ire,** to go
19. **dare,** to give
20. **videre,** to see

Practice Exercise No. 71

1. **paravi,** I (have) prepared
2. **incitavi,** I (have) aroused
3. **aravi,** I (have) ploughed
4. **debui,** I (have) owed
5. **liberavi,** I (have) freed
6. **locavi,** I (have) placed
7. **terrui,** I (have) frightened
8. **aedificavi,** I (have) built
9. **habitavi,** I (have) lived in
10. **monui,** I (have) warned
11. **fui,** I have been, I was
12. **habui,** I (have) had
13. **dedi,** I have given, I gave
14. **tenui,** I (have) held, kept
15. **servavi,** I (have) preserved, kept
16. **monstravi,** I have shown, I showed
17. **timui,** I (have) feared
18. **ii,** I have gone, I went
19. **movi,** I (have) moved
20. **mansi,** I (have) remained, stayed

Practice Exercise No. 72

1. **amatus,** having been loved
2. **habitus,** having been had
3. **liberatus,** having been freed
4. **necatus,** having been killed
5. **monitus,** having been warned
6. **exspectatus,** having been waited for
7. **narratus,** having been told
8. **territus,** having been frightened
9. **occupatus,** having been seized
10. **portatus,** having been carried
11. **datus,** having been given
12. **nuntiatus,** having been announced
13. **servatus,** having been saved
14. **iutus,** having been helped
15. **visus,** having been seen, seemed
16. **adoratus,** having been worshipped
17. **motus,** having been moved
18. **spectatus,** having been watched
19. **obtentus,** having been obtained
20. **locatus,** having been placed, put

Practice Exercise No. 73

1. Both your mother and your father were giving advice about courage.
2. In the middle of the town there were many buildings.
3. The report will be carried to my nation by the messengers.
4. The girl and the boy are swimming under the water.
5. We ought to walk around the city and see many things.
6. You remember many bad things, don't you?
7. The sun seemed to be on the top of the water.
8. The nations of Europe will not always fight.
9. Sailors sail on seas and oceans.
10. Roman soldiers have great courage.

Practice Exercise No. 74

1. **dolere**
2. **terrere**
3. **movere**
4. **vocare**
5. **obtinere**
6. **dare**
7. **spectare**
8. **volare**
9. **laudare**
10. **manere**
11. **debere**
12. **timere**
13. **habere**
14. **videre**
15. **necare**
16. **parare**
17. **occupare**
18. **stare**
19. **iuvare**
20. **monere**

Practice Exercise No. 75

1. **spectavi**
2. **curare**
3. **moneo**
4. **dedi**
5. **motus**
6. **paravi**
7. **servatus**
8. **territus**
9. **habito**
10. **laudare**

Practice Exercise No. 76

1. of the animals and men
2. by the father
3. by the mothers
4. the sea and star
5. fathers and mothers
6. speed and size
7. by Mercury
8. by the soldiers
9. by Pluto
10. war and peace

Practice Exercise No. 77

1. he, she, it was being praised
2. they will grieve
3. we were being warned
4. they are being killed
5. you are being called
6. we shall obtain, secure
7. you are being seen; you seem
8. you were helping
9. I shall have
10. you will be moved
11. they are being occupied, seized
12. they were fearing
13. he, she, it will be prepared
14. you will give
15. you are being saved
16. we were being prepared
17. it will be owed
18. you were being cared for
19. we were being watched, looked at
20. they will frighten, terrify

Practice Exercise No. 78

1. **paravi**
2. **laudavi**
3. **monui**
4. **debui**
5. **portavi**
6. **servavi**
7. **vocavi**
8. **movi**
9. **dedi**
10. **rogavi**

Practice Exercise No. 79

1. The Farmer was working in the fields.
   His daughter brought water.
2. The leader was watching the enemy.
   The enemy attacked the camp.
3. The woman was asking money for the books.
   Tarquinius did not give her the money.
4. The woman went into the temple.
   We were watching the women.
5. The soldiers captured the town.
   The people were afraid.
6. Rome was in great danger.
   Cincinnatus saved Rome.
7. Horatius was standing on the bridge without help.
   He slew a soldier of the enemy.
8. The Germans used to live in the woods, because they were uncivilized.
   The Romans went into the woods and attacked the Germans.
9. The gladiator was standing in the amphitheatre and was watching the large animal.
   He remained there and killed the animal with his sword.
10. Ceres was grieving because Pluto had carried Proserpina to the dead.
    She went to Jupiter and asked for help.

Practice Exercise No. 80

1. I had walked
2. they had adored
3. he, she, it had ploughed
4. they had moved
5. we had remained, stayed
6. you had seen
7. you had prepared
8. you had given
9. you had held, kept
10. I had stood
11. he, she, it had prepared
12. they had been
13. you had stirred up, aroused
14. you had cared for
15. I had swum
16. we had grieved
17. he, she, it had asked
18. they had gone
19. he, she, it had seen
20. you had called

Practice Exercise No. 81

1. you will have loved
2. he, she, it will have cared for
3. I shall have praised
4. we shall have placed
5. they will have had
6. he, she, it will have frightened
7. he, she, it will have moved
8. they will have given
9. you will have stood
10. he, she, it will have held
11. we shall have been
12. I shall have saved
13. he, she, it will have carried
14. they will have prepared
15. you will have announced
16. we shall have gone
17. you will have had
18. he, she, it will have owed
19. they will have worshipped
20. you will have walked

Practice Exercise No. 82

1. they have been
2. he, she has walked
3. he has been carried
4. they have been loved
5. you have been cared for
6. they have been praised
7. I have been warned
8. we have owed, ought to have
9. you have stood
10. it has been related, told
11. we have been called
12. I have swum
13. you have been saved
14. it has been announced
15. they have been moved
16. you have feared
17. he has been prepared
18. they have been placed
19. they have praised
20. you have moved

Practice Exercise No. 83

1. they had given
2. he, she, it had moved
3. he had been frightened
4. you had remained, stayed
5. you had held
6. he, she, it had fought
7. I had been praised
8. they had been cared for
9. you had been loved
10. you had been aroused, incited
11. they had been prepared
12. you had occupied, seized
13. you had been freed
14. he had been killed
15. we had been saved
16. he had warned, advised
17. you had had
18. you had held, kept
19. we had been helped
20. they had worshipped

Practice Exercise No. 84

1. I shall have warned, advised
2. he, she, it will have been
3. it will have been carried
4. they will have been warned
5. they will have had
6. you will have frightened
7. we shall have moved
8. you will have been seen; you will have seemed
9. he, she, it will have feared
10. she will have been moved
11. we shall have given
12. they will have stood
13. we shall have been
14. you will have been killed
15. we shall have been praised
16. you will have been armed
17. they will have been cared for
18. It will have been placed
19. they will have been; there will have been
20. she will have been saved

Practice Exercise No. 85

1. **portatum**
2. **oppugnata**
3. **mota**
4. **Servatae**
5. **narratae**
6. **incitati**
7. **occupatus**
8. **visi**
9. **laudatus**
10. **dati**

Practice Exercise No. 86

1. for many years
2. in the next year
3. for many hours
4. in the next hour
5. for seven hours
6. in the middle of the year
7. in six hours
8. for long years
9. in twelve hours
10. for twelve hours

Practice Exercise No. 87

1. **urbem**
2. **oppido**
3. **domi**
4. **forum**
5. **aqua**
6. **agros**
7. **Proserpina**
8. **matribus**
9. **collem**
10. **ruri**

Practice Exercise No. 88

1. I shall see
2. he, she, it had fought
3. you were standing
4. we shall work
5. he, she, it had been; there had been
6. they will obtain
7. we were swimming
8. he, she, it will be; there will be
9. we see
10. it has been looked at
11. he, she, it will be moved
12. they had been built
13. you have been
14. we were being attacked
15. they have remained, stayed

Practice Exercise No. 89

1. Next year we shall go to Rome.
2. For six hours they remained in the city.
3. They had been attacked on top of the hill.
4. I stayed in Italy for many hours.
5. He (she) will swim for an hour.
6. They will work for many years, won't they?
7. He walked towards the town for many long hours.
8. He has not been freed by the king.
9. Are they in the garden with the boys?
10. I walked for seven miles from the city.

Practice Exercise No. 90

1. they are sending
2. I have been shown, taught
3. we are being sought
4. he, she, it ought; owes
5. you had been warned
6. they will have been prepared
7. he, she, it has led
8. you have freed
9. I was worshipping
10. he, she, it will have sent
11. he, she, it will order
12. we were being watched, looked at
13. you are showing
14. they will ask
15. you were leading
16. he, she, it will send
17. I have saved, preserved
18. you had feared
19. you had sought
20. they have remained, stayed

Practice Exercise No. 91

1. on account of the injury
2. out of the battles
3. for six hours
4. on the march, journey
5. out of the territory
6. towards Gaul
7. away from the hill
8. in the letter
9. by the men; away from the men
10. into the river bank

Practice Exercise No. 92

1. **eum**
2. **ea**
3. **ea**
4. **eo**
5. **ei**
6. **eis**
7. **id**
8. **eius**
9. **ea**
10. **eorum**

Practice Exercise No. 93

1. **ducitur**
2. **ductus sum**
3. **ducebam**
4. **duxerunt**
5. **ducar**
6. **missus es**
7. **mittebant**
8. **mittetis**
9. **misisti**
10. **missus erat**
11. **petiti sunt**
12. **petiverimus**
13. **petetur**
14. **petit**
15. **petebas**

Practice Exercise No. 94

1. in, on the feet
2. away from the hill
3. towards the rivers
4. out of the fields
5. into the fire
6. in, on the walls
7. about the body
8. in the country
9. from Rome
10. to Rome
11. at home
12. out of the city

Practice Exercise No. 95

1. he, she, it had been; there had been
2. we have ruled
3. he has been asked
4. you will have carried
5. they have given
6. they have placed
7. they have been given
8. you have sent
9. it will have been sought
10. it had been increased
11. we have moved
12. we have been
13. they had been aroused
14. you had hurried
15. they will have been; there will have been
16. I have been asked
17. he, she, it stood
18. you have gone
19. we shall have been praised
20. he had had

Practice Exercise No. 96

1. in the next year
2. for seven hours
3. in the next hours
4. in the first year
5. for six years
6. on that night
7. for those nights
8. for those years
9. in that year
10. in that hour

Practice Exercise No. 97

1. his, hers, its
2. them
3. they
4. to, for him, her, it; they
5. it
6. them
7. she; they; them; from, with, by her
8. their
9. to, for, from, with, by them
10. him
11. they
12. from, with, by it

Practice Exercise No. 98

1. that love
2. of that boldness
3. those names
4. those causes
5. to, for, from, with, by those territories
6. of those journeys
7. those apples
8. to, for that woman
9. that body
10. of that place
11. to, for that king
12. that night
13. those laws
14. from, with, by that mountain
15. of that signal

Practice Exercise No. 99

1. because of the delay
2. because of my care
3. because of the dangers
4. because of fear
5. because of death
6. because of diligence
7. because of speed
8. because of boldness
9. because of the delays
10. because of the time

Practice Exercise No. 100

1. with zeal, eagerness
2. with great care
3. with great diligence, care
4. with great fear
5. with speed
6. with much zeal, eagerness
7. with great zeal, eagerness
8. with delay
9. with great speed
10. with great delay

Practice Exercise No. 101

1. **posui**
2. **superare**
3. **dedi**
4. **capere**
5. **servatus**
6. **facio**
7. **verti**
8. **terrui**
9. **duco**
10. **paratus**

Practice Exercise No. 102

1. he, she, it has ordered
2. you have led
3. they have shown
4. he, she, it wishes
5. we have made, done
6. he, she, it is being taught
7. you are being sent; will be sent
8. you are being taken, seized
9. you prefer
10. we shall increase
11. they will seek
12. they were flying
13. you prefer
14. he, she, it was being turned
15. he, she, it had terrified
16. you had sought
17. they had taken, seized
18. they will have been moved
19. we had been led
20. they do not wish

Practice Exercise No. 103

1. because of the hour
2. because of the weapon
3. in front of the camp
4. from the city
5. down from the tree; about the tree
6. by the king; away from the king
7. out of the trees
8. into that place
9. with the father
10. with great care
11. in, on the water
12. under the ocean
13. around the walls
14. against him
15. between, among the towns
16. through the field
17. behind the camp
18. without them
19. across the sea
20. about, concerning the men

Practice Exercise No. 104

1. this wall
2. that city
3. in that place
4. these leaders
5. to, for those soldiers
6. to, for that lieutenant
7. these commanders
8. those plans
9. of that ocean
10. of these men
11. in that garden
12. that goddess
13. of that foot soldier
14. about this master
15. out of that tree
16. this hindrance
17. to, for these fathers
18. these ships
19. that book
20. to that girl
21. these weapons
22. of these parts
23. about that peace
24. of those sands
25. in these years
26. for that hour
27. that sign, standard
28. of this horse
29. towards these women
30. those messengers

Practice Exercise No. 105

1. his, her, its
2. he
3. to, for him, her, it; they
4. them
5. to, for, from, with, by them
6. of them, their
7. it; from, with, by him, it
8. to, for him, her, it
9. she; from, with, by her; they; them
10. they
11. she; they; them
12. her
13. them
14. him
15. them

Practice Exercise No. 106

1. the goddess herself, the very goddess
2. out of the temples themselves, out of the very temples
3. the same city
4. the men themselves, the very men
5. by the same youth
6. the same name
7. of the same nation
8. with the same horsemen
9. the same journeys, ways
10. to, for, from, with, by the same men
11. out of the field itself, out of the very field
12. in the years themselves, in the very years
13. the boys themselves, the very boys
14. of the lieutenant himself, of the very lieutenant
15. the same hour; in the same hour
16. the law itself, the very law
17. the mountain itself, the very mountain
18. the girls themselves, the very girls
19. the same journey
20. by the women themselves, by the very women
21. at the same time
22. of the same generals
23. the same towns
24. in the cities themselves, in the very cities
25. of the same people
26. the same men
27. out of the same places
28. in the same years
29. on the night itself, on the very night
30. peace itself, the very peace

Practice Exercise No. 107

1. **ipsi**
2. **eodem**
3. **hos**
4. **illi**
5. **earundem**
6. **huius**
7. **ipsum**
8. **hi, illi**
9. **haec**
10. **eiusdem**

Practice Exercise No. 108

1. they were able to lead
2. you wish to stay
3. he, she, does not wish to worship
4. he, she, it will be able to free
5. they can care for
6. we prefer to kill
7. I had been able to order
8. you can teach
9. we will be willing to ask
10. I was not willing to increase
11. we shall be able to help
12. you were unwilling to fight
13. they have not been able to call
14. they had been unwilling to work
15. you have been able to stay

Practice Exercise No. 109

1. in one year
2. no care
3. of which gift
4. to, for any ship
5. for all the years
6. with the father alone
7. of no deaths
8. to neither nation
9. in the other road
10. with, by another name
11. to which river
12. of any hill
13. to, for one book
14. for no reasons
15. by neither man

Practice Exercise No. 110

1. they had feared
2. you have been
3. they will send
4. he, she, it took
5. he, she, it will fear
6. they were looking at
7. they will be held
8. I shall be sent
9. they have been praised
10. it had been done, made
11. you were sailing
12. they were being given
13. he, she, it carries on
14. they had been; there had been
15. they have had

Practice Exercise No. 111

1. one is large, the other small
2. at no time
3. of any war
4. towards which camp
5. the women themselves alone
6. of neither youth
7. other cities
8. one part
9. about neither girl
10. another journey

Practice Exercise No. 112

1. in a short hour
2. of a bold slave
3. swift horse
4. in, on a swift river
5. by bold men
6. for all times; all times
7. by a keen lieutenant
8. short life
9. at all hours
10. in a swift ship
11. bold work
12. in a short time
13. active troops
14. of a swift horse
15. active women
16. swift death, quick death
17. short journeys
18. to a bold man
19. for a short year
20. in every place

Practice Exercise No. 113

1. of the golden sun
2. out of neither place
3. on the top of the mountain
4. of an easy journey
5. any hours, of any hour
6. grave punishments
7. of the nearest nations
8. bold citizen
9. strong body
10. of swift rivers
11. Latin books
12. other men
13. your ship
14. of many fathers
15. of each king

Practice Exercise No. 114

1. Who are you?
2. To whom did he give those things?
3. Whom shall I see?
4. Whose eyes?
5. What things does he know?
6. With whom does he (she) walk?
7. By whom has he been captured?
8. Who is shouting?
9. Who is fighting?
10. Whose weapons?
11. What do you have?
12. Whom has he (she) killed?
13. To whom shall I give it?
14. What has been asked?
15. To whom have you given the gift?
16. Whom do you like?
17. Who is fleeing?
18. What is easy?
19. Whose is it?
20. With whom?
21. Whom will he send?
22. What is he doing?
23. Who are hastening?
24. By whom has the war been waged?
25. Who is calling?

Practice Exercise No. 115

1. **portare**
2. **mittere**
3. **regere**
4. **dare**
5. **laudare**
6. **rogare**
7. **scribere**
8. **videre**
9. **cognoscere**
10. **necare**
11. **capere**
12. **iubere**
13. **habere**
14. **movere**
15. **parare**
16. **ducere**
17. **augere**
18. **servare**
19. **vincere**
20. **terrere**

Practice Exercise No. 116

1. **demonstrari**
2. **duci**
3. **moveri**
4. **iuberi**
5. **verti**
6. **armari**
7. **amari**
8. **capi**
9. **doceri**
10. **occupari**
11. **mitti**
12. **geri**
13. **accipi**
14. **terreri**
15. **vocari**
16. **interfici**
17. **iuvari**
18. **teneri**
19. **cognosci**
20. **simulari**

Practice Exercise No. 117

1. they take, seize
2. it had been learned
3. they have been conquered
4. they will turn
5. we were killing
6. they have done, made
7. you had taken, seized
8. he, she, it was fleeing
9. he, she, it will be put
10. they will have carried on, waged
11. he, she, it writes
12. you throw
13. they will hurry
14. they have been put
15. it has been carried on, waged

Practice Exercise No. 118

1. because of death
2. because of injury
3. with great diligence
4. because of the general
5. because of food
6. because of the fleets
7. with a small punishment, fine
8. with great zeal, eagerness
9. because of the hindrance
10. because of the sand

Practice Exercise No. 119

1. him
2. his, hers, its
3. them
4. that
5. he himself
6. their
7. the same things; she
8. his, hers, its
9. he
10. of them themselves
11. whom
12. what
13. whose
14. to, for whom
15. with whom

Practice Exercise No. 120

1. he, she wished to shout
2. they were unwilling to take
3. you can do, make
4. we are unwilling to put, place
5. you have been able to conquer
6. he, she will be able to hurry
7. they preferred to write
8. we were able to recognize, learn
9. you will be unwilling to turn
10. they are able to carry on, wage

Practice Exercise No. 121

1. of one work
2. of all the citizens
3. another hindrance
4. new weapons
5. in a short time
6. with a sharp stone
7. of no foot soldier
8. any injury
9. bold horsemen, knights
10. swift punishment

Practice Exercise No. 122

1. **pulchre,** beautifully
2. **longe,** far, distant
3. **magnopere,** greatly
4. **bene,** well
5. **acriter,** keenly
6. **graviter,** seriously
7. **breviter,** briefly
8. **alte,** high, on high
9. **grate,** with pleasure
10. **audacter,** boldly
11. **misere,** wretchedly
12. **proxime,** next, most recently
13. **fortiter,** bravely
14. **celeriter,** swiftly
15. **libere,** freely

Practice Exercise No. 123

1. you carry, do carry
2. I have
3. they lead, are leading
4. he throws, is throwing
5. you have heard
6. he has been freed
7. they had been seen, had seemed
8. they have been heard
9. you have been received, accepted
10. I had been heard
11. they were becoming, being made, being done
12. he will have been prepared
13. he, she, it will hear
14. they have sought
15. they hear, do hear
16. they will become, be made, be done
17. we were being heard
18. we were turning
19. they will be taken, seized
20. you will be heard
21. you are being heard
22. he, she, it has done, made
23. they will ask
24. we have heard
25. they had become, been made, been done

Practice Exercise No. 124

1. they are fighting bravely
2. we saw very recently
3. he, she, it carried on the war bravely
4. they will be widely accepted
5. we are being taught well
6. he, she walks far
7. they stand well
8. he easily recognized
9. he, she liked greatly
10. not keenly enough

Practice Exercise No. 125

1. The place will be defended easily.
2. At first nothing was able to be prepared.
3. Because of fear you did not fight bravely.
4. Which door do you like?
5. Everything is being done.
6. Not only the king but also the queen heard it.
7. About whom has he (she) written boldly?
8. In that year we were preparing many things.
9. Eurydice lived unhappily under the earth.
10. He led them far from this place.

Practice Exercise No. 126

1. 1. who are making the journey with their forces
   2. The men, who are making the journey with their forces, are brave.
2. 1. which he built
   2. The tower, which he built, was keeping the barbarians from the town.
3. 1. with whom I was walking
   2. The woman, with whom I was walking, is my mother.

4. 1. whose name we cannot see
   2. The ship, whose name we cannot see, is sailing towards Italy.
5. 1. to whom I gave the letter
   2. The boy, to whom I gave the letter, will come quickly.
6. 1. which you will have
   2. The fear, which you will have, soon will not be remembered.
7. 1. to which they were fleeing
   2. The river, to which they were fleeing, was deep and wide.
8. 1. about which he wrote
   2. The place, about which he wrote, is a very beautiful city.
9. 1. which he had
   2. Everything, which he had, now is mine.
10. 1. whose sons you see
    2. The men, whose sons you see, are friends.

Practice Exercise No. 127

1. in what places?
2. which man?
3. what town?
4. what booty?
5. which men?
6. with what speed?
7. in what year?
8. of what name?
9. at what hour?
10. at what time?
11. with what soldiers?
12. of what citizens?
13. what baggage?, what hindrances?
14. of what size?
15. with what plan?

Practice Exercise No. 128

1. they make, do
2. he, she, it will order
3. you have hindered
4. he, she, it will arrive
5. to be had
6. he, she, it was preferring
7. he, she, it had been
8. he, she, it took, seized
9. they have observed
10. it was happening
11. you hear
12. you have arrived
13. he, she, it was fighting, hurrying
14. they had given
15. to be seen; to seem
16. they have prohibited
17. they will be; there will be
18. I shall be seen; I shall seem
19. to be asked
20. I shall become, be made, be done

Practice Exercise No. 129

1. he, she, it has not been able
2. of that place
3. your sons
4. others come; some come
5. he, she wishes to come
6. brave people
7. because of the storm
8. with great zeal
9. he, she remained at home
10. of (that) nation
11. in the next year
12. O my friend
13. all men
14. he, she fears nothing
15. not only your mother

Practice Exercise No. 130

1. for many paces
2. your group; your hand
3. long attack
4. because of his arrival
5. each wing
6. of our armies
7. on your wing
8. out of the army
9. into the house
10. for six miles
11. against the armies
12. because of your arrival
13. the attack (attacks) of the enemy
14. group (groups) of soldiers
15. by the army

Practice Exercise No. 131

1. their battle lines
2. on that day
3. on the next day
4. because of these things
5. of any hope
6. the whole thing
7. for one day
8. of what things
9. our battle lines
10. what things
11. in what battle line
12. of each day
13. because of that thing
14. in these battle lines
15. much hope

Practice Exercise No. 132

1. he, she has walked
2. we are seen; we seem
3. they were; there were
4. he, she, it had done, made
5. he, she was fleeing
6. he, she, it hinders
7. it had been given
8. he, she, it can, is able
9. it has been drawn up
10. to be seen; to seem
11. they have been left behind
12. we shall become, be made, be done
13. he, she, it has drawn up
14. he, she makes a journey
15. they will be heard

Practice Exercise No. 133

1. All things seem to be easy.
2. After six days neither soldier had any hope.
3. The captives whom you led back came out of their army.
4. Who hindered the strong attack greatly?
5. In one hour the men will come home.
6. For what reason was he drawing up his battle line on the hill?
7. Among these things which we have is a small supply of water.
8. The soldiers are turning their horses from that wing towards the enemy.
9. Neither the wing nor the battle line saw hope.
10. Who among these peoples hold the royal power?

Practice Exercise No. 134

1. you
2. we; us
3. by you
4. their; of them
5. she; they; them; from, with, by her
6. to, for her, him, it; they
7. you; from, with, by you
8. I
9. him
10. to, for me
11. with us
12. you
13. to, for you; from, with, by you
14. them
15. that; it
16. to him, her, it
17. his, her, its
18. with you
19. their; of them
20. towards you
21. to you
22. of you
23. of us
24. about me
25. to, for them; from, with, by them
26. about them
27. she; from, with, by her; they; them
28. with her
29. their; of them
30. them

Practice Exercise No. 135

1. to, for himself, herself, itself; to, for themselves
2. yourself; from, with, by yourself

3. from, by myself
4. yourselves
5. himself, herself, itself; themselves; from, with, by himself, herself, itself, themselves
6. to, for yourselves; from, with, by yourselves
7. to, for myself
8. to, for ourselves; from, with, by ourselves
9. myself; from, with, by myself
10. ourselves

Practice Exercise No. 136

1. The man himself sees us.
2. I sent help to you.
3. We found you in this place.
4. Will you come with me?
5. You give books to us.
6. You do not hear him.
7. They were fleeing towards us.
8. He sent these things to me.
9. He (She) will not be able to walk home with you.
10. This is your native country.
11. You will tell that to them.
12. We shall lead him home.
13. They were seeking peace from them.
14. I was being terrified by you and your sword.
15. We had saved ourselves at that time.
16. You can help us, can't you?
17. He saw their city.
18. We ourselves shall order them to come.
19. You will point out those things to us.
20. His spirit did not frighten me long.

Practice Exercise No. 137

1. **late**, widely
2. **acriter**, keenly
3. **facile**, easily
4. **misere**, wretchedly
5. **longe**, far
6. **magnopere**, greatly
7. **laete**, happily
8. **libere**, freely
9. **bene**, well
10. **anguste**, narrowly

Practice Exercise No. 138

1. I shall come
2. he, she knew
3. he has been heard
4. we were arriving
5. they will be hindered
6. they find, discover
7. you were being heard
8. it had been known
9. they have wished
10. you will be heard

Practice Exercise No. 139

1. whose
2. whom
3. who, which
4. who
5. with whom
6. we; us
7. to, for me
8. me; from, with, by me
9. of you
10. to, for you
11. with you
12. his, her, its; of him, her, it
13. their, of them
14. him
15. her

Practice Exercise No. 140

1. to, for the army
2. the things; things
3. of the horn, wing
4. the battle line
5. hope
6. of the hands, groups
7. on, from, with, by the day
8. to, for, from, with, by the attacks
9. the arrival
10. home; the house
11. to, for, from, with, by the things
12. horns, wings
13. of the armies
14. to, for the hand, group
15. to, for hope

Practice Exercise No. 141

1. fifteen
2. nine
3. twenty
4. five
5. sixteen
6. ten
7. three
8. seventeen
9. four
10. eleven
11. one hundred
12. fourteen
13. eight
14. nineteen
15. two
16. thirteen
17. seven
18. one
19. eighteen
20. one thousand
21. twelve
22. six

Practice Exercise No. 142

1. fourth
2. eighth
3. tenth
4. third
5. seventh
6. second
7. fifth
8. ninth
9. first
10. sixth

Practice Exercise No. 143

1. a thousand ships
2. three men
3. thousands of soldiers
4. for fourteen days
5. of one man
6. twenty miles
7. a hundred boys
8. for five years
9. six of the soldiers
10. in seven hours
11. in a hundred years
12. eight of the boys
13. for two days
14. of ten laws
15. three places
16. two of the provinces
17. in twelve days
18. of six animals
19. eighteen of the kings
20. in three years

Practice Exercise No. 144

1. to, for, of the tenth girl
2. on the eighth day
3. in the sixth hour; the sixth hour
4. the seventh ship
5. in the fifth summer
6. for the third day
7. in the tenth winter
8. the seventh attack
9. to, for, of the ninth hour; ninth hours
10. in the first year

Practice Exercise No. 145

1. a difficult way, road
2. a wretched home
3. of the free men
4. keen fears
5. similar armies
6. a long day, for a long day
7. on a high mountain
8. swift rivers
9. wide streets
10. of pretty girls

Practice Exercise No. 146

1. narrower streets
2. a taller boy
3. of happier girls
4. a friendlier people
5. a longer journey, way
6. in more pleasing places
7. of more famous sisters
8. a longer winter, for a longer winter
9. wider rivers
10. a bolder man

Practice Exercise No. 147

1. of a very sweet spring
2. out of very pretty gardens
3. a very narrow temple
4. because of very wretched memories
5. very famous oracles
6. a very happy citizen
7. out of a very wide field
8. with very pretty mothers
9. on a very new ship
10. very short names

Practice Exercise No. 148

1. That is a very wretched place.
2. The bravest men arrived at the island.
3. The very keen horses were running swiftly.
4. This is an easier journey.
5. The people of Italy are very free.
6. This is the narrower part of the river.
7. These things are also very similar.
8. We saw a very deep and rather wide river.
9. Our men chose a shorter way.
10. You can see a high building from this place.

Practice Exercise No. 149

1. These towers are higher than those.
2. You are taller than your father.
3. Those roads are not easier than others.
4. You are more like your father than your mother.
5. Men are much stronger than women.
6. His house is newer than mine.
7. The boy is happier than his sister.
8. The barbarians are much bolder than their neighbours.
9. He will be friendlier to you than to me.
10. Is the hand quicker than the eye?

Practice Exercise No. 150

1. they will be; there will be
2. it has been carried
3. he, she, it has decided
4. he, she, it will be prepared
5. they were leading
6. he has been left behind
7. he, she, it will be sent
8. you are being carried
9. we were seeing
10. he, she has walked

Practice Exercise No. 151

1. more things
2. better
3. of the worst
4. of a bigger
5. of smaller
6. of very many
7. to, for, from, with, by more
8. the next
9. more suitable; of more suitable
10. most suitable

Practice Exercise No. 152

1. in very many cities
2. out of smaller springs
3. the greatest courage
4. best voice
5. down from higher walls
6. more water
7. more suitable time
8. of the worst thing; to, for the worst thing
9. towards a better part
10. with a bigger army
11. on a longer day
12. very many states
13. worse end
14. best years
15. smallest sister
16. of very many difficulties
17. better journey
18. of the worst summer
19. very many gifts
20. of a smaller ship

Practice Exercise No. 153

1. wide
2. widely
3. wider
4. more widely
5. very wide
6. very widely
7. free
8. freely
9. more free
10. very free
11. more freely
12. very freely
13. pretty
14. more pretty
15. very pretty
16. prettily
17. more prettily
18. very prettily
19. swift
20. swiftly
21. swifter
22. more swiftly
23. very swift
24. very swiftly
25. keen
26. keenly
27. keener
28. more keenly
29. keenest
30. most keenly

Practice Exercise No. 154

1. They were being attacked for a very long time.
2. He fights more bravely.
3. They have been burned quickly.
4. They will speak much more briefly.
5. He will be warned very boldly.
6. They drew up the battle line very quickly.
7. He waged war more keenly.
8. They walk proudly.
9. He gave more freely.
10. He is praised very greatly.
11. They have been sent more widely.
12. He gave very freely.
13. He sails very far.
14. He runs more quickly.
15. They were seen more clearly.
16. They remain longer.
17. He will fear very keenly.
18. They have been taken boldly.
19. He was speaking very briefly.
20. They fight bravely.

Practice Exercise No. 155

1. well
2. greatly
3. badly
4. much
5. too little
6. long
7. often
8. longer
9. more
10. more
11. better
12. worse
13. less
14. more often
15. most
16. most
17. longest
18. most often
19. best
20. worst
21. least

Practice Exercise No. 156

1. They arrive more often.
2. He fought as long as possible.
3. He has been aroused more.
4. He was being hindered more.
5. You have ruled very well.
6. That has been heard most often.
7. He walks very easily.
8. They are very powerful among us.
9. He flies more swiftly.
10. He will stay much longer.

Practice Exercise No. 157

1. one of the sisters
2. three rivers
3. two years; for two years
4. a thousand years
5. two wives
6. a hundred words
7. of one voice
8. twenty springs, fountains
9. the fourth hour; in the fourth hour
10. on the fifth day
11. in the second year
12. the seventh word
13. the first oracle
14. in the fourth harbour, port
15. out of the sixth gate, door

Practice Exercise No. 158

1. the longer winter; for the longer winter
2. the very pretty summer
3. of the longest years
4. the sweeter word
5. a very similar burden
6. of an immortal voice
7. easier journey
8. clearer lights
9. of a very great difficulty
10. of stronger husbands

Practice Exercise No. 159

1. sweet, sweeter, sweetest
2. keen, keener, keenest
3. long, longer, longest
4. similar, more similar, most similar
5. high, higher, highest
6. free, freer, freest
7. swift, swifter, swiftest
8. wide, wider, widest
9. clear, clearer, clearest
10. bold, bolder, boldest

Practice Exercise No. 160

1. big, bigger, biggest
2. small, smaller, smallest
3. good, better, best
4. bad, worse, worst
5. much, more, most
6. many, more, very many
7. suitable, more suitable, most suitable

Practice Exercise No. 161

1. he was walking more quickly
2. he has been oppressed miserably
3. he sleeps too little
4. it will burn for a very long time
5. they have been very greatly aroused
6. they were touching more
7. they have surrendered more easily
8. they are very powerful
9. it, he, she will be more powerful
10. they will be forced less easily

Practice Exercise No. 162

1. you are being loved, are loved
2. you wish, are willing
3. you are being carried, are carried
4. it had been had
5. he, she, it prefers
6. he, she, it had borne, carried
7. you become, are made, are done
8. I shall have ruled
9. it was necessary, it behoved
10. they had gone
11. it vexes
12. we are unwilling, do not wish
13. I shall hear
14. it will be unbecoming
15. we have made, done
16. you are; be
17. it was lawful
18. it repented
19. he, she, it was able, could
20. it will shame

Practice Exercise No. 163

1. **consilii**
2. **Mihi**
3. **nos**
4. **militem**
5. **belli**
6. **Antonium**
7. **patri Romano**
8. **civium**
9. **Virtus**
10. **Caesarem**

Practice Exercise No. 164

1. It is becoming for soldiers to fight as bravely as possible for their country.
2. While it is raining, it is not lawful for the girls (*or* the girls are not allowed) to go out.
3. Do you pity the Sabine women whom the Romans captured?
4. If it is snowing, it behoves us (*or* we ought) to remain at home.
5. It was not pleasing to Venus to help Psyche.
6. It did not behove Psyche to look at her husband. *or* Psyche ought not to have looked at her husband.
7. I shall soon be weary of the Latin language.
8. What will it behove us to do? *or* What ought we to do?
9. Why did Psyche's sisters not repent of their foolishness?
10. Cupid said that he had loved Psyche against his mother's command.

Practice Exercise No. 165

1. to warn
2. to have increased
3. to be thrown
4. to be about to place
5. to have fled
6. to hinder
7. to have swum
8. to be about to frighten
9. to have remained
10. to be about to hear
11. to have written
12. to be about to fight
13. to be about to praise
14. to be aroused
15. to have been sought
16. to send
17. to be touched
18. to have been attacked
19. to be about to be praised
20. to be about to carry on
21. to be received
22. to have been conquered
23. to wish
24. to be about to walk
25. to have feared

Practice Exercise No. 166

1. **petere,** to seek
2. **cepisse,** to have taken
3. **habere,** to have
4. **rexisse,** to have ruled
5. **portare,** to carry
6. **vocavisse,** to have called
7. **facere,** to do, make
8. **dedisse,** to have given
9. **instruere,** to draw up
10. **vertere,** to turn

Practice Exercise No. 167

1. **narrari,** to be told
2. **defensus esse,** to have been defended
3. **videri,** to be seen; to seem
4. **iuvari,** to be helped
5. **laudatus esse,** to have been praised
6. **motus esse,** to have been moved
7. **vocatum iri,** to be about to be called
8. **inveniri,** to be found
9. **necatus esse,** to have been killed
10. **relinqui,** to be left

Practice Exercise No. 168

1. **futurus esse,** to be about to be
2. **iussurus esse,** to be about to order
3. **facturus esse,** to be about to make
4. **defensurus esse,** to be about to defend
5. **oppugnaturus esse,** to be about to attack
6. **properaturus esse,** to be about to hurry
7. **capturus esse,** to be about to take
8. **inventurus esse,** to be about to find
9. **daturus esse,** to be about to give
10. **positurus esse,** to be about to place

Practice Exercise No. 169

1. **necatos esse**
2. **transiturum esse**
3. **se**
4. **vidisse**
5. **esse**
6. **agricolas**
7. **captam esse**
8. **se**
9. **facere, adventurum esse**
10. **impeditum iri**

Practice Exercise No. 170

1. Those soldiers said that they would give aid to the men.
2. Do you think your work has been done?
3. We were hoping the enemy would come as quickly as possible.
4. The girls seem to be happy.
5. This king wished to rule well.
6. He will not want to be called back.
7. To defend our town is best.
8. To have hoped was better than to have retreated.
9. He announced that the speed could be increased.
10. He ordered us to find a better place.

Practice Exercise No. 171

1. calling
2. having been moved
3. about to send
4. receiving
5. about to come
6. having been watched
7. arriving
8. about to take
9. placing, putting
10. having been announced
11. having been warned
12. fearing
13. about to say
14. having been aroused
15. going

Practice Exercise No. 172

1. the ships, sailing
2. the leader, about to order
3. they, having been attacked
4. the men, about to arrive
5. seeking peace
6. the dog, running
7. the cities, having been captured
8. the temples, having been built
9. the harbours, having been found
10. the rivers running

Practice Exercise No. 173

1. The people of the cities, which had been captured, were very brave.
2. The men, who were about to arrive, were making the journey as quickly as possible.
3. The king, who is now ruling your country, seems to be timid.
4. The woman will give aid, when (if) she sees your difficulty.
5. Since Psyche was about to journey to the kingdom of the dead, she feared many things.
6. The father had great joy, because he was about to see his sons.
7. They were running as fast as possible, because they fear our men.
8. The men, who (because they) had been defeated, were very frightened.
9. When she arrived at the town, she told her story.
10. Those who were defending the gate, were not friends.

Practice Exercise No. 174

1. **Urbe capta**
2. **Urbem captam**
3. **Te ducem**
4. **Te duce**
5. **Hostibus oppressis**
6. **Hostes oppressos**
7. **Puellam natantem**
8. **Puella natante**
9. **Milites mare spectantes**
10. **Militibus mare spectantibus**

Practice Exercise No. 175

1. bravely
2. as quickly as possible
3. least, not at all
4. for a very long time
5. more keenly
6. very well, best
7. very easily
8. better
9. badly
10. greatly
11. more often
12. very unhappily

Practice Exercise No. 176

1. When the oracle had been heard, many people decided to come to our land.
2. When the signal had been given, they made an attack on the field.
3. Although their weapons had been lost, the men fought bravely.
4. Because many soldiers had been killed, they sought peace.
5. Since the war has been finished, the soldiers will be received at home with great joy.
6. When this thing has been done, the boys will come home.
7. If he is the leader, we shall do it without difficulty.
8. When these things had been reported, I wanted to make a journey from the city.
9. If these have been killed, the people will be ruled better.
10. When the day had been set, they prepared everything as quickly as possible.
11. Because the door was open, he was able to come into the cottage.
12. He had no hope, because the city had been captured.
13. When these things had been done, the king was more powerful.
14. If the rest have been seen, we shall run towards the forest.
15. When his father is the leader, they do everything boldly.
16. When peace has been made, he will sail away from the island.
17. If many are timid, we shall not be able to find the rivers.
18. Since the allies have been conquered, no help will arrive.
19. Because the place is suitable, you wish to stay here longer.
20. Because help was given, there was great joy.

Practice Exercise No. 177

1. to be
2. to have been
3. to be about to find out
4. to be about to be found
5. to have been thought
6. to have thought
7. to carry back, report
8. to be about to carry back, report
9. to have hoped
10. to be about to hope
11. to be led
12. to have led
13. to have been had
14. to have
15. to wish, want
16. to be wished, wanted
17. to have been able
18. to be able
19. to have fought
20. to have been praised
21. to be warned
22. to have warned
23. to have said
24. to be said
25. to have been willing
26. to have feared
27. to have been made, done, become
28. to be about to make, do
29. to be seen; to seem
30. to be going to be seen, seem

Practice Exercise No. 178

1. leading
2. about to lead
3. having, holding
4. having been had
5. having been thought
6. about to think
7. finding out
8. having been found out
9. carrying back, reporting
10. about to carry back, report
11. hoping
12. about to hope
13. about to move
14. moving
15. coming
16. about to come
17. fearing
18. having been frightened
19. about to go
20. going
21. sending
22. having been sent
23. about to see
24. seeing
25. about to say
26. saying
27. warning
28. having been warned
29. having been placed, put
30. placing, putting

Practice Exercise No. 179

1. they having been seen
2. he, it having been captured
3. these having been said
4. the war having been made
5. the men being afraid
6. the girl walking
7. the leaders being afraid
8. the arms having been lost
9. sleep coming
10. the soldiers fighting
11. the city having been captured
12. the remaining speaking
13. the word having been heard
14. hope having been found
15. many having been killed

Practice Exercise No. 180

1. **laudem**
2. **videam**
3. **dicam**
4. **faciam**
5. **veniam**
6. **sim**
7. **eam**
8. **feram**
9. **coner**
10. **verear**
11. **sequar**
12. **aggrediar**
13. **ordiar**
14. **velim**
15. **nolim**
16. **malim**
17. **possim**
18. **fiam**
19. **inscribam**
20. **vindicem**

Practice Exercise No. 181

1. **eamus**
2. **congregentur**
3. **possimus**
4. **volo**
5. **amemus**
6. **secuti**
7. **possim**
8. **invenias**
9. **moriamur**
10. **profecti**

Practice Exercise No. 182

1. The enemy will run so quickly that it will be difficult to attack them.
2. The speech is such that everyone praises Cicero.
3. When he had encouraged the soldiers, Caesar ordered them to make an attack on the camp of the enemy.
4. Let us follow Cicero; let us not allow Catalina to overcome Rome.
5. After Troy had been besieged for ten years, the Greeks built a great horse.
6. Let us always be willing to love and preserve the state.
7. The Gods are so great that we fear and worship them.
8. Since Leander has died, Hero does not wish to live.
9. Venus said that Psyche had not herself put the grain in order.
10. So many Persians are making an attack that we can not conquer.

Practice Exercise No. 183

1. **natarem**
2. **viderem**
3. **scriberem**
4. **fugerem**
5. **dormirem**
6. **essem**
7. **irem**
8. **ferrem**
9. **fierem**
10. **hortarer**
11. **vererer**
12. **loquerer**
13. **morerer**
14. **orirer**
15. **vellem**
16. **nollem**
17. **mallem**
18. **exponerem**
19. **ignorarem**
20. **agerem**

Practice Exercise No. 184

1. **spectaverim**
2. **tenuerim**
3. **miserim**
4. **iecerim**
5. **sciverim**
6. **fuerim**
7. **ierim**
8. **tulerim**
9. **factus sim**
10. **conatus sim**
11. **veritus sim**
12. **profectus sim**
13. **passus sim**
14. **potitus sim**
15. **voluerim**
16. **noluerim**
17. **maluerim**
18. **vigilaverim**
19. **consumpserim**
20. **comprehenderim**

Practice Exercise No. 185

1. **ambulavissem**
2. **debuissem**
3. **incendissem**
4. **interfecissem**
5. **cupivissem**
6. **fuissem**
7. **iissem**
8. **tulissem**
9. **factus essem**
10. **insidiatus essem**
11. **veritus essem**
12. **secutus essem**
13. **aggressus essem**
14. **molitus essem**
15. **voluissem**
16. **noluissem**
17. **maluissem**
18. **secessissem**
19. **sensissem**
20. **circumstetissem**

Practice Exercise No. 186

1. **transiret**
2. **sit**
3. **capta esset**
4. **velim**
5. **feceris**
6. **videret**
7. **veniam, eam**
8. **faciant**
9. **posset**
10. **reciperet**

Practice Exercise No. 187

1. The Gauls did not know what was happening.
2. The Gauls did not know what had happened.
3. Caesar tried to find out where the Gauls had placed their camp.
4. Caesar tried to find out where the Gauls were placing their camp.
5. The leader asks how many ships have been lost.
6. The leader asks how many ships are being lost.
7. I do not know what kind of soldier he is.
8. I do not know what kind of soldier he was.
9. Now let us find out what Caesar is doing in Gaul.
10. Now let us find out what Caesar did in Gaul.

Practice Exercise No. 188

1. **Currendo**
2. **vincendi**
3. **recipiendi**
4. **eundo**
5. **conficiendas**
6. **discenda**
7. **faciendo**
8. **patienda**
9. **laudandi**
10. **interficiendi**

Practice Exercise No. 189

1. To learn the Latin language here I sit alone.
2. To learn the Latin language here I sit alone.
3. You are tired of learning the Latin language, aren't you?
4. The envoys announced to Caesar that there was no hope of saving the army.
5. The Trojans did not know what was in the horse.
6. When Athens had been captured the citizens took the women to the islands so that they would not be killed by the Persians.
7. The Helvetii said that those things were to be completed by Orgetorix.
8. The sea is so wide that we cannot cross it by swimming.
9. It did not behove Psyche to know what sort of husband she had.
10. Psyche did not know whether her sisters were to be listened to or not.

Practice Exercise No. 190

1. **ut**
2. **cur**
3. **ne**
4. **quin**
5. **quin**
6. **ut** *or* **ne** according to sense
7. **ut**
8. **ne**
9. **quin**
10. **utrum**

Practice Exercise No. 191

1. Orgetorix persuaded the citizens to leave their territory with all their forces.
2. We could not warn our men to withdraw.
3. The soldiers feared that the enemy would surround and conquer them.
4. There is no doubt that Caesar excels all men in courage.
5. Venus forbade Psyche to look at her husband.
6. Cupid used to come to Psyche at night so that she would not see him.
7. Her sisters used to ask Psyche who her husband was and if she had seen him.
8. The soldiers asked Caesar to lead them against the enemy.
9. Orgetorix asked the people if they were willing to allow him to undertake the embassies to the states.
10. What will Caesar do to prevent Orgetorix, Casticus and Dumnorix from gaining the mastery of all Gaul?

Practice Exercise No. 192

1. **possemus**
2. **vicimus**
3. **abiit**
4. **redirent**
5. **ceperant**
6. **facimus**
7. **spectaret**
8. **spectavisset**
9. **vidit**
10. **pervenerunt**

Practice Exercise No. 193

1. When the camp had been captured we withdrew to the mountains.
2. When the camp had been captured we withdrew to the mountains.
3. When the camp had been captured we withdrew to the mountains.
4. After the camp had been captured we withdrew to the mountains.
5. Hero was afraid that Leander was dead.
6. While the city was burning, Aeneas returned to find his wife.
7. Pluto ordered Orpheus not to look at Eurydice.
8. Theseus was so brave that he killed the Minotaur.
9. Caesar was unwilling to punish Dumnorix before he had spoken with Diviciacus.
10. Caesar asked Diviciacus whether he himself ought to decide about Dumnorix or if he wished to order the state to decide.

Practice Exercise No. 194

1. **fecerimus**
2. **iissemus**
3. **esset**
4. **laborabimus**
5. **possit**
6. **veretur**
7. **pugnaremus**
8. **haberent**
9. **servetur**
10. **intraret**

Practice Exercise No. 195

1. If we were at Rome, we would be able to go to the Circus Maximus.
2. Even if Orgetorix had not died, he would not have gained the mastery of all Gaul.
3. Although Catalina had left Rome, Cicero knew that his allies and friends were in the city.
4. After the enemy had left the town, the inhabitants asked whether they were allowed to return or not.
5. We learn some things by reading and writing, other things by doing.
6. Although Troy was burning, Aeneas returned to seek his wife.
7. Orpheus went to the dead in order to recover his wife.
8. We prevented the the enemy from crossing the river by burning the bridge.
9. If Psyche had not seen her husband, she would not have repented of her foolishness.
10. Although we like Tiro, let us now find out what Caesar is doing in Gaul.

Practice Exercise No. 196

1. **confectum erat**
2. **confectum esset**
3. **petivi**
4. **petiverim**
5. **erat**
6. **esset**
7. **erat**
8. **esset**
9. **receperunt**
10. **recepissent**

Practice Exercise No. 197

Caesar had decided to have Dumnorix especially with him because he had discovered that he was desirous of changes, desirous of power, a man of great spirit and of great authority among the Gauls. There was added to this the fact that Dumnorix had said in the council of the Aedui that the kingship of the state was being offered to him by Caesar. Caesar had heard of that event from his friends. Dumnorix at first strove by every kind of entreaty to ask that he should be left in Gaul, partly because he was unused to sailing and feared the sea, partly because he said he was prevented by religious scruples. After he had seen that that was being resolutely denied him, he began to incite the leaders of Gaul and to urge them to remain on the continent: [he said that] it was not happening without reason that Gaul was being robbed of all its nobility; it was Caesar's plan to take across to Britain and kill all those whom he was afraid to kill in sight of Gaul; he was demanding an oath that they should control by a common policy what they perceived was to the advantage of Gaul. These things were reported to Caesar from many sources.

Practice Exercise No. 198

1. **vigilem, vigilarem, vigilaverim, vigilavissem**
2. **sedeam, sederem, sederim, sedissem**
3. **agam, agerem, egerim, egissem**
4. **perficiam, perficerem, perfecerim, perfecissem**
5. **sentiam, sentirem, senserim, sensissem**
6. **coner, conarer, conatus sim, conatus essem**
7. **verear, vererer, veritus sim, veritus essem**
8. **utar, uterer, usus sim, usus essem**
9. **patiar, paterer, passus sim, passus essem**
10. **moliar, molirer, molitus sim, molitus essem**
11. **sim, essem, fuerim, fuissem**
12. **eam, irem, ierim, iissem**
13. **fiam, fierem, factus sim, factus essem**
14. **feram, ferrem, tulerim, tulissem**
15. **velim, vellem, voluerim, voluissem**

Practice Exercise No. 199

1. The Gauls thought that they would conquer our men very easily.
2. The battle has been so long that I can scarcely stand.
3. Dumnorix is not allowed to stay in Gaul until Caesar returns from Britain, is he?
4. If we had asked, the inhabitants of that town would have told us where the enemy had put their camp.
5. When Caesar had set out for Italy the enemy attacked the camp.
6. Although you are sick, we shall come to Rome in order to see you.
7. The general ordered the Greeks to enter the horse in order to capture Troy.
8. By reading books we can become wise.
9. We ought to become wise so that we shall not be ashamed of our foolishness.
10. If you have read this book carefully, you know how difficult the Latin language is.

Practice Exercise No. 200

When this was known Caesar decided that Dumnorix must be repressed and prevented by whatever means he could. And so after staying in that place for about twenty-five days, because the north-westerly wind was preventing the sailing, the wind which is accustomed to blow for a great part of all time in those regions, he gave attention to keeping Dumnorix in his duty. At length after he had obtained suitable weather, he ordered the soldiers and the cavalry to embark on the ships. But when everyone's mind was occupied, without Caesar's knowing, Dumnorix with the cavalry of the Aedui began to leave the camp for home. When this was reported, Caesar interrupted the departure, laid aside everything, sent a large detachment of cavalry to pursue him and ordered that he be brought back; if he used force and did not obey, he ordered that he be killed. Dumnorix, however, when he was recalled began to resist and to protect himself by force and to appeal to the loyalty of his men, often crying aloud that he was a free man and a citizen of a free state. The cavalrymen, as had been ordered, surrounded the man and killed him: but the cavalry of the Aedui all returned to Caesar.

THE VERB: FIRST CONJUGATION

amo

INDICATIVE

	Active		*Passive*	
PRESENT	**amo**	**amamus**	**amor**	**amamur**
	amas	**amatis**	**amaris**	**amamini**
	amat	**amant**	**amatur**	**amantur**
FUTURE SIMPLE	**amabo**	**amabimus**	**amabor**	**amabimur**
	amabis	**amabitis**	**amaberis**	**amabimini**
	amabit	**amabunt**	**amabitur**	**amabuntur**
IMPERFECT	**amabam**	**amabamus**	**amabar**	**amabamur**
	amabas	**amabatis**	**amabaris**	**amabamini**
	amabat	**amabant**	**amabatur**	**amabantur**
PERFECT	**amavi**	**amavimus**	**amatus sum**	**amati sumus**
	amavisti	**amavistis**	**amatus es**	**amati estis**
	amavit	**amaverunt**	**amatus est**	**amati sunt**
FUTURE PERFECT	**amavero**	**amaverimus**	**amatus ero**	**amati erimus**
	amaveris	**amaveritis**	**amatus eris**	**amati eritis**
	amaverit	**amaverint**	**amatus erit**	**amati erunt**
PLUPERFECT	**amaveram**	**amaveramus**	**amatus eram**	**amati eramus**
	amaveras	**amaveratis**	**amatus eras**	**amati eratis**
	amaverat	**amaverant**	**amatus erat**	**amati erant**

THE VERB: FIRST CONJUGATION (*continued*)

amo

SUBJUNCTIVE

	Active		*Passive*	
PRESENT	**amem**	**amemus**	**amer**	**amemur**
	ames	**ametis**	**ameris**	**amemini**
	amet	**ament**	**ametur**	**amentur**
IMPERFECT	**amarem**	**amaremus**	**amarer**	**amaremur**
	amares	**amaretis**	**amareris**	**amaremini**
	amaret	**amarent**	**amaretur**	**amarentur**
PERFECT	**amaverim**	**amaverimus**	**amatus sim**	**amati simus**
	amaveris	**amaveritis**	**amatus sis**	**amati sitis**
	amaverit	**amaverint**	**amatus sit**	**amati sint**
PLUPERFECT	**amavissem**	**amavissemus**	**amatus essem**	**amati essemus**
	amavisses	**amavissetis**	**amatus esses**	**amati essetis**
	amavisset	**amavissent**	**amatus esset**	**amati essent**

IMPERATIVE

ama	**amare**
amate	**amamini**

INFINITIVES

PRESENT	**amare**	**amari**
PERFECT	**amavisse**	**amatus esse**
FUTURE	**amaturus esse**	**amatum iri**

PARTICIPLES			
PRESENT ACTIVE	**amans**	SUPINE	**amatum**
PERFECT PASSIVE	**amatus**	GERUND	**amandum**
FUTURE ACTIVE	**amaturus**	GERUNDIVE	**amandus**

THE VERB: SECOND CONJUGATION

habes

INDICATIVE

	Active		*Passive*	
PRESENT	**habeo**	**habemus**	**habeor**	**habemur**
	habes	**habetis**	**haberis**	**habemini**
	habet	**habent**	**habetur**	**habentur**
FUTURE SIMPLE	**habebo**	**habebimus**	**habebor**	**habebimur**
	habebis	**habebitis**	**habeberis**	**habebimini**
	habebit	**habebunt**	**habebitur**	**habebuntur**
IMPERFECT	**habebam**	**habebamus**	**habebar**	**habebamur**
	habebas	**habebatis**	**habebaris**	**habebamini**
	habebat	**habebant**	**habebatur**	**habebantur**

PERFECT TENSES Formed from Perfect Stem and Perfect Participle Passive as for **amo.**

SUBJUNCTIVE

	Active		*Passive*	
PRESENT	**habeam**	**habeamus**	**habear**	**habeamur**
	habeas	**habeatis**	**habearis**	**habeamini**
	habeat	**habeant**	**habeatur**	**habeantur**
IMPERFECT	**haberem**	**haberemus**	**haberer**	**haberemur**
	haberes	**haberetis**	**habereris**	**haberemini**
	haberet	**haberent**	**haberetur**	**haberentur**

PERFECT TENSES As for **amo**

IMPERATIVE

habe	**habere**
habete	**habemini**

INFINITIVES

PRESENT	**habere**	**haberi**
PERFECT	**habuisse**	**habitus esse**
FUTURE	**habiturus esse**	**habitum iri**

PARTICIPLES

PRESENT ACTIVE	**habens**	SUPINE	**habitum**
PERFECT PASSIVE	**habitus**	GERUND	**habendum**
FUTURE ACTIVE	**habiturus**	GERUNDIVE	**habendus**

THE VERB: THIRD CONJUGATION

duco and capio

INDICATIVE

	Active		*Passive*	
PRESENT	**duco**	**capio**	**ducor**	**capior**
	ducis	**capis**	**duceris**	**caperis**
	ducit	**capit**	**ducitur**	**capitur**

	Active		*Passive*	
	ducimus	**capimus**	**ducimur**	**capimur**
	ducitis	**capitis**	**ducimini**	**capimini**
	ducunt	**capiunt**	**ducuntur**	**capiuntur**
FUTURE SIMPLE	**ducam**	**capiam**	**ducar**	**capiar**
	duces	**capies**	**duceris**	**capieris**
	ducet	**capiet**	**ducetur**	**capietur**
	ducemus	**capiemus**	**ducemur**	**capiemur**
	ducetis	**capietis**	**ducemini**	**capiemini**
	ducent	**capient**	**ducentur**	**capientur**
IMPERFECT	**ducebam**	**capiebam**	**ducebar**	**capiebar**
	ducebas	**capiebas**	**ducebaris**	**capiebaris**
	ducebat	**capiebat**	**ducebatur**	**capiebatur**
	ducebamus	**capiebamus**	**ducebamur**	**capiebamur**
	ducebatis	**capiebatis**	**ducebamini**	**capiebamini**
	ducebant	**capiebant**	**ducebantur**	**capiebantur**

PERFECT TENSES As for **amo**

SUBJUNCTIVE

PRESENT	**ducam**	**capiam**	**ducar**	**capiar**
	ducas	**capias**	**ducaris**	**capiaris**
	ducat	**capiat**	**ducatur**	**capiatur**
	ducamus	**capiamus**	**ducamur**	**capiamur**
	ducatis	**capiatis**	**ducamini**	**capiamini**
	ducant	**capiant**	**ducantur**	**capiantur**
IMPERFECT	**ducerem**	**caperem**	**ducerer**	**caperer**
	duceres	**caperes**	**ducereris**	**capereris**
	duceret	**caperet**	**duceretur**	**caperetur**
	duceremus	**caperemus**	**duceremur**	**caperemur**
	duceretis	**caparetis**	**duceremini**	**caperemini**
	ducerent	**caperent**	**ducerentur**	**caperentur**

PERFECT TENSES As for **amo**

IMPERATIVE

	duc	**cape**	**ducere**	**capere**
(irregular—usually -e)				
	ducite	**capite**	**ducimini**	**capimini**

INFINITIVES

PRESENT	**ducere**	**capere**	**duci**	**capi**
PERFECT	**duxisse**	**cepisse**	**ductus esse**	**captus esse**
FUTURE	**ducturus esse**	**capturus esse**	**ductum iri**	**captum iri**

PARTICIPLES

PRESENT ACTIVE	**ducens**	**capiens**	SUPINE	**ductum**	**captum**
PERFECT PASSIVE	**ductus**	**captus**	GERUND	**ducendum**	**capiendum**
FUTURE ACTIVE	**ducturus**	**capturus**	GERUNDIVE	**ducendus**	**capiendus**

THE VERB: FOURTH CONJUGATION

audio

INDICATIVE

	Active		*Passive*	
PRESENT	**audio**	**audimus**	**audior**	**audimur**
	audis	**auditis**	**audiris**	**audimini**
	audit	**audiunt**	**auditur**	**audiuntur**
FUTURE SIMPLE	**audiam**	**audiemus**	**audiar**	**audiemur**
	audies	**audietis**	**audieris**	**audiemini**
	audiet	**audient**	**audietur**	**audientur**
IMPERFECT	**audiebam**	**audiebamus**	**audiebar**	**audiebamur**
	audiebas	**audiebatis**	**audiebaris**	**audiebamini**
	audiebat	**audiebant**	**audiebatur**	**audiebantur**

PERFECT TENSES As for **amo**

SUBJUNCTIVE

PRESENT	**audiam**	**audiamus**	**audiar**	**audiamur**
	audias	**audiatis**	**audiaris**	**audiamini**
	audiat	**audiant**	**audiatur**	**audiantur**
IMPERFECT	**audirem**	**audiremus**	**audirer**	**audiremur**
	audires	**audiretis**	**audireris**	**audiremini**
	audiret	**audirent**	**audiretur**	**audirentur**

PERFECT TENSES As for **amo**

IMPERATIVE

Active	Passive
audi	**audire**
audite	**audimini**

INFINITIVES

	Active	Passive
PRESENT	**audire**	**audiri**
PERFECT	**audivisse, audiisse**	**auditus esse**
FUTURE	**auditurus esse**	**auditum iri**

PARTICIPLES

PRESENT ACTIVE	**audiens**	SUPINE	**auditum**
PERFECT PASSIVE	**auditus**	GERUND	**audiendum**
FUTURE ACTIVE	**auditurus**	GERUNDIVE	**audiendus**

THE VERB: IRREGULAR VERBS

	sum	possum	eo	fio	volo	nolo	malo	fero	
								Active	*Passive*
				INDICATIVE					
PRESENT	sum	possum	eo	fio	volo	nolo	malo	fero	feror
	es	potes	is	fis	vis	nonvis	mavis	fers	ferris
	est	potest	it	fit	vult	nonvult	mavult	fert	fertur
	sumus	possumus	imus	—	volumus	nolumus	malumus	ferimus	ferimur
	estis	potestis	itis	—	vultis	nonvultis	mavultis	fertis	ferimini
	sunt	possunt	eunt	fiunt	volunt	nolunt	malunt	ferunt	feruntur
FUTURE SIMPLE	ero	potero	ibo	fiam	volam	nolam	malam	feram	ferar
	eris	poteris	ibis	fies	voles	noles	males	feres	fereris
	erit	poterit	ibit	fiet	volet	nolet	malet	feret	feretur
	erimus	poterimus	ibimus	fiemus	volemus	nolemus	malemus	feremus	feremur
	eritis	poteritis	ibitis	fietis	voletis	noletis	maletis	feretis	feremini
	erunt	poterunt	ibunt	fient	volent	nolent	malent	ferent	ferentur
IMPERFECT	eram	poteram	ibam	fiebam	volebam	nolebam	malebam	ferebam	ferebar
	eras	poteras	ibas	fiebas	volebas	nolebas	malebas	ferebas	ferebaris
	erat	poterat	ibat	fiebat	volebat	nolebat	malebat	ferebat	ferebatur
	eramus	poteramus	ibamus	fiebamus	volebamus	nolebamus	malebamus	ferebamus	ferebamur
	eratis	poteratis	ibatis	fiebatis	volebatis	nolebatis	malebatis	ferebatis	ferebamini
	erant	poterant	ibant	fiebant	volebant	nolebant	malebant	ferebant	ferebantur
PERFECT TENSES	fui	potui	ii, ivi	factus sum	volui	nolui	malui	tuli	latus sum
	etc.	etc.	etc.	etc.	etc.	etc.	etc.	etc.	etc.
				SUBJUNCTIVE					
PRESENT	sim	possim	eam	fiam	velim	nolim	malim	feram	ferar
	sis	possis	eas	fias	velis	nolis	malis	feras	feraris
	sit	possit	eat	fiat	velit	nolit	malit	ferat	feratur
	simus	possimus	eamus	fiamus	velimus	nolimus	malimus	feramus	feramur
	sitis	possitis	eatis	fiatis	velitis	nolitis	malitis	feratis	feramini
	sint	possint	eant	fiant	velint	nolint	malint	ferant	ferantur

IMPERFECT	essem	possem	irem	fierem	vellem	nollem	mallem	ferrem	ferrer
	esses	posses	ires	fieres	velles	nolles	malles	ferres	ferreris
	esset	posset	iret	fieret	vellet	nollet	mallet	ferret	ferretur
	essemus	possemus	iremus	fieremus	vellemus	nollemus	mallemus	ferremus	ferremur
	essetis	possetis	iretis	fieretis	velletis	nolletis	malletis	ferretis	ferremini
	essent	possent	irent	fierent	vellent	nollent	mallent	ferrent	ferrentur
PERFECT TENSES	See above.								
					IMPERATIVE				
	es	—	i	—	—	noli	—	fer	ferre
	este	—	ite	—	—	nolite	—	ferte	ferimini
					INFINITIVES				
PRESENT	esse	posse	ire	fieri	velle	nolle	malle	ferre	ferri
PERFECT	fuisse	potuisse	iisse, ivisse	factus esse	voluisse	noluisse	maluisse	tulisse	latus esse
FUTURE	futurus esse *or* fore	—	iturus esse	fore *or* futurus esse	—	—	—	laturus esse	latum iri
					PARTICIPLES				
PRESENT	—	—	iens, euntis	—	volens	nolens	—	ferens	
PERFECT	—	—	—	—	—	—	—	—	latus
FUTURE	futurus	—	iturus	futurus	—	—	—	laturus	—
					SUPINES				
	—	—	—	—	—	—	—	latum	—
					GERUNDS				
	—	—	eundum	—	—	—	—	ferendum	—
					GERUNDIVES				
	—	—	—	—	—	—	—	ferendus	—

THE NOUN

FIRST DECLENSION

puella	
puella	puellae
puella	puellae
puellam	puellas
puellae	puellarum
puellae	puellis
puella	puellis

SECOND DECLENSION

amicus		puer		ager		bellum	
amicus	amici	puer	pueri	ager	agri	bellum	bella
amice	amici	puer	pueri	ager	agri	bellum	bella
amicum	amicos	puerum	pueros	agrum	agros	bellum	bella
amici	amicorum	pueri	puerorum	agri	agrorum	belli	bellorum
amico	amicis	puero	pueris	agro	agris	bello	bellis
amico	amicis	puero	pueris	agro	agris	bello	bellis

THIRD DECLENSION

homo, hominis		caput, capitis		mare, maris	
homo	homines	caput	capita	mare	maria
homo	homines	caput	capita	mare	maria
hominem	homines	caput	capita	mare	maria
hominis	hominum	capitis	capitum	maris	marium
homini	hominibus	capiti	capitibus	mari	maribus
homine	hominibus	capite	capitibus	mari	maribus

FOURTH DECLENSION

exercitus		cornu	
exercitus	exercitus	cornu	cornua
exercitus	exercitus	cornu	cornua
exercitum	exercitus	cornu	cornua
exercitus	exercituum	cornus	cornuum
exercitui	exercitibus	cornu	cornibus
exercitu	exercitibus	cornu	cornibus

FIFTH DECLENSION

res	
res	res
res	res
rem	res
rei	rerum
rei	rebus
re	rebus

THE ADJECTIVE

FIRST AND SECOND DECLENSION

bonus

bonus	**bona**	**bonum**	**boni**	**bonae**	**bona**
bone	**bona**	**bonum**	**boni**	**bonae**	**bona**
bonum	**bonam**	**bonum**	**bonos**	**bonas**	**bona**
boni	**bonae**	**boni**	**bonorum**	**bonarum**	**bonorum**
bono	**bonae**	**bono**		**bonis**	
bono	**bona**	**bono**		**bonis**	

miser

miser	**misera**	**miserum**
miser	**misera**	**miserum**
miserum	**miseram**	**miserum**
	etc.	

pulcher

pulcher	**pulchra**	**pulchrum**
pulcher	**pulchra**	**pulchrum**
pulchrum	**pulchram**	**pulchrum**
	etc.	

THIRD DECLENSION

omnis

omnis	**omnis**	**omne**	**omnes**	**omnes**	**omnia**
omnis	**omnis**	**omne**	**omnes**	**omnes**	**omnia**
omnem	**omnem**	**omne**	**omnes**	**omnes**	**omnia**
	omnis			**omnium**	
	omni			**omnibus**	
	omni			**omnibus**	

audax

audax	**audax**	**audax**
audax	**audax**	**audax**
audacem	**audacem**	**audax**
	audacis	
	etc.	

celer

celer	**celeris**	**celere**
celer	**celeris**	**celere**
celerem	**celerem**	**celere**
	celeris	
	etc.	

acer

acer	**acris**	**acre**
acer	**acris**	**acre**
acrem	**acrem**	**acre**
	acris	
	etc.	

THE COMPARATIVE ADJECTIVE

longior

longior	**longior**	**longius**	**longiores**	**longiores**	**longiora**
longior	**longior**	**longius**	**longiores**	**longiores**	**longiora**
longiorem	**longiorem**	**longius**	**longiores**	**longiores**	**longiora**
	longioris			**longiorum**	
	longiori			**longioribus**	
	longiore			**longioribus**	

THE PRONOUN

PERSONAL PRONOUNS

First Person		*Second Person*	
ego	**nos**	**tu**	**vos**
me	**nos**	**te**	**vos**
mei	**nostrum, nostri**	**tui**	**vestrum, vestri**
mihi	**nobis**	**tibi**	**vobis**
me	**nobis**	**te**	**vobis**

REFLEXIVE (THIRD PERSON) SINGULAR OR PLURAL

—
se
sui
sibi
se

DEMONSTRATIVE PRONOUNS

hic

hic	**haec**	**hoc**	**hi**	**hae**	**haec**
hunc	**hanc**	**hoc**	**hos**	**has**	**haec**
	huius		**horum**	**harum**	**horum**
	huic			**his**	
hoc	**hac**	**hoc**		**his**	

ille

ille	**illa**	**illud**	**illi**	**illae**	**illa**
illum	**illam**	**illud**	**illos**	**illas**	**illa**
	illius		**illorum**	**illarum**	**illorum**
	illi			**illis**	
illo	**illa**	**illo**		**illis**	

is

is	**ea**	**id**	**ei, ii**	**eae**	**ea**
eum	**eam**	**id**	**eos**	**eas**	**ea**
	eius		**eorum**	**earum**	**eorum**
	ei			**eis, iis**	
eo	**ea**	**eo**		**eis, iis**	

THE RELATIVE PRONOUN

qui	**quae**	**quod**	**qui**	**quae**	**quae**
quem	**quam**	**quod**	**quos**	**quas**	**quae**
	cuius		**quorum**	**quarum**	**quorum**
	cui			**quibus**	
quo	**qua**	**quo**		**quibus**	

VOCABULARY—LATIN-ENGLISH

A

a, ab, from, away from; by
abeo, abire, abii, abitus, go away
absum, abesse, afui, be absent
accedo, accedere, accessi, accessurus, approach, be added, to agree, support
accido, accidere, accidi, happen
acer, acris, acre, sharp, active, keen
acerbus, acerba, acerbum, harsh, bitter
acies, aciei, *f.*, battle line
ad, to, towards
addo, addere, addidi, additus, put on, add
adfero, adferre, attuli, adlatus, bring
administro, administrare, administravi, administratus, manage, control, rule
adoro, adorare, adoravi, adoratus, worship, adore
adsum, adesse, adfui (adfuturus), be present
adulescens, adulescentis, *m.*, youth
advenio, advenire, adveni, adventus, come to, reach, arrive at
adventus, adventus, *m.*, arrival, approach
aedificium, aedificii or **aedifici,** *n.*, building
aedifico, aedificare, aedificavi, aedificatus, build
aeger, aegra, aegrum, sick, ill
aequus, aequa, aequum, equal, level, fair
aestas, aestatis, *f.*, summer
Africa, Africae, *f.*, Africa
ager, agri, *m.*, field
aggredior, aggredi, aggressus sum, approach, attack
ago, agere, egi, actus, put in motion, carry on, do
agricola, agricolae, *m.*, farmer
ala, alae, *f.*, wing
aliquis, aliqua, aliquod, someone, anyone, some, any
alius, alia, aliud, other, another
alter, altera, alterum, the one, the other
altus, alta, altum, high, deep
ambulo, ambulare, ambulavi, ambulatus, walk
amicus, amica, amicum, friendly
amicus, amici, *m.*, friend
amitto, amittere, amisi, amissus, send away, lose
amo, amare, amavi, amatus, like, love
amor, amoris, *m.*, love
amphitheatrum, amphitheatri, *n.*, amphitheatre
angustus, angusta, angustum, narrow
animal, animalis, *n.*, animal
animus, animi, *m.*, mind, spirit
annus, anni, *m.*, year
ante, before, in front of
antea, before
antequam, before
antiquus, antiqua, antiquum, ancient, old
antrum, antri, *n.*, cave
apertus, aperta, apertum, open
Apollo, Apollinis, *m.*, Apollo
appello, appellare, appellavi, appellatus, address, call, name
Aprilis, Aprile, of April
apud, among, in the presence of
aqua, aquae, *f.*, water
arbor, arboris, *f.*, tree
arca, arcae, *f.*, chest, box
ardeo, ardere, arsi, arsus, be on fire, burn
arena, arenae, *f.*, sand
Ariadne, Ariadnes, *f.*, Ariadne
arma, armorum, *n. pl.*, arms, weapons
armo, armare, armavi, armatus, arm
aro, arare, aravi, aratus, plough
at, but
Atalanta, Atalantae, *f.*, Atalanta
Athenae, Athenarum, *f. pl.*, Athens
Atlas, Atlantis, *m.*, Atlas
atque, ac, and also, also
auctoritas, auctoritatis, *f.*, power, authority, prestige
audacia, audaciae, *f.*, boldness, daring
audax, audacis, bold
augeo, augere, auxi, auctus, increase, enlarge
Augustus, Augusta, Augustum, of August
aureus, aurea, aureum, golden
aurum, auri, *n.*, gold
aut, or

aut . . . aut, either . . . or
autem, but, however
auxilium, auxilii or **auxili**, *n.*, aid, help
avunculus, avunculi, *m.*, uncle

B

Bacchus, Bacchi, *m.*, Bacchus
barbarus, barbara, barbarum, savage, uncivilized, barbarian
barbarus, barbari, *m.*, barbarian
belle, prettily, neatly, well
bellum, belli, *n.*, war
bene, well
biennium, biennii or **bienni**, *n.*, a period of two years
bis, twice
bonus, bona, bonum, good
brevis, breve, short, brief
Britannia, Britanniae, *f.*, Britain

C

cado, cadere, cecidi, casus, fall
caedes, caedis, *f.*, slaughter, murder
caelum, caeli, *n.*, sky, heaven
canis, canis, *m.* and *f.*, dog
capio, capere, cepi, captus, take, seize, capture
captivus, captivi, *m.*, captive
caput, capitis, *n.*, head
carcer, carceris, *n.*, prison
careo, carere, carui, caritus (with Ablative case), be without, lack
carrus, carri, *m.*, baggage waggon
casa, casae, *f.*, cottage
castra, castrorum, *n. pl.*, camp
Caurus, Cauri, *m.*, the northwest wind
causa, causae, *f.*, cause, reason
causa (following a Genitive case), for the sake of
cedo, cedere, cessi, cessus, go away, withdraw, yield
celer, celeris, celere, quick, swift
celeritas, celeritatis, *f.*, speed, swiftness
centiens, a hundred times
cera, cerae, *f.*, wax
Cerberus, Cerberi, *m.*, Cerberus
Ceres, Cereris, *f.*, Ceres
certe, certainly, surely, indeed
certus, certa, certum, certain, sure
Charon, Charontis, *m.*, Charon
cibus, cibi, *m.*, food
Cincinnatus, Cincinnati, *m.*, Cincinnatus
circiter, about
circum, around, about
circumsisto, circumsistere, circumsteti, —, stand around, surround
circumsto, circumstare, circumsteti, —, stand around, surround
civis, civis, *m.* and *f.*, citizen
civitas, civitatis, *f.*, state
clamito, clamitare, clamitavi, clamitatus, cry aloud, proclaim
clamo, clamare, clamavi, clamatus, shout, cry
clarus, clara, clarum, clear, famous, bright
classis, classis, *f.*, fleet
coemo, coemere, coemi, coemptus, purchase, buy up
(coepio), coepere, coepi, coeptus, begin
coerceo, coercere, coercui, coercitus, surround, confine, repress, restrain
cognosco, cognoscere, cognovi, cognitus, learn, recognize, know
cogo, cogere, coegi, coactus, collect, drive, compel
collis, collis, *m.*, hill
colloquor, colloqui, collocutus sum, speak with
Colosseum, Colossei, *n.*, The Colosseum
commonefacio, commonefacere, commonefeci, commonefactus, remind
commoror, commorari, commoratus sum, linger, abide, remain, stay
communis, commune, common, general
comparo, comparare, comparavi, comparatus, bring together, compare
comperio, comperire, comperi, compertus, find out, learn, discover
complures, complura (or **compluria**), several, many
comprehendo, comprehendere, comprehendi, comprehensus, seize, apprehend, discover
concilio, conciliare, conciliavi, conciliatus, reconcile, win over, win
concilium, concilii or **concili**, *n.*, council
confero, conferre, contuli, conlatus, bring together, collect, apply
conficio, conficere, confeci, confectus, finish, complete, carry out
confirmo, confirmare, confirmavi, confirmatus, establish, strengthen, confirm
congrego, congregare, congregavi, congregatus, assemble, gather together
coniuratio, coniurationis, *f.*, alliance, plot
conloco, conlocare, conlocavi, conlocatus, place, station

conor, conari, conatus sum, try
conscendo, conscendere, conscendi, conscensus, mount, ascend, embark
consensio, consensionis, *f.,* agreement, unanimity
consensus, consensus, *m.,* agreement, consensus
conservo, conservare, conservavi, conservatus, keep safe, preserve
consilium, consilii or **consili,** *n.,* plan, advice
conspectus, conspectus, *m.,* sight, view
conspicio, conspicere, conspexi, conspectus, observe
constituo, constituere, constitui, constitutus, decide, establish
consuesco, consuescere, consuevi, consuetus, accustom, be accustomed
consumo, consumere, consumpsi, consumptus, use up, consume, spend
contendo, contendere, contendi, contentus, hasten, strive, contend
contineo, continere, continui, contentus, hold together, limit, enclose, keep, repress, comprise
contra, against
convenio, convenire, conveni, conventus, come together, assemble
copia, copiae, *f.,* supply, abundance
copiae, copiarum, *f. pl.,* troops
coquus, coqui, *m.,* cook
cornu, cornus, *n.,* horn, wing
corpus, corporis, *n.,* body
cotidianus, cotidiana, cotidianum, daily, usual
cras, tomorrow
Creta, Cretae, *f.,* Crete
Creusa, Creusae, *f.,* Creusa
cum, with; when, while
cupiditas, cupiditatis, *f.,* desire
Cupido, Cupidinis, *m.,* Cupid
cupidus, cupida, cupidum, desirous, eager
cupio, cupere, cupivi, cupitus, desire, wish, want
cur, why
cura, curae, *f.,* care
curia, curiae, *f.,* the senate-house
curo, curare, curari, curatus, care for, cure
curro, currere, cucurri, cursus, run
Cyclops, Cyclopis, *m.,* Cyclops

D

Daedalus, Daedali, *m.,* Daedalus
de, about, concerning, down from
dea, deae, *f.,* goddess
debeo, debere, debui, debitus, owe, ought
decem, ten
December, Decembris, Decembre, of December
decet, decere, decuit, —, it becomes, it is fitting
dedecet, dedecere, dedecuit, —, it is unbecoming, unseemly
dedo, dedere, dedidi, deditus, give up, surrender
defendo, defendere, defendi, defensus, ward off, repel, defend
defero, deferre, detuli, delatus, bring away, carry off, offer, report
deinde, then, next
deligo, deligere, delegi, delectus, choose, select
demonstro, demonstrare, demonstravi, demonstratus, point out, show
denique, finally, at last
desino, desinere, desii, desitus, cease, desist
desisto, desistere, destiti, destitus, cease, desist
deterreo, deterrere, deterrui, deterritus, frighten off, deter, prevent, hinder
deus, dei, *m.,* god
dico, dicere, dixi, dictus, say, speak
dictator, dictatoris, *m.,* dictator
dies, diei, *m.* and *f.,* day
difficilis, difficile, difficult, hard
difficultas, difficultatis, *f.,* difficulty
diligenter, carefully
diligentia, diligentiae, *f.,* diligence, care
diligo, diligere, dilexi, delectus, value, love
discedo, discedere, discessi, discessus, withdraw, go away, leave
disco, discere, didici, —, learn
diu, long, for a long time
dives, divitis, rich
do, dare, dedi, datus, give
doceo, docere, docui, doctus, teach, show
doleo, dolere, dolui, dolitus, grieve, be sorry
domi, at home
domicilium, domicilii or **domicili,** *n.* dwelling, domicile
domina, dominae, *f.,* mistress
dominus, domini, *m.,* master
domus, domus, *f.,* house, home
donec, until
donum, doni, *n.,* gift, present
dormio, dormire, dormivi, dormitus, sleep

dubito, dubitare, dubitavi, dubitatus, doubt
dubius, dubia, dubium, doubtful, uncertain
duco, ducere, duxi, ductus, lead
dulcis, dulce, sweet
dum, while
duodecim, twelve
dux, ducis, *m.*, leader

E

e, ex, from, out from
edo, edere, or **esse, edi, esus,** eat
educo, educere, eduxi, eductus, lead out
effugio, effugere, effugi, —, flee away, escape
ego, mei, I
egregius, egregia, egregium, excellent, outstanding
emo, emere, emi, emptus, buy
enim, for
enuntio, enuntiare, enuntiavi, enuntiatus, speak out, disclose, make known
eo, for that reason
eo, ire, ii or **ivi, iturus,** go
epistola, epistolae, *f.*, letter
eques, equitis, *m.*, horseman, knight
equus, equi, *m.*, horse
et, and
et . . . et, both . . . and
etiam, even, also
etiamsi, even if
etsi, even if, although
Europa, Europae, *f.*, Europe
Eurydice, Eurydices, *f.*, Eurydice
Eurystheus, Eurysthei, *m.*, Eurystheus
ex, e, from, out from
excito, excitare, excitavi, excitatus, arouse, stir up
exeo, exire, exii, exitus, go out, go away, withdraw
exercitus, exercitus, *m.*, army
expono, exponere, exposui, expositus, set forth, exhibit, explain
exspecto, exspectare, exspectavi, exspectatus, await, expect, wait for

F

fabula, fabulae, *f.*, story
facilis, facile, easy
facio, facere, feci, factus, make, do
fama, famae, *f.*, rumour, renown, report
familiaris, familiaris, *m.* or *f.*, friend
febris, febris, *f.*, fever
Februarius, Februaria, Februarium, of February
femina, feminae, *f.*, woman
fero, ferre, tuli, latus, bear, carry; **me fero,** move, hasten
fides, fidei, *f.*, faith, pledge
filia, filiae, *f.*, daughter
filius, filii or **fili,** *m.*, son
finis, finis, *m.*, end, border
fines, finium, *m. pl.*, territory
finitimus, finitima, finitimum, neighbouring
finitimus, finitimi, *m.*, neighbour
fio, fieri, factus sum, become, be made, be done
firmo, firmare, firmavi, firmatus, make firm, strengthen
firmus, firma, firmum, firm, strong
flo, flare, flavi, flatus, blow
floreo, florere, florui, —, bloom, flourish
flumen, fluminis, *n.*, river
fons, fontis, *m.*, fountain, spring
formica, formicae, *f.*, ant
fortis, forte, brave, strong
fortuna, fortunae, *f.*, fortune, fate, luck
forum, fori, *n.*, forum, market place
fossa, fossae, *f.*, ditch
frater, fratris, *m.*, brother
fructuosus, fructuosa, fructuosum, fruitful, abundant
frumentum, frumenti, *n.*, grain
fuga, fugae, *f.*, flight, escape
fugio, fugere, fugi, fugiturus, flee, run away, escape
furur, furoris, *m.*, rage, fury, passion

G

Gallia, Galliae, *f.*, Gaul
Gallus, Galli, *m.*, a Gaul
gaudium, gaudii or **gaudi,** *n.*, joy
genus, generis, *n.*, kind, class
Germania, Germaniae, *f.*, Germany
Germanus, Germani, *m.*, a German
gero, gerere, gessi, gestus, carry on, wage
gladiator, gladiatoris, *m.*, gladiator
gladius, gladii or **gladi,** *m.*, sword
gloria, gloriae, *f.*, glory
Graecia, Graeciae, *f.*, Greece
Graecus, Graeca, Graecum, Greek
gratulor, gratulari, gratulatus sum, be glad, congratulate
gratus, grata, gratum, pleasing
gravis, grave, heavy, severe, serious

H

habeo, habere, habui, habitus, have, hold
habito, habitare, habitavi, habitatus, dwell, live
Hannibal, Hannibalis, *m.*, Hannibal
Hellespontus, Hellesponti, *m.*, The Hellespont
Hercules, Herculis, *m.*, Hercules
Hero, Herus, *f.*, Hero
Hesperides, Hesperidum, *f. pl.*, the Hesperides
hic, here, in this place
hic, haec, hoc, this; he, she, it
hiems, hiemis, *f.*, winter
Hippomenes, Hippominis, *m.*, Hippomenes
Hispania, Hispaniae, *f.*, Spain
hodie, today
Homerus, Homeri, *m.*, Homer
homo, hominis, *m.*, man
hora, horae, *f.*, hour
Horatius, Horati, *m.*, Horatius
hortor, hortari, hortatus sum, urge, encourage, exhort
hortus, horti, *m.*, garden
hospes, hospitis, *m.*, host, guest, friend
hostis, hostis, *m.*, enemy
huc, to this place, hither, to this

I

iaceo, iacere, iacui, —, lie, be recumbent, be situated
iacio, iacere, ieci, iactus, throw
iam, now, already
Ianuarius, Ianuaria, Ianuarium, of January
ibi, there, in that place
Icarus, Icari, *m.*, Icarus
idem, eadem, idem, the same; he, she, it
idoneus, idonea, idoneum, fit, suitable
Idus, Iduum, *f.*, the Ides
ignis, ignis, *m.*, fire
ignoro, ignorare, ignoravi, ignoratus, not know, be ignorant
ille, illa, illud, that; he, she, it
illustro, illustrare, illustravi, illustratus, make clear, disclose
immortalis, immortale, immortal
impedimentum, impedimenti, *n.*, hindrance
impedio, impedire, impedivi, impeditus, hinder
imperator, imperatoris, *m.*, commander, general, emperor
imperium, imperii or **imperi,** *n.*, command
impero, imperare, imperavi, imperatus (with Dative case), command, order
impetus, impetus, *m.*, attack
imploro, implorare, imploravi, imploratus, appeal to, beseech, implore
improbus, improba, improbum, bad, wicked
in, in, on; into, onto
incendo, incendere, incendi, incensus, set fire to, burn
incito, incitare, incitavi, incitatus, arouse, stir up, incite
incola, incolae, *m.* or *f.*, inhabitant
incredibilis, incredibile, unbelievable
indico, indicere, indixi, indictus, proclaim, appoint, summon
induco, inducere, induxi, inductus, lead in, lead on, induce, excite
ineo, inire, inii, initus, go in, enter
Inferi, Inferorum, *m. pl.*, Those Below, the dead
infero, inferre, intuli, inlatus, bring in, introduce; **bellum infero,** make war
inhumanus, inhumana, inhumanum, rude, uncultured
inimicus, inimica, inimicum, unfriendly
inimicus, inimici, *m.*, personal enemy
iniuria, iniuriae, *f.*, injury, harm
inopia, inopiae, *f.*, want, scarcity
inquam (Defective verb. Perfect **inquii**), say
insciens, inscientis, unknowing, unaware
inscribo, inscribere, inscripsi, inscriptus, write on
insequor, insequi, insecutus sum, follow, follow after, pursue
insidiae, insidiarum, *f.*, trap, snare, ambush
insidior, insidiari, insidiatus sum, lie in ambush
instruo, instruere, instruxi, instructus, draw up, form, train
insuetus, insueta, insuetum, unaccustomed, unused
insula, insulae, *f.*, island
intellego, intellegere, intellexi, intellectus, understand
inter, among, between
intercessio, intercessionis, *f.*, mediation, intervention, protest, veto
interea, meanwhile
interficio, interficere, interfeci, interfectus, kill
intermitto, intermittere, intermisi, inter-

missus, leave off, omit, interrupt, neglect
interpres, interpretis, *m.* or *f.*, interpreter
intro, intrare, intravi, intratus, enter
invenio, invenire, inveni, inventus, find, come upon
investigo, investigare, investigavi, investigatus, search after, discover, investigate
ipse, ipsa, ipsum, himself, herself, itself; very
is, ea, id, he, she, it; that
ita, thus, so; yes
Italia, Italiae, *f.*, Italy
itaque, and so, therefore
item, moreover, also
iter, itineris, *n.*, journey, march, way
iterum, again
iubeo, iubere, iussi, iussus, order, command
iudico, iudicare, iudicavi, iudicatus, judge, decide
Iulia, Iuliae, *f.*, Julia
Iulius, Iulia, Iulium, of Julius
iumentum, iumenti, *n.*, beast of burden, mule, ass
Iunius, Iunia, Iunium, of June
Iuno, Iunonis, *f.*, Juno
Iuppiter, Iovis, *m.*, Jupiter
ius iurandum, iuris iurandi, *n.*, oath
iustitia, iustitiae, *f.*, justice
iuvo, iuvare, iuvi, iutus, help, aid

K

Kalendae, Kalendarum, *f.*, the Kalends, first day of the month

L

labor, laboris, *m.*, work, toil, labour
laboro, laborare, laboravi, laboratus, work
labyrinthus, labyrinthi, *m.*, labyrinth
laetus, laeta, laetum, happy
lana, lanae, *f.*, wool
Latinus, Latina, Latinum, Latin
Latinus, Latini, *m.*, Latinus
Latium, Lati, *n.*, Latium
latus, lata, latum, wide
laudo, laudare, laudavi, laudatus, praise
Leander, Leandri, *m.*, Leander
legatio, legationis, *f.*, embassy, legation
legatus, legati, *m.*, lieutenant, legate
lego, legere, legi, lectus, read
lex, legis, *f.*, law
libenter, gladly, with pleasure
liber, libera, liberum, free
liber, libri, *m.*, book
libero, liberare, liberavi, liberatus, free, set free
libet, libere, libuit (Impersonal verb), it pleases, it is pleasing
licet, licere, licuit (Impersonal verb), it is lawful, it is allowed
lingua, linguae, *f.*, language
littera, litterae, *f.*, letter
litterula, litterulae, *f.*, little letter
loco, locare, locavi, locatus, place, put
locus, loci, *m.*, place
longus, longa, longum, long
loquor, loqui, locutus sum, speak, talk, say
ludus, ludi, *m.*, game
luna, lunae, *f.*, moon
lupa, lupae, *f.*, wolf
lux, lucis, *f.*, light

M

magis, more
magnitudo, magnitudinis, *f.*, size, great size
magnopere, greatly
magnus, magna, magnum, large, great
maior, maius, larger
Maius, Maia, Maium, of May
male, badly
malo, malle, malui, —, prefer
malus, mala, malum, bad, evil
mando, mandare, mandavi, mandatus, commit, entrust, order
mane, in the morning
maneo, manere, mansi, mansus, remain, stay
manifestus, manifesta, manifestum, clear, evident, manifest
manus, manus, *f.*, hand; group
Marathonius, Marathonia, Marathonium, of Marathon
mare, maris, *n.*, sea
maritus, mariti, *m.*, husband
Martius, Martia, Martium, of Mars, of March
mater, matris, *f.*, mother
matrimonium, matrimonii or **matrimoni,** *n.*, marriage
maxime, most, especially
maximus, maxima, maximum, largest
medius, media, medium, middle, middle of

melior, melius, better
memoria, memoriae, *f.*, memory
Mercurius, Mercuri, *m.*, Mercury
meus, mea, meum, my, mine
Midas, Midae, *m.*, Midas
miles, militis, *m.*, soldier
mille, a thousand
mille passus, mile
milia passuum, miles
minime, by no means, not at all, very little
minimus, minima, minimum, smallest
minor, minus, smaller
Minos, Minois, *m.*, Minos
Minotaurus, Minotauri, *m.*, the Minotaur
mirus, mira, mirum, wonderful, surprising
miser, misera, miserum, wretched, unhappy
miseret, miserere, miseruit (Impersonal verb), it distresses, it pities
misericordia, misericordiae, *f.*, pity, compassion, mercy
mitto, mittere, misi, missus, send
modus, modi, *m.*, manner, way
molior, moliri, molitus sum, endeavour, struggle, attempt
moneo, monere, monui, monitus, warn, advise
mons, montis, *m.*, mountain, mount
monstro, monstrare, monstravi, monstratus, point out, show
mora, morae, *f.*, delay
morbus, morbi, *m.*, disease, sickness
morior, mori, mortuus sum, die
moror, morari, moratus sum, delay
mors, mortis, *f.*, death
mortalis, mortale, mortal
mortuus, mortua, mortuum, dead
moveo, movere, movi, motus, move
mox, soon, presently
mulier, mulieris, *f.*, woman
multitudo, multitudinis, *f.*, great number, multitude
multo, much, by much
multus, multa, multum, much
murus, muri, *m.*, wall

N

nam, for
nanciscor, nancisci, nactus sum or **nanctus sum**, get, obtain, receive
narro, narrare, narravi, narratus, tell, relate
nascor, nasci, natus sum, be born
natio, nationis, *f.*, nation
nato, natare, natavi, natatus, swim
natura, naturae, *f.*, nature
nauta, nautae, *m.*, sailor
navigatio, navigationis, *f.*, sailing, voyage
navigo, navigare, navigavi, navigatus, sail, cruise
navis, navis, *f.*, ship
-ne, indicates a question
ne, that not, lest
necesse (Adjective with only Nom. and Acc. Sing. Neuter, used with **esse**), necessary
neco, necare, necavi, necatus, kill
nego, negare, negavi, negatus, deny, say not
nemo, neminem, —, nemini, nemine, *m.* + *f.*, no one, no man, nobody
neque, and not
neque . . . neque, neither . . . nor
nescio, nescire, nescivi, —, not know, be ignorant
nihil, nil, *n.*, nothing
ningit, ningere, ninguit (Impersonal verb), it snows
nisi, if not, unless
nobilis, nobile, famous, noble
nobilitas, nobilitatis, *f.*, fame, nobility
noctu, at night
nolo, nolle, nolui, —, wish not, be unwilling
nomen, nominis, *n.*, name
non, not
Nonae, Nonarum, *f.*, the Nones
nonne, indicates a question expecting the answer 'yes'
nos, nostrum, we
noster, nostra, nostrum, our, ours
novem, nine
November, Novembris, Novembre, of November
novus, nova, novum, new
nox, noctis, *f.*, night
nullus, nulla, nullum, no, none
num, indicates a question expecting the answer 'no'
numerus, numeri, *m.*, number
numquam, never
nunc, now
nuntio, nuntiare, nuntiavi, nuntiatus, announce, report
nuntius, nuntii or **nunti**, *m.*, message, messenger

O

ob, on account of, because of
obsideo, obsidere, obsedi, obsessus, besiege
obstinatus, obstinata, obstinatum, determined, resolute, obstinate
obtineo, obtinere, obtinui, obtentus, secure, obtain
occupo, occupare, occupavi, occupatus, seize, take possession of
oceanus, oceani, *m.*, ocean
October, Octobris, Octobre, of October
oculus, oculi, *m.*, eye
offendo, offendere, offendi, offensus, wound, offend
officium, officii, or **offici**, *n.*, service, favour, obligation, duty
olim, formerly, once
omnis, omne, all, every
onus, oneris, *n*, burden, weight
opera, operae, *f.*, service, pains, work; **operam do**, take pains, give attention
oportet, oportere, oportuit (Impersonal verb), it is necessary, it behoves
oppidum, oppidi, *n.*, town
opportunus, opportuna, opportunum, suitable, opportune
opprimo, opprimere, oppressi, oppressus, overcome, crush
oppugno, oppugnare, oppugnavi, oppugnatus, attack
optimus, optima, optimum, best
opto, optare, optavi, optatus, choose, wish for, desire
opus, operis, *n.*, work
oraculum, oraculi, *n.*, oracle
ordino, ordinare, ordinavi, ordinatus, order, set in order, arrange
ordior, ordiri, orsus sum, begin, commence
ordo, ordinis, *m.*, rank, order
orior, oriri, ortus sum, rise, appear
Orpheus, Orphei, *m.*, Orpheus
ostendo, ostendere, ostendi, ostentus, point out, show
ovis, ovis, *f.*, sheep

P

paene, almost, nearly
paeninsula, paeninsulae, *f.*, peninsula
paenitet, paenitere, paenituit (Impersonal verb), it repents
pareo, parere, parui, —, appear, be visible, obey, comply (with Dative case)
paro, parare, paravi, paratus, prepare, get ready
pars, partis, *f.*, part
partim, partly, in part
parum, too little, not enough
parvus, parva, parvum, small
passus, passus, *m.*, pace
patefacio, patefacere, patefeci, patefactus, open, reveal
pater, patris, *m.*, father
patior, pati, passus sum, bear, suffer, allow
patria, patriae, *f.*, native country
pauci, paucae, pauca, few
pax, pacis, *f.*, peace
pecunia, pecuniae, *f.*, money
pedes, peditis, *m.*, foot soldier
peior, peius, worse
per, through
perfacilis, perfacile, very easy
perficio, perficere, perfeci, perfectus, carry out, accomplish, finish
periculum, periculi, *n.*, danger
permitto, permittere, permisi, permissus, let pass, give up, surrender, let, allow
permoveo, permovere, permovi, permotus, move deeply, excite, arouse
Persae, Persarum, *m. pl.*, the Persians
persuadeo, persuadere, persuasi, persuasus (with Dative case), convince, persuade
pertineo, pertinere, pertinui, —, reach, relate, concern, pertain
pervenio, pervenire, perveni, perventus, arrive
pes, pedis, *m.*, foot
pessimus, pessima, pessimum, worst
peto, petere, petivi or **petii, petitus**, seek
piget, pigere, piguit (Impersonal verb), it grieves, it vexes
piscis, piscis, *m.*, fish
plane, plainly, completely
plebs, plebis, *f.*, the common people
pluit, pluere, pluit or **pluvit** (Impersonal verb), it rains
plurimum posse, be most powerful
plurimus, plurima, plurimum, most
plus, pluris, more
plus posse, be more powerful
Pluto, Plutonis, *m.*, Pluto
poena, poenae, *f.*, punishment, retribution; **poenas sumo**, inflict punishment
poeta, poetae, *m.*, poet
polliceor, polliceri, pollicitus sum, promise
Polyphemus, Polyphemi, *m.*, Polyphemus
pomum, pomi, *n.*, apple

pono, ponere, posui, positus, put, place
pons, pontis, *m.*, bridge
populus, populi, *m.*, people
porta, portae, *f.*, gate, door, entrance
porto, portare, portavi, portatus, carry
portus, portus, *m.*, harbour, port
posco, poscere, poposci, —, ask, beg, demand
possum, posse, potui, be able
post, behind, at the back of
postea, afterwards
posterus, postera, posterum, next, following
postpono, postponere, postposui, postpositus, put after, lay aside, neglect, disregard
postquam, after, when
postridie, on the next day
potens, potentis, able, mighty, powerful, potent
potestas, potestatis, *f.*, ability, power
potior, potiri, potitus sum (with Ablative case), become master of, get, obtain
potius, rather
praeda, praedae, *f.*, booty, plunder
praemium, praemii or **praemi,** *n.*, reward
praesens, praesentis, present
praesidium, praesidii or **praesidi,** *n.*, guard, garrison
praesto, praestare, praestiti, praestitus, stand out, excel
praetor, praetoris, *m.*, praetor
pretium, pretii or **preti,** *n.*, price
(prex, precis) (defective noun having only Acc., Dat. and Abl. Sing. and all Plural cases), *f.*, prayer, entreaty
primum, primo, first, at first
primus, prima, primum, first
princeps, principis, *m.*, leader
principatus, principatus, *m.*, leadership, sovereignty
principio, in the beginning
prius, before, previously
priusquam, before
pro, in front of; for, instead of; for, in behalf of
probo, probare, probavi, probatus, approve, show, prove
proelium, proelii or **proeli,** *n.*, battle
profectio, profectionis, *f.*, departure
proficiscor, proficisci, profectus sum, set out, depart
prohibeo, prohibere, prohibui, prohibitus, keep off, hinder, prohibit, prevent
propero, properare, properavi, properatus, hurry, hasten
propinquus, propinqua, propinquum, near
propter, because of, on account of
propterea, therefore, on that account
Proserpina, Proserpinae, *f.*, Proserpina
provideo, providere, providi, provisus, foresee, take precautions
provincia, provinciae, *f.*, province
proximus, proxima, proximum, next, nearest, most recent
Psyche, Psyches, *f.*, Psyche
pudet, pudere, puduit (Impersonal verb), it shames
puella, puellae, *f.*, girl
puer, pueri, *m.*, boy
pugna, pugnae, *f.*, fight
pugno, pugnare, pugnavi, pugnatus, fight
pulcher, pulchra, pulchrum, pretty, beautiful
pulchritudo, pulchritudinis, *f.*, beauty
puto, putare, putavi, putatus, think, believe
Pythia, Pythiae, *f.*, Pythia

Q

qualis, quale, of what sort
quam, as possible; than
quam diu, how long
quamquam, although
quamvis, although
quantus, quanta, quantum, how much, how great
quare, by what means, how, wherefore, therefore
-que, and
quem ad modum, in what manner, how
qui, quae, quod, who, which, that; which, what
quia, because
quicumque, quaecumque, quodcumque, whoever, whatever
quin, but that
Quiris, Quiritis, *m.*, a Roman citizen, Quirite
quis, quid, who, what
quisquam, any, anyone
quisque, whoever, each (of more than two)
quod, because
quominus, whereby the less
quoque, also
quot (indeclinable adjective), how many

R

ratio, rationis, *f.*, account, affair, method
recipio, recipere, recepi, receptus, take back, receive; **me recipio,** withdraw, retire, retreat
redeo, redire, redii, reditus, go back, return
reduco, reducere, reduxi, reductus, lead back
regina, reginae, *f.*, queen
regio, regionis, *f.*, region, boundary
regno, regnare, regnavi, regnatus, rule
regnum, regni, *n.*, kingdom
rego, regere, rexi, rectus, rule
religio, religionis, *f.*, duty, piety, religious scruple
relinquo, relinquere, reliqui, relictus, leave, leave behind
reliquus, reliqua, reliquum, remaining, rest of
remaneo, remanere, remansi, —, remain, stay behind
removeo, removere, removi, remotus, remove, send away
reperio, reperire, repperi, repertus, find, discover
repeto, repetere, repetivi, repetitus, seek again, demand, exact
reporto, reportare, reportavi, reportatus, carry back, bring back
repugno, repugnare, repugnavi, repugnatus, resist, oppose
res, rei, *f.*, thing
resisto, resistere, restiti, —, stand still, halt, withstand, oppose, resist
res publica, rei publicae, *f.*, state
retraho, retrahere, retraxi, retractus, draw back, call back, bring back
revertor, reverti, reversus sum or **reverti,** turn back, return
revoco, revocare, revocavi, revocatus, call again, call back, recall
rex, regis, *m.*, king
ripa, ripae, *f.*, river bank
robustus, robusta, robustum, strong, robust
rogo, rogare, rogavi, rogatus, ask, ask for
Roma, Romae, *f.*, Rome
Romanus, Romana, Romanum, Roman
Romanus, Romani, *m.*, a Roman
ruri, in the country

S

Sabini, Sabinorum, *m. pl.*, the Sabines
sacrosanctus, sacrosancta, sacrosanctum, inviolable
saepe, often
sagitta, sagittae, *f.*, arrow
sagittarius, sagittarii or **sagittari,** *m.*, archer
salus, salutis, *f.*, health, safety, greeting
salvus, salva, salvum, safe
sancio, sancire, sanxi, sanctus, make sacred, ratify
sapientia, sapientiae, *f.*, wisdom
satis, enough
saxum, saxi, *n.*, stone, rock
scelus, sceleris, *n.*, crime, wickedness
scio, scire, scivi, scitus, know
scribo, scribere, scripsi, scriptus, write
se, him, her, it (reflexive)
secedo, secedere, secessi, secessus, go away, withdraw
secerno, secernere, secrevi, secretus, divide, separate, set apart
sed, but
sedeo, sedere, sedi, sessurus, sit
sementis, sementis, *f.*, a sowing
semper, always
sentio, sentire, sensi, sensus, feel, perceive
separatim, separately
septem, seven
September, Septembris, Septembre, of September
septimus, septima, septimum, seventh
sequor, sequi, secutus sum, follow
serpens, serpentis, *f.*, snake, serpent
servo, servare, servavi, servatus, save, preserve
servus, servi, *m.*, slave, servant
sex, six
si, if
Sibyllinus, Sibyllina, Sibyllinum, Sibylline
sicut, so as, just as, as
signum, signi, *n.*, signal, standard
Silenus, Sileni, *m.*, Silenus
silva, silvae, *f.*, forest, woods
similis, like, similar
simulo, simulare, simulavi, simulatus, pretend
sine, without
sino, sinere, sivi, situs, let, suffer, allow
socius, socii or **soci,** *m.*, comrade, ally
sol, solis, *m.*, sun
sollicito, sollicitare, sollicitavi, sollicitatus, disturb, agitate, excite, incite
sollicitudo, sollicitudinis, *f.*, anxiety, solicitude

solum, alone, only
solus, sola, solum, alone, only
somnus, somni, *m.*, sleep
soror, sororis, *f.*, sister
Sparta, Spartae, *f.*, Sparta
specto, spectare, spectavi, spectatus, look at, watch
spero, sperare, speravi, speratus, hope
spes, spei, *f.*, hope
spolio, spoliare, spoliavi, spoliatus, strip, rob, plunder
statuo, statuere, statui, statutus, decide, judge
stella, stellae, *f.*, star
stipendiarius, stipendiaria, stipendiarium, tributary
sto, stare, steti, status, stand
studium, studii or **studi,** *n.*, zeal, eagerness
stultitia, stultitiae, *f.*, folly, foolishness
sub, under
sum, esse, fui, futurus, be
summus, summa, summum, greatest, highest, top of
sumo, sumere, sumpsi, sumptus, take, take up, assume, undertake, spend; **poenas sumo,** exact punishment
superbus, superba, superbum, proud, haughty
supero, superare, superavi, superatus, surpass, overcome, conquer
suppeto, suppetere, suppetivi, suppetitus, be available, suffice
supplicium, supplicii or **supplici,** *n.*, punishment
supra, over, above
suscipio, suscipere, suscepi, susceptus, take up, undertake
suspicio, suspicionis, *f.*, suspicion
suus, sua, suum, his, her, its, their

T

taedet, taedere (Impersonal verb), it wearies
talis, tale, such, of such a kind
tam, so
tamen, however, nevertheless
tametsi, even if
tandem, finally
tango, tangere, tetigi, tactus, touch
tantus, tanta, tantum, so great
Tarquinius, Tarquini, *m.*, Tarquin
telum, teli, *n.*, weapon
temperantia, temperantiae, *f.*, moderation, self-control, temperance
tempestas, tempestatis, *f.*, storm, bad weather
templum, templi, *n.*, temple
tempus, temporis, *n.*, time
teneo, tenere, tenui, tentus, hold, keep, have
terra, terrae, *f.*, land, earth
terreo, terrere, terrui, territus, frighten, scare, terrify
Thermopylae, Thermopylarum, *f. pl.*, Thermopylae
Theseus, Thesei, *m.*, Theseus
timeo, timere, timui, fear, be afraid of
timidus, timida, timidum, timid
timor, timoris, *m.*, fear, dread
tonat, tonare, tonuit (Impersonal verb), it thunders
tot (indeclinable adjective), so many
totus, tota, totum, all, whole
trado, tradere, tradidi, traditus, give up, surrender
traduco, traducere, traduxi, traductus, lead across, take across
traho, trahere, traxi, tractus, draw, drag
trans, across
transeo, transire, transii, transitus, go over, go across, cross over
tribunal, tribunalis, *n.*, platform, tribunal
Troia, Troiae, *f.*, Troy
tu, tui, you
tum, then, at that time
turris, turris, *f.*, tower
tuus, tua, tuum, your, yours

U

ubi, where, when
Ulixes, Ulixis, *m.*, Ulysses
ultimus, ultima, ultimum, last, farthest
umerus, umeri, *m.*, shoulder
umquam, ever
unus, una, unum, one
urbanus, urbana, urbanum, of the city
urbs, urbis, *f.*, city
usus, usus, *m.*, use, advantage; **ex usu,** of advantage
ut (Adverb), as, when
ut (conjunction), that, so that, in order that
uterque, utraque, utrumque, each, every
utilis, utile, useful
utor, uti, usus sum (with Ablative case), use
uxor, uxoris, *f.*, wife

V

vacillo, vacillare, vacillavi, vacillatus, stagger, waver, vacillate
valetudo, valetudinis, *f.*, health, state of health
venio, venire, veni, ventus, come
ventus, venti, *m.*, wind
Venus, Veneris, *f.*, Venus
verbum, verbi, *n.*, word
vereor, vereri, veritus sum, respect, fear, be afraid
vero, truly, in truth
verto, vertere, verti, versus, turn
vester, vestra, vestrum, your, yours
veto, vetare, vetui, vetitus, forbid, prohibit
vetus, veteris, old
via, viae, *f.*, road, way, street
victoria, victoriae, *f.*, victory
video, videre, vidi, visus, see
vigilo, vigilare, vigilavi, vigilatus, be awake, keep watch
vinco, vincere, vici, victus, conquer
vindico, vindicare, vindicavi, vindicatus, save, avenge
vir, viri, *m.*, man
virtus, virtutis, *f.*, courage, valour
vis, vis, *f.*, force
Plural **vires, virium,** strength
vita, vitae, *f.*, life
vix, with difficulty, scarcely
voco, vocare, vocavi, vocatus, call
volo, velle, volui, —, wish, be willing
volo, volare, volavi, volatus, fly
voluntas, voluntatis, *f.*, wish, will, good will
vos, vestrum, you
vox, vocis, *f.*, voice
vulnus, vulneris, *n.*, wound

Z

Zephyrus, Zephyri, *m.*, Zephyr, west wind